ADVENTURE IN FAITH:
The First 300 Years
of First Baptist Church,
Charleston, South Carolina

ADVENTURE IN FAITH:

The First 300 Years of First Baptist Church, Charleston, South Carolina

Robert A. Baker & Paul J. Craven, Jr.

Broadman Press
Nashville, Tennessee

Inside photographs: Terry Richardson, Arnold Eaves, and the Baptist Historical Collection of
Furman University Library.

© Copyright 1982 ● Broadman Press.

All rights reserved.

4265-63

ISBN: 0-8054-6563-4

Scriptures marked ASV are from the American Standard
Version of the Bible © 1901, Thomas Nelson & Sons.

Dewey Decimal Classification: 286.1757

Subject Heading: CHARLESTON. FIRST BAPTIST CHURCH

Library of Congress Catalog Card Number: 82-71559

Printed in the United States of America

To those individuals across the centuries
who have comprised the membership of the
First Baptist Church, Charleston, South Carolina,
many of whose identities are unknown
but all of whom are members of the
Church Eternal,
this volume is dedicated.

Now unto him that is able to do exceeding abundantly above all
that we ask or think, according to the power that worketh in us,
Unto him be glory in the church by Christ Jesus throughout all
ages, world without end. Amen.

Ephesians 3:20-21

Preface I

More than forty years ago, I was introduced to the history of the First Baptist Church, Charleston, South Carolina. I learned that source materials concerning this, the oldest Baptist church in the South, were quite fragmentary. When Basil Manly, pastor from 1826 to 1837, entered into research in order to observe the 150th anniversary of the church in 1832, he bewailed the fact that hurricanes, water, fire, and war had destroyed the records of the church up to almost the very time he was preparing his anniversary sermons. It is not surprising that he titled his sermons, "Fragments of the history."

I was pleased when the church asked me to work with Dr. Paul J. Craven, Jr., then pastor, to prepare this tricentennial history, for I had been collecting bits and pieces of the story for over four decades. In conference with Dr. Craven, we agreed that the story must be as complete as possible, using all collateral material such as wills, deeds, diaries, biographies, and the like to fill in the areas where the source documents had been lost or destroyed. Also, it was agreed that the story must be well documented, to insure accuracy and to identify the sources for possible further study. I have been fortunate to find several items that had been previously unknown or unrecognized.

Several observations should be made about this story. Because of the change in dating following the adoption of the Gregorian calendar in England in 1752, there may be slight dating inaccuracies carried over from earlier accounts. Some of the documents may have been identified as New Style when they were actually Old Style, but if this is true, it makes a difference of only eleven days at most. Some of the material had been recopied and, in some cases, corrected in style and spelling in the secondary works where they were preserved, while other documents retained the original language and dating of the source. It was necessary to accept these at face value in the absence of the original material itself. In cases where actual quotations contain the older type of spelling (or misspelling), no attempt has been made to insert [sic] to identify these, for if this were done the documents would be almost unreadable due to the continuous insertion of [sic]. Instead, if the reader discovers a misspelled word or a contextual error in a quotation, he should assume that this was the form in which the original was cast.

Documentation can usually be made without problem, but occasionally it becomes necessary to be less precise than is desired. For example, the large collection of Oliver Hart papers, diaries, sermons and sermon notes, and the like has not been collated and put into orderly form which would allow specific source documentation. In this case, the date and identification of the item involved are included in the text with an initial footnote explaining the situation and giving the location of the material to which reference has been made.

Many people have assisted me in my research for this story. My thanks go to Dr. William G. McLoughlin, Brown University, Providence, Rhode Island; Dr. William H. Brackney, Director of the American Baptist Historical Society, Rochester, New York; and Dr. Ellis O'Neal and Diana Yount of Andover-Newton Theological Seminary and the Franklin Trask Library, Newton Centre, Massachusetts.

Dr. Keith Wills, Cecil White, and Robert Phillips and the staff of Fleming Library, The Southwestern Baptist Theological Seminary, Fort Worth, have been helpful. Sara Walls, Tuscaloosa, Alabama, located some source material involving Richard Furman and the Charleston church. Dr. Robert G. Gardner, Shorter College, Rome, Georgia, generously shared with me some significant correspondence of 1735 between the General Baptists of the Charleston church and the General Baptist Church at Newport, Rhode Island. The Baptist Historical Society of London, England, granted permission to quote from their publications some significant material from the minutes of the Western Baptist Association. Dr. Richard Land allowed me to use his copy of the Luppit Church Records, Devonshire, which he discovered in the Angus Library at Regent's Park College, Oxford. These records opened new sources of information about William Screven. Dr. Lynn May and the staff of the Historical Commission of the Southern Baptist Convention have been of great assistance at many points. Dr. James A. Rogers, Florence, South Carolina, official biographer of Richard Furman, has shared some of his insights.

Most of all, I must express my sincere thanks and deep obligation to Dr. Loulie Latimer Owens and Dr. J. Glenwood Clayton. Dr. Owens graciously read my portion of the manuscript and made many valuable suggestions for its improvement, in addition to sharing much excellent material gleaned from her thorough knowledge of South Carolina Baptists. Dr. Clayton, as curator of the Baptist Historical Collection, Furman University, Greenville, South Carolina, has sent me source material and made helpful suggestions.

My secretaries, Sue Rainey and Carolyn Lacy, have typed the manuscript and caught many of my errors. However, any remaining are my own responsibility. Again I express my gratitude to my companion at home for understanding the demands of an "after hours" ministry in preparing this story.

ROBERT A. BAKER

Preface II

From my earliest childhood I was told fascinating portions of the history of the First Baptist Church of Charleston, South Carolina. Across the years these stories have lingered, and I have experienced a growing awareness of the diverse influence this church has had during its three centuries. These three hundred years have brought a myriad of historical contexts which have shaped and been shaped by the life of the First Baptist Church. A dilemma which both Dr. Baker and I faced was how to limit the material to a volume of practical size. We have endeavored to show the part each pastoral period played in the ongoing story and to provide guidance to those who might do additional study in any given period.

I join Dr. Baker in thanking those individuals he has mentioned. In addition I express thanks to those on the present church staff of the First Baptist Church who offered invaluable support and assistance. I also express sincere appreciation to the History Subcommittee of the Tricentennial celebration, Dr. John A. Hamrick, Lester L. Hamilton, and Dr. Malcolm C. Clark whose assistance was of great encouragement.

My secretaries, Mrs. Kathrine Blackmon and Mrs. June Burcham, have provided sustained help in seeing this project through to a successful completion. Finally, I thank Joye for her unwavering support and our four daughters who were often willing to have their plans and wishes subordinated to their father's research and writing schedule.

PAUL J. CRAVEN, JR.

Contents

A List of Pastors in First Baptist Church

1682 –1706	William Screven
1706(?)– ?	_____ White
–1710(?)	William Screven
1713(?)–1717	
or 1718	_____ Sanford (or Sandiford)
1718 –1722	William Peart
1725 –1744	Thomas Simmons
1746 –1749	Isaac Chanler (or Chandler)
1750 –1780	Oliver Hart
1787 –1825	Richard Furman
1826 –1837	Basil Manly, Sr.
1837 –1844	William Theophilus Brantly, Sr.
1845 –1847	Nathaniel Macon Crawford
1847 –1854	James Ryland Kendrick
1854 –1868	Edwin Theodore Winkler
1868 –1869	William H. Williams
1870 –1882	Lewis Hall Shuck
1883 –1887	Andrew Jackson Spears Thomas
1887 –1890	Robert Wilkins Lide
1891 –1899	Lucius Cuthbert
1900 –1901	Arthur Crane
1902 –1906	R. H. White
1908 –1911	Beverly Lacy Hoge
1912 –1913	T. G. Phillips
1913 –1914	C. N. Donaldson
1914 –1915	J. C. Cullum
1915 –1918	Robert W. Sanders
1918 –1920	John Bomar
1920 –1921	D. O. Rivers
1921 –1923	Stacy P. Poag
1924 –1929	Oswell Smith
1930 –1934	Cornelius A. Westbrook
1934 –1939	Vance A. Havner
1940 –1968	John Asa Hamrick
1969 –1981	Paul John Craven, Jr.

1

A Divine Preparation

It was a bright day for the cause of Christ when the First Baptist Church of Charleston, South Carolina, the first Baptist body in the South, was organized three centuries ago. This church was a child of the heroic days of Baptists when giants like Roger Williams, John Clarke, Henry Jessey, Thomas Collier, William Kiffin, and John Bunyan walked the earth. The church was related, either immediately or more remotely, with the first Baptist churches in Great Britain and the American colonies. From her have come pioneer leaders of great stature, men like William Screven, Oliver Hart, Richard Furman, Basil Manly, William T. Brantly, and James P. Boyce, to name but a few. Her creative activity provided the initial thrust among Southern Baptists in missions, Christian education, and organizational life. She shared in the sweeping revivals of Christianity that blessed America in the eighteenth and nineteenth centuries and played a noble part in the inspiring and dangerous events that brought the United States into existence.

When W. W. Barnes delivered an address at the observance of the 250th anniversary of this church, he remarked:

> We stand at the fountainhead of Southern Baptist history; at a center from
> which has gone out influences in missions and education that reach to the
> end of the earth. . . . This spot should be sacred to every Southern Baptist
> that reveres the past, loves the present, and has hope for the future.

The tercentenary anniversary of the church in 1982 provides a proper occasion to recall the unusual providences that have marked the growth of this church from her British roots, the triumphs and tragedies that she has encountered through three centuries, and the rich contributions that she has made all along the journey.

God Prepares a People

All historians, Baptist and secular, point to the British Isles as the seedbed for the earliest members of the First Baptist Church, Charleston. Basil Manly, pastor of the church from 1826 to 1837, commenced his story of the church

13

by focusing on seventeenth-century England. This was the right place to begin. The church was organized in an English colony, her first pastor was an Englishman, and all of her first members were English subjects who were seeking in the New World what they could not attain in the homeland— freedom to worship God according to their beliefs.

The atmosphere of England pervaded the American colonies of the seventeenth century. The northeastern area was appropriately called New England, and her towns reproduced names from the mother country: Boston, Cambridge, York, Amesbury, Salisbury, Plymouth, Portland, Gloucester, and the like. In the South, likewise, a Britisher would feel quite at home with names such as Virginia, Maryland, and Carolina, as well as Jamestown, Charles Town, Somerton, Isle of Wight, and so on. These American names from Great Britain reflect the fact that most of the early colonists had already known a happy life in towns with similar names at home. Why else would they have reproduced these names in the new land?

There is a prior question, however: Why would they leave their pleasant homes which they loved and seek a new life in the distant and dangerous colonies of America? Some, of course, sought fortune; some, adventure; but many of the Baptist pioneers were forced to flee from religious persecution in Great Britain and were willing to undergo the privations and perils of the American wilderness in order to secure liberty of conscience.

A word of background is needed to explain how this persecution occurred. Church and state had been united in Great Britain since 1534 when King Henry VIII wrenched the Church of England from the Roman Catholic Church and became her titular head. Continuing the precedent set by the Roman Catholic Church for over a millennium, Henry determined to crush any dissent from his religious views just as rigorously as he would smite a political enemy. This meant that all subjects of the king were required to agree with him in his religious beliefs as well as in his political views.

It was difficult enough for his people to agree wholeheartedly with Henry in religious matters, for he wavered somewhat in his doctrines. This problem, moreover, was compounded when he died in 1547 and his young son and heir (Edward VI) moved from Henry's Roman Catholic beliefs toward Protestant doctrines. Six years later, when Edward died, his half-sister Mary promptly brought the nation back to the bosom of the Roman Catholic Church, and presumably all of the citizens immediately left Protestantism and became Roman Catholics overnight. When Elizabeth I succeeded Mary Tudor in 1558, she soon severed England again from the Roman Catholic Church, and the people were supposed to renounce their Roman Catholic views promptly and become Protestants. Such a situation was intolerable for anyone who held religious convictions of any kind.

So when James I succeeded Elizabeth in 1603, the people of the realm watched intently to determine what religious beliefs he would hold. He had come from Scotland, where he had lived under the influence of Presbyterianism, but his mother, Mary Queen of Scots, had been a devoted Roman Catholic. James followed the Anglican model of Elizabeth and demanded that all his subjects adopt these religious views or he would "harry them out of the land." This meant that all British subjects must accept the authority of the bishops of the Church of England in matters of church government and doctrine; that infants must be baptized for salvation and partake of the saving sacraments of the Church of England as they grew older; and that those differing with the king in religious doctrine or practice were both heretical and traitorous.

The confrontation between King James and the Baptists occurred early in the history of British Baptist life. There were two principal kinds of Baptists in seventeenth-century Britain—General Baptists and Particular Baptists. Since friction between these two kinds of Baptists later brought a schism in the First Baptist Church of Charleston in America, it is helpful to understand their differences. General Baptists, influenced by the Arminians and Mennonites during their exile in the Low Countries, disagreed with Particular Baptists principally in the related doctrines of Christ's atonement and of election. General Baptists believed that Christ made atonement on the cross for all people in the world and that anyone who confessed faith in Christ was elected by God to share in this atonement and be saved. Particular Baptists, on the other hand, stressed God's total sovereignty, asserting that before the creation of the world God had elected a particular group to be saved and that on the cross Christ had made atonement only for these who were so elected. Others could not be saved because Christ had not died for them.

The earlier General Baptists were first to defy the king. Thomas Helwys, the pastor of what became the first General Baptist church in England, wrote in 1611 that authority in a church did not come from the king or the bishops but from Christ through each autonomous congregation; that baptism "in no wise apperteyneth to infants"; and that "man is justified onely by the righteousness of Christ, apprehended by faith" and not by sacramental observances.[1] In the following year, he prepared a short tract entitled "The Mistery [Mystery] of Iniquity," which clearly asserted that every person must be allowed liberty of conscience in matters of religion. This was the first cry for religious liberty in the English tongue. In a presentation copy addressed to King James, Helwys bluntly said that he was a loyal subject to his king in temporal matters but that the king was only a man, not God, and was not qualified, therefore, to control the consciences of his subjects. For this defiance of the king, Helwys was imprisoned at Newgate until his death several years later.

This reflected the attitude of other British Baptists. Both General and

Particular Baptists incurred the wrath of the dragon of persecution, but they never retreated from their belief that only God was able to bind their consciences in spiritual matters. An enemy, Robert Baillie, counted this to be one of their main characteristics. In a tract attacking Baptists in 1646, he asserted that "they are a people very fond of religious liberty, and very unwilling to be brought under the bondage of the judgment of any other."[2]

Despite intense persecution, both General and Particular Baptists grew rapidly in Great Britain during mid-century. Baillie remarked that they had "increased their number above all the sects in the land."[3] In 1661 when General Baptists presented a petition and confession of faith to Charles II, it was approved by over twenty thousand Baptists and signed by forty-one of their principal ministers.[4]

Particular Baptist churches numbered over 125, dotting the countryside from Northumberland on the Scottish border in the far north of England to Cornwall, Devon, Dorset, and Hampshire on the English Channel in the far south, and from Pembroke on the Bristol Channel on the extreme west of Wales to Norfolk, Suffolk, Essex, and Kent on the eastern shore of England's Midlands. Approximately seventy pastors of these Particular Baptist churches were named in this list.

In addition, Joseph Ivimey, the British historian, mentioned the existence of ten Baptist churches in Ireland in 1653: Dublin, Waterford, Clonmel, Kilkenny, Cork, Limerick, Galloway, Wexford, Carrick Fergus, and Kerry.[5]

Even Presbyterian Scotland had Baptist churches during this period. Rippon's *Register* in 1796 described how Baptist congregations at Leith and Edinburgh had published a confession of faith in 1653 signed by Thomas Spencer, Abraham Holmes, Thomas Powell, and John Brady. The *Register* believed that the church had been formed by Baptists who had been a part of Oliver Cromwell's army, which was garrisoned in various parts of Scotland during the civil war between 1641 and 1649, and speculated that perhaps the violence of the persecution under Charles II had caused the church to disperse and move elsewhere.

The presence of these Baptist churches in every part of Great Britain was most significant. When Dissenters from almost anywhere in the British Isles embarked on the long sea voyage to seek liberty of conscience in the American colonies, it is quite likely that Baptists were among their number, both because of the Baptist emphasis on religious liberty and because immediate conditions of coercion and persecution for conscience were intolerable.

The time factor was also important. Persecution of British Baptists and other Dissenters slowed in the 1640s because of civil war between Charles I and Parliament and in the 1650s because Oliver Cromwell, the victorious general of the parliamentary forces, became ruler of the nation after Charles was tried and executed in 1649. Cromwell allowed toleration of all religious groups except Roman Catholics.

With the death of Cromwell, however, the royal monarchy was restored. Charles II, the older son of Charles I, made glowing promises to grant religious liberty if he were restored to the throne; but when he returned in 1660 as king, with the prompting of a vindictive Anglican parliament, he forgot all of his promises and intensified the persecution of Dissenters from the Church of England. Even worse, in the minds of many Dissenters, Charles openly favored the Roman Catholic Church and secretly plotted to restore England to the bosom of that Church during his fifteen-year reign.

Charles II's persecution of Dissenters was more devastating than all of the indignities they had suffered under his father (Charles I) or his grandfather (James I). In 1661 all Dissenters were forbidden to take any part in local or regional government. In the next year, all Dissenters were banished from the pulpits of England, and all teachers who did not conform to the Church of England's doctrines were forbidden to teach in public or private schools. The Conventicle Act of 1664 forbade Dissenters from meeting for worship. In the following year, all dissenting ministers were prohibited from approaching within five miles of any city or town or of any church in which they had ministered. In 1673, Dissenters were excluded from all civil and military positions.[6] There is not room in this brief account even to list the many examples of imprisonment and suffering that these persecuting acts brought to Baptists in Great Britain. Ivimey described many of them in detail. The records of most Baptist churches either were not kept or were deliberately destroyed by the churches in order to eliminate documents that could be used in evidence to imprison them. Enough records remain, however, to preserve for history the terrible malignity of these persecuting acts against those who refused to stifle their consciences.[7]

It was this persecution under Charles II after 1660 that caused many British Baptists to determine to leave their homes and loved ones and seek a place where they might worship God according to the convictions of their consciences. But where should they go?

God Prepares a Land

It seems providential that at the very height of this persecution, when there was widespread fear that Charles II might be successful in replacing the Anglican Church with the Roman Catholic, a new colony offering liberty of conscience was founded in America. The attitudes of the older American colonies had caused misgiving to those seeking religious liberty. Virginia, which had been settled in 1607, was an intolerant Anglican colony, and had passed an act in 1661-62 punishing any schismatical persons who "out of their averseness to the orthodox established religion, or out of the new fangled conceit of their own heretical inventions, do refuse to have their children baptized."[8] Massachusetts Bay Colony, founded in 1620 by the Pilgrims, was persecuting any Dissenters from the Congregational way. The Roman Catholic colony of Maryland, attempting to attract settlers, had promised limited toleration in 1649. But this colony did not appeal to British Baptists since their persecutor, King Charles II, was Roman Catholic in spirit and already openly favoring Roman Catholics in his realm. Even the Baptist colony of Rhode Island (Providence Plantations and Newport), which did offer religious liberty, was a place of uneasy isolation from constant attacks. John Clarke had published his tract in England in 1652 entitled "Ill News from New England" which described the imprisonment and whipping of Baptist preachers who had ventured from Rhode Island to preach to a blind man in Massachusetts.

But God was preparing a haven for British Dissenters. Financiers and adventurers, always eager to find profitable investments—particularly since the end of the civil war in England in 1649 and the Thirty Years War on the continent in 1648—eyed the "wide and empty territory" that stretched southward from the Virginia colony toward Spanish Saint Augustine. Earlier, in 1629, King Charles I had granted this area south of Virginia to Sir Robert Heath, one of his officials. Its nearness to Spanish holdings, general inaccessibility, and rumors of a poor climate kept it somewhat isolated in its early years, and Heath did little to establish a colony here.

However, it was evident that this new area would be explored and settled. Francis Yeardley, son of a former governor of Virginia, wrote a letter on May 8, 1654, to John Ferrar in Huntingdonshire, England, describing his exploration of this land which he called "South Virginia or Carolina," and spoke of the "most fertile, gallant, rich soil, . . . serene air, and temperate clime."[9] From Virginia came the initial move to settle the area. The Reverend Roger Green of Nansemond, Virginia, was granted ten thousand acres of land on the condition that he could induce one hundred persons to settle south of the Chowan River. Evidently a steady stream of colonists from Virginia moved here.[10] New England adventurers also had begun exploration of the country around Cape Fear and had been interested enough in colonizing it to secure Henry Vassall as an agent to represent their interests in England.

The most significant of the efforts to colonize what is now South Carolina, however, stemmed from the tiny island of Barbados located off the northern coast of South America and settled by the English in 1625. The limited size of the island required the allotment of land in small parcels, which made it difficult for the sugar planters to secure enough acreage to enlarge their profitable enterprise. A bold Barbadian entrepreneur, Colonel John Colleton, who served as a high official of Barbados during the Protectorate of Oliver Cromwell (1653-58), returned to England at the time Charles II was brought to the throne to restore the Stuart monarchy in 1660. Colleton became a member of the Council for Foreign Plantations. He was a close friend to Lord Ashley Cooper. It is likely that these two initiated the project to secure a large land area like Carolina for the ambitious Barbadian planters. However, both Colleton and Ashley had served during the Protectorate under Oliver Cromwell, which tarnished their loyalty to the crown. They therefore felt that in order to secure a grant from the new Stuart king (Charles II), they must ally themselves with other important men who commanded the king's confidence. They found such associates in Edward Hyde, earl of Clarendon, who was lord chancellor of England; George Monck, duke of Albemarle, who was master of the king's horse and captain-general of all his forces; William Lord Craven, an old friend of the king's father who had strongly supported the king's cause; John Lord Berkeley, who had defended the Crown in the civil war; Sir George Carteret, vice-chancellor of the king's household; and Sir William Berkeley, governor of Virginia, who had led that colony to maintain loyalty to Charles II even while the king was still in exile.

So, on March 20, 1663, along with these royal favorites, Colleton and Ashley Cooper were named the eight lords proprietors of a grant to the land from the thirty-first to the thirty-sixth parallel and westward to the "South Seas," wherever that was. However, the proprietors desired to reap the advantages of the promising settlement already established in the Albemarle region and discovered that their grant did not include the area this far north. So on June 30, 1665, the eight proprietors secured from the king an additional grant extending their boundary north to the border of Virginia. The prior grant gave them the country southward into Florida almost to Cape Kennedy. The total grant included the territory northward from twenty-nine degrees to thirty-six degrees and thirty minutes latitude.

Thus, the shrewd plan fashioned by John Colleton, the Barbadian adventurer, finally began to develop. His brother Peter Colleton, along with Thomas Moodyford, aided in this project, and these men also employed Henry Vassall as their agent in England.

This brief background will help explain how the new colony could grant liberty of conscience in religious matters from the beginning to all who would come, for the Barbadians already possessed religious liberty in their original charter. The strong Barbadian desire to enlarge their land holdings gave rise to an exploratory trip by Captain William Hilton in 1663 to what is now North Carolina. Contrary to the reports of New England adventurers, he highly praised the area around the Cape Fear River. Citizens of Barbados united to send Captain Hilton and others to explore the land south of Cape Fear. Hilton's groups reached the present coast of South Carolina on August 26, 1663 and explored the area. Hilton and company published their report in London in 1664. The last of the eight proposals they made for colonizing this

South Carolina area urged that the people "shall have the freedom of Trade, Immunity of Customes, and Liberty of Conscience."[11]

"Liberty of conscience" was a large word in 1664, and British Baptists and other Dissenters began to weigh the risks of the long ocean voyage to this new colony. This was the first use of this expression relative to South Carolina. It came not simply from the developing ideas that had been proclaimed during the civil war in England and the efforts of proprietors to induce settlers to come to their new colonies, but was a privilege that had already been a part of the earlier Barbadian charter granted in 1652 which specifically permitted liberty of conscience.

In 1666, the proprietors published a tract about Carolina (mainly the northern area) which was intended to induce settlers to colonize the new land. As a result, many persons migrated to the South Carolina area also. In this account, the advantages of settling in the new colony were enumerated. The first of these asserted that there was "full and free Liberty of Conscience granted to all, so that no man is to be molested or called in question for matters of Religious Concern." Such an advertisement appearing in London at the very time the most intense persecution of Dissenters was taking place in Great Britain reinforced the desire of many Baptists there to seek the new land which offered such a great boon as religious liberty.

The Barbadian influence in the settlement of Carolina was apparent. Robert Sanford accompanied Sir John Yeamans and others in October, 1665, from Barbados in an exploration of the lower coast of Carolina to determine the best location for a colony. Although the Yeamans' colony in the northern area had failed by 1667, with some of the settlers going to Albemarle, some to Virginia, and some to England, this expedition into Carolina was a stepping-stone to the settlement of Charles Town, South Carolina. In his exploration, Sanford met an Indian cassique, or chief, of the Kiawah tribe, who urged him to come further south to the broad and deep harbor of his country (where Charleston is now situated). A. S. Salley remarked that it was the pride which the Kiawah chief took in his harbor and his country that was responsible for the settling around Charles Town of the first English colony in South Carolina.[12]

This narrative so influenced the proprietors in England that they quickly sent three vessels with ninety-two settlers from England, picked up sixty more settlers from Barbados, and established the first colony in South Carolina about March, 1670. The settlement was made at Bulls Bay, about twenty-five miles northeast of the present city, and William Sayle, an aged Puritan Dissenter, became governor. Most of the party were Dissenters, as had been practically all of the settlers in the northern area of Carolina. Despite instructions from the proprietors, the South Carolina settlers found that Bulls Bay was not the best place for a town, so they moved about twenty-five miles to the western bank of the Ashley River and named the spot Charles Town.[13]

The difficulties of the first year and the lack of revenue to the lords proprietors made the prospects for survival of Charles Town rather dim. What seems to have been another providential development, however, changed the picture. Lord Ashley, the most active of the diminishing proprietors' group, secured another grant from Charles II on November 1, 1670, consisting of the Bahama Islands. His grand scheme now was to unite Albemarle, Charles Town, and Bermuda (and perhaps other locations later) into a cooperative trade unit that on paper seemed to promise good financial returns. This made the new settlement at Charles Town much more important as one base of the new trade unit. Ashley increased his efforts to strengthen Charles Town. From Barbados the *John* and the *Thomas* brought forty-two new settlers on February 16, 1671. About a week later the *Carolina* brought sixty-four more. On May 14, 1671, the *Blessing* arrived from England with another large accession to the colony. By 1672, the settlement had 263 men able to bear arms, 69 women, and 59 persons under sixteen years of age.[14]

The coming of so many settlers demanded that the town enlarge beyond the limits of what was then Charles Town. By 1672 the council authorized laying out three colonies of twelve thousand acres each: one was Charles Town where the original settlement was made; one was called James Town; and the third was titled Oyster Point. It was this last-named town, Oyster Point, that became the focal point of this story. Warrants for town lots there date from the spring of 1677. The settlers found this area to be the most favorable of all locations, situated as it was at the confluence of the Ashley and Cooper Rivers where the Kiawah chieftain had boasted of the fine harbor.

By June 1680 the official center of the colony was moved to Oyster Point, and it became known as New Charles Town or later simply Charleston.[15] It will be called Charleston hereafter in this account, although this spelling was not officially adopted until 1783.

Charleston's population began to increase greatly. In April 1680 the *Richmond* arrived with forty-five French Huguenots whom the proprietors hoped could introduce the cultivation of silk. They presaged a large number of French Calvinists in this area. In one month Joseph Morton brought five hundred Dissenters from western England (the hotbed of English Baptists). Ireland, Scotland, and Wales sent their people, as well.

In about 1682 Thomas Ashe lavishly praised the new city of Charleston, which he estimated to have about a thousand or twelve hundred people.[16] Samuel Wilson viewed the city at the same time and judged that the new town had increased from a few houses a year or two before to about one hundred houses in this "pleasant and fertile country," and noted that on one day there had been sixteen vessels (some upward of two hundred tons) riding in the Charleston harbor.[17] Thomas Newe, in May, 1682, wondered why all of these one hundred houses were made of wood, since there was so much excellent brick made in the area.[18]

So, by the 1670s and 1680s, during a time of continuous persecution for their religious views, British Baptists learned that there was a new colony in America which provided complete liberty of conscience. They also learned from Samuel Wilson's tract that many persons had gone there as servants but now had been able to acquire good stocks of cattle and servants of their own; that many who had been in good financial condition when they arrived were now living "in a very plentiful condition, and their estates still encreasing"; and that "six men will in six weeks time, Fall, Clear, Fence in, and fit for Planting, six Acres of Land."[19]

Like the early Christians in Jerusalem, Baptists in Great Britain were shaken loose from their moorings at home by persecution and scattered into new areas carrying the word of faith. These hardships turned out to the furtherance of the gospel. A new country was opened at the very time the situation in Great Britain became unbearable to Dissenters, and this new colony offered more than good financial prospects and personal gain. It promised complete liberty of conscience. As Article XXXIX of the *Fundamental Constitutions* of Carolina specifically said: "No person whatsoever shall disturb, molest, or persecute another for his opinion in religion, or way of worship."

The Baptist Migration

Who were these British Baptists that came to South Carolina during this early period? This is a difficult question because all of the eyewitnesses who described the settling of the land simply identified all non-Anglicans who arrived as "Dissenters," without referring to them as Presbyterians, Congregationalists, Quakers, Puritans, Baptists, or whatever. This was true of Robert Sanford, Maurice Matthews, Nicholas Carteret, Joseph West, William Sayle, Thomas Ashe, Samuel Wilson, William Pratt, Edward Randolph, and John Archdale, the writers of firsthand accounts. Daniel Defoe's tract was written from England, as was the history by John Oldmixon, and these are valuable for their points of view but not as actual eyewitness accounts.

The principal story of Baptists in early South Carolina evidently was preserved by Oliver Hart, who served from 1750 to 1780 as the pastor of the Charleston church. South Carolina historians generally reckon him to be the fourth regular pastor of the church (Screven, Peart, Simmons, and Hart). When Basil Manly, the sixth regular pastor of the church, delivered his historical discourse at the sesquicentennial celebration in 1832, he remarked:

> It is to be regretted, however, that the Church has no records to direct our enquiries; a series of calamities having deprived them of nearly every vestige of their own progress, which could be considered as properly their own, and within the last twelve years. In the year 1752, September 15, occurred the dreadful hurricane and inundation with which Charles-

ton was visited. Among other and great injury sustained in all parts of the city, the south west corner of the Baptist Meeting House, was carried away by a vessel of nine or ten feet draft, which had been driven from her anchors through the mouth of Vanderhorst's Creek; and all the books and papers perished in the flood. The vessel afterwards grounded on the west side of Meeting street. About thirty years after, viz: on January 3, 1782, the British troops visited St. Thomas's Parish, and from the dwelling of Col. Thomas Screven, then the acting Trustee of the Church, they took, and either carried off or destroyed, "the old book kept by the Trustees of said Church, and also all the indents, acts, papers, &c. of the church."

The records and papers which had accumulated after that period were again destroyed, in the conflagration which consumed, among others, the house of Mr. Robert Brodie, the Church Clerk, in the year 1819. Thus the water, the fire, and the hand of the enemy, each in its turn, have deprived the Church of the means of relating its own history. Some printed documents, however, remain, and some papers preserved among the Screven family, and handed over to Deacon William Inglesby, who was allied to the family by marriage. We have also a curious manuscript volume, (in Roman Character) of the Rev. Mr. Morgan Edwards, A. M., containing "materials towards a history of the Baptists in the provinces of Maryland, Virginia, North and South Carolina," collected by him, during a pedestrian journey in 1772. With the aid of these sources of information, we venture to present you with the following imperfect sketch of the History of the oldest Baptist Church in South Carolina.[20]

Although Manly did not mention it here, the Charleston Association minutes were another source of information about the church. After the destruction of the minute books of the church in the hurricane of September 15, 1752, the Charleston Association immediately ordered that a historical sketch of the First Baptist Church be included in their associational records; so, a few weeks after the storm, this historical sketch was evidently prepared by Oliver Hart, in whose home the church minutes had been kept at the time of the hurricane. Following so soon after the loss of the original church book, this sketch must have been rather accurate as recalled by Hart. It was from this sketch in the Charleston Association minutes that Manly secured some of his information. Wood Furman prepared a history of the Charleston Association in 1811, and his account of the beginnings of the First Baptist Church was also taken from these associational minutes. It should be said, also, that Hart was very close to his pastoral successor, Richard Furman, whose account of the early days of the church is quite similar to the material in Edwards, Manly, and Wood Furman.

Manly made reference to the "curious manuscript volume" of Morgan Edwards as another source of his information. Edwards undoubtedly got his information about the Charleston church principally from Oliver Hart also. Edwards was a scholarly Welshman who at the age of thirty-nine had come to

America in May 1761 to be pastor of the First Baptist Church, Philadelphia, Pennsylvania. Resigning this post in 1770, he spent most of the remainder of his twenty-five years of life gathering materials for the history of Baptists in America. He traveled extensively from New Hampshire to Georgia and later prepared manuscript or printed histories of Baptist beginnings in many of the colonies.

According to the diary of Oliver Hart, Edwards arrived in Charleston on January 23, 1772, and remained until the following February 11 taking notes on the history of the Charleston church and other nearby Baptist churches. Edwards evidently thoroughly discussed the early history of the church with Oliver Hart, who had been pastor of the church for about twenty-three years (although only forty-nine years old in 1772). Hart had read the original minutes and, as his diaries indicate, was quite careful in his recollection and account of events. His daughter had married a Screven, the great-grandson of the first pastor of the church, who may have provided Hart with additional information. Neither Edwards nor Hart states how much of the story Edwards got from the pastor, but certainly Hart must have supplied most of it.

Edwards could also have talked with Mrs. Catherine Stoll Screven, the wife of William Screven, Jr., son of the first preacher. She died in 1772. Many of the grandchildren of preacher Screven were still located around Charleston, and Edwards doubtless spent some of his time with them during these two weeks of research. In addition, the children and grandchildren of pioneer families of the church were also numerous around Charleston, so Edwards was undoubtedly able to preserve a great deal of fairly accurate information about Baptist beginnings in Charleston almost a century before.

One of the Charleston Baptist traditions that Edwards discovered was the story about the distinguished Blake family and their relationship with the Baptists. The famous British Admiral Robert Blake (1599-1657) had been one of the heroes of the civil war between Parliament and the Crown. Placed in charge of the British Navy, this former army officer had pursued royalist ships into the Mediterranean and even across the Atlantic Ocean. In the colonies he demanded and received the allegiance of Virginia and Barbados who had refused heretofore to recognize the parliamentary government. He also became well known as a protector of the British Isles themselves by attacking Dutch and Spanish ships in the English Channel.

Admiral Blake died before Oliver Cromwell completed his reign and Charles II (1660-85) began his persecution of Dissenters, so it is difficult to know how much loyalty this Blake had to the Anglican Church. There is no doubt, however, that the American Blakes were strong Dissenters from the Church of England. Benjamin Blake, the admiral's brother, lived in Somersetshire, England, a hotbed of English Baptists and other Dissenters. There he had bitterly criticized the Church of England and, with the accession of

Charles II in 1660, had greatly feared the possible return of the Roman Catholic Church as the official church of England. John Oldmixon (who wrote his history of the British Empire in 1708) recalled his acquaintance with Benjamin Blake:

> 'Twas about this time (1683), that the Persecution rais'd by the Popish Faction, and their Adherents, in England, against the Protestant Dissenters, was at the height; and no Part of this kingdom suffer'd more by it than Somersetshire. The Author of this History liv'd at that time with Mr. Blake, Brother to the famous General of that name, being educated by his Son-in-law, who taught School in Bridgewater, and remembers, tho then very young, the Reasons old Mr. Blake us'd to give for leaving England: One of which was, That the Miseries they endur'd, meaning the Dissenters then, were nothing to what he foresaw would attend the Reign of a Popish Successor; wherefore he resolv'd to remove to Carolina: And he had so great an Interest among Persons of his Principles, I mean Dissenters, that many honest substantial Persons engag'd to go over with him. . . .
>
> I say the more of Mr. Blake, because his Family is one of the most considerable in this Province; where he arriv'd in the Year 1683, with several other Families, the followers of his fortune. What Estate he had in England, he sold, to carry the Effects along with him; . . .[21]

The date for the coming of Benjamin Blake and company to South Carolina probably should be 1683. A. S. Salley identified a grant of land to Benjamin Blake and twenty-one persons in 1683.[22] Elsewhere, Salley recorded that on March 28, 1683, the Grand Council directed the surveyor-general to lay out one thousand acres of land to Benjamin Blake, which were purchased by him from the lords proprietors by a conveyance dated June 6, 1682.[23] It is likely that other land grants to a Benjamin Blake, which showed him as coming to the colony in 1681, referred to a different man with the same name.[24]

It appears that Benjamin Blake's family who accompanied him to South Carolina included his son Joseph and his daughter Elizabeth. Joseph became acting governor of South Carolina about the middle of 1696 (the year that William Screven left Maine for South Carolina) and was confirmed as governor on April 25, 1697. He was twice married. His first wife was Deborah Morton, daughter of Joseph Morton, an influential Dissenter and governor of the colony in 1682. A. S. Salley said that Morton had been named governor of the colony in 1682 as a means of inducing many Dissenters to leave Britain and come to South Carolina.[25] It is interesting that Governor Morton, although identified by no one as being friendly to the Baptists, left £5 in his will to Nehemiah Coxe, the London Baptist minister.[26] Perhaps the Mortons had contacts with London Baptists and were able to influence some of them to migrate to South Carolina.

Deborah Morton Blake died after 1678. Blake's second wife was from an equally prominent family of English Dissenters, the Axtells. The American Daniel Axtell's will was dated August 3, 1678. In it he showed that with him at that time in South Carolina were his wife, Rebecca, two minor sons (Daniel and Holland), and five unmarried daughters (Sibilia, Mary, Rebecca, Elizabeth, and Ann), all unmarried and under twenty-one.[27]

Joseph Blake died in 1700. His wife, Lady Elizabeth Axtell Blake, and her mother, Lady Rebecca (spelled in various ways) Axtell, widowed before September 27, 1683, were strong Dissenters from the Church of England. Joseph Blake seems to have been a Presbyterian, according to the context of his will.[28] It seems certain that his wife, Lady Elizabeth Axtell Blake, was an active Baptist. At the time her will was proved on July 23, 1726, she left £50 for the building of a parsonage for the Baptist church at Charleston, along with a sum of £20 a year for sustaining the minister of the Baptist church.[29] Her mother, Lady Rebecca Axtell, was quite friendly with the Baptists. Among other things, she gave the church the glass chandelier which was still hanging in the old Baptist church building when Basil Manly prepared his history of the church in 1832.[30]

Another Baptist tradition that Edwards encountered was the story that Paul Grimball, the noted secretary of the province, who seems to have come to South Carolina about 1681-82, was also a Baptist. Grimball, along with Joseph Blake and several others, was a part of the committee to revise the *Fundamental Constitutions* of John Locke for use in governing the colony. However, Paul Grimball died before February 20, 1696, when his will was proved. Although he may have been a Baptist, there is no evidence that this was so. Doubtless the tradition developed because his son Thomas and daughter Providence Grimball were baptized by William Screven on Edisto Island about 1700, four years after their father died. These children were loyal Baptists, and it is possible, of course, that they could have been influenced in this direction by their father before his death.

Morgan Edwards and Basil Manly also encountered the tradition that in the 1680s Henry Lord Cardross had brought a company from Scotland and north England which included a number of Baptists. Manly identified some familiar names as a part of this group: William Fry, Thomas Grimball, Providence Grimball, Ephraim Mikell, Joseph Sealy, Joseph Parmenter, Isaac Parmenter, Thomas Parmenter, and William Tilly. This group, said Manly, "attached themselves to Mr. Screven's Church, still worshipping at Somerton."[31]

This is now known to be inaccurate. The people named by Manly were converted under the preaching of William Screven about 1700, several years after the church was functioning in Charleston, so they could not have joined the Somerton body. The actual names of the Cardross party are given in a land warrant issued to him on October 6, 1685, as follows: "William Stevenson,

Peter Allen, Alexandr Mrtis, James Martine, Carpenter and Martha his Wife, James Martine Junior, Anna Martine, Deborah Martine, Priscilla Martine, Charles Campble, Mary Huttchison, Martha Martine, spinster, Moses Martine, Mary Martine, Mary Foulton, and James Foulton."[32] The party settled on Port Royal Island, but were forced by Indian and Spanish attacks in 1686 to move to the mouth of the Edisto River, and Cardross returned to Scotland. None of the names of this party appear in Baptist life in Charleston, but it is possible that some of the women may have intermarried with Baptists and preserved this tradition. It was impossible for them to have joined Screven's church in the 1680s, whether at Somerton or Charleston, for Screven had not yet come to South Carolina.

In his material, Morgan Edwards specifically identified Baptist families who had come from Great Britain to form the early Baptist community at Charleston as being the Atwells, Bullines, Elliotts, Bakers, Ravens, Blakes, Barkers, Butlers, Chapmans, Childs, Caters, Whitakers, Bryants, and others. His "and others" leaves much to be desired by those who search meticulously for any kind of identification of the pioneers of the church, but the specific family names are helpful. His listing of only the family names gives a sense of authenticity, as his sources did not attempt to remember in detail all of the husbands, wives, brothers, sisters, and children in the family. Anyone familiar with the history of this period gets a feeling that Morgan Edwards was being quite discriminative in naming this group. For one thing, the names were not given in alphabetical order, nor in the order of importance, nor in the order of their coming; rather, Edwards seems to have listed first those whom his informers knew most about and confidently identified as being among the pioneers. Then, too, some familiar and early families who were prominent in the church, such as the Bedons, the Shepherds, the Filbins, the Gibbes, the Mikells, the Sealys, the Frys, and many others, were not listed by Edwards as among the pioneers even though they mingled with them quite early. This kind of discrimination increases one's confidence in Edwards' material which evidently came principally from Oliver Hart.

All of the names mentioned by Edwards as being founders of the Baptist community in Charleston have been identified by Henry A. M. Smith as being early settlers along the Ashley and Cooper Rivers or in Charleston itself.[33] Also, a surprisingly large number of these names appear in the early warrants for land in South Carolina.[34]

The first name—the Atwells—can easily be identified, although it is questionable whether this family should be counted among the pre-Screven Baptists in Charleston. This was Joseph Atwell, William Screven's adopted son who evidently accompanied Screven to South Carolina in 1696 from Kittery, Maine. He lived on James Island with his wife, two sons (Joseph and Benjamin), and two daughters (Mary and Abigail). His will was proved on

February 14, 1723.[35] It identifies him as a carpenter, and his principal executor was Samuel Screven, perhaps the oldest son of William Screven the preacher.

The Bulline family (spelled variously as Bullein, Bullen, Bulling, etc.) certainly included some Baptists, although A. H. Hirsch identifies one of them with the French Huguenots.[36] John Bulline secured warrants for land in 1677 and 1678, as well as a town lot at Oyster Point (later Charleston) in 1677 before the city had moved to that location. Either he or his son was trustee of the Ashley River Baptist Church in 1725. Thomas Bulline was doubtless related to John Bullen who had land warrants in 1677, and Joseph Bullen, who had a warrant in 1684. Thomas Bulline may have known William Screven before the preacher came to South Carolina, as will be mentioned later. Thomas secured a warrant for land at "Summer towne" on December 7, 1696, and elsewhere later on. He became a trustee of the first lot owned by the church in Charleston in 1699.

The Elliotts became one of the most prosperous and influential families in the early Charleston church. On July 18, 1699, William Elliott gave the lot at 62 Church Street for the building of a Baptist meetinghouse. As will be noted later, Elliott was a General Baptist from England. Between February 6, 1692, and April 23, 1711, he secured twelve warrants for thousands of acres of land. His sons William Jr., John, Joseph, and Thomas also secured many land warrants from 1693 onward. There were a number of Elliotts in Charleston about this time, and most of them seem to have been related to one another.

The Baker family evidently included Richard Baker, who secured a land warrant on the Ashley River in 1681, and he and his family were active in the Ashley River branch of the Charleston church (organized May 24, 1736). Richard and Susanna Baker, a part of this family who were longtime members of the Ashley River church, made generous gifts to their church in the 1760s.

The Raven family seems to have arrived in Charleston about 1672, when John Raven came as a servant. He secured five land warrants between 1684 and 1702. He was a trustee of the first Baptist church lot in Charleston donated by William Elliott in 1699. He and his son John Jr. were also trustees of the second deed to the property in 1712. The family must have been well respected by their neighbors, for John is shown several times as a member of the Commons House of Assembly from Colleton County.

The Blake family has already been discussed. The Barker family evidently dated from 1674 when Jonathan Barker arrived in the first fleet and secured a land warrant. Charles Barker was active for over a generation in the work of the church, taking part in the organization of the Charleston Association in 1751 and serving as trustee of a gift to the Ashley River Baptist Church in the following year.

The Butler family included Richard Butler, who was named a trustee in 1712 of the lot on which the first church building was erected. It is not known when the first Butler came. A Richard Butler secured a land warrant on March 4, 1678, and made his will on September 12, 1696. However, in this will there was no mention of a son bearing the same name, so probably the Richard Butler who was a Baptist pioneer and perhaps had a son by the same name must have been another person. Richard Butler is shown witnessing several wills between 1714 and 1723, one for a brother, Shem Butler. On November 22, 1725, Richard Butler and his wife gave six acres of land to the Baptists at Ashley River for building a meetinghouse.[37]

The Chapman family came to the colony before 1681 when William was granted lot 78 on Church Street. He was a tanner by trade. He was closely related, perhaps by blood or marriage, to the Richard Caper family and to Susannah Griffin, the widow of his mariner friend Benjamin Griffin, who witnessed his will. He gave Susannah Griffin a lot and house in Charleston on January 7, 1704, before his death in January, 1712. Tradition has it that the church met in either Chapman's home or in a house of his on King Street before the building was erected about 1699-1700, so evidently he secured several city lots in Charleston quite early. His will indicated that he also owned a plantation on James Island before his death.

It is not known when the Child (or Childs) family arrived in the province. Benjamin Child was one of the members of the Charleston church who worshiped at the Ashley River branch and became one of the constituent members of the Ashley River church when it was organized in 1736. Morgan Edwards said that Benjamin Child gave one thousand pounds in currency and twenty acres of land to the Ashley River church not long after that church was formed. Perhaps a Joseph Child was related to Benjamin, for he named his son Benjamin; if so, the family was in Charleston in 1692 when Joseph witnessed a will there. There were several families of Childs in the Charleston area. In his will in 1738, the Baptist William Elliott mentioned his daughter, Hanah Child, now deceased, who may have been related to the Benjamin Child family.

The Cater (or Cator) family came before 1682 when Thomas Cater secured a warrant for land on Ashley River. The Caters (Thomas and his son William), the Lady Joseph Blake, and her mother Lady Rebecca Axtell must have had a close relationship, for each of them secured land warrants on September 4, 1707, for five hundred acres of land on "Combee Island," evidently adjoining tracts for the four of them.[38] In his will of February 1, 1730, proved on April 26, 1731, Thomas Cater mentioned his son William; two daughters, Susannah Bradwell and Mary Lashly; five grandsons under twenty-one years of age; and four granddaughters, Elizabeth Bullen, Ann and Mary Hamblin, and Mary Shephard. His will also left ten pounds to Thomas Simmons, pastor of the Baptist church in Charleston.[39]

Practically nothing is known of the Whitaker or Bryant families, mentioned in the list of Morgan Edwards. These family names are not found in the later history of the church, and this adds coincidental evidence that Edwards was not simply recounting the names of prominent Baptists in the Charleston church as he listed the founders. As mentioned earlier, the order of listing was not totally alphabetical, chronological, or according to their importance, but apparently gave the more familiar names early, since all of Edwards' sources recalled them as pioneers, while the later names were those less familiar. The Whitakers and Bryants were in this last category. Edwards' use of "and others" suggests that perhaps some of the older members with whom he talked would name one family as being an early pioneer, while others might not include that particular family. It would be unreal to suppose that the memories of all his informants provided identical names.

Thus, from historical materials and legal records of various sorts, it seems rather clear that there were many Baptists among the "Dissenters" who migrated from England to South Carolina in the 1670s, 1680s, and 1690s. It is inconceivable that very many of them, having fled from Great Britain to find liberty of worship, would not meet for worship with fellow Baptists in this new colony where religious liberty was guaranteed. The intermarrying of Baptist families and the scores of wills where known Baptists signed as witnesses or acted as executors, as will be discussed briefly in a succeeding chapter, indicate that they were a close-knit community and joined one another to confront the social and legal problems of the day.

There can be little doubt that they also worshiped together. A tradition of Charleston, separate from that of New England, speaks of Baptist gatherings for worship in the 1680s. This could very well have happened. It was not at all unusual for a group of Baptists in America (as in England) to worship together for years without a pastor and without a building. It is also possible that the Charleston group, as did the church herself later, sought a pastor in England, Europe, and the other American colonies through correspondence. The coming of William Screven from New England to become the first pastor of the Charleston church could have resulted, as will be discussed later, from an appeal by some of the Somersetshire neighbors of Screven who had come to Charleston with Benjamin Blake and his son Joseph, later governor of the province.

This, then, was the source of the earliest Baptists in Charleston. Driven from their homes in many parts of Great Britain by persecution under Charles II, these Britishers chose the land that God had prepared for them by providing religious liberty for all Dissenters. God was already preparing the man who would come to serve them as their first pastor.

Notes

1. William L. Lumpkin, *Baptist Confessions of Faith* (Philadelphia: The Judson Press, 1959), pp. 114 ff.

2. Joseph Ivimey, *A History of the English Baptists,* 4 vols. (London: 1811-1830), I:175.

3. Ibid.

4. Ibid., pp. 277-78.

5. Ibid., pp. 240 ff.

6. For these documents, see Henry Gee and William John Hardy, *Documents Illustrative of English Church History* (London: Macmillan and Co., Limited, 1914), pp. 594 ff.

7. See Ivimey, vols. I and II.

8. Robert A. Baker, *A Baptist Source Book* (Nashville: Broadman Press, 1966), p. 7.

9. Alexander S. Salley, Jr., ed., *Narratives of Early Carolina, 1650-1708* (New York: Charles Scribner's Sons, 1911), p. 25. This volume is included in the series *Original Narratives of Early American History,* J. Franklin Jameson, gen. ed., reproduced under the auspices of the American Historical Association.

10. William S. Powell, "Why Carolina Was Granted to the Proprietors," eds. Ernest M. Lander, Jr. and Robert K. Ackerman, *Perspectives in South Carolina History* (Columbia: University of South Carolina Press, 1973), pp. 3-5.

11. Salley, *Narratives,* p. 61.

12. Ibid., p. 94.

13. Wesley Frank Craven, "The Early Settlement," in *Perspectives,* p. 19.

14. Ibid.

15. Ibid., p. 22.

16. Salley, *Narratives,* pp. 157-58.

17. Ibid., p. 167.

18. Ibid., p. 181.

19. Ibid., p. 167.

20. Basil Manly, *Mercy and Judgment, A Discourse Containing Some Fragments of the History of the Baptist Church in Charleston S.C.* (n.p.: Press of Knowles, Vose and Co., 1837), pp. 6-7. This will be referred to hereafter as Manly, *Discourse.*

21. Salley, *Narratives,* pp. 329-31.

22. Leah Townsend, *South Carolina Baptists 1670-1805* (Florence, S.C.: The Florence Printing Company, 1935), p. 10 n.

23. Salley, *Narratives,* p. 331 n.

24. Alexander S. Salley, Jr., ed., *Warrants for Lands in South Carolina 1692-1711* (Columbia: The Historical Commission of South Carolina, 1915), pp. 47, 50.

25. Salley, *Narratives,* p. 329 n.

26. The will of Joseph Morton's father, proved on November 20, 1688, indicates that he had lived in Somersetshire before coming to South Carolina. For the reference to the money left to Cox by Joseph Morton, see the *South Carolina Historical and Genealogical Magazine* (Charleston: 1900 on), V:108. Cited hereafter as SCH&GM.

27. Caroline T. Moore and Agatha Aimar Simmons, comps. and eds., *Abstracts of*

the Wills of the State of South Carolina 1670-1740 (Columbia: The R. L. Bryan Company, 1960), p. 4.

28. Ibid., p. 21.

29. Ibid., p. 124.

30. Manly, *Discourse,* p. 12.

31. Ibid., p. 13.

32. Salley, *Narratives,* p. 292 n. Herbert L. Osgood, *The American Colonies in the Seventeenth Century* (Gloucester, Mass.: Peter Smith, 1957), II:219, identifies Cardross and followers as Scotch Presbyterians endeavoring to escape from persecution by the Duke of York and Claverhouse.

33. Much of this information may be found in Townsend, p. 10 n.

34. For warrants mentioned hereafter see Salley, *Warrants,* passim.

35. For all of the wills mentioned hereafter see Moore & Simmons, *Wills,* and Caroline T. Moore, comp. and ed., *Abstracts of the Wills of the State of South Carolina 1740-1760* (Columbia: The R. L. Bryan Company, 1964).

36. Arthur Henry Hirsch, *The Huguenots of Colonial South Carolina* (Durham, N.C.: Duke University Press, 1928), p. 8.

37. Townsend, pp. 32-33.

38. Salley, *Warrants,* pp. 207-8.

39. Moore & Simmons, *Wills,* p. 156.

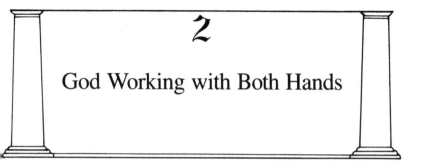

God Working with Both Hands

What a remarkable providence brought a pastor to these South Carolina Baptists! The man whom God chose for them had doubtless known some of them in western England before any of them left for the New World. Since the South Carolina colony guaranteeing religious liberty did not exist when the future pastor migrated to America, he spent almost thirty years in a circuitous route before finally reaching the place of his greatest service in Charleston at the age of sixty-seven. But when he did arrive there in 1696, he was the seasoned and tested pastor who was needed to meet the peculiar problems facing Charleston Baptists at that time. So God, who with one hand had gathered a people from Great Britain and provided a refuge for them in a distant land, with his other hand selected a man who would find his way to South Carolina to become the first pastor of the gathered people.

Get Thee Out

William Screven (sometimes spelled Scriven, Sereven, Screeven, Scrivine, or Scrivener) was the man whom God chose for the South Carolina Baptists. Until recently, little was known about his English background. When he died on October 10, 1713, at the age of eighty-four, near Georgetown, South Carolina, his youngest son Elisha was living with him and inherited most of his property. Evidently, Elisha informed Oliver Hart about the exact age and date of the death of the pioneer preacher and his birth in Somerton, England, in 1629, and Hart gave this information to Morgan Edwards, the Baptist historian, in 1772.

The only documented fact previously found in English records was that a William Screven had signed the Somerset Confession of Faith in 1656 as a representative from the Baptist church at Somerton. Most Baptist historians followed the views of Henry S. Burrage, who probably did more research than anyone else on William Screven. Burrage identified the English Screven as the American pastor until he learned that the American Screven was baptized by the Baptist church at Boston, Massachusetts, on June 21, 1681.

He then judged that the American Screven was probably the son of the English Screven.[1]

An excellent piece of recent research, however, has added much information about the English Screven. The discovery was made by Professor Richard Dale Land during the writing of his Oxford dissertation on Thomas Collier. As Professor Land searched for material on Collier in the Angus Library at Regent's Park College, Oxford, England, he came upon a six-page document which proved to be the first church records of the Luppit Baptist Church in Devon. These records showed that Collier baptized thirteen men and women to form the Luppit church on May 5, 1652 (by present dating). But there was more. The next entry in the church book revealed that four men were baptized on

> the one and twentyth day of the third month in 1652 [May 31, 1652, by present dating] by *Willm Hare* & Willm Screven, two gifted brethren, & members of the Church of Somerton, acting among us by our consent, & by the approbation of Brother Collyer aforesayd, & also by the approbation of the aforesayd Church—of Somerton.[2]

Evidently William Hare of Somerton left Luppit at this time, for the records showed that Screven alone then baptized four persons on or about June 17 (present dating), six persons on September 17 (present dating), one person about a month earlier, and three persons on September 24, 1652 (present dating). Thereafter, the baptizing was done by Edmond Burford, who himself had been baptized by Screven on September 17, and the record seems to end about 1655. Burford is also described in the records as a "gifted brother."

The last page of the document contains a list of fourteen "Orders & Instructions" for the Luppit church which were prepared by William Hare and William Screven on May 31, 1652. This was the date when together they had baptized four men, evidently after Collier had departed, and these two "gifted brethren" seem to have collaborated on these instructions for the church before Hare left Screven alone with the church.

The second, third, and twelfth of these instructions are quite interesting. The second reads: "That whosoever comes to preach in this church, except our brethren aforesayd, Willm Hare & Willm Screven, we ought to require a letter of Recommendation from the Church where he is." The third reads: "That he is to be tried in ye Church, before we suffer him to preach in ye world." The twelfth reads: "That Lucas Cyril may preach in the Church & at Otterford, & elsewhere for some time; but may not goe forth to the world as a Gospel Minister, without ye approbation of ye Church of Luppit & of the Church of Somerton."[3]

This new document provides a great deal of information about William Screven. It relates to him in at least four areas.

In the first place, a close relationship of Screven to Thomas Collier is indicated. Even before this new material was discovered, it had been conjectured that Screven probably had been won to Christ and baptized by Collier, for Collier was one of the earliest and most important Baptist evangelists and church organizers in western England. W. T. Whitley, the outstanding English Baptist historian, called Collier "the absolute head of all the Baptist work in the West country."[4] He sketched a brief history of Collier in 1908 in the Baptist historical journal of England, urging that more research should be done on "this great evangelist of the West."[5] Whitley pointed out that two letters of Collier stolen by his enemies showed that he had been founding churches in the South and West of England as early as 1645. Thomas Edwards, one of the principal antagonists of English Baptists, quoted others to the effect that Collier was "an illiterate Carter, or an Husbandman (for so he is by his calling, I heare) though now by usurpation, a Preacher . . ." and was "the first who sowed the seeds of Anabaptism, Anti-sabbatarianism, and some Arminianisme among the sect in these parts."[6] Edwards also said that Collier had "emissaries under him, whom he sends abroad and commands to several parts, as Syms, Rowe, &c. and supply his places in his absence."[7]

Collier could very well have founded the Somerton church in the same way the new records show that he began the church at Luppit. He had organized several churches around Somerton before 1652. He was the principal figure in the organization of the Western Baptist Association, which probably should be dated before 1653.[8] Most historians credit him with the authorship of the Somerset Confession of Faith in 1656 which was set forth by the Western Baptist Association. W. L. Lumpkin said that this confession represented "the earliest important effort at bringing Particular and General Baptists into agreement and union."[9]

The numerous writings of Collier showed his eloquence and zeal, but they also revealed his erratic doctrinal and ecclesiological views. In the late 1640s he seems to have been influenced by the new Quaker emphasis on the ordinances of the church as being spiritual. There is uncertainty about his own ordination. Some writers call Collier a "lay-evangelist." Some speculate that he had been ordained earlier but may have renounced the ordination when he became enamored with some Quaker doctrines. In May, 1654, he was ordained at the meeting of the Western Baptist Association, evidently for the distinctive work of evangelism. The ambiguous language of the record at that time probably has given rise to some of the different views. A few in the association scrupled against Collier's ordination at the associational meeting in 1654, but the majority of the representatives in attendance

> concluded it there duty to procede in a further and more orderly
> ordaining and appoyntinge our deerly beloved brother Thomas Collier in

the name of our Lord Jesus and of his churches who were in it, to the
worke of the ministrey to the worlde and in the churches which was
performed by two brethren of Luppitt who were formerly ordained and
now called thereunto as their duty being desiered by the rest of their
brethren.[10]

Before 1677, however, Collier had receded considerably from the orthodox
posture he displayed between 1652 and 1659. Nehemiah Coxe, a scholarly
London Baptist, wrote a resounding blast against Collier in 1677, accusing
him of "Pelagian, Jesuitical & Socinian" heresies. This pamphlet was
endorsed by the principal ministers of London Baptists, including such
stalwarts as William Kiffin, Daniel Dyke, and William Collins. In that same
year, London Baptists prepared a confession of faith which was quite similar
to the Presbyterian Westminster Confession of Faith (save in the form of
baptism and the candidate). Collier replied with a counterconfession and
subsequently defended his doctrinal position in writings that made it plain he
had developed ideas quite remote from the Baptist position, especially in the
sensitive area of soteriology. He was a controversial figure until his death in
1690.[11]

This, then, was the Thomas Collier who probably won and baptized both
William Hare and William Screven. He was in his orthodox period in the
1650s when he sent word to these two "gifted brethren" to come to Luppit to
assist him in the preaching and baptizing. The language of the church records
suggests that Hare and Screven had been at Luppit before they baptized the
four men on June 1, perhaps preaching in the area after Collier went
elsewhere after May 6.

It is significant that Hare and Screven were described in the church records
as "gifted brethren," and Burford was given the same title. This was a term
identified with Thomas Collier and had become a technical title by 1652. In
several of his tracts, Collier defended his enlistment of "private persons" or
unordained men whom he identified as "gifted persons" for preaching.[12] To
insure an orderly ministry, Collier insisted that any such "gifted persons"
must first be approved by their own churches before being allowed to preach.
The Luppit records reflected this emphasis of Collier when they specifically
identified Hare and Screven, as well as Edmond Burford, as "gifted
brethren." Evidently Lucas Cyril was in the process of being certified as a
gifted brother in the twelfth item of the Orders and Instructions prepared by
Hare and Screven. He had just been baptized by Hare or Screven on June 1,
1652, and must have had some Christian experience prior to that time since he
was permitted to preach on the same day.

Thus, William Screven in 1652 can be identified as a Baptist layman from
Somerton, as a person known well enough for Thomas Collier to entrust him
with the fostering of the new Luppit church, and as one who had displayed

such spiritual gifts that Collier, the Somerton church, and the Luppit church would approve him as a "gifted brother."

In the second place, this new material suggests that William Screven may have been a preacher of more prominence than had been realized. He had been approved as a "gifted brother" before 1652, at least, and by the time he signed the Somerset confession in 1656 he may have had many opportunities of service similar to the one at Luppit. Three of the Luppit men whom Screven had baptized became "gifted brethren"—Samuel Ham, Edmond Burford, and Lucas Cyril. Perhaps he had assisted others to gain this standing in the four years between 1652 and 1656. Both Ham and Burford signed the Somerset confession, and these men would certainly look to Screven as a talented leader. Screven would also have been well-acquainted with William Hare, his companion at Luppit in 1652, who had become a pastor by 1656 and signed the Somerset confession in that year.

More than likely, Screven also attended other meetings of the Western Baptist Association after 1652 which were dominated by his mentor Thomas Collier. The association evidently planned to meet regularly each spring and fall, but special meetings for specific purposes were also convened. Between 1653 and 1659, regular general meetings took place four times at Wells (about ten miles north of Somerton); once at Taunton (about fifteen miles west of Somerton); three times at Bridgwater (about twelve miles west of Somerton); two times at Chard (about twenty miles southwest of Somerton); once at Tiverton (about thirty-five miles southwest of Somerton); and once at Dorchester (about thirty miles south of Somerton). Some of the special meetings occurred immediately preceding or following the regular general meetings. This seems to have been true at Wells in November, 1653, and April, 1656, and at Tiverton in September, 1657. The meeting at Exeter (about forty-five miles southwest of Somerton) in October, 1656, was evidently a special meeting about one month before the regular general meeting at Bridgwater.[13] It can be seen that these meetings of the association were not far distant from Somerton, so Screven could have attended. With the possible exception of the meeting adopting the Somerset Confession of 1656, none of the records showed all individuals in attendance, so it is difficult to be certain about Screven's presence at other than the 1656 session.

Thus, the closeness of Screven to Collier, Screven's influence in baptizing and inducting new "gifted brethren" into ministry, and his acquaintance with William Hare and perhaps many others attending the associational meetings reveal that Screven was no solitary Baptist figure in a small house-church in Somerton but was recognized as an active participant in a large and dedicated fellowship of ministering brethren. It is significant that when Henry Jessey, the notable London preacher, toured the western churches about 1655 at the invitation of Baptists at Bristol, he stopped at the Somerton house-church, doubtless visiting with Screven and other members of the congregation.

In the third place, this material may provide a clue to the activity of William Screven during the "silent years" between 1656 and 1668. As is true in the life of Thomas Collier, there are several blocks of time (both in England and in America) when Screven cannot be found in the records. No references have been found to the Somerton church after Screven represented her at the associational meeting in 1656. When Charles II permitted the licensing of dissenting preachers and places of preaching in 1672, Thomas Collier was licensed to preach at the North Bradley church in Wilts. Many other friends of Screven in the West were also licensed, but there is no record of a license for William Screven or any preacher or house at Somerton.[14] This indicates that the Somerton congregation may have disappeared before that time.

There were good reasons for the disappearance of many Baptist congregations in England between 1656 and 1668. Screven lived in England during some of the most tumultuous and unstable years in all English history. He probably was baptized during the civil war between Charles I and parliament from 1641 to 1649. Even the execution of the king in 1649 did not end the turmoil. As late as March 1655, for example, Colonel John Penruddock marched a Royalist force from Yeovil directly through the Luppit area north of Honiton, then proceded to South Moulton by way of Cullompton and Tiverton. Captain Unton Croke endeavored to engage Pendruddock but, missing him at Luppit, wheeled to the west and defeated him at South Moulton.[15] The turmoil of Cromwell's struggle for power had barely subsided before his death in 1658.

Even worse for the Baptists, however, the restoration of Charles II as king in 1660 initiated a period of the most rigorous persecution of Dissenters that the nation had known, as mentioned in the previous chapter. Two particularly vicious persecutions were the Conventicle Act of 1664, which forbade religious meetings by Dissenters, and the Five Mile Act of 1665, which permitted no dissenting minister to come within five miles of any city, town, or parish in which he had formerly served.

This severe persecution after 1660 caused many Baptist congregations to destroy their records lest they be used as evidence against them. Many of the small churches disappeared. This was a silent period in the life of Screven. However, the newly found Luppit records may hint at the activity of Screven during this time. There must have been a close relationship between the Somerton and the Luppit churches. In the Orders and Instructions prepared by Hare and Screven on May 31, 1652, the twelfth article specifically provided that Lucas Cyril must receive the approval of both the Luppit and the Somerton churches before going into the world as a gospel minister. When Cyril was baptized on May 31 by Hare or Screven, he was shown as being from Otterford, a few miles north of Luppit. Unless there was some overseeing relationship between the Luppit and the Somerton churches, it is difficult to understand why the Somerton church would need to approve Cyril's preaching.

Because of its location, Luppit became one of the most important meeting places for Baptists in the West during the intense persecution under Charles II. The community was situated near the hamlet of Upottery, where the counties of Devon, Somerset, and Dorset joined, and, as well, where five Anglican parishes came together. When some county or parish authority issued a warrant for the arrest of these Baptists, they could quickly cross the border into another county and parish out of the jurisdiction of the authorities pursuing them. Thus, the church came to be known as Luppit-Upottery as she moved about to escape the officers. Located on the highest spot in the entire area, the church worshiped "underground," posting a watch to warn the people about the approach of hostile authorities. Churches from miles around, finding themselves forced to discontinue their own services for fear of the authorities, spread the word that the safest place to worship was at Luppit-Upottery. The historian of Tiverton, for example, wrote:

> The Five Mile Act pressed severely on our fathers. Unable to meet in their own borough or its vicinity, their devotion made it impossible for them to forsake their assemblies for worship, and they therefore walked to Upottery, twenty-one miles distant. This place was chosen on account of its isolation, it being seven miles from any town containing a Nonconformist church. Another feature which greatly commended it to the persecuted Baptists was that at that time five parishes and three counties met there, so that when they were forbidden to meet in one county or parish it was easy to cross over into another, and so for a while they were undisturbed. To this spot came Baptists from all the country round, from Taunton, Wellington, Honiton, Tiverton, and even from Exeter.
>
> There is a tradition still in Upottery that the Baptists from Tiverton were accustomed to start from their homes with staff and provisions on the Saturday in order to cover the twenty-one miles in good time for the Sunday morning worship; and immediately the evening service was ended they would wish their brethren farewell, and walk back through the night, not reaching Tiverton until the early hours of Monday morning.[16]

But spies were everywhere and were encouraged to report unauthorized conventicles by giving the informant a share of the possessions of those arrested. The Luppit-Upottery historian wrote:

> Their meetings at and around Newhouse [Luppit-Upottery] were narrowly watched. Rarely could assemblies be held twice in the same place. Hence the baptisms by night in the pool, and also in the court yard of one Thomas Quick, a yeoman, and member of the Church, and probably at Fair Oak Farm. Near Taunton a number of friends were found meeting in a house. They were brought before the justices, convicted of a "conventi-

cle," and sentenced to pay £3 each or go to prison for 60 days. Nearly all
went to prison. Many of the Upottery Baptists suffered imprisonment and
transportation, and more emigrated to America.[17]

The reference to "transportation" meant that those arrested were banished
from England, often to the West Indies.

William Screven could have worshiped at Luppit-Upottery during the early
period of Anglican persecution. He may have been apprehended and placed in
jail without any record remaining. He could have been "transported." He
must have been familiar with the extreme sufferings endured by his Luppit-
Upottery friends. Joseph Allein, for example, was arrested while on his way
to preach at Luppit-Upottery. His letters to the church from prison in 1664
expressed his willingness to suffer martyrdom, which he did in prison in 1668
at the age of 35.[18] Probably Screven also knew about Abraham Cheare,
another Devon pastor and poet, who was arrested in 1661 and jailed at Exeter
for encouraging religious assemblies. Cheare was banished and, after much
suffering at the hands of the authorities, died in 1668 also.[19] The American
William Screven first appeared in the Massachusetts records in the very year
that Allein and Cheare died.

Finally, this new material from Luppit provides additional support for the
belief that the English William Screven was indeed the American Screven, not
a son by the same name. As mentioned earlier, Burrage initially held the view
that the American Screven was the English preacher but upon learning that the
American Screven had been baptized in Boston in 1681, he had conjectured
that the American Screven had been the unconverted son of the English
Screven, thus accounting for the baptism in America. Burrage's new position,
of course, would vitiate the position that religious persecution drove the
English Screven to America. More significant than that, however, as will be
noted, this view ignores the recognizable fact that the American Screven gave
many evidences of having been an experienced Baptist long before he was
immersed at Boston in 1681. A short time thereafter he displayed much
spiritual maturity; possessed a clear understanding of Baptist theology and
church order; utilized a Baptist vocabulary that could hardly have been
acquired quickly; was baptized, licensed, and ordained by a staid church that
refused to lay hands suddenly on anyone; and, notably, prepared a distinctive
church covenant after the English pattern. These developments occurred just a
few months after his baptism at Boston, as will be noted shortly.

Is there any hypothesis that can harmonize these seemingly contradictory
facts? There seems to be a better answer than producing a son by the same
name. Everyone who has studied the records of early American Baptist life
has noticed the sensitiveness of Baptist churches in striving to protect the
ordinances and ordination of the churches. If some stranger appeared for
membership and could not produce satisfactory evidence of a proper baptism,

he would be required to undergo the ordinance of baptism again, or he might be required to be ordained again should there be any evidence of an irregularity in a previous ordination.

When William Screven presented himself for membership in the Boston church by 1681, he probably conferred with John Myles, who had come to Boston to assist the church while she was without a pastor. Myles had brought his Baptist church from Wales to Massachusetts in 1663 to escape the same persecution that probably drove Screven from Somerton. It takes little imagination to reconstruct the dialogue between the two:

> Myles: Brother Screven, you have been worshiping with us for some time now, and we are impressed with your Christian understanding and spirit. And now you would like to join our church?
>
> Screven: Yes, Brother Myles. I was baptized at Somerton by Thomas Collier over thirty years ago. I preached as a "gifted brother."
>
> Myles: Do you have a recommendation from the Somerton church?
>
> Screven: No, the church met in my home, and when persecution came we were unable to worship together any more.
>
> Myles: I have experienced some of that, Brother Screven. You say that Thomas Collier baptized you?
>
> Screven: Yes, that is right.
>
> Myles: I knew about Mr. Collier and the questions about his ordination when I was pastor in Swansea, about sixty miles from Somerton by water and overland. You know that our London brethren have condemned him as a heretic, do you not?
>
> Screven: I have heard reports of it.
>
> Myles: Brother Screven, since you can get no church recommendation and Mr. Collier baptized you, I think that the church would prefer that you come as a candidate for baptism. This would eliminate any question about your baptism being done properly and would encourage your Congregational wife and her family to do the same.
>
> Screven: I agree. Bridget and I will come as candidates for baptism.

This solution to the identity of the American Screven would provide the simplest explanation that would cover all of the known facts. It is supported by many coincidental factors which, although not conclusive in themselves, combine to make such an hypothesis more attractive. All that is known about the character of William Screven in England, for example, harmonizes well with the American Screven: his zeal and unsparing labor, the ability to serve in an "underground" ministry effectively, and a spiritual maturity and understanding born of long experience in Baptist life. Furthermore, the American Screven (according to the reliable American chronology) was thirty-eight or thirty-nine years old when he arrived in Massachusetts. It would hardly seem logical for a man of this age to pull up his English roots and migrate to a strange land unless motivated by something like religious persecution. The fact that he apprenticed himself to learn a trade also suggests that he had no dependents, for such an occupation would hardly support a family. His religious zeal, the troubled times, and the incessant persecution could explain why he had not married earlier in England.

In addition, the sequence of time seems to fit better with the English preacher than with a possible son. If the English Screven were the American, he was born in 1629 at Somerton; was baptized by 1652; ministered at Luppit and probably elsewhere from 1652 until 1668, signing the Somerset Confession of Faith in 1656; and fled to America in 1668 to escape persecution. It would be more difficult to get a father into this picture. The fact that William Hare's name always came first in the Luppit records when he and Screven are mentioned together may suggest that Hare was the older man in 1652. A father of the American Screven would have probably been in his fifties.

When Humphrey Churchwood described William Screven to the Boston church in 1682, he said that Screven had "the spirit of the veterans." How could a man baptized only a few months earlier have this kind of spirit in Christian work unless he had some experiences comparable to those of the English Screven behind him?

Perhaps another coincidental detail is also relevant. The Kittery church was organized on September 25, 1682. It promptly adopted a church covenant, a most unusual practice for American Baptist churches.[20] As will be noted, the church covenant, evidently prepared by Screven, reflects the form of English Baptist church covenants in speaking of the purpose of serving God and one another and living holy lives. But it has a distinct Thomas Collier and Western Baptist Association flavor in it. Screven spoke in this church covenant of the "light att present through his grace given us, or here after he shall please to discover & make knowne to us thro his Holy Spirit." When this is compared with the language of Collier and the Western Association, there is much similarity. For example, in the reply by Collier to a query at the Taunton meeting of the association in 1654, he said, "onely we desire to wait on the Lord for further light for the full clearing of it." At the Bridgwater meeting in 1656, Collier replied to a query by saying, "We cannot at present determine this question but desire to waite on the Lord for further light on it." At the same meeting, he closed an answer to a query by saying, "This is our present light."[21] Other English Baptists occasionally used such expressions, but Collier was noted for this language.

Finally, the efforts of Collier and the Somerset Confession of Faith to tone down the doctrinal differences between General and Particular Baptists in the 1640s and 1650s seem to be reflected in the willingness of the American William Screven, after arriving at Charleston in 1696, to accept both groups into the church there, although by that time in England there was a considerable amount of tension between the two parties.

A New Land

There are no specific records showing when and how William Screven left England. Assuming that it was he and not his son who left, he could have embarked from Bristol where a rather substantial Baptist church existed. Doubtless he had met many Bristol members at the Western Baptist Association meetings. Bristol was only about thirty miles from Somerton. Depending upon favorable winds and weather, he could have arrived in Massachusetts in several months. His name first appeared in American records in 1668 when he witnessed a deed in Salisbury, Massachusetts, a few miles south of the Maine and New Hampshire line.[22] It probably was not a coincidence that this area had been settled by people from the strongly dissenting counties of Somerset, Devon, and Dorset in England. Indeed, many of the towns in that part of Massachusetts were named after similar towns in western England, such as Salisbury, Amesbury, Wells, and Portsmouth.

On May 10, 1669, Screven bound himself for four years "after the manner of an apprentice" to George Carr, a shipwright in Amesbury, about three miles west of Salisbury. There were already Baptists in this vicinity as will be noted hereafter. The Carr family had been engaged in the shipping business here for many years before Screven apprenticed himself to them, and they remained in Amesbury for many years after he left. Nothing is known about their religious background.[23]

There is no description anywhere of the person of William Screven. He must have been strong of body, for the use of hammer and saw in his daily work and the strenuous activity he maintained as a preacher for the next forty-three years would make harsh demands upon his physical stamina. He continued his work as a shipwright and carpenter until almost the time of his death at the age of eighty-four. Since he entered into a legal contract to bind himself to George Carr as an apprentice, he evidently came alone to America. There is no hint in the records that he had been married before coming to the New World.

On the Fringe of New England

William Screven's apprenticeship at Amesbury ended on May 10, 1673. On November 15 of that year he purchased from Elizabeth Seeley ten acres of land on Spruce Creek in Kittery, Maine, a few miles to the north of Amesbury.[24] He probably chose this area just out of the Massachusetts colony because he knew (as many did) that Kittery, Maine, and Portsmouth, New Hampshire (just across the Piscataqua River from Kittery), were a "haven for dissent." This community was Screven's world for over twenty years.

It must have seemed to William Screven, however, that he had hopped from the frying pan into the fire by leaving England for America. At the very time he appeared in northern Massachusetts and Maine, the Massachusetts colony was just as intolerant religiously as England had been. For over thirty years this colony and the Royal Commission in England had been sparring over the political rights of the colony, and only the civil war between parliament and Charles I prevented a possible revocation of the Massachusetts patent and royal seizure of the colony in the 1640s. The internal problems of England seemed to cause Massachusetts to become increasingly bolder in her relations with the Crown. During the English civil war, this colony defiantly laid claim to the provinces of Maine and New Hampshire, despite knowing that this claim would anger the royal authorities. If Massachusetts could have maintained this claim, it would have made little difference for William Screven whether he moved from Massachusetts into Maine or New Hampshire to escape persecution, for he would still have been under the suzerainty of Massachusetts and her theocracy.

When Charles II assumed the throne in 1660, political, economic, and religious reasons impelled him to take specific action to settle this quarrel with the Massachusetts colony. Politically, Massachusetts had befriended the regicides (the judges who had sentenced the king's father to death in 1649) and had aggressively resisted efforts by England to curb the sovereignty of the colony. Economically, Massachusetts, like most of the other American colonies, had been evading the laws of the mercantile system that had been instituted by England as a means of bringing more revenue to the mother country and keeping the colonies dependent upon her. Religiously, the theocratic ideas of the colony's leadership in Massachusetts had made a religious outcast of everyone not a Congregationalist including Church of England members in Massachusetts. Not only so, but only Congregationalists had a vote in the elections of the Massachusetts colonial government, and all other religious groups were politically disfranchised.

A critical stage in the struggle between Massachusetts and the Crown developed just a few years after William Screven moved to Maine. The Maine and New Hampshire area had been claimed by the heirs of Sir Ferdinando Gorges and Captain John Mason because of a royal grant from James I in 1620. The tension between the Gorges' heirs and the Massachusetts colony became critical. In 1663 John Archdale, a Quaker who later became one of the governors of South Carolina, visited New England as an agent of the Gorges-Mason interests to combat Massachusetts' claim to Maine and New Hampshire. The confrontation became so abrasive between Archdale and Massachusetts that it almost led to violence. Another event heightened the friction. In 1665 the four principal towns of New Hampshire (led by Portsmouth, just across the river from Kittery) presented a petition to the royal commissioners of England in which they accused Massachusetts of usurping the rights of the people and oppressing the king's loyal subjects in New Hampshire.[25] Another similar petition quickly followed urging that the New Hampshire colony be attached to Maine and that both be brought under the protection of the king.[26] However, the third war with Holland and internal dissension in England prevented vigorous action by the Crown until 1675.

In 1676 King Charles II sent Edward Randolph to inform Massachusetts that the crown was now ready to take action against her as a rebellious colony.[27] Randolph spent a month in the area, visiting Portsmouth, New Hampshire, and Kittery, Maine; and William Screven probably rejoiced to hear Randolph declare publicly that the Crown would soon intervene to bring Massachusetts to her knees and permit religious liberty for all inhabitants. The crisis deepened in March, 1678, when Massachusetts, in defiance of the king, purchased the Maine patent from the Gorges-Mason heirs. On July 24, 1679, Charles strongly rebuked Massachusetts for making this purchase and said that the Crown would assume ownership of the Maine patent after reimbursing Massachusetts for the price she had paid to the Gorges-Mason heirs. The Massachusetts leaders, however, voted to defy the king and, on February 24, 1680, appointed commissioners to supervise Maine. The king and Massachusetts were now in open conflict. Boston began to fortify her harbor.

So, about seven years after moving to Kittery, William Screven stood in the midst of a revolution. Apart from the religious issues involved, he was ready to take sides. He had developed close ties in the communities of Kittery and Portsmouth with persons who were opposed to Massachusetts authority, such as Captain Francis Champernowne, Nicholas Shapleigh, Robert Cutt (or Cutts), Robert Jordan, Thomas Withers, Henry Jocelyn, Edward Hilton, Abraham Corbett, and John Hole.[28] Highborn Champernowne was the outstanding man in the entire Kittery community at this time, owning most of the land in the area. He had lived in the West Indies in his earlier years and occasionally would spend a winter in Barbados during his residence near Kittery. He was a merchant in Kittery and a close friend to William Screven. The other outstanding member of this group of friends was Robert Cutt, one of three influential brothers. Evidently he had been a traveling merchant, having come to Maine from Barbados. He had married Mary Hole, probably while they were in Barbados; her brother, John Hole, later came from Barbados to Kittery to live.

Robert Cutt had six children. The youngest was Robert Cutt, Jr., born in 1673, just one year before his father died. On July 23, 1674, about a month after Robert Cutt, Sr., died, William Screven married Bridget, evidently the oldest daughter of Robert and Mary Hole Cutt. The one-year-old child, Robert, was put into the home of Screven and his new wife, perhaps while the widow (Mary Hole Cutt) returned to her original home in Barbados with her brother John Hole for a time. By 1682 Mary Hole Cutt had returned to Kittery and soon married Captain Francis Champernowne.[29]

William Screven had also become a rather prominent civic figure and shipwright in Kittery, Maine. He was named constable for lower Kittery in 1676 and served on the grand jury in 1678 and 1679. Furthermore, during King Phillip's war with the Indians between 1675 and 1678, he took Joseph, the minor child of Benjamin Atwell, into his own home and later became his official guardian. Screven soon identified his position relative to the Massachusetts conflict with the Crown. On July 24, 1679, Charles II wrote Massachusetts that he expected her to permit freedom of conscience so that members of the Church of England, and others who did not wish to worship in the Congregational way, might be unhindered in their religious practices and not subject to fines, forfeitures, or other punishment, "which is a severity the more to be wondered at, when liberty of Conscience was made one principal motive for your first transportation to those parts."[30]

Later that year a dramatic scene took place. Over one hundred citizens of Kittery, knowing their minority status and disdaining the reprisals that they knew would come, stood quietly to sign a petition to the king. They reviewed the struggle between the Crown and the Massachusetts colony since 1661 and reminded the king that the colony had flaunted his royal authority. This sturdy document closed with a prayer that the king "take the premise into your royal consideration and by your gracious letters to reestablish and confirm us under your royal authority granting liberty to tender consciences." On his feet to support this petition and to sign it was William Screven.[31] This scene was repeated in the following year when Screven signed a second provocative petition to the king in which the Crown was asked to establish a royal government in Maine.[32]

This open identification of his opposition to the Congregational theocracy of Massachusetts by William Screven speaks of his willingness to risk the reprisals that such a position was bound to bring. There seems to be little doubt why he chose this side. It was the party of his mother-in-law and her brother John Hole, his distinguished friend Francis Champernowne, and many of his neighbors and close friends in the community. The repeated promises of liberty of conscience made by the Crown, not only for Maine and New Hampshire but for Dissenters in Massachusetts as well, also exerted no little influence upon his choice. This side also was the one any Baptist would have to take.

Screven Steps into Baptist Leadership

There are no records to picture the religious life of William Screven in America before 1681. For some time before June, 1681, he must have been riding horseback from Kittery to attend the Baptist church at Boston, Massachusetts, a distance of about fifty miles each way. The Baptist church at Boston had been organized in June, 1665, by seven men and two women under the leadership of Thomas Gould, after several of its charter members had been meeting for about ten years in private homes. Three of the men and two of the women had been Baptists in England (Richard Goodall from William Kiffin's Baptist church in London, William Turner and Robert Lambert from Robert Steed's Baptist church in Dartmouth, and Goodall's wife and Mary Newell from other English Baptist churches).[33] Thomas Gould, Thomas Osborne, Edward Drinker, and John George became members by baptism, the first two from the Congregational church, and the latter two upon profession of faith and without any prior church relationship, although they had lived in the colony for many years.[34]

This Boston church was persecuted for the first fifteen years of her life. Following the example of Baptist churches in England, the church often moved here and there to escape harrassment. This constant movement posed no problem because the church had no house of worship. Sometimes they met in Charlestown, Massachusetts, and often on Noddle's Island in east Boston, out of the jurisdiction of the Boston authorities. The imprisonment of William Turner and John Farnum on July 30, 1668, by the Boston court for holding Baptist services brought some surprising results. Congregationalists in England, upon hearing of this persecution, strongly urged their New England counterparts not to persecute the Baptists. In a long letter, one said:

> And what! is that horrid principle crept into precious New England, who have felt what persecution is, and have always pleaded for liberty of conscience? Have not these (Baptists) run equal hazards with you for the enjoyment of their liberties; and how do you cast a reproach upon us, that are Congregational in England, and furnish our adversaries with weapons against us? We blush and are filled with shame and confusion of face, when we hear of these things.[35]

Another said:

> Anabaptists are neither spirited nor principled to injure nor hurt your government nor your liberties; but rather these be a means to preserve your churches from apostasy, and provoke them to their primitive purity.[36]

In July, 1679, after the death of Gould and a brief interim pastorate by John Myles from Swansea, Massachusetts, John Russell of Woburn was ordained as pastor of the Boston church.[37] Meanwhile, a plain meetinghouse had been erected in Boston for worship by the Baptists by February 15, 1679. Several of the Baptist leaders were promptly arrested, and the doors to the meeting-house were sealed. After many arrests and threatenings, Boston Baptists were able to occupy this building for worship in 1680. The pastor, John Russell, died December 21, 1680, and it appears that John Myles returned to Boston from Swansea to assist the Boston church by his ministry. The church records showed that he baptized Mary Dill at the church on November 12, 1681. Isaac (Isaack) Hull was probably not ordained as pastor of this church until 1682.

That William Screven had visited this Boston Baptist church during the pastorates of Gould, Myles, and Russell seems likely, as will be pointed out later. The church record simply said, however, that on June 21, 1681, William Screven, his wife, and Humphrey Churchwood, all of Kittery, Maine, were baptized into the fellowship of the church. It would appear that they were baptized by John Myles. Why would Screven step out so boldly at this time?

On the face of it, there were political and personal factors involved in this action by Screven and his friends. From a political point of view, for a man with dissenting ideas this was the very time to step out into the open. The religious intolerance of the Massachusetts colony was now being vigorously attacked by no less an authority than the Crown of England. Not only was the Crown promising liberty of conscience, but at this very time Boston Baptists were holding public services in their own building. Imprisonment and banishment of Baptists had now been replaced by occasional fines and literary attacks. The accusations of political disloyalty by Baptists had been given the lie by the heroic actions of members of the Boston Baptist church who helped defend Massachusetts during the Indian attacks of the 1660s. Edward Drinker and William Turner, for example, were officers in the Massachusetts militia, and Turner lost his life in fighting for Massachusetts at the Deerfield engagement of 1676.

When Increase Mather published in March, 1679, a denunciatory blast against Baptists entitled "The Divine Rite of Infant Baptism," John Russell, pastor of the Boston Baptist church, replied in a dispassionate *Narrative* in the following year. He answered completely the eight charges Mather made against the Baptists: that they were a schismatical company; that they were scandalous persons; that they were disorderly persons; that they were disturbers of the public peace; that they were underminers of the church; that they neglected the public worship of God on the Lord's day; that they were idolators; and that they were enemies of civil government. The reply of Russell was printed in England and introduced by six prominent English Baptist ministers who pointed out that Congregationalists in England "do equally plead for our liberties as for their own," and continued as follows:

> And it seems most strange that such of the same way in New-England, yea even such (a generation not yet extinct, or the very next successors of them) also chose rather (with liberal estates) to depart from their native Soil into a Wilderness, than be under the imposition and lash of those who upon Religious pretences took delight to smite their Fellow-Ser-

vants; should exercise towards others the like severity that themselves with so great hazard and hardship fought to avoid; Especially considering that it is against their Brethren, who avowedly profess and appeal to the same rule with themselves for their guidance in, and decision of all matters relating to the Worship of God, and the ordering of their whole Conversation.[38]

Probably the simplest explanation of why Screven took this step is that this was the same William Screven who had signed the Somerset Confession in 1656 in England. As his children were born and pressure was exerted on him to have them sprinkled as babies, he increasingly realized that it was impossible to remain "underground" about his Baptist convictions.

The hypothesis as to why the English Screven would need to be baptized in Boston has already been outlined. The best evidence points to the American William Screven as being the English "gifted person" by that name, not his son. The Boston church simply would not have baptized, licensed, and ordained a new convert as pastor of the Kittery church, as will be described shortly, in the few months between June 21, 1681, and September 25, 1682. This American William Screven was not a new convert or an inexperienced Baptist. The description in his license to preach, which was issued by the Boston church about six months after his baptism, solemnly affirmed that his spiritual gifts had been tried in Boston and the church had found him "to be a man whom God hath qualified and furnished with the gifts of his Holy Spirit and grace, enabling him to open and apply the word of God."

As will be noted hereafter, the Boston church would never have taken this hasty action in the case of a new Christian. This William Screven must have possessed and exercised unusual spiritual gifts before he came to the Boston church for baptism. His Christian maturity will be glimpsed in his letters and those of Humphrey Churchwood written to the Boston church. His Christian vocabulary reflected long experience in speaking the language of Zion. The church covenant prepared by Screven when the Kittery church was organized demanded much more background in Baptist life than a few months of walking in the Christian way. As will be noted, the correspondence of Screven and Churchwood makes it clear that both were quite familiar with Baptist polity, Baptist events of previous years, and the Baptist situation that existed in America and England about this time.

What about Screven's "silent" years in Kittery between 1673 and 1681? It is possible that in the midst of a dissenting community like Kittery during these years, when no record can be found about Screven's religious activity, the Somerton William Screven could have been relatively active in his Baptist convictions without incurring the wrath of the authorities. An example of this was Seth Sweester, who had been a Baptist in Hertfordshire, England, and in 1638 came to Boston, where he quickly prospered. He was unmolested for twenty-four years. He died in 1662 (before the Boston church was organized) but had been active with those preparing to organize a Baptist church in Boston. His son Benjamin became a member of the Boston church before 1669 and was ordained a deacon in 1688. So, even in Boston itself, little attention was paid to those who were not faithful to the Puritan God, unless overt and noisome activity demanded reprisal.[39] Many second-generation Congregationalists were turning away from their own churches, and the Half-Way Covenant of 1662 marked a distinct lowering of Congregational religious vitality.

Thus, although there would be little problem if the American William Screven were the son of the English William Screven, the whole picture seems to suggest that the American Screven was in fact the Somerton Screven who signed the 1656 Somerset Confession. If not, the story that the American Screven died as an old man in 1713 is difficult to accept.

The Church Organized

The records were silent about any persecution which these new members of the Boston Baptist church may have suffered during the remainder of 1681, but on January 3, 1682, Humphrey Churchwood wrote a long letter to the Boston church as follows:

> Humphrey, a servant of Jesus Christ to the church which is at Boston; grace be with you, and peace, from God, even the Father of our Lord Jesus Christ, the Father of mercies and the God of all comforts, who comforteth us in all our tribulations that we may be able to comfort them that are in any trouble, as we are comforted of God. Most dearly beloved brethren and friends, as I am, through free grace, a member of the same body and joined to the same Head, Christ Jesus, I thought it my special duty to inform you that the tender mercy of God in and through Jesus Christ, hath shined upon us by giving light to them that sit in darkness, and to guide our feet in the way of peace; for a great door, and effectual, is opened in these parts, and there are many adversaries, according to the 1st of Corinthians, 16.9. Therefore, dearly beloved, having a desire to the service of Christ, which is perfect freedom, and the propagating of his glorious gospel of peace and salvation, and eyeing that precious promise in Daniel the 12th, 3d, 'They that turn many to righteousness shall shine as the stars forever'; therefore I signify unto you, that here [are] a competent number of well established people whose hearts the Lord hath opened insomuch that they have gladly received the word and do seriously profess their hearty desire to the following of Christ and to partake of all his holy ordinances, according to his blessed institution and divine appointment; therefore I present my ardent desire to your serious consideration, which is, if the Lord see it fit, to have a gospel church planted here in this place; and in order hereunto, we think it meet that our

beloved brother, William Screven, who is, through free grace, gifted and endued, with the spirit of veterans to preach the gospel; who, being called by us, who are visibly joined to the church. When our beloved brother is ordained according to the sacred rule of the Lord Jesus, our humble petition is to God that he will be pleased to carry on this good work to the glory of his holy name, and to the enlarging of the kingdom of his beloved Son, our dear Redeemer, who will add daily to his church such as shall be saved; and we desire you in the name of our Lord Jesus not to be slack in this good work, believing verily that you will not, and that you are always abounding in the work of the Lord, and we humbly crave your petitions for us to the throne of grace, and we commend you to God and the good word of his grace, which is able to build you up and to give you an inheritance among them that are sanctified.[40]

There are several interesting references in this letter. Evidently Humphrey Churchwood was familiar enough with the history of the Boston church and the practice of Baptists to request that a Baptist church be formed at Kittery by the Boston church. This was not an unusual request from the standpoint of British Baptists or of Boston Baptists. For example, Richard Goodall and his wife Mary, both of whom had been faithful Baptists before emigrating from England, had come to Massachusetts and settled at Newberry (Newbury) by 1638, finally locating at Salisbury in 1639-40. They became members of the Boston church at the time it was founded in 1665. They probably lived in Salisbury when William Screven witnessed a deed there in 1668. Amesbury, where Screven spent four years as an apprentice, was only a few miles from Salisbury. He may have known the Goodalls there. George Little and his wife had been baptized by the Boston church in 1676; William Sayer and wife, Benjamin Moss and wife, Edward Woodman and wife, John Sayer, and Abel Merrill were baptized in Boston on July 1, 1681—all of them residents of Newberry. These last-named persons were baptized in Boston just a few weeks after William Screven and wife and Humphrey Churchwood were immersed. In 1682 the Boston church "assented to the settling of the church at Newberry." This Newberry Baptist church was only a few miles from Kittery on the Boston road. Screven must have known about it and may have stopped there on one of his many trips to Boston. The church was in existence in 1689 and perhaps thereafter, although the records have disappeared entirely.[41]

A somewhat similar situation occurred at Woburn, Massachusetts, about halfway between Boston and Kittery, Maine. There were Baptists at Woburn and Billerica at least by 1669. Two years later Isaac Cole, Francis Wiman, Francis Kendall, Robert Pierce, Matthew Smith, Joseph Wright, John Johnson, Hopestill Foster, John Pierce, John Russell, and Matthew Johnson were summoned to court "for absence from Church and opposition to infant Baptism."[42] Most of these later became members of the Boston Baptist church. They desired to form a separate church at Woburn but finally decided that the Woburn group should continue meeting with the Boston church "until ye said Church att Boston be supplyed with A sufficient Able ministry settled with them in Boston."[43] John Russell, Jr., one of these Woburn Baptists, had displayed gifts for pastoral leadership. After conference with John Myles, pastor of the Baptist church at Swansea (whom the Boston church wanted as pastor but could not get the Swansea church to release him), the church ordained John Russell on July 28, 1679, as pastor of the Boston church. The Woburn group, not being able to find a pastor, did not form a separate church.

So, in a fashion duplicating the method of British Baptists in forming new Baptist churches, the Boston church was already working with groups of Baptists in several parts of Massachusetts to do the very thing that Humphrey Churchwood wanted them to do at Kittery: to settle a new Baptist church at Kittery, Maine, where some of the Boston members lived. That both Churchwood and Screven were familiar with this contemporary history of Baptist groups at Newberry, Woburn, and Billerica can hardly be doubted.

Churchwood's letter suggested that he also had been a Christian for longer than the six months since he was baptized at Boston. The quoting and paraphrasing of many scriptural passages and the typical Baptist vocabulary of the letter revealed considerable Christian and Baptist maturity. His use of the expression "free grace" reproduced a favorite phrase in English Baptist Calvinistic confessions of faith, and although he, like William Screven, was baptized by the Boston church six months earlier, his Baptist background evidently went back much farther.

The letter also indicated that he and William Screven had been witnessing to others, since there was in Kittery "a competent number of well established people whose hearts the Lord hath opened insomuch that they have gladly received the word and do seriously profess their hearty desire to the following of Christ." He does not give specific names of "well established people," but they doubtless included some of those who later signed the church covenant at Kittery.

It should be noticed that in this letter Churchwood described Screven as one "who is, through free grace, gifted and endued, with the spirit of veterans to preach the gospel." This is hardly the language that would be used of a man who had been converted about six months earlier. Screven must have been active in an American "underground" witness similar to the one he followed in England during the days of persecution there.

This letter was personally delivered by Screven to the Boston church. It would be interesting to know what route he took. Perhaps he mounted his horse at Kittery early on a snowy or icy January Monday morning and rode to Amesbury and Salisbury, eighteen miles south, where he could have spent the night with friends whom he had known there since his apprentice days. Then on the following day he may have ridden to Newberry, five miles farther south, where many Baptists were located and where a new Baptist church would be established by Boston Baptists during that year. After visiting briefly there, he may have ridden twenty miles farther to Billerica and Woburn, where he could have spent the second night with Baptist friends. From Woburn it was only about ten miles farther to Boston. Recalling the frigid and usually snowy weather of Maine and Massachusetts in early January, one must reflect about the stamina and conviction needed to journey several hundred miles on horseback from Kittery to Boston (and probably on to Swansea, Massachusetts) before returning home.

The request of Churchwood that Screven be set apart for Christian ministry brought immediate action. In fact, this action must have come at the very first church meeting after Screven arrived in Boston with Churchwood's letter of January 3. On January 11, 1682, the following action was taken by the church:

> To All Whom It May Concern:—These are to certify, that our beloved brother William Screven is a member in communion with us, and having had trial of his gifts among us, and finding him to be a man whom God hath qualified and furnished with the gifts of his Holy Spirit and grace, enabling him to open and apply the word of God, which through the blessing of the Lord Jesus may be useful in his hand, for the begetting and building up of souls in the knowledge of God, do therefore appoint, approve and encourage him, to exercise his gift in the place where he lives, or elsewhere, as the providence of God may cast him; and so the Lord help him to eye his glory in all things, and to walk humbly in the fear of his name.[44]

The rapid action of the church, as well as the statement that his gifts had been tried and that he was a man qualified to open and apply the Word of God, makes it plain that Screven had been well known to the church long before this time. The Boston church, like other Baptist churches, was not inclined to lay hands suddenly on anyone in ordination or even to grant a license of this sort until the members were satisfied that the candidate possessed gifts for ministry. Ellis Callender, for example, was a lay preacher in the Boston church for about thirty years and had led in public worship in the absence of the pastor many times between 1669 (when he became a member of the church) and 1708 when he was ordained and called as pastor of the church.[45]

Furthermore, the particular office that the Boston church seemed to envision for Screven was that of pastor. Early New England Baptist churches often had three types of elders—the pastor, a teaching elder, and a ruling elder. The pastor was the leader and preacher; the teaching elder taught the Bible and often moved from that post to become pastor; the ruling elder visited the sick, rebuked, and administered discipline. The license of William

Screven did not look toward the teaching or ruling eldership but spelled out the qualifications for pastoral leadership. It should be emphasized that this document of the Boston church was a license for William Screven and not ordination, as some writers have thought. It professed confidence in Screven as a man gifted by the Holy Spirit for applying the Word of God and reaching souls for Christ.

When Screven did not return to Kittery from Boston after about three weeks, Churchwood wrote a second letter to the Boston church dated January 25, 1682, which read:

> Grace be multiplied, and peace, from God our Father, and from the Lord Jesus Christ. Most dearly beloved brethren and Christian friends, I thought good to inform you that since our beloved brother Screven went from us, who, I trust is by God's mercy, now with you, by his long absence from us, has given great advantage to our adversaries to triumph and to endeavor to beat down that good beginning which God, by his poor instrument hath begun amongst us; and our magistrate, Mr. Hucke, is almost every day summoning and threatening the people by fines and other penalties, if they ever come to our meetings any more, five shillings for every such offense. And yesterday, being the twenty-third of this instant January, I was fetched before him by a summons, whither being come, he demanded of how I spent my time; being informed, as I understood, that I made it my business to go from house to house as a seducer; but after I gave him to understand that I was joined to the baptized church of Boston, in covenant and fellowship, he told me that he was very sorry that I was deluded and misled; and our minister, Mr. Woodbridge, being present, he began to rail upon you, and especially of being built upon excommunicate persons, naming one John Farnum, who, he said was a grievous, censorious man; and would not let Mr. Mader [Mather] alone till he had cast him out of his church. Then I gave him the book set forth by Elder John Russell, and told him, if he would impartially read that book, he would not speak so evilly of them. But Woodbridge told him that he would affirm that there were many palpable untruths in that book; but I said there were many grievous, false scandals and false insinuations in their book entitled *The Divine Rite of Infant Baptism*, falsely laid upon those who professed believers' baptism which had been fully answered by a letter from one Kiffin, of London, and confuted by all sober men, and taken to arise from a spirit of inveternation of ministers, and that none might preach except called by men, I affirmed that it is written God's people shall all be taught of him, and therefore, as every man has received the gift of God, so let him administer the same as good stewards of the manifold grace of God. Then Mr. Hucke answered, saying, Behold your great Doctor, Mr. Miles of Swanzey, for he now leaves his profession and is come away, and will not teach his people any more, because he is like to perish for want, and his gathered church and people will not help him. I answered, it was a great

untruth, but he said he could bring two sufficient men to testify that they had it from his own mouth at Boston. Dear brethren, I cannot harbor any such thing, but it is in every one's mouth, and it is a great stumbling block to many tender consciences; therefore, I request you not to fail, as soon as you can possibly, if this letter come to your hand before Brother Screven cometh from thence, that you would send an answer to this thing, for the satisfaction of our friends here, and I hope you will take that into serious consideration which I sent by Brother Screven. And the good will of him that dwelt in the bush, be with you to guide you in all your undertakings. And so, humbly craving your prayers for us, and that you will dispatch Brother Screven as soon as he cometh back from Swanzey, for his long tarrying maketh us conclude that he is gone thither. All our friends here are well, blessed by God! and we hope the same by you, which is the tenor of our prayers.[46]

Evidently Screven was the chief means of communication between the Kittery group and Boston, for Churchwood had not yet received the news that the Boston church had already licensed Screven to preach about two weeks earlier. This letter showed Screven to be the center and strength of the Kittery band. It also revealed the extensive familiarity of Churchwood (and Screven) with the contemporary Baptist situation. Churchwood had given Benjamin Woolbridge, the Congregational minister at Kittery, a copy of the very rare tract by John Russell answering that attack by Increase Mather against the Baptists. Francis Hooke, who had been a Congregational preacher at Saco, Maine, about 1660 and a political opportunist after he left the ministry, claimed to have personal knowledge of problems faced by John Myles, Baptist pastor at Swansea on the Rhode Island border. It would be interesting to know the identity of the "two sufficient men" (who also were untruthful men) that Hooke said had heard Myles dolefully discuss the Swansea situation. These Kittery Congregationalists seemed to follow Baptist matters rather carefully. The whole picture emphasizes the closeness of the Baptist community in Massachusetts and Maine.

One reason for the delay in the return of Screven to Kittery may have been the fact that exactly one week after Screven was licensed, Leonard Drown (Drowne), a thirty-six-year-old shipwright living at Sturgeon Creek, about seven miles from Portsmouth and Kittery, was baptized by the Baptist church at Boston. He became a part of the Kittery church when it was organized. In 1692 he moved to Boston because of the Indian uprisings. One of his sons, Shem Drown, became an active leader and deacon in the First Baptist Church of Boston, where he was baptized in 1713.[47]

There is no record of the date when Screven returned to Kittery, but on March 13, 1682, he was brought on a special warrant before the Provincial Council at York which was made up of Deputy-President John Davees, Edward Rishworth, and Francis Hooke. The record read:

William Scrivine upon rumors & reports from a Comman fame of some presumptuos if not blasfeamous speeches about the holy ordinance of baptisme which should pass from him, whereof being Informed, wee sent for sd Scrivine by a spetiall Warrant to Yorke where upon examination, hee did not absolutely deney his Charge, but after It was proved hee, seemd to own & Justify the matter of his speeches, in his secund Charge, though hee possitively denyd the first about his Child, for Infant Baptisms hee sayd was an ordinance of the Devill, as the testimonys declare, hee replyd that hee Conceived it no ordinance (5:107) of God but an Invention of man, what was It? & put us to prove by any possitive Command in the Gospell or scriptures that there was Infant baptisme, & according to our understandings hee Indeavored to make good the matter of his words, & to put the manner of them into a smoother dress, minceing the matter as Edw: Rishworth tould him, whose reply was that minceing was to put it in better tearmes then It deserved, chargeing Mr. Hooke with prejudice who brought him thither, & desired not to bee Judgd by him.

After some further discourse wee required sd Scrivine to give in security sufficient to the Treasurer of the province of a bond of one hundred pounds to answere his charge at the next Court of pleas houlden for this Province, or wee must make him his Mittimus & send him to the Gaole. which sd Scrivine refuseing accordingly was done.[48]

Evidently Screven had refused to have one of his children sprinkled and plainly told the court that infant baptism was not taught in the Scriptures and inquired where the authority for this ordinance was found. He did not deny that he had made speeches against infant baptism. Screven's statement that Francis Hooke was prejudiced against him probably stemmed from a long relationship. Hooke had signed the protest of 1668 to the king, along with Screven and others, asking that royal control be established in Maine. However, when Massachusetts gained control, Hooke had jumped to that side and had been named a justice of the peace. Perhaps he and Screven had exchanged warm words about integrity and consistency. Later on, Hooke would shift back to the royal side before his death in 1695.[49] Screven refused to give a bond for one hundred pounds (which seems excessive for this sort of charge) and was put into jail to insure his appearance at the Court of Pleas. How long he remained in jail is not clear, but from the language of the court on April 12, he evidently was released before that hearing.

The records of the Boston Baptist church revealed that someone was active in witnessing during this time, for on March 20, 1682, the following Kittery residents were baptized at Boston: William Adams, Humphrey Axill (sometimes spelled Axtell, Axtall, etc.), Timothy Davis, George Litten (sometimes spelled Liddon, Litton, Lytton, Leddon, etc.), and John Morgradge (a rare old Somerset name, sometimes spelled Morgrage, Morgradye, etc.). Adams was a relatively young man who had come to Kittery from England and apprenticed himself to Thomas Withers, a strong anti-Massachusetts leader of Kittery. He will be discussed later in connection with the South Carolina church. Little is known of the previous background of Humphrey Axill, but he became a part of the South Carolina group. Timothy Davis was a young Welshman who worked as a joiner in Portsmouth. George Litten was a mariner who first purchased land in Kittery in 1667. John Morgradge was a bricklayer of Kittery and was well known as an anti-Massachusetts figure.[50]

How much William Screven had to do with winning these converts from Kittery is not known. When the Court of Pleas met on April 12, their verdict said:

> This Court haveing Considered the offencive speeches of William Scrivine, by his rash inconsiderate words tending to blasfemy, do Adjudg the Delinquent for his offence to pay ten pounds in to the Treasury of the Countey, or province, And further the Court doth further discharge the sd Scrivine under any pretence to keepe any private exercise at his own house or else where upon the Lords dayes either in Kittery or any other place within the lymitts of this province, and is for the future Injoyned to observe the publique worship of God in our publique Assemblys upon the Lords days according to the laws here Established in this province, upon such poenultys as the law requires, upon his Neglect of the Premisses.[51]

It appears that William Screven was holding religious services on Sunday in his own home and perhaps other places nearby and was not attending the Congregational religious services.

On June 28, 1682, Screven was brought before the General Assembly, the highest provincial court. Evidently he had continued to hold Baptist meetings in defiance of the order of the Court of Pleas and had refused to attend services of the Congregational church. The record of the General Assembly said:

> William Scrivine appeareing before this Court & being before Convicted of the Contempt of his Majestys authority, by refuseing to submitt him selfe to the sentence of the former Court, prohibiting his publique exerciseing, referring to some irreligious speeches uttered by him & upon examination before this Court declareing his resolution still to persist in the same Course, The Court tendered him lyberty to returne home to his family in case he would forbeare such kind of disorderly & turbulent practises, & amend for the future, but hee refuseing, the Court required him to give bond for his good behaviour, & to forbeare such Contemptuos behaviours for the future, & ordered that the delinquent should stand Committed untill the Judgment of this Court herein bee

fullfilld, after which sd Scrivine Comeing into the Court did in the
presence of the sd Court & President promiss and Ingage to depart out of
this province with in a very short time.[52]

What did William Screven mean when he said that he intended to depart
from the province within a short time? There are some interesting possibilities. For one thing, the Boston church may have made overtures for him
to become her pastor. Elder Russell had died on December 21, 1680, and the
church was without a pastor until Isaac Hull was ordained about two years
later. Hull was aged and could not carry on the work. The church had written
to London for a minister in 1681, saying, "Our minister is very aged and
feeble, and often incapable of his ministerial work."[53] On July 23, 1683, a
Brother Browne was admitted to the Boston church "to administer the Word
amongst us," but the church did not retain him.[54] Baptist preachers were a
rare item in those days. Another possibility is that John Myles had requested
Screven to take his place at Swansea. Myles was nearly at the point of death at
this time, finally passing away on February 3, 1683.

Most intriguing of the possibilities, however, is that someone from the
Blake or Bulline or Smith families in South Carolina, who had come from
Somersetshire (Screven's home in England) or nearby counties in the early
1680s, had corresponded with William Screven after arriving in the southern
colony. If so, as early as 1682 Screven may have considered moving to the
colony which freely offered religious liberty, and it may be more than
coincidence that when he did go to South Carolina, Joseph Blake had just
become governor.

Whatever Screven may have meant in saying that he would depart out of the
province shortly, it is evident that between June and September, 1682, he
changed his mind. Perhaps his continued success in witnessing among the
Kittery people encouraged him to think in terms of organizing a Baptist
church at Kittery. This is suggested by the fact that in July, 1682, three other
Kittery residents were baptized by the Boston church: Richard Cutt, Robert
Williams, and a Mr. Landall.[55] Nothing further is known about Landall. Cutt
was the twenty-two-year-old son of Robert and Mary (Hole) Cutt, father and
mother of Screven's wife. Through his family the Cutt name was carried into
the twentieth century in Maine. Robert Williams was a joiner from Portsmouth, just across the river from Kittery.

Another reason for Screven's change of mind may have been the increasing
evidence that the Crown would soon force Massachusetts to grant liberty of
conscience, which would allow a Baptist church to worship in Kittery
without molestation. So, instead of leaving the province, Screven reiterated
his defiance of the authorities. On September 13, 1682, Screven wrote to
Thomas Skinner, son-in-law of the founder of the Boston church and at this
time a deacon in the church, as follows:

To Thomas Skinner, Boston, for the church: Dearly beloved brethren in the Lord Jesus Christ, the King of saints. I and my wife salute you with our Christian love in our Lord Jesus, hoping through grace these few lines will find you in health of body and mind. Blessed be God for Jesus Christ, in whom he is pleased to account his saints meet to be partakers of the blessed rest provided for them in his mansion-house eternally in the heavens. That will be happy day when all the saints shall join together in sounding of his praise. The good Lord enable us to prepare for that blessed day. To that end, brethren, let us pray, every one himself, for himself, and for one another, that God would please to search our hearts and reins, so as that we may walk with God here, and hereafter dwell with him in glory.

I had thought to have been with you last church-meeting, but my wife's condition was such I could not come, and this time by providence, I have taken some hurt, so that I cannot ride so far as yet. I hope to be with you next month, if the Lord will. And we have sent you our apprehensions about our present state. I hope we are conscientious in what we have said to you. I believe you will not judge otherwise. I am persuaded it will do much for the honor of God to have it done here. Besides, my mother-in-law hath desired to follow Christ in that ordinance. We all conceive it will be more honorable and expedient that it be done by the Elder Hull, that is so truly praised here. I pray you to consider these things. Both may be done when the messengers come up to us. My humble request to you is, that you will grant us what we have conscientiously treated you for. I conceive we are all agreed to leave our burdens, and you to agree on the time. No more at present; but rest, your unworthy brother in gospel relation.[56]

Screven remarked here that he had planned to attend the last church meeting at Boston but had been deterred by an injury to himself and by the condition of his wife (probably awaiting the birth of another child). He indicated that he would probably be with them at the next monthly church meeting. This suggests that he was no stranger to the monthly church meetings of the Boston church, even though attendance involved a ride on horseback of about one hundred miles. His reference to the desire of Mrs. Cutt (his mother-in-law) to be baptized, as well as the possible organization of a church at Kittery, may reflect some of his reasons for deciding not to leave the province.

The letter brought a quick response. In less than two weeks, despite his age and infirmities, Isaac Hull, along with Thomas Skinner and Philip Squire, made the journey from Boston to Kittery, conducted a strict examination of the group desiring to form the church, approved their doctrinal stance, helped ordain Screven and Churchwood as pastor and deacon respectively, declared the Kittery congregation now to be a properly organized Baptist church, and evidently baptized Mrs. Cutt. The date for the organization of the church was September 25, 1682. The Boston church record said:

Upon serious & Solemn Consideration of the Church About A motion
or Request made by severall members that lived att Kittery, yt they might
become A Church & that they might p-ceed therein provided they were
such as should be Approved for such a Foundacon work, the Church gave
there grant and att ye time Appointed did send severall messengers to
make yt strict Inquiry & Examinason as they ought in such A case who
att there Returne brought ye Coppys here Inserted 26th of 7mo 1682.

The Church of Christ att Boston yt is baptized upon profession of faith
haveing taken into serious consideration ye Request of our Brethren att
Kittery Relateing to there being A Church by themselves yt soe they
might Injoy the precious ordinances of Christ which by reson of distance
of habitason they butt seldome could injoy have therefore thought meet to
make Choice of us whose names are underwritten as Messengers to
Assist them in ye same and coming up to them we have found them A
Competent Number and in ye same faith with us for upon careful
examination of them in matters of Doctrine & practise & soe finding one
with us by there (we hope) Conshiencous Acknowledgmtt of ye Confession of faith putt forth by ye Edlers & Brethren of ye Churches in
London and ye Contry in England dated in ye year 1682.

And they haveing given themselves up to ye Lord & too one Another in
A Solemn Covenant to walk as said Covenant may Express & alsoe
haveing Chosen theire officers whome they with us have Appointed &
ordained, we doe therefore in ye name of ye Lord Jesus & by the
Appointmtt of his Church deliver them to be A Church of Christ in ye
faith and order of ye Gospel.[57]

The reference to the 1682 confession of faith of the churches in London and
thereabouts evidently meant the Assembly or Second London Confession of
1677, reaffirmed in a meeting in 1682 and again in 1689.[58] Hull was the
pastor of the Boston church. Thomas Skinner was a deacon and son-in-law of
Thomas Gould, founder of the Boston church. Philip Squire was an
influential member of the church who, with Ellis Callender, had owned the
ground on Salem Street on which the first building of the Boston church was
erected.[59]

The Kittery church adopted a covenant which may be the oldest Baptist
church covenant in America. It read:

Wee whose names are here underwritten doe solemnly & on good
Consideration God Assisting us by his grace give up our selves to ye
Lord & to one another in Solem Covenant, wherein wee doe Covenant &
promise to walk with God & one with another In A dew and faithfull
observance of all his most holy & blessed Commandm.tts Ordinances
Institutions or Appointments, Revealed to us in his sacred word of ye
ould & new Testament and according to ye grace of God & light att
present through his grace given us, or here after he shall please to
discover & make knowne to us thro his Holy Spiritt according to ye same

blessed word all ye Dayes of our lives and this will wee doe, If ye Lord graciously please to Assist us by his grace and Spiritt & to give us Divine wisdome, strength, knowledg, & understanding from Above to p-forme ye same without which we cann doe nothing John 15:4; 2 Corinthians 3:5.[60]

Those making this covenant were William Screven (Screeven) as elder, Humphrey Churchwood as deacon, Robert Williams, John Morgradge, Richard Cutt, Timothy Davis, Leonard Drown, William Adams, Humphrey Axill, and George Litten. Seven sisters also owned the covenant, although their names are not shown. Doubtless one of these women was Bridget Screven, baptized with her husband in Boston. Another was Mrs. Mary Hole Cutt, Screven's mother-in-law. She later married Captain Francis Champernowne after she had become a Baptist. Following his death in December 1687, she cast her lot with William Screven and the church group in the South Carolina migration in 1696. Her name is found many times in the legal records of York County, Maine, both before her departure to South Carolina and as late as 1702. No record of her will has been found in either Maine or South Carolina, and it is possible that she died at her old home in Barbados.

A third woman signing the covenant was probably Mrs. Sarah Morgandy (Morgradye), who was baptized in Boston in July 1682. Two of the blood sisters of Bridget Screven were evidently among the signers. One was Elizabeth, who married Robert Elliott between 1684 and 1686. After his death, she married Robert Wetherick (Watherick, Witherick) and accompanied the Screven party to South Carolina in 1696, becoming a part of the Baptist group there. The other sister, Mary, became the wife of Humphrey Churchwood after 1686 and likely signed the covenant. It is quite certain that Leonard Drown's wife was one of the signers, for her family remained Baptist after moving to Boston in 1692, where her son later became a deacon in the church there. It is known that Churchwood, Cutt, Adams, and Axill were unmarried at this time, but the other woman signing the covenant may have been the wife of Williams, Davis, or Litten.

This was the Baptist church organized at Kittery, Maine, on September 25, 1682, which would migrate in 1696 to Charleston, South Carolina, with her pastor and most of the living members to constitute the first Baptist church in the South. These ten men and seven sisters evidently met for worship in Screven's house, which was located just west of the Cutt mansion near Spruce Creek in Kittery. This was the first Baptist church organized in Maine. At this time, there were only two Baptist churches in Massachusetts (Swansea, organized in 1663, and Boston, in 1665) and six in Rhode Island (some of which were Six Principle and some Seventh Day Baptist churches).

After this bold action by Kittery Baptists in organizing the church, it would be expected that the authorities would take threatening action. However, none of the members except the pastor, William Screven, was brought into court. Over a year later, on October 9, 1683, Screven appeared in the Court of Sessions at Wells, and the record said:

> William Scrivine being brought before this Court for not departing the Province, according to a former consession of Court, & his own Choyce, & denying now to fullfill it, This Court doth declare that the sentence of the Generall Assembly, beareing date the 28th of June 1682: stands good & in full force against the sayd William Scrivine, dureing the Courts pleasure.[61]

Screven did not desist from his religious activities, for in the Court of Pleas on May 27, 1684, "an order to bee sent for William Scrivine to appeare before the Generall Assembly in June next" was issued. The records of the General Assembly in June said nothing about Screven.

Henry Burrage and others relying on his interpretation asserted that Screven and his group departed for South Carolina instead of appearing in court in June, 1684, thus explaining the lack of further persecution of Screven and maintaining the integrity of the preacher. If the preacher Screven had been in Maine, it was felt, he would have been faithful to his Baptist convictions and would have continued to be persecuted. Another interpretation pointed to the oft-recurring name of William Screven in Maine records after 1684 as indicating that he had remained there until 1696. Burrage had accounted for the name by suggesting that the William Screven in Maine was the son of the preacher by a first wife, for which there is no documentation at all.

Neither of these views was substantiated by incontrovertible proof, for pointing to chronological sequence alone was basically an argument from silence. William Screven, the father, need not have purchased land immediately upon arriving in South Carolina. There are numerous instances of inhabitants settling in this colony rather early but for various reasons not securing land warrants until many years after their arrival.[62] Furthermore, William Screven did have a son named after him, and under some circumstances this could justify Burrage in his view. As a matter of fact, in the genealogy of William Screven in South Carolina, it is most difficult to identify the William Screvens (the son, grandsons, etc.) after about 1725.

But there is indisputable evidence that William Screven, the Baptist preacher, retained Kittery, Maine, as his principal place of residence until 1696, and that the name of William Screven in the records of Maine could not have been that of the son by the same name.

In the first place, the very exacting legal requirements of that day provide incontrovertible evidence that William Screven, the preacher-father, was the man in Maine from 1684 to 1696. A William Screven purchased ten acres of land on the west side of Spruce Creek in Kittery on November 15, 1673. On

July 22, 1686, a William Screven purchased twenty acres of land at Spruce Creek near the bridge in Kittery from Richard Cutt. If the theory is correct that William Screven the preacher went to South Carolina in 1683-84, it could not have been the preacher who purchased the land in 1686, so it must have been his son by the same name. However, in 1704 Robert Screven, who titled himself as from South Carolina and "attorney to my honored father, William Screven of ye same place Shipwright" secured power of attorney *from his father* dated June 12, 1704, placed the same on record with the court at York, Maine, and pursuant thereto sold *all of the above land.* This means that there could have been only one William Screven of legal record who purchased land in Maine both in 1673 and 1686. Were this not true, Robert Screven would have had to secure a power of attorney from his brother, William, as well as from his father. This fact, of course, is exact and conclusive and leaves no room for further doubt at this point.

There is additional evidence that the William Screven on the records of Maine repeatedly from 1684 until 1696 could not have been the son of the preacher. In all of the lists of the children of preacher Screven, William, Jr., is always far down the line, never the first or the last; evidently he was neither the oldest nor the youngest of the children. It is significant that Robert was sent back to act as the father's attorney in selling the land, not William, Jr., and that Samuel (and no other sons) acted as a legal witness in 1696 in Maine.

It is known that William, Jr., married Catherine Stoll of Charleston, South Carolina, and died after 1750. This means that all of the time the son was in Maine he was a young man (probably not old enough to be a legal witness) and unmarried. Henry Burrage had no grounds for supposing that this William was a child by a former marriage, except a desire to make him old enough to do the important things which were done under the name William Screven in Maine between 1684 and 1696.

Furthermore, some of the Kittery residents are known to have accompanied Screven to South Carolina, yet these appear repeatedly in the records after 1684. On February 25, 1691, Humphrey Axill was on a jury for a trial. On June 2, 1691, he was on the grand jury in Kittery. In 1694 he was referred to in the records as having *lately* fenced his orchard. On July 4, 1694, a court case against Mrs. Mary Champernowne indicated that she was in Kittery at that time. If Screven had gone to South Carolina in 1684, Humphrey Churchwood would have gone with him, but Churchwood died in New England about 1693. Screven's son Samuel was in Maine in 1696. Many more examples could be cited.[63]

With this legal and collateral evidence that shows conclusively the presence of William Screven, the Baptist preacher, in Maine until 1696, a serious question must be raised. If Screven were faithful to his Baptist views in Kittery between 1684 and 1696, why was he not prosecuted? The answer is to be found in the very unstable political situation. The Puritan theocracy was disintegrating. In Portsmouth, New Hampshire, Governor Edward Cranfield, the royalist head of the province, had filled the New Hampshire Assembly with royal supporters like Captain Francis Champernowne, now the father-in-law of William Screven. Cranfield had vowed to break the power of the Puritan theocracy and had jailed the Reverend Joshua Moody, head of the Portsmouth Puritan party, for thirteen weeks beginning February 6, 1684, during which time there was no Congregational worship in Portsmouth. As a result of this, Moody had given up the fight in Portsmouth and had moved to Boston after his release from jail in May. He did not return to Portsmouth until 1693.[64]

In addition, Massachusetts was in dire straits. In February, 1684, Edward Randolph had returned to England with a recommendation that the Massachusetts charter be canceled immediately. Everywhere the word was spoken that this action was imminent. It took place in October, 1684, dissolving the General Court in Boston and leaving political and religious matters in the province of Maine in a perplexing legal snarl. Thus, with royal control completely established in New Hampshire and imminent in Maine and Massachusetts, it appears that the authorities in Maine were unwilling to make an issue of liberty of conscience, particularly in view of the repeated demands by the Crown that this be granted. Similar political circumstances had protected Boston Baptists just a few years before. Now Screven seems to have profited by them.

From 1684 to 1691, when complete royal control of these colonies was finally put into effect, there was considerable confusion, politically and religiously. Before the revocation of the Massachusetts patent could be implemented, Charles II died in 1685. James II succeeded him and served until 1688 when the Bloodless Revolution installed William and Mary on the English throne. Immediately, an Act of Toleration was passed which brought legal status to Baptists in Great Britain, although its application in the colonies was slow and not always just.

It is incredible to suppose that William Screven would defy the Puritan leadership while it was in power, as he did on June 28, 1682, and then leave his convictions and compromise with the Puritan side after the triumph of royal control and religious liberty had been proclaimed. There can be no question of "changing sides" on the part of Screven. He remained consistently Royalist in his sympathies. The several public offices he held after 1684, similar to those he held before 1684, were evidence of the esteem with which he was held in the community. To quote a non-Baptist authority,

> he seems to have been able because of his apparent ability and position, aided doubtless by the decline of governmental authority in matters religious as Massachusetts' dispute with the crown became more serious,

to remain a respected citizen of Kittery, honored with election to important office and trusted with important commissions.[65]

Screven's warm and zealous faith, when he can be clearly glimpsed in the records, makes it unreasonable to believe that in this obscure period he was anything but faithful to his convictions. There was still a halfhearted attempt to follow some of the "blue laws" that had prevailed under the old regime, but admonitions were mild and cases few. Even Screven himself was involved in a case of this kind.[66] However, it is likely that no religious person, whether Congregationalist or Baptist, was molested for attending religious services according to his conscience. As W. D. Williamson pointed out, idolatry and heresy, which had once been capital offenses, were no longer punishable by law, and all Christians except Roman Catholics were expressly allowed liberty of conscience by the charter of William and Mary for Maine dated October 7, 1691.[67]

Thus, William Screven, the Baptist preacher, remained in Kittery between 1684 and 1696 and became an outstanding civic leader. The offices that he held were among the highest that could be granted by the people of the community. But what about the Kittery church during this time? The loss of records and the misunderstandings about when and why Screven left Maine have brought much confusion to the story.

The Continuing Church

New information on the condition of the Kittery church between 1684 and 1696 has been uncovered since the story was first published by Isaac Backus in 1777. Backus worked only from available records around Boston, and particularly those of the First Baptist Church, Boston, which were often incomplete. He did not investigate the Kittery materials nor the South Carolina records, and his statement that the Kittery church disbanded and the members returned to their connection with the Boston church (in less than one year after its formation, according to the interpretation of Backus by Joshua Millet and David Weston) is palpably incorrect. Backus corrected himself in his 1804 volume, written after he had consulted the materials of Morgan Edwards, and the revision noted that "cruel persecution soon scattered them, some to South-Carolina, some to New-Jersey, and some to Boston again."[68] In this modified statement, Backus still reflected his basic mistake of thinking that William Screven had fled from Kittery in 1683-84 to escape persecution by the Puritan theocracy when, as has been demonstrated by incontrovertible evidence, Screven did not leave Kittery until 1696 and was not fleeing from Puritan persecution, which had practically ceased by 1684 in Massachusetts, Maine, and New Hampshire.

Much of the difficulty in establishing the true story stems from the fact that all Baptist historians from Backus to the present generation have perpetuated these radical errors of Backus about the date when Screven migrated to South Carolina and about the reason for such migration. This point of view vitiates the conclusions of such eminent historians as Morgan Edwards, David Benedict, Basil Manly, Joshua Millet, David Weston, Henry Burrage, H. A. Tupper, and A. H. Newman. Their acceptance of the date of 1683 for the migration of Screven to South Carolina and the Puritan persecution as the reason for it gives them an improper focus which affects all of their conclusions.

The corrective to this must come, of course, from the effective establishment of 1696 as the date when Screven settled in South Carolina and the evidence that his church was not scattered by the Puritan persecution of 1683. The date of 1696 has been determined by legal records in New England, as well as by supportive proof in land warrants in South Carolina, while the history of New England reveals the cessation of Puritan persecution, even in Boston, by the early 1680s. The several reasons for the move by William Screven and his group in 1696 from Kittery, Maine, to South Carolina will be sketched shortly.

The collation of the New England and the South Carolina materials has added many details to the older story. Although the Kittery church records were probably destroyed with the early Charleston church records in the hurricane of September 15, 1752, there is adequate evidence to assert that the Kittery church was alive and active during the silent period between 1684 and 1696. The fact that earlier historians thought that Screven and company had left Maine in 1683-84 may account for the view that the silence of the Maine records after 1684 about the Baptist church at Kittery meant that the church had died. But, on the contrary, the lack of persecution did not stem from the absence or death of the church. It is well known that Screven himself was still a strong Baptist, as seen by his activities later in South Carolina, and had the Puritan persecution been taking place in Kittery between 1684 and 1696, Screven himself would have experienced it. The fact that he was not persecuted but rather was elected by the community to high offices in Kittery speaks louder than the silent records about the cessation of persecution.

The Baptist church at Newberry, Massachusetts, provides a similar example. This Newberry church was founded about the same time as the church at Kittery and was located only a few miles to the south. There is a long period of silence in the history of the Newberry church and one could speculate that it had died, but historians have located a letter of 1689 which showed that the Newberry church was active, although unpublicized.

Another evidence that the Kittery church was alive between 1684 and 1696 was the growth that she experienced. The original church covenant at Kittery was signed by ten men and seven unnamed sisters. When Screven left for

South Carolina in 1696, two of the men (Churchwood and Litten) were known to be dead, and perhaps one other also. One (Drown) had moved to Boston in 1692. Of the six or seven remaining, Richard Cutt had vast holdings in Maine and had no reason to leave. Through him, the Cutt name was continued into the twentieth century. Three of the men (Screven, Adams, and Axill) migrated to South Carolina. The identity of the seven sisters signing the covenant is not known, but almost certainly Mrs. Bridget Cutt Screven, her mother Mrs. Champernowne, her two sisters Elizabeth Elliott Wetherick and Mary Churchwood, and Mrs. Leonard Drown were five of the seven. The Drown family had moved to Boston in 1692 to escape the Indians, but most of the original seven sisters signing the church covenant accompanied Screven to South Carolina in 1696.

The church had grown since her founding in 1682. Undoubtedly, the preacher won and baptized his twelve children, and some of them may have married in Maine and brought their spouses into Baptist life. At least it is clear that his five daughters (Mercy, Sarah, Bridget, Elizabeth, and Patience) and his seven sons (Samuel, Robert, Joshua, William, Joseph, Permanus or Permanow, and Aaron) accompanied him to South Carolina and were active in the church there. Also accompanying the preacher to South Carolina was the family of Humphrey Axill or Axtell. In this group were John Green, Mrs. Axtell's son by a previous marriage, and five daughters (Mary, Elizabeth, Hannah, Lydia, and Sarah), also by the previous marriage. Joseph Atwell, the adopted son of William Screven, was in the party, and probably Joseph's wife also. Mrs. Champernowne (Screven's mother-in-law), Screven's wife's sister (Mrs. Wetherick), and Mrs. Elizabeth Cutt Elliott Wetherick's two sons by her first husband (Champernowne and Robert Elliott) also made the journey. It is probable that Robert Wetherick, Elizabeth's second husband, was a part of the group. Thus, a large party of Baptist people accompanied William Screven to South Carolina, and it is more than likely that Screven had baptized most of them between 1684 and 1696. The wills of this and the following period confirm the Baptist relationship of these migrants from Maine to South Carolina. The earliest reference to the membership of the church at Charleston affirmed that these people from Kittery formed the majority of the original Charleston church.[69]

One of the most persuasive reasons for believing that the Kittery church continued her existence in the silent period between 1684 and 1696 is the nature of William Screven himself. He had boldly confronted every inferior and superior judicature in Maine with his convictions between 1682 and 1684. His active witness became less dramatic when Puritan persecution ceased in 1684, but the moment he appears in the South Carolina records he is found serving actively in Baptist work and continued in this fashion until his death at a very advanced age. Can an argument from silence prove that this kind of person did not continue faithfully between 1684 and 1696 after all hindrances to his witness were eliminated? Evidently the Boston church, which was probably familiar with the Kittery situation, did not think so. When they were without a pastor in 1707, they so esteemed Screven that they were willing to invite a very old man to return to Boston as their regular pastor. Had Screven's conduct in these silent years been anything but impeccable, these Boston Baptists would not have issued such an invitation even in their great need.

Finally, it must not be overlooked that there is no hint in the South Carolina records that William Screven and his Kittery church ever contemplated organizing a new church body when they arrived at Charleston. All of the old accounts said that the Kittery party worshiped together as a church for a considerable time at Somerton before settling in Charleston. Whether this tradition is correct in all of its details or not, its very existence suggests that the transplanted Kittery church continued her worship before there was an integration with South Carolina Baptists.

The Church Leaves Maine

The Baptists of Charleston still waited for the pastor whom God was preparing for them. In 1696 William Screven, accompanied by most of the living charter members of the Kittery church and a large company of Baptists, left Maine in the fall before ice had covered the region, making the long and generally stormy voyage southward to Charleston, South Carolina. What persecution had not accomplished, other factors did. From a human standpoint, one could make a long and detailed list of reasons for a sixty-seven-year-old preacher to break the continuity of his life in the Kittery community for the past twenty-three years and lead his large family and others on a journey of over nine hundred miles to begin life anew. The Indian raids during what has been called King William's War had almost depopulated Kittery by 1696, and it was not safe even to attend church. The supply of timber for ship masts was depleted around Kittery, and the fierce Indians precluded seeking this commodity farther away. Robert Cutt, who had been reared in the home of Screven, was now grown and would soon be married. He would become one of the most influential inhabitants of Kittery. Many of Screven's close friends had contacts with South Carolina, and these doubtless urged him to forsake the rigorous climate and marauding Indians of Maine to enjoy the milder climate of the southern colony. Samuel Screven, perhaps the oldest son, was coowner of a twenty-five-ton sloop built in Boston and was carrying on trade with Carolina. The father himself may have had an interest in some of the vessels plying the route regularly to Carolina, since he was a shipwright.[70]

It is likely that several of the church group were even related to Baptists in the South Carolina colony: Screven's mother-in-law, Mrs. Mary Hole Cutt

Champernowne, may have had relatives there. His wife's sister Elizabeth, who had married Robert Elliott, doubtless was related through him to the influential and numerous Baptist Elliotts of Charleston. Perhaps even Humphrey Axill (Axtell) was related distantly to the outstanding Axtell family of South Carolina.

Some of Screven's friends may have already gone to South Carolina to live and written him about the numerous Baptists living in and around Charleston. William Adams, who had been baptized in the Boston church on March 20, 1682, was quite likely the same William Adams who left Kittery about 1686. He probably witnessed a will in South Carolina in 1693 and in his own will in 1707 identified himself as one of the inner circle of Baptists in Charleston.[71] A close friend of Adams in South Carolina was William Sadler, one of the first trustees of the Baptist church in Charleston. It is possible that Sadler was the same William Sadler who had opposed the Puritan ministers in Kittery in 1681 and had left Kittery in 1684.[72] If this is so, Sadler, like Adams, could have corresponded with William Screven and urged him to make the journey. Another Kittery friend who secured a land warrant in Charleston several months before Screven and company arrived was John Green, the son of Humphrey Axill's (or Axtell's) wife by her first husband.[73]

It is not at all unlikely that the appointment of Joseph Blake as acting governor of South Carolina about the middle of the year 1696 may have influenced Screven. Joseph's father, Benjamin Blake, had been a prominent merchant in England at Bridgwater, only about ten to twelve miles from Somerton where Screven lived. Screven was often in Bridgwater, especially in attendance at the meetings of the Western Baptist Association there. He could not have failed to know the Blake family of Bridgwater, for they were outstanding Dissenters. He may have known Joseph, who probably was about the same age as Screven. Joseph's second wife was a Baptist woman. Can it be a coincidence that Screven told the General Court in Kittery when being persecuted in 1682 (the year that Benjamin Blake brought a large group of Somersetshire Dissenters to South Carolina) that he might leave the province of Maine shortly? Was it another coincidence that within a few months after Joseph Blake, Screven's neighbor in England, was named governor, the entire Screven family left Maine for South Carolina?

Finally, Screven may have had correspondence with other Baptists or other Dissenters living in and around Charleston, some of whom he may have known in England. An old tradition suggested this earlier English connection.[74]

Whatever may have been the personal, economic, social, and political factors involved, it should be kept in mind that many of the living charter members of the Baptist church formed at Kittery on September 25, 1682, and many more who had joined the Baptist company thereafter, accompanied

William Screven on this journey. The migration assumed a religious character, since all of these approximately thirty people who came with Screven seem to have been Baptists. In the commingling of human exigencies and divine purpose, so familiar in Scripture and to the Christian historian, William Screven finally completed the long and arduous preparation that he had begun over forty years earlier at Somerton, England. He was on his way toward making his most significant contribution to the cause of Christ after the sixty-seventh year of his life.

Notes

1. Henry S. Burrage, *History of the Baptists in Maine* (Portland: Marks Printing House, 1906), pp. 24-25.

2. Luppit—Church Records, mss., Angus Library, Regent's Park College, Oxford, England.

3. Ibid.

4. "The Baptist Licenses of 1672," in W. T. Whitley, ed., *Transactions of the Baptist Historical Society* (London: Baptist Union Publication Department, 1908 on), I:168.

5. Ibid., pp. 121-22.

6. Ivimey, II:141-45.

7. Ibid., p. 142. See also B. R. White, "Thomas Collier and Gangraena Edwards," in *The Baptist Quarterly* (replaced *Transactions,* London, 1908 on), XXIV, No. 3, pp. 99-107.

8. J. G. Fuller, *A Brief History of the Western Association* (Bristol: I. Hemmons, 1843), pp. 4-6. See also Douglas Jackson, *Baptists in the West Country* (Dorchester: The Western Baptist Association, 1953), pp. 1-7.

9. Lumpkin, *Confessions,* pp. 201-202. See also Whitley, *Transactions,* V:174.

10. B. R. White, ed. *Association Records of the Particular Baptists of England, Wales, and Ireland to 1660. Part 2, The West Country and Ireland* (London: The Baptist Historical Society, 1973), p. 103. Quoted by permission.

11. Nehemiah Coxe, *Vindiciae Veritatis* (London: Printed for Nath. Ponder at the Peacock in the Poultry near Corn-Hill, and in Chancery-lane near Fleet-street, 1677). The best account of Thomas Collier and his views is the unpublished doctoral dissertation of Richard Dale Land, "Doctrinal Controversies of English Particular Baptists (1644-1691) as Illustrated by the Career and Writings of Thomas Collier," submitted to Oxford University, Oxford, England, Spring term, 1980.

12. See Thomas Collier, "The Pulpit-guard routed in its strong holds. Or, a brief answer, to a large and lawless discourse, written by one Thomas Hall of Kings-Norton, entitled the Pulpit guarded with twenty arguments, pretending to prove the unlawfulness and sinfulness of private men's preaching. Wherein the arguments being weighed in the Balance of the Sanctuary, are found too light; and the lawfulness of private men's preaching (as Thomas Hall calls them) viz. Gifted Brethren, is cleared and confirmed in opposition to all gainsayers." See this document discussed briefly in

Ivimey, II:143. See also Thomas Collier, "An Answer to a Book Written by one Richard Sanders of Kenlishbeer," pp. 15-18. This pamphlet is on microfilm in the library, The Southwestern Baptist Theological Seminary, Fort Worth, Texas.

13. White, ed., *Association Records*, Part II:53-104.

14. Whitley, "The Baptist Licenses," pp. 156-177.

15. Samuel Rawson Gardiner, *History of the Commonwealth and Protectorate, 1649-1660* (London: Longmans, Green, and Co., 1901), pp. 136-141.

16. H. B. Case, *The History of the Baptist Church of Tiverton 1607 to 1907* (Tiverton, Devon: Gregory & Son, 1907), p. 15.

17. W. T. Andress, comp., *The History of Newhouse Upottery* (n.p.: 1932), p. 4.

18. Ibid., pp. 5-6.

19. Ivimey, II:103-116.

20. Whitley, *Transactions,* VII:227. See also Champlin Burrage, *The Church Covenant Idea* (Philadelphia, 1904), esp. pp. 181-82.

21. White, ed., *Association Records,* II:58, 65, and 66.

22. Sybil Noyes, Charles T. Libby, and Walter G. Davis, *Genealogical Dictionary of Maine and New Hampshire* (Portland, Maine: 1928-39), p. 615.

23. Ibid., p. 129. For the Carr family, see *Records and Files of the Quarterly Courts of Essex County, Massachusetts* (Salem: 1913), III:405 and IV:183.

24. Ibid., p. 615. See also SCH&GM, IX:230-31.

25. Everett S. Stackpole, *History of New Hampshire* (New York: 1916), I:55 ff. See also Stackpole, *Old Kittery and Her Families* (Lewiston, Maine: 1903), p. 211. Compare Charles E. Banks, *Topographical Dictionary of 2885 English Emigrants to New England—1620-50* (Baltimore, 1957), passim.

26. Ibid., p. 55.

27. Osgood, III:309 ff.

28. These sentences will sum up material in Robert A. Baker, *The First Southern Baptists* (Nashville: Broadman Press, 1966), pp. 10-14, which utilized specific references to many sources.

29. *New England Historical and Genealogical Register* (1889), XLIII:356 ff. Cited hereafter as NEH&GR.

30. Robert E. Moody, *Province and Court Records of Maine* (Portland, Maine: 1947), III:x-xii.

31. William Willis, ed., *Collections of the Maine Historical Society* (Portland, Maine: 1865), I:400-401.

32. Moody, III:xiii.

33. Nathan E. Wood, *The History of the First Baptist Church of Boston* (Philadelphia: American Baptist Publication Society, 1899), pp. 57 ff.

34. Ibid., pp. 31 ff.

35. A. H. Newman, *A History of the Baptist Churches in the United States,* rev. ed. (Philadelphia: American Baptist Publication Society, 1898), p. 185.

36. Ibid., p. 186.

37. This summary is taken from Wood, pp. 121 ff.

38. Ibid., p. 150.

39. Wood, p. 194.

40. Isaac Backus, *A History of New England with Particular Reference to the*

Denomination of Christians Called Baptists, 2nd ed., 2 vols. (Newton, Mass.: Backus Historical Society, 1871), I:401.

41. Wood, pp. 58, 178-79.
42. Ibid., p. 129.
43. Ibid., p. 130.
44. Ibid., pp. 179-80.
45. Ibid., pp. 57, 195.
46. Backus, I:402-3.
47. See Burrage, p. 20 n., and Wood, p. 204. Burrage said that the Boston records showed that Screven's mother-in-law, Mrs. Robert (Mary) Cutt, was also baptized in Boston on January 17, 1682, at the same time Drown received the ordinance, but in view of the letter of Screven dated September 13, 1682, and the context of the whole story, it would appear that Mrs. Cutt was not baptized until later.
48. Moody, III:160.
49. William D. Williamson, *The History of the State of Maine,* 2 vols. (Hallowell, Me.: 1832), I:679.
50. Baker, *First Southern Baptists,* pp. 31 ff.
51. Moody, III:165.
52. Ibid., p. 33.
53. Wood, p. 189.
54. Ibid., p. 191.
55. Burrage, p. 20 n.
56. Backus, I:404.
57. Wood, p. 180.
58. Burrage, p. 22.
59. Wood, passim.
60. Ibid., pp. 181-82.
61. Moody, III:182.
62. See, for example, SCH&GM, I:341. Major Charles Colleton came to South Carolina in 1686 but purchased land in 1696 from Landgrave Thomas Smith.
63. For documentation of this material on the preacher Screven, see Baker, *First Southern Baptists,* pp. 36-38.
64. Stackpole, *History,* I:146-47. See also Nathaniel Adams, *Annals of Portsmouth* (Portsmouth, N.H.: 1825), p. 80.
65. Moody, III:xxiv-xxxix.
66. *York Deeds* (Portland, Me.: 188 on), Book V, Part II, Folio 22.
67. Williamson, II:18-21.
68. Backus, IV:129-30.
69. Manly, *Discourse,* p. 10 n.
70. Moody, III:xxiv-xxix.
71. Moore & Simmons, *Wills,* p. 24. See also Baker, *First Southern Baptists,* p. 43.
72. See the discussion in Baker, *First Southern Baptists,* pp. 43-44.
73. Salley, *Warrants,* p. 130.
74. NEH&GR, XLIII:356.

3

The Church at Charleston

When William Screven sailed into the harbor at Charleston in 1696, probably aboard the sloop of Samuel Screven, he glimpsed a "fair and pleasant" land which contrasted in many ways with the rugged landscape and harsh physical conditions that he had known at Kittery. As a visitor in this area wrote a few years later:

> The climate of Carolina and of the adjoining region, now called Georgia, was one of the finest in the world. The soil of both countries was marvellously rich. Where cultivated, oranges, olives, rice, indigo, wheat, peas, and Indian corn were grown in great abundance. Most of the land, however, was entirely untilled, and consisted of swamps of black fat earth, immense forests of oaks and pines, and, here and there, luxuriant glades, overrun with flowering shrubs and plants the most beautiful.[1]

Screven may have observed that most of the houses of every kind in Charleston were made of wood, since as a carpenter and shipbuilder he had a considerable interest in the available supply of timber. He surely must have noticed also the magnificent natural harbor and the almost imperceptible rise of the land from the sea level, as contrasted with the "stern and rockbound coast" of New England. The most probable time of his arrival was October, 1696, (when his son Samuel had served as a witness in Kittery), before hard winter had yet gripped New England.

The New Home

The events of the first years of William Screven in South Carolina are shadowed by many diverse traditions. Most of the problems have arisen over the question of chronology. All of the older historians followed the mistakes of Baptist historian Isaac Backus in assuming that William Screven fled from the persecution of the Massachusetts theocracy in about 1684 when, as a matter of fact, Screven and his party did not journey to South Carolina until 1696 and most certainly were not fleeing to escape religious persecution. All later historians agree that by the early 1680s even Boston itself, the very heart of the Puritan theocracy, permitted Baptists and others to worship openly in their midst.[2] The older historians also had not researched the records of both Maine and South Carolina and consequently overlooked much material about the migration of Screven and his party that could come only from a collation of these records.

Typical of the early South Carolina accounts of the arrival of William Screven and party from Kittery, Maine, was that of Basil Manly, who delivered the sesquicentennial address on the history of the First Baptist Church, Charleston, in 1832. Briefly, Manly's chronology asserted that (1) Screven came to South Carolina in 1682 and went with his party immediately to Somerton, about forty miles northwest of the city; (2) about 1682-83, Joseph Blake brought a group of Dissenters from western England, and some of these joined the Screven church at Somerton; (3) Lord Cardross brought some Dissenters from northern England, and before 1686 some of these had joined the Somerton church; (4) by 1693 most of the Somerton group had moved to Charleston and begun meeting in the house of William Chapman; (5) in 1699 William Elliott gave the lot on Church Street, and before 1701 a building for worship had been erected there; and (6) in 1700 the church adopted the 1689 confession of faith of English Particular Baptists.[3] The best modern research modified this story, principally by noting that Screven probably did not come to South Carolina until 1696.[4]

Fresh research and a long look at the material demand that Manly's traditional story be altered at several points. Traditions are almost always grounded in actual historical events, but oftentimes these recollections garble the dates and sequences. That probably has occurred in the story of Screven's arrival in South Carolina.

When Screven and his rather large party arrived in Charleston in the fall of 1696, where did they go? Even contemporary writers have followed the old story that they went immediately to Somerton, although there was a twelve-year gap between the earlier chronology and the corrective. It appeared reasonable that Screven and party secured the Somerton land and went immediately there in 1696 when the official land warrants showed that Screven secured two grants of land on December 7 and December 17, 1696, totaling fifteen hundred acres.[5]

However, this sequence could not have occurred. Henry A. M. Smith, the widely respected historian of South Carolina, conducted a thorough research in an effort to identify the exact place at Somerton to which Screven and party allegedly went when they arrived in South Carolina. He found that the warrants for fifteen hundred acres secured by Screven on December 7 and 17, 1696, did not involve the Somerton area. Rather, on January 23, 1698, William Screven purchased from John Stewart a tract of 804 acres which had been granted to Stewart on October 14, 1696. This land was situated at a locality known as "Wampee" on the west side of the Pooshee or Biggin Swamp, one of the headwaters of the Cooper River, about forty miles northwest of Charleston. Evidently this adjoined the land warrant secured by Thomas Bulling (Bulline) on December 7, 1696.[6] Writing in 1912, Smith said that he had seen an old map of the Somerton settlement and that none of the plantation buildings were on this first tract. On January 11, 1700, Screven purchased 300 additional acres at Wampee adjoining to the east the 804-acre tract. These two tracts, aggregating 1,104 acres, constituted the holdings of William Screven at Somerton (never a town or village but simply the title of an area).

Incidentally, the tradition that William Screven gave the name to this area in memory of his English home was incorrect, for grants to Thomas Bulling and Robert Wetherick long before Screven purchased the land in that vicinity were called by the name of Somerton or Summerton.[7] It should be said also that there were a number of areas called Somerton up and down the coast. After describing these tracts and evidently not realizing what it meant to the *time* of Screven's residence at Somerton, Smith positively asserted that the old map of the Somerton area showed all of the plantation buildings to be on the three hundred acres purchased in 1700.[8] With other collateral information to support this view, it appears, then, that William Screven and company did not go immediately to Somerton in 1696 and probably did not move out to the Somerton plantation until after January 11, 1700, when Screven purchased the three hundred acres that contained all of the buildings.

Part of that collateral information is the fact that Screven owned a house in Charleston before February, 1700. On February 28, 1700, the *Journal of the Commons House of Assembly* reported the burning of the house and all the goods of William Screven in Charleston. An attempt to give him aid was defeated by the Provincial Council.[9] There was no hint in the records as to how long Screven had been living in Charleston, but if there were no buildings on his plantation at Somerton until he purchased the additional tract on January 11, 1700, he must have lived in Charleston after his arrival in late 1696 before moving to the Somerton plantation. The circumstances surrounding the purchase of 300 acres adjoining the 804-acre tract he already owned at Somerton make it appear that he may have desired the additional acreage *because* it had houses on it.

This view is also enhanced by the fact that there was really no gathering of the Screven clan at the Somerton area until after he had purchased the 300 acres on January 11, 1700. It is true that at the time William Screven secured a warrant for 500 acres of land on December 17, 1696, his wife's sister's husband, Robert Wetherick, received a warrant for 100 acres of land "att

Summerton."[10] Wetherick probably lived there briefly, for in an oral will on his deathbed on September 5, 1700, he styled himself as "late of New England, then of Somerton in the country aforesaid [Berkeley County]."[11] However, on May 17, 1701, subsequent to the purchase of the 300 acres by Screven on January 11, 1700, Wetherick's widow Elizabeth (the sister of Screven's wife) secured 325 additional acres at Somerton. On November 6, 1704, Champernowne (Champernoun) Elliott (Elizabeth's son by her first husband), Permanow Screven (the preacher's son), and Humphrey Axtell (Axill), all a part of the Screven company, secured grants in the Somerton area.[12] If this revised chronology of events is correct, William Screven and most of his party must have remained in Charleston for several years after arriving in 1696.

As pointed out, Screven brought with him a large number of people. One writer remarked that this would have been necessary before Screven could have secured land warrants for as much as fifteen hundred acres, which he did in December, 1696. Since Samuel Screven, the oldest son, is known to have owned a sloop of substantial size, it is quite possible that some of the other grown sons or even the shipwright father himself also had vessels. If this many people came to South Carolina together, it seems probable that they must have made some arrangements in advance for lodging and other accommodations until they could get settled. There is an old tradition that William Screven and company went directly to the plantation of a friend whom Screven had known in England, Landgrave Thomas Smith, when they arrived at Charleston.[13] According to the Crisp maps of 1680 and 1704, Smith's Charleston house was located at "the half moon" on the Cooper River (so-called evidently because of the land formation jutting into the river). Smith had larger plantations outside of Charleston, for he secured many land warrants between 1693 and this time, in addition to inheriting much land.[14] Screven could have sailed right up the Cooper River to the wharf and docked in the front yard of this city property. Some credence should be given to this tradition since Landgrave Smith's granddaughter later married the grandson of William Screven, and Smith also provided land for the building of a Baptist church.[15]

It is possible, of course, that William Adams, John Green, or William Sadler, former New England associates, may have arranged accommodations; or perhaps Mrs. Mary Hole Cutt Champernowne, who undoubtedly had stopped at Charleston many times in her travels between her home in the Barbados and Kittery, had friends or relatives who might have entertained some of this large group. Some have believed that the numerous family of Elliotts in South Carolina was related to Humphrey Elliott of New England, who had married Elizabeth Cutt, sister of William Screven's wife; if so, this party could have been welcomed in many substantial homes.[16] Indeed, if the numerous Baptists around Charleston in the 1680s and 1690s had written letters to Europe, Great Britain, and all parts of the American colonies seeking pastoral leadership, as they did at other times during their history, it is possible that William Screven had corresponded with some Charleston Baptists as early as 1682 when he talked about leaving the province of Maine and later on when he did leave.

There may be a hint in the records that the old Charleston family of the Bullines, well-known Baptists, could have had some earlier communication with William Screven before he came to South Carolina. It must be more than coincidental that in the record of the warrant for one thousand acres of land secured by William Screven shortly after he arrived in South Carolina, the very next item on the page showed that Thomas Bulling (Bulline) secured a warrant for "five hundred acres of Land Lying at Summer towne on the West Side of Stewarts Line." The warrants of both William Screven and Thomas Bulling were dated December 7, 1696.[17] Since Screven later purchased the land of John Stewart as the location for his plantation, and a few years thereafter a number of Screven's family and party from New England purchased adjacent land, it would appear that Thomas Bulling and William Screven, both Baptists and soon to become neighbors, securing land warrants on the same day, perhaps at the same time, could have been friends prior to Screven's coming to Carolina. In whatever fashion it occurred, it seems clear that the large company of Baptists from Maine was quickly and easily integrated into the Charleston community.

Thus, from the best documented chronology, it appears that the Screven party was accommodated somewhere around Charleston upon arriving, perhaps at the plantation of Landgrave Thomas Smith; that Screven purchased a house and lived in Charleston before securing his Somerton residence; that Screven did not name the area Somerton after his old home in England, since others had already affixed that name; that Elisha, the last son of William Screven, was probably born in Charleston on September 1, 1698, before the family had moved to Somerton; and that the church had erected her building in Charleston while Screven still had his residence in the city. He may have purchased the Somerton acreage containing plantation buildings as a result of the burning of his house and the loss of his goods in Charleston before January 11, 1700, even though the Commons House of Assembly did not take up the question of assisting him until February 28. Evidently Screven was living in Charleston when William Elliott gave the lot to the church on July 18, 1699, and it appears that Screven immediately began to build the meeting-house which was completed before January 20, 1701. This new chronology should offer no serious problems. Most of the older story was traditional and without documentation. It was basically accurate except for dating and sequence of events. It is difficult to be exact about these last two items without written records after the passing of several generations.

Settling the Church

This new sequence makes it much easier to understand the rapid amalgamation of the Charleston Baptist community (which included both Particular and General Baptists) and the New England group. An old tradition said that Screven and his Kittery church met for worship together for a rather extended period before the Charleston Baptists were integrated into the church.[18] Here again the tradition must have garbled some of the sequences and dating, but the existence of the story explains why there was evidently no record in the original church books about the organization or constitution of a new church at Charleston, as will be discussed later. It was the personal contact of Screven with the people that enabled the church to secure a lot by 1699 and a building before 1701. The tradition that Charleston Baptists had been worshiping as a "house church" without a pastor for many years, while quite possible and perhaps probable, cannot be at all documented. It would be helpful to know if the Charleston group and the New England party united in a single service or if the uniting process were gradual.

There is no evidence to suggest that any consideration was given to organizing a new church when worship services were begun in South Carolina. Even if the church books had not been destroyed on September 15, 1752, it is possible that not a great deal would be added to what is known about these early years. Church records were not well kept in most Baptist churches at this time. The First Baptist Church of Boston, for example, would be expected to have kept rather accurate and complete records after she moved into her permanent house of worship in 1679 when persecution had virtually ceased. Yet the records of that church after 1679 are incomplete at many points and leave many questions unanswered. The Kittery church, meeting here and there in the midst of very unfavorable circumstances in Maine, may have kept some records, but they were probably rather sketchy at best.

What evidence is there in South Carolina records to suggest that the Kittery church, organized on September 25, 1682, simply migrated as a church when her pastor and a large number of her members moved to South Carolina in 1696? There are several coincidental facts that support this story.

The principal source for the South Carolina account of the beginning of the Charleston church was Oliver Hart, pastor of the church from 1750 to 1780. He was the only person who had actually seen the original record books of the church that can be identified as passing on the story he had read there. He became pastor of the church in early 1750. The great hurricane of September 15, 1752, destroyed the parsonage of the church and with it the church books.

Undoubtedly Hart had read these minute books which were in his possession for almost three years. Three times he was asked to describe the beginnings of the church. The first time occurred in the year the hurricane destroyed the records. In that year the Charleston Association, organized the year before at the initiative of Hart and meeting only a month or so after the loss of the records, placed in their minutes an account of the beginnings of the Charleston church, undoubtedly prepared by the pastor Oliver Hart. These associational minutes of 1752 were used by Wood Furman in 1811 in writing the history of the Charleston Association. Basil Manly, Sr., pastor of the church from 1826 to 1837, used them when he brought the 150th anniversary messages to the church in 1832. These minutes were subsequently lost.

The second time Oliver Hart was interrogated about the beginnings of the Charleston church came in 1772, twenty years later. In his diary Hart mentioned that Morgan Edwards, the noted Baptist church historian, had come to Charleston on January 23 and remained until February 11, 1772, securing information about Baptist beginnings in South Carolina. Isaac Backus used this Edwards material in his history in 1804, and Richard Furman was sent a copy of it, which he annotated with his recollections.

The third occasion when Hart provided information on the beginnings of the church came in his discussions with Richard Furman, his successor as pastor of the church. Furman had been close to Hart and secured his information about the church from Hart and from Morgan Edwards, who secured his material from Hart also.

What, then, can be found in these three direct inquiries addressed to a scholarly, historically-minded man who had read the original minutes of the church? Very little. Not once did Oliver Hart suggest that a new church was constituted by William Screven after coming to South Carolina in 1696. The only statement that surfaced was that the people from Maine formed the majority of the early Charleston church.[19] None of the voluminous diaries and other writings of Oliver Hart make reference to how the Charleston and Maine groups were united or anything about the first years of the Charleston church. To anyone who has read the extant writings of Hart and is acquainted with his specific dating of storms, births, deaths, marriages, revivals, journeys, sermons, and historic events, it is inconceivable to believe that if the church records had shown a specific date for the founding of the Charleston church or had described anything about her constitution, Oliver Hart would have failed to mention it. When the story of the beginning of the church in the Charleston Association minutes, the manuscripts of Morgan Edwards, and the writings of Richard Furman offer no more information at this point, it must mean that the church records themselves, which Oliver Hart had read, were silent about the constitution of a new church in Charleston after the arrival of William Screven.

And why should there have been a separate organization of a new church in Charleston by Screven when most of the charter members of the Kittery church and a substantial number of new Kittery additions to the church accompanied their pastor to South Carolina, where they worshiped alone for some time before any of the South Carolina Baptists were integrated into the church? No Baptist church remained in Kittery after Screven departed.

There was no 50th anniversary celebration by the church because at that very time the church had been almost destroyed by controversy, as will be seen. The centennial celebration was not held because the Revolutionary War had brought the fall of Charleston, the flight of the pastor, and the near destruction of the church. On the 150th anniversary of the church, however, the pastor, Basil Manly, was asked to prepare an address on the history of the church. From his diary it is evident that Manly spent at least two years in a careful study of all of the records in South Carolina in the preparation of his *Discourse,* which was printed and later published in the *American Baptist Memorial.* As will be seen later, Manly delivered the historical message on two Sundays exactly 150 years after the forming of the Kittery church. Of particular interest here is the statement that he made about the beginning of the Charleston church, a conclusion that he arrived at after a long and careful study of all the records. After describing the founding of the Kittery church, Manly wrote:

> To the constitution, and subscription of a covenant above mentioned at Kittery, September 25, 1682, the Baptist church in Charleston traces its origin;—and from all the means of information now accessible, it is most probably concluded that their settlement about Charleston was only a transfer of the seat of worship of the persecuted flock (or a majority of it) which had been gathered on the Piscataqua.[20]

The first evidence of rapid union of the Kittery and Charleston groups was the report that the church was meeting in a temporary building or in the home of William Chapman on King Street. No date for this can be determined. An exact landmark in the church's history, however, came on July 18, 1699 when William Elliott executed a deed in which he gave to the church in trust lot 62 on Church Street in Charleston. This lot had originally belonged to a mariner, Josiah Willis, and Elliott purchased it for twenty pounds from Elizabeth Willis, the only daughter of the deceased Josiah.[21] The gift of this lot by William Elliott was made

> in consideration of the brotherly love which he hath for, and doth bear unto the people of the Church of Christ, baptized on profession of faith, distinguished from all others by the name of Antipaedobaptists, of which Church he professeth himself a member, as to *promote* and encourage so good and pious a work as *the building* a place for the said people to meet and worship, &c.[22]

The lot measured 230 by 100 feet, according to Morgan Edwards. The church named William Sadler, John Raven, Thomas Bulline, Thomas Graves, and John Elliott as trustees.[23] It cannot be known exactly when the first meetinghouse was built. Edwards said that a building measuring 47 by 37 feet was erected on the lot, which left enough room to build a parsonage later. Likely the church building was a wooden structure, and William Screven probably helped construct it. How he must have rejoiced in the first building for worship that he had ever known as a preacher! The earliest exact date that can be assigned to this building is from a deed of sale which referred to a tract of land as being "to the northward upon the Baptist Meeting House." This was recorded on January 20, 1701.[24]

The tradition that in about 1700 the church adopted the London or Philadelphia Confession of Faith, omitting the articles on laying on of hands and ruling elders, presents many problems.[25] For one thing, the London Particular Baptist Confession of 1677 (and adopted again several times thereafter) did not include articles on laying on of hands and ruling elders. When Benjamin Keach and his son Elias revised this confession in 1697 for their two London congregations, they added articles on laying on of hands and singing, but these articles were never counted a part of the 1677 confession. The Philadelphia Association, which was not formed until 1707 (seven years after the supposed adoption of this confession by the Charleston church), referred to the 1677 confession for the first time in 1724. The articles on laying on of hands and singing were not adopted by the Philadelphia Association until they distributed the confession in 1742.[26] Finally, if the church did adopt the 1677 confession (reaffirmed in 1689) of London Particular Baptists, it seems strange that in his last message to the church in 1713 William Screven would urge the church to get a pastor who "does own the confession of faith put forth by our brethren in London in 1689." Why would the pastor ignore the confession of faith adopted by his own church about 1700 and urge that a new pastor own the London confession that was identical to that of his own church?

Since some of these difficulties are insuperable, the argument that the adoption of this Calvinistic or Particular Baptist confession of faith proved that the majority of the Charleston church were Particular Baptists cannot be sustained. It is true, however, apart from this tradition, that the majority of the Charleston church were indeed Particular Baptists, for as Manly noted from the Charleston Association minutes, most of the early Charleston church consisted of the Piscataqua migrants. None of these was a General Baptist, and from later controversies it seems clear that most of the Charleston congregation were Particular Baptists in their doctrinal views.

It is certain that there were some General Baptists in the Charleston group that united with the Screven party. About forty years later, in litigation over the church property before the Commons House of Assembly, William Elliott, the donor of the lot on which the first Baptist church building was erected, was identified by his son as being a General Baptist at the time the father became a member of the Charleston church. William Elliott came from a General Baptist background in England. From later events, it seems probable that there were other General Baptists in the church quite early. It is a tribute to the gracious spirit as well as the spiritual gifts of William Screven that he had the ability to unite into a single church those Baptists in Charleston who had various backgrounds and held different doctrinal points of view. At this very time in England, the General Assembly of General Baptists was instructing its constituent churches quite specifically not to allow those holding Particular Baptist views to remain in their membership. Screven may have gotten this conciliatory spirit from Thomas Collier or Henry Jessey.

The presence of important General Baptists in the membership of the Charleston church at this time probably explains why the General Assembly of General Baptist Churches in England passed a resolution in June, 1702, which read:

> Whereas, our Brethren of the Baptist perswation and of the Generall Faith who haue their aboad in Caralina haue desierd us to Supply them with a Ministry or with books, we being not able to present to doe the former haue collected ye Sum of Seuen pounds twelve Shillings wch wth wt can be farther obtain'd we haue put into the hands of our Bror S Keeling to Supply ym wth ye latter. & yt ye sd Bror Keeling doe wright a letter to them in the name of this Assembly.[27]

It had been thought that the letter mentioned could not have come from the Charleston church to the General Baptists of England because the Charleston church was made up of Particular Baptists. However, as indicated, there was a General Baptist strain in the Charleston group which united with Screven. Thus, it is possible and even likely that the General Baptists of Charleston wrote this letter to the General Assembly of General Baptists in London, appealing for someone to replace Screven, who was getting old and feeble. They wrote a similar letter later on, as will be seen.

The Somerton Center

The tradition that related William Screven and his party with the area known as "Somerton" was substantially accurate. As suggested earlier, William Screven purchased the three-hundred-acre tract on which there were plantation buildings and probably moved there in 1700, perhaps after his house in Charleston burned. He doubtless kept a house in Charleston also. Owning both a plantation and a city house was the practice of many at this time, and the extant wills of his sons and grandsons showed them to have done the same. As mentioned, on May 17, 1701, his wife's sister, Elizabeth

Wetherick, secured an additional grant of 325 acres adjoining the tract of Screven. Mrs. Wetherick's son by her first marriage, Champernowne Elliott, secured a thousand-acre tract on November 6, 1704; while Permanow Screven, the preacher's son, and Humphrey Axtell, who came with the preacher from New England, secured adjoining tracts at the same time.[28] The first actual reference to Screven's residence at Somerton came, as will be seen, in September 1702.

Progress Despite Difficulties

The presence of William Screven in South Carolina did not go unnoticed by antagonistic religious leaders. The first non-Baptist record of his aggressive preaching was contained in a letter written February 21, 1699, by Joseph Lord, a Congregationalist preacher who had brought his congregation from Dorchester, Massachusetts, to South Carolina in 1695. Lord visited New England in March, 1698, and, after returning to South Carolina in December of that year, wrote his New England friends, saying:

> When I came up to Dorchester, I found that a certain Anabaptist teacher (named Scrivan), who came from New England, had taken advantage of my absence to insinuate unto some of the people about us, and to endeavor to make proselytes, not by public preaching of his own tenets, nor by disputations, but by employing some of his most officious and trusty adherents to gain upon such as they had interest in, and thereby to set an example to others that are too apt to be led by any thing that is new. And he had like to have prevailed: but Mr. Cotton's and my coming has a little obstructed them.[29]

Lord wrote again in September, 1702, to complain about the work of Screven, as follows:

> Mr. Hugh Adams a while since sent Mr. Screven the Anabaptist preacher here a Challenge to a Dispute; but after the appointment of time & place & Mr. Adam's Going to Charlestown for that End, Mr. Screven Waved it; which disturbed several of his followers so, that they (as it were) compelled him to send Mr. Adams a Challenge; so that time & place was appointed a second time. But that morning that the Dispute was to have been Mr. Adams had word the Mr. Screven was sick; whereupon haveing waited that day & the next, & seeing no likelihood of a Dispute he went home & so did Mr. Screven shortly after; About which things I was lately in Discourse with a man, who told me that it was thought Mr. Screven would be sick at Somerton these Six Months. However, the Anabaptists are much at a loss what excuse to make for the man that has been much extolled by them; for it is believed by many his sickness was feigned.[30]

The nonconformist preacher, Hugh Adams, referred to in this second letter, also gave an account of this incident concerning "William Scrivener, originally of Kittery in New England, a ship carpenter, but then pretending to be a mighty preacher of the Anabaptist error." Adams wrote that "Said Anabaptist Prater . . . in his Shame and Confusion Retired about 50 miles out of the Town into the Countrey, not appearing again There for about 4 months."[31]

In addition to questioning the accuracy of these accounts, one must smile to hear the accusation that a man who had endured persecution as an active Dissenter in England, who had openly confronted the Massachusetts theocracy when it was persecuting Baptists, and who had defended his beliefs before all the provincial courts of Maine for over a decade, would deliberately feign illness to keep from debating a person like Adams. Perhaps it never occurred to Lord and Adams that this seventy-three-year-old preacher, who had ridden the gospel chariot over rough terrain for at least forty-five years, might actually have been ill when he retired to his Somerton plantation in 1702.

As a matter of fact, the years were beginning to tell on the doughty Baptist champion. He did not succumb to the terrible smallpox epidemic of 1698 in Charleston when 300 persons died, as did 160 others in the following year. As stated earlier, his house and goods in Charleston burned in late 1699 or early 1700, which may have been the reason that he purchased the Somerton plantation in early 1700. There is a hint that some of his children may have died in these first years in Charleston, although that is conjectural. His brother-in-law, Robert Wetherick, died on September 5, 1700, evidently rather suddenly, judging from the place and character of his oral will. A legal memorandum prepared by a doctor, Nathaniel Snow, on September 9 described how Wetherick had called him and three other witnesses into the room where Wetherick lay and had haltingly given his last will and testament. He was buried there on Snow's plantation in Berkeley County.[32] Adding to Screven's hardships were the French, Spanish, Indian, and pirate depredations of these years which will be described in the next chapter. A letter by Screven's hand in 1708 said that he had been brought very low by illness at about that time.

Yet these were productive years for this aged preacher. He had a part in the rapid increase of Baptists in and around Charleston. Some idea of this growth beyond the city may be glimpsed from the reports of the missionaries of the Society for the Propagation of the Gospel in Foreign Parts. This society had been authorized by the British Crown in 1701 to minister to the Anglican people in the colonies. They reported that everywhere they went, they were stumbling over Baptists. Missionary Samuel Thomas arrived in Charleston on December 25, 1701, and wrote that there were many Anabaptists on the eastern branch of the Cooper River, "there being preachers of that sort here."[33] On February 17, 1703, Nicholas Trott wrote to the Bishop of London that "we are here very much infected with the sect of the Anabaptists" and requested five hundred copies of a tract written by John Philpott against their errors.[34] Thomas wrote again on January 18, 1706, to report that among other denominations in the several areas around Charleston, he had observed that Baptists had two families on Goose Creek, almost thirty families on the western branch of the Cooper River, two families on the eastern branch of the Cooper, and perhaps as many as thirty families on Stono River.[35] In Charleston itself in 1708, Governor Nathaniel Johnson reported the white population as being 4,180, of which he estimated that 10 percent were Baptists.[36]

Not only is there evidence of the presence of many Baptists in and about Charleston, but after the settling of the church, the "spirit of veterans" often displayed by William Screven sent him in about 1700 to preach on Edisto Island, twenty-five miles southeast of Charleston at the mouth of the Edisto River. Here he baptized William Fry; Thomas and Providence Grimball; Joseph Sealy; Ephraim Mikell; Joseph, Isaac, and Thomas Parmenter; and others.

Many of the Charleston church members had settled very early along the Ashley River to the northwest of the city and either attended the Charleston services or had the minister from the church come out to lead meetings for them. Two decades after the death of Screven, their number had increased enough that they were able to form a separate congregation.

Some important members of the Charleston church also lived on the Stono River about sixteen miles west of Charleston and evidently commuted to the services in Charleston during the lifetime of Screven.[37] This group later formed a separate General Baptist church. So, in the early ministry of William Screven at Charleston, despite opposition from many sides and personal hardships, he laid the foundations for Baptist expansion in the entire section.

A Painful Setback

Political factors in the colony were responsible for the development of a situation that led directly to the establishment of the Anglican Church in the colony of South Carolina in 1706.[38] Hirsch wrote that the long and noisy religious controversy that accompanied the establishment of the Church of England in South Carolina caused many Dissenters to move to Pennsylvania after 1706. There is no specific record of the reaction from William Screven and his party, although Lady Elizabeth Blake addressed to the proprietors a long and vigorous protest against Governor Moore.[39] Richard Furman later wrote that it was not known what part Baptists took in this controversy, but that doubtless they had opposed the establishment.[40] Perhaps coincidentally,

William Screven moved to Winyah Bay on the site of what is now Georgetown about this time. Evidently he purchased this land about 1710, although that is uncertain.[41] One of his letters in 1707 was sent from Jameston.[42] When the preacher died in 1713, followed by the death of his wife in 1717, this land was inherited by Elisha Screven, who laid out the town of Georgetown in about 1730, although subsequent litigation revealed a clouded title to the property.[43]

Although moving to the plantation on Winyah Bay before 1710, having disposed of his Somerton property on October 15, 1708, Screven evidently retained his town house in Charleston and ministered to the church there on a part-time basis. His February 10, 1708, letter to Ellis Callender of Boston was written from the city. Oldmixon called him the Anabaptist minister at Charleston in 1708.[44] The establishment of the Church of England, while using public tax monies to support that church, did not affect the liberty of the people of other denominations to worship in their own fashion and support their own churches also. This situation continued until the Revolutionary War.

The Charleston Church in 1708

Fortunately, some of the letters of William Screven, written in his last years, have been preserved. In 1707 the Boston church, which had ordained Screven, wrote to him asking that he return to New England and become her pastor. This action certainly refutes any conjecture that Screven had not been a faithful and committed Baptist pastor in Kittery between 1684 and 1696, else this strict Boston group, so quick to excommunicate members for almost any offense, would not have issued this invitation.[45] In reply, Screven wrote on June 2, 1707:

> To the Church of Christ at Boston, your old christian friend saluteth you in our dear Lord; wishing you all grace, mercy, and peace, from God our Father, and from Jesus Christ our Lord.
>
> Dearly Beloved—This may inform you that I have many thoughts of heart about you, and am much concerned for you; and I hope I can say, my prayers are to God for you, though I am not with you, nor can I come to you, as I was inclined to do if I could; our help being taken from us: for our Minister that came from England is dead, and I can by no means be spared. I must say, 'tis a great loss, and to me a great disappointment; but the will of the Lord is done, and in his will I must be satisfied. I pray the Lord to sanctify all his dispensations; especially such awful ones as this is to us, and to me especially. I do not now see how I can be helpful to you, otherwise than in my prayers to God for you, or in writing to you. The Lord help us to pity one another in our affliction as the Gospel counselleth, if one member be afflicted all mourn. I pray the Lord help us that we may do so; for surely it concerneth the churches of Christ, being members of the same body, to sympathize with one another in their

afflictions. And now, my dear friends, my counsel and advice to you is, that for as much as you are destitute of a Minister of your own, in the same faith and order of the Gospel, (if you are not supplied since I last heard from you, by my dear brother Callender's letter,) that you keep together nevertheless, and that you keep up your meetings; otherwise you will give a great step to the losing of the cause, and give the adversary occasion to rejoice: for how fair soever they carry it to you, they are expecting your dissolution or coming to nothing—the which I pray God forbid.

It is my heart's desire that you might thrive and grow in grace, and abound in every good work, to the glory and praise of God. I have longed to hear that were you supplied with an able Minister that might break the bread of life among you; but if the Lord do not think meet to supply you in the way you have expected, your way will be to improve your own gifts, you have among you in the Church. Brother Callender, and brother Joseph Russell whom I was well acquainted with, I know have gifts that may tend to the church's edification, if improved. I think you should call one, or both of them to it; and if either should refuse, except on weighty good grounds, I do not see how they can answer it. I would have you remember that God hath all along carried on his work among you, by such persons and means as were despicable in the eye of the world; therefore I desire you to improve the gifts you have, if possibly you can persuade to it, and be thankful and content. It may be, 'tis that God looks for from you; and our God is abundantly able to supply all your wants by Jesus Christ. And I hope he will be found of you in the way of your duty, and increase both your gifts and graces. I shall be glad to hear from you, and of your prosperity, and how all my old friends do, especially brother Hull, Sweetser, and Hillier, and indeed all the rest. I shall be glad to hear how it is with you, with respect to the Indians.

My kind love, with my wife's, to you all. In haste, I rest your constant remembrancer, assured friend, and christian brother, in Gospel Bonds.[46]

This letter showed that Screven was inclined to return to Boston as their pastor, but that the "minister who came from England" had died, so the Charleston church depended upon Screven for assistance. Who was this minister? Morgan Edwards identified the preacher as a Mr. White, who served briefly in 1706. This would match the date of the letter by Screven in 1707. W. T. Whitley, the England Baptist historian, attempted to identify this White with the Thomas White who was sent to America by the General Assembly of General Baptists.[47] This could not have been the same man. It is true that occasionally dates are in error where the memory tries to recall them, but in this instance the letter of William Screven was definitely dated, and the minutes of the General Assembly of General Baptists specifically gave the date as May 19, 1714, when Robert Norden and Thomas White were appointed to go to Virginia. Thomas White did not live long enough to land in

America, but died on the voyage, and thus could not have been the man who served briefly in Charleston with William Screven.[48] Also, Screven would not have been pleased to install a *General Baptist preacher* in the Charleston church as his possible successor when his last word to the church urged her to get a *Particular Baptist pastor* quickly. Leah Townsend thought that this White was probably the man referred to by Samuel Thomas, missionary of the Church of England, who wrote in 1706 that "the Dissenters have at present 4 ministers among them besides one Anabaptist Preacher lately gone into Carolina from Biddiford in the West of England."[49]

The Boston church took Screven's advice and called as pastor one of her own members, Ellis Callender, who had been preaching for about thirty years in and around Boston. Screven's reference to Isaac Hull suggests that he had not corresponded with Boston recently, for Hull had died in 1699.[50]

A beautiful letter of Christian comfort and greetings was sent from Charleston by Screven to Callender at Boston on February 10, 1708, which read:

> My Dear Brother—My christian love, with my wife's, presented to you and your wife; hoping and earnestly desiring your prosperity in all spiritual and temporal blessings. This may inform you that I received yours of the 25th of August last, in which you inform me of the state of New-England. I am much concerned for New England in general, because of the great afflictions God hath laid upon it. I know it hath been very great also. That there should be such a spirit of infatuation on the spirits of your forces as to go to Port-Royal, and not so much as ask it, as you tell me, is unaccountable, and so it is indeed. But what shall we say to these things? It is the Lord who doth all that he pleaseth in the Heavens and Earth. But, my dear brother, give me leave to tell you, that although all our sins are great, and every one ought to cry to God for pardon, and New-England is guilty of many sins, I cannot but think that the sin of persecution is one, if not the chief, for which God is thus contending with them. For you know how it hath been. But I hope the Lord hath a peculiar people there, for whose sake, or at least for his mercy's sake, he will not have New-England under the cruel stroke of a cruel enemy. I pray God to grant a thorough reformation; then may you and we expect deliverance from all our troubles.
>
> As to your particular church state, I am more concerned, as a member of the same body with you; that the cause is so low with you, that your endeavors to obtain a Minister from England are disappointed, and that there is none stirred up among you, seems to me to be very sad. And indeed it is sad with a people when there is no open vision; and indeed, with respect to the administration of ordinances according to our faith and order, it is so with you though your meeting be upheld by one of a contrary mind. I pray God to pity your case, for his mercy's sake. I doubt not but 'tis your prayer, and I hope it shall be mine, that he will send forth

labourers into his vineyard, and so in his due time supply you. In the meantime, I pray the God of all grace to support your spirits under all your exercises, that when you have been tried, (for this is a trying time for you,) you may come forth as gold out of the fire, being more purified, and so more meet for your great Master's use. I am concerned to think of your loss of that good friend you tell me of; that when you had some hope of help all should become dark, as in that solemn providence it was to you. But O my brother, what a depth is there in Divine Providence! His works are past finding out. The Lord grant us such grace that we may lie low at his feet, and say, just and right are thy ways, O thou King of Saints! Our congregation here are, I think, growing in health, and I hope thriving in grace; blessed be the Lord! I can't enlarge, but I pray you to present my kind love to brother Hillier and his wife, brother John Russell and his wife, and my dear sister Procter, and brother Sweetser; and the rest of our friends which to me may be unknown. I shall be glad to hear from you by every opportunity, and hope I shall give you to know how we do. So wishing you well, desiring your prayers, I commend you to the grace of God, and subscribe myself your christian brother in the best of bonds.[51]

On August 6, 1708, Screven wrote his last letter of record. It was addressed to Ellis Callender and written from Charleston. It read:

My Dear Brother—I salute you, and your dear wife and family; praying all suitable grace and favor may be communicated to you, for your spiritual and temporal supplies, from God our Father and our Lord Jesus Christ. This may inform you that I received yours of June 12th, for which I thank you, and of which I am glad. I heard of your sickness, and that you were like to die, if not dead; therefore I sent my last to brother Hillier; but am glad the Lord hath raised you up from the gates of death; I hope, for his own glory, his church's and your own good. I rejoice that you are inclined to, and employed in, the blessed work of the Lord, for the support of his cause, and the comfort of his saints left of that poor languishing church with you; as it must and will be, if you have the blessed ordinances of the holy Jesus among you again. I am glad you have reason to hope the cause hath gained some credit, among some who did judge too hardly of us; but am grieved to hear of such a censorious spirit in any of those that bear the name by which we are called among men. I pray God to be with your spirit, and strengthen you to the great work to which you are called, and that the little vine may be flourishing under your hand. I hope it will make both you and me glad, you may assure yourself my heart hath been with you, and should have been glad to have come over to your help if I could; but I hope I can say that I have not forgotten to pray for our Mother Sion, or her daughters our sister churches, but more especially you, of whom I count myself a poor unworthy member. I have been, of late, brought very low by sickness; but I bless the Lord I was helped to preach and administer the communion last Lord's day, but am still very weak; therefore can write but a little to you now. I want to know who of our friends with you are dead since I left you. Our Society are, for the most part I think, in health, and I hope thriving in grace. We are about ninety in all. I shall be glad to hear from you by all opportunities, and to hear of the thriving of the church with you. My dear love to brother Russell, and brother Hillier and their good wives, and sister Proctor, and the whole church with you.

So commending you and yours, and all your great concerns to the Lord and the blessing of his grace, desiring your prayers, promising you mine, I rest your brother and fellow-laborer in the best of services, for the best rewards.[52]

Who were these ninety Baptists referred to in this letter? It is not difficult to list the names of about ninety who might have been members of this church in 1708. This antedated the formation of a separate Ashley River church in 1736, the schism of General Baptists in that year, and the separate organization of the Edisto Island group in 1746. There are three rather trustworthy sources for the names of Baptists in this early period. These are: (1) the names of the legal trustees of the property of the church in 1699 and 1712; (2) the names of the group which Screven brought down from Kittery; (3) the material by Morgan Edwards. Another source, admittedly less reliable, consists of wills, land grants, church litigation, family genealogies, and similar material. From a study of these several sources, it is possible that the following were the ninety members referred to by William Screven in 1708.

Perhaps as many as twenty of these members consisted of the trustees of the property and their wives. On July 18, 1699, William Elliott gave the lot at 62 Church Street for the building of a house of worship for the Baptists. The trustees were William Sadler, John Raven, Thomas Bulline, Thomas Graves, and John Elliott. There can be little doubt that these five trustees and William Elliott were Baptist members at this time. On August 4, 1712, another deed was executed, showing some new trustees for this lot upon which the Baptists had built a meetinghouse. There were five new names in this list of trustees. Together with their wives this would add an additional ten to the church roll. The trustees in the 1712 deed were John Raven, Sr., Richard Butler, Ephraim Mikell, Lawrence Dennis, John Raven, Jr., and Henry Turner.[53] Thus, because they were trustees of this particular lot, it is certain that these eleven men were members of this first church in Charleston. None of these trustees accompanied William Screven from New England.

In addition to these twenty or more (including their wives), the Screven group certainly comprised a part of the membership of this early church. This would include the preacher, his wife (Bridget), his wife's mother (Mrs. Mary Hole Cutt Champernowne) and sister (Elizabeth Wetherick), Humphrey Axtell, and William Adams, all of whom were probably members of the original Baptist church in Kittery. The eight boys (Samuel, Robert, Joshua, William, Joseph, Permanus or Permanow, Aaron, and Elisha) and the five daughters (Mercy, Sarah, Bridget, Elizabeth, and Patience) were doubtless members of this church also. Elisha was the last child, born in 1698. From a review of the later history of this church and those that came out of it, as well as the wills and other documents that are extant, it is evident that the succeeding Screvens were faithful to the convictions of the head of their tribe.[54]

It would be of considerable assistance to know the names of the men to whom the five Screven daughters were married, as well as the five daughters of Mrs. Humphrey Axtell. Undoubtedly some of these were a part of the Baptist group. It is not certain whether Mrs. Champernowne's grandsons, Champernowne and Robert Elliott, were part of the church or not, but they probably were. Champernowne Elliott became a well-known surveyor in the area. The brother Robert made his will in July, 1727, and in this he referred to two sons, Artemus and Humphrey, both under twenty, and two daughters, Dorothy and Elizabeth, both under sixteen years of age. His mother, Elizabeth Wetherick, was still living and was named as executor, but there was a hint that she was not well, for the will mentioned that at her death three Baptists, Richard Butler and Thomas and John Bullen, were to act in that capacity.[55] She sold her Somerton holdings the next year.[56]

As suggested earlier, it is probable that Mrs. Champernowne's daughter (Elizabeth Wetherick) was one of the seven sisters referred to by William Screven as members of the church when it was organized in 1682. The wife of Humphrey Axtell and his foster son (John Green) were from an outstanding Dissenter family in Kittery. Both Mrs. Axtell's first husband and her father signed the anti-Massachusetts petition of 1679. In 1705 Axtell and his wife and John Green, identifying themselves as residents of Charleston, South Carolina, arranged to sell their land in and about Kittery. Green was apparently of legal age at this time.[57] Counting the thirteen children of Screven and the wives of the sons (but not the husbands of the daughters), together with Mrs. Elizabeth Wetherick and her two sons, and the wife and foster son of Humphrey Axtell, all of whom very probably were a part of this church, this would add twenty-six more members.

The third rather trustworthy source for the names of the members of this first church is Morgan Edwards. As suggested, his sources were excellent, and the more the entire story is studied the more evident it becomes that he was quite accurate in most of his information. He said that at the time William Screven baptized Ephraim Mikell on Edisto Island about 1700, he also baptized William Fry; Thomas and Providence Grimball; Joseph, Isaac, and Thomas Parmenter; Joseph Sealy; "and others."[58]

Edwards gave the last names of other families who made up the membership in 1699. It is evident that he was careful in listing the family names who belonged to this first congregation, for there are many other families, like the Bedons and Shepherds, who were shown quite early in the Baptist membership at Charleston, but Edwards did not include these family names in his list. It is possible that these were a part of the "and others," mentioned by Edwards, but apparently names were not listed indiscriminately.

Edwards named as a part of the early congregation the Atwells, Bullines, Elliotts, Ravens, and Butlers, who have already been mentioned; and in addition he mentioned the Bakers, Barkers, Blakes, Chapmans, Childs, Caters, Whitakers, Bryants, "and others." Most of these names were quite familiar in Baptist life of this period. The names of the Bakers, Barkers, Childs, and the Caters appeared many times in the history of the undivided Charleston church.[59] The name of Governor Joseph Blake had been related to the Baptists, although there is considerable uncertainty about his membership. There is no doubt that his wife, Lady Elizabeth Blake, was an active Baptist. Her will, in 1725, provided a generous gift and a sustaining sum annually for the Baptists. Her mother, Lady Rebecca Axtell, was probably also related to the Baptists.

The name of William Chapman as an active and generous Baptist was well known. Evidently he provided the meeting place for the earliest church gathering in Charleston. Little is known about the Whitakers and the Bryants. It is significant that these names were included, even though the early church records did not include their descendants by name. Their daughters may have been members under the names of their husbands.

Another source of information, not as trustworthy as those mentioned heretofore, are the wills of the period. It is recognized that care must be exercised about reading back into the early period from even a decade or two later. Furthermore, it is easy to make a person a member of the church by association when that was not actually the case. Simply because a number of Baptists signed a will or acted as executors does not necessarily mean the one making the will was a Baptist. It is true that by proximity and intermarriage, numbers of people of other denominations were influenced toward the Baptists. For example, Quaker families like the Witters and the Ladsons intermarried with the Baptists.[60]

William Chapman, Jr., was an executor of James Witter's will; and Witter and wife witnessed the will of Joseph Atwell, a known Baptist; but this still did not make Witter a Baptist. The Ladsons were known Quakers,[61] but the name Ladson showed up in Baptist ranks also. Thomas Ladson, in his will, left twenty pounds to the Baptist minister, and his will was witnessed by several Baptists of the community.[62] William Screven, Jr., married Catherine Stoll, daughter of Justinus Stoll of Charleston, and before long the name of Justinus Stoll showed up on a Baptist church roll. Landgrave Thomas Smith, evidently not related to the early Baptist movement, gave his daughter in marriage to James Screven and provided land for a Baptist church later on in laying out a town. One is tempted to include Thomas Quarterman, who married William Cater's daughter; Samuel Commander, whose daughter married Elisha Screven; and Henry Bower, whose will showed Joseph Sealy as executor and both the father and son Ephraim Mikell as witnesses.[63] Despite these close associations with the Baptists, one cannot determine if they were members or not.

However, when a will showed a cluster of Baptists as executors and witnesses (especially a Baptist preacher), when a person gave money in his will to the Baptists, and when the person's age was such that he could have been a member in 1708, there is good reason to include him in the membership of ninety mentioned by William Screven.

One is inclined to put into this category William Skipper, who died about 1725. He was the nephew of Thomas Elliott and in his will gave fourteen pounds to the poor of the Baptist church.[64] Thomas Ladson, who, like Skipper had a Quaker background, but whose will contained the names of several Baptists, at his death gave twenty pounds to the Baptist minister.[65] Mary Wyatt, whose will in 1724 showed Joseph Sealy as executor, gave fifty pounds to the Baptist church in Charleston.[66]

One name in the wills was that of William Adams, who has already been mentioned as probably being the man by that name who was a member of the church in Kittery. He came to Charleston before 1695, signed a will by his mark in 1693, and secured a number of land warrants beginning May 20, 1696.[67] His will was dated June, 1707, and in it he mentioned that his daughter Elizabeth had married Thomas Grimball, a well-known Baptist; his son William was to be apprenticed to William Elliott until twenty-one years of age; his daughter Lidiah was to attend the school of Mrs. Elizabeth Wetherick. The executors and witnesses were William Elliott, William Sadler, and John Child.[68]

As suggested previously, the dates of William Adams's activity in Charleston preceded those of William Screven by several years. It is possible that he was a key figure in bringing Screven to South Carolina. He may have been killed by the Indians in the fall of 1707, which could account for his making a will in the late summer of 1707, when he still had a young family. Many people made their wills when taking a hazardous journey, and the outbreak of Indian troubles may have caused Adams to make his will. If this were the William Adams who was killed, he was identified as a "New England" man.[69]

One interesting will was that of Florence Soreney, whose name was never mentioned anywhere else in connection with Baptist life. Evidently the name *Florence* was that of a man, for his will in 1720 mentioned a wife named Ann. The interesting thing about this will is that there were three Baptists named as executors: *Captain* Lawrence Dennis, John Shepherd, and, most significantly, William Pert. This may be the only time the name of the Baptist preacher who preceded Thomas Simmons as pastor of the Charleston church is found in any of these legal records.[70]

A careless totaling of all of these mentioned as likely members of the Charleston church in 1708 brings the number to approximately ninety. It is true that there cannot be certainty as to some of the names, but there are good grounds for each one.

Screven's Last Days

Not long after writing his final letter of record to the Boston pastor, William Screven and his wife made a major decision. On October 15, 1708, they conveyed the Somerton plantation to René Ravenel. Although the plantation was not named in the transfer, the Ravenel family owned it for nearly a century and a half, and it was always known by the name of Somerton. On March 26, 1728, Elizabeth Wetherick sold the 325 acres adjoining the Somerton plantation to Paul Ravenel, who evidently incorporated it into the original Somerton.[71] All of this area is now under Lake Moultrie.

Screven probably served a brief additional period at Charleston and then, after purchasing lands at what is now Georgetown, moved to that area about 1710.[72] The fact that the correspondence between the Charleston church and the Devonshire church in 1711 was addressed to Fry and Sadler at the Charleston church, with no mention made of Screven, suggests that he was not in Charleston at that time. However, there is a reference dated "about 1713" in the report of Commissary Gideon Johnston to London which speaks of Mr. Screven the ship carpenter as the Anabaptist teacher in Charleston at that time, along with Mr. Sandford.[73] Either Screven returned there for a brief period or the dating is inaccurate. It is known that he died in what is now Georgetown on October 10, 1713, in his eighty-fourth year, and was buried in what later became lot 66 of the town.[74]

He left a writing known as *An Ornament for Church Members,* which was printed after his death. No copy is known to exist, but Morgan Edwards preserved one section of it, which read:

> And now for a close of all (my dear brethren and sisters, whom God hath made me, poor unworthy me, an instrument of gathering and settling in the faith and order of the gospel) my request is, that you, as speedily as possible, supply yourselves with an able and faithful minister. Be sure you take care that the person be orthodox in faith, and of blameless life, and does own the confession of faith put forth by our brethren in London in 1689, etc.

The urging of Screven to the church to secure promptly a Particular Baptist as pastor might suggest that Screven was well aware of the growing strength of the General Baptists led by William Elliott. It is quite possible that Elliott, becoming wealthy and influential rather quickly, was the one who addressed the General Assembly of General Baptists in London in 1702 asking for a General Baptist preacher to come to South Carolina. He certainly did so later, as will be noted. The existence of a growing General Baptist party may account for Screven's effort to continue his ministry at Charleston until a Particular Baptist preacher could be secured from England and also may explain Screven's language in his last message to the church, urging her to secure a Particular Baptist pastor promptly. Basil Manly quoted from Morgan Edwards these pungent words: "Had they attended to this counsel, the distractions, and almost destruction of the Church, which happened twenty-six years after, would have been prevented."[75]

Notes

1. L. Tyerman, *Rev. George Whitefield,* 2 vols. (New York: Anson D. F. Randolph & Company, 1877), I:129.
2. Wood, p. 144.
3. Manly, *Discourse,* pp. 11 ff.
4. Townsend, pp. 6-8.
5. Salley, *Warrants,* p. 137.
6. Ibid.
7. Ibid.
8. Henry A. M. Smith, "Some Forgotten Towns in Lower South Carolina," in SCH&GM, XIV:134-36.
9. *Journal of the Commons House of Assembly* (Columbia: South Carolina Archives Department), February 28, 1700. Cited hereafter as JCHA.
10. Salley, *Warrants,* p. 137.
11. SCH&GM, XII:148-49.
12. Ibid., XIV:134-36.
13. NEH&GR, XLIII:356.
14. Salley, *Warrants,* p. 4 and passim.
15. Cecil Hampden Cutts Howard, *Genealogy of the Cutts Family in America* (Albany, N.Y.: 1892), p. 51. See also Noyes et al., pp. 177-79, and Townsend, p. 58.
16. Howard, pp. 494 ff.
17. Salley, *Warrants,* p. 137.
18. Manly, *Discourse,* p. 12-13.
19. Ibid., p. 10 n. Diaries, sermon notes and records, and correspondence of Oliver Hart have been collected by Mrs. Loulie Latimer Owens. They have not been collated into permanent form, so references to the material must be by date, which will usually be shown in the body of the text. Copies of this material are found in the Baptist History Collection, Furman University Library, Greenville, South Carolina, and elsewhere.

20. Ibid., p. 11.

21. Ibid., p. 14 n.

22. Townsend, p. 10.

23. Ibid., p. 15.

24. Ibid., p. 11 n.

25. Ibid., p. 11.

26. Lumpkin, *Confessions,* pp. 239-40, 349-50.

27. W. T. Whitley, ed., *Minutes of the General Assembly of the General Baptist Church in England,* 2 vols. (London: Baptist Historical Society, 1909-10), I:75.

28. SCH&GM, XIV:135-36.

29. Moody, III:xxxiv ff.

30. Ibid.

31. Ibid.

32. *Wills and Miscellaneous Records* (Columbia, S.C.: Historical Commission), LII:26.

33. SCH&GM, V:32-35, 38.

34. Letter of Nicholas Trott to Bishop of London, dated February 17, 1703. Library of Congress, Fulham Palace MSS, South Carolina Box, no. 245.

35. SCH&GM, V:32-35, 38.

36. Robert G. Rhet, *Charleston—An Epic of Carolina* (Richmond, Va.: 1940), p. 55.

37. SCH&GM, V:32-35, 38.

38. For this story, see Osgood, II:326-30. See also, Salley, *Narratives,* pp. 221-23, 267-68.

39. Salley, *Narratives,* pp. 251-52.

40. Manly, *Discourse,* pp. 74-75.

41. Henry A. M. Smith, "Georgetown—The Original Plan and the Earliest Settlers," SCH&GM, IX(1908):85-101. Also George C. Rogers, Jr., *The History of Georgetown County, South Carolina* (Columbia, S.C.: University of South Carolina Press, 1970), pp. 32-34.

42. Manly, *Discourse,* Appendix p. 70. See also ibid., p. 17 and 17 n.

43. See Henry A. M. Smith, SCH&GM, IX (1908):85-101.

44. Salley, *Narratives,* p. 364.

45. See Wood, pp. 192-93, for an example.

46. Isaac Backus sent this letter to Colonel Thomas Screven in 1796 when the latter was collecting materials about his great-grandfather. Manly, pp. 70-71.

47. W. T. Whitley, *The Crozer Quarterly,* January 1936, pp. 21-32.

48. Garnett Ryland, *The Baptists of Virginia 1699-1926* (Richmond: The Virginia Baptist Board of Missions and Education, 1955), p. 5.

49. Townsend, p. 271.

50. Wood, p. 190.

51. Manly, *Discourse,* p. 72.

52. Isaac Backus sent this letter to Colonel Thomas Screven in 1796. Manly, pp. 72-73.

53. Townsend, p. 15.

54. See, for example, Reuben A. Guild, *Chaplain Smith and the Baptists* (Philadelphia: American Baptist Publication Society, 1885), p. 38 n.

55. Moore & Simmons, *Wills,* p. 125.

56. SCH&GM, XIV:135 ff.

57. *York Deeds,* Book VII, Folios 33-34.

58. Morgan Edwards, *Materials Towards a History of the Baptists in the Province of South Carolina,* 1772, p. 2. Crozer manuscript in the Library of the American Baptist Historical Society, Rochester, N.Y.

59. Townsend, p. 33.

60. See wills of James Witter and Thomas Ladson in Moore & Simmons, *Wills,* pp. 154, 166.

61. SCH&GM, XXVIII:22-43.

62. Moore & Simmons, *Wills,* p. 166.

63. Ibid., p. 222 for Quarterman's will; p. 216 for Commander's will; p. 94 for Bower's will.

64. Ibid., p. 109.

65. Ibid., p. 166.

66. Ibid., p. 98.

67. Salley, *Warrants,* pp. 119, 135, 169.

68. Moore & Simmons, *Wills,* p. 24.

69. SCH&GM, XL:76.

70. Moore & Simmons, *Wills,* p. 62.

71. SCH&GM, XIV:134-36.

72. Ibid.

73. Hirsch, p. 309.

74. SCH&GM, XVI:93-95.

75. Manly, *Discourse,* p. 16.

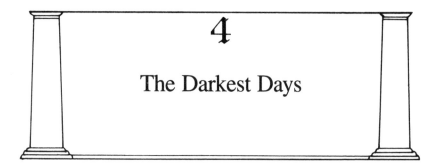

4

The Darkest Days

It appeared that the First Baptist Church of Charleston would enjoy a period of budding and blossoming in the generation that followed the death in 1713 of William Screven, her first pastor. There were many reasons for this optimism.

The church was rapidly developing a broad base of faithful and prospering members. The first pastor's family was an example. None of his sons entered the ministry, so far as is known, but it appears that all continued their love and support for the church.

Bridget, the preacher's wife, outlived him by only four years. This, with other circumstances, may suggest that she was the oldest of the daughters of Robert Cutt when Screven, at the age of forty-five, took her to be his wife in 1674. The four or five daughters in Screven's family lost their name identities in historical record through marriage. It is known that Elizabeth married her cousin, Robert Elliott, and died before 1726 when he remarried.[1] Screven's children and scores of grandchildren may be glimpsed in the meager records of the Charleston church and her offspring long beyond the end of this period in her history. They added much to the strength and witness of the church by their faithfulness.

In addition, the wills of early Charleston Baptists showed that there was a great deal of intermarrying among the families in the church. In some instances, known Baptists intermarried with non-Baptists, and soon their children were listed in Baptist ranks. The Screvens married the Brisbanes, the Dixons, the Fowlers, the Boutwells, the Sandifords, and the Witters; the William Elliotts married the Skippers; the Thomas Elliotts married the Fitchs; the Caters married the Quartermans, the Bakers, the Childs, the Bradwells, and the Bullines; the Childs married the Quartermans; the Mikells married the Hazards; the Hutchinsons married the Grimballs; the Riverses married the Witters; the Butlers married the Elliotts; the Adamses married the Grimballs; the Fowlers married the Brisbanes, the Bedons, and the Bakers; and the intermarrying went on and on. Some Baptists married into prominent families. As noted, William, the son of the preacher, married Catherine Stoll of a fine Charleston family, and their son James married Mary H. Smith, the daughter of Landgrave Thomas Smith.

This broadening base of membership may also be seen in the numerous additions to the leadership of the church. The names of trustees for the church property provide an example. The original trustees of lot 62 were William Sadler, John Raven, Thomas Bulline, Thomas Graves, and John Elliott. In 1712 a confirming deed included new names for this property: Richard Butler, Ephraim Mikell, Lawrence Dennis, John Raven, Jr., and Henry Turner. In 1730, when a tract of land was purchased on Edisto Island to provide a meeting place for members of the Charleston church living there, the trustees were Charles Odingsell, Joseph Sealy, Sr., William Elliott, Sr., John Sheppard, and Samuel Screven. The names of new leaders like this spring up constantly in the records during this period.

In addition to new Baptist churches in Virginia and North Carolina, another center of Baptist influence was formed in South Carolina. In 1738 thirty of the Welsh Tract Baptists from what is now Delaware organized a church on the fertile lands by the Peedee River near present-day Society Hill, South Carolina. In 1743 this Baptist group was integrated into older South Carolina Baptist life when Philip James was ordained by Isaac Chanler and Thomas Simmons of Ashley River and Charleston.[2]

These, then, were the other Baptists who had organized churches in the Southland during the period from 1713 to 1750. The presence of these Baptists might be expected to encourage and strengthen the witness of the Charleston church. However, these optimistic prospects were quickly dimmed by other factors that almost destroyed the Charleston church during this same period.

In the several decades after the death of William Screven in 1713, the members of the church in Charleston, along with other inhabitants of the city and province, experienced much suffering and harrassment. Typhonic hurricanes inundated and pounded the city sporadically, bringing death and destruction. Intermittent "pestilential fever" ravaged Charleston time and again. In May, 1715, the former allies of the colonists, the Yemassee Indians, perhaps in retaliation for the aid South Carolina had given in subduing the Tuscaroras to the north, began their attacks at almost the very door of Charleston. The Indians had a force of between eight and ten thousand warriors, while only twelve hundred whites were available to defend the small South Carolina settlements. It appeared that Charleston itself would be destroyed. However, Governor Craven defeated the Indians in engagements to the west and south, and this menace was diminished, although the cost in life was great.

Another serious crisis for the city occurred in the summer of 1718. The War of the Spanish Succession on the continent (known as Queen Anne's War in America) had ended in 1713. All nations in this war had continued the old practice of licensing ship owners to fit out their own vessels with heavy arms and engage as "privateers" to prey on the commerce of the enemy. After peace was restored, many of these privateers altered their visage from patriotism to piracy and continued to seize and loot other vessels, often those of their own nation.

The close of Queen Anne's War multiplied the number of these pirates, and many had their headquarters in the uncharted islands of the West Indies. From here they would cruise to the north and ravage shipping from Charleston, then continue on to secondary bases in North Carolina. Armed vessels stationed themselves within sight of the city of Charleston, waiting like birds of prey for their victims to sally forth with their cargoes.

All trade was well-nigh destroyed. In vain Governor Johnson appealed to England for assistance. The Crown was engaged in serious internal political problems. Consequently, Johnson decided that if anything were to be done, the colonists would have to do it themselves. In the fall of 1718, a small force led by Colonel William Rhett was able to capture the notorious pirate Stede Bonnet. Fearful of pirate reprisals, Governor Johnson himself prepared four ships. By strategic maneuvering and hard fighting he defeated the infamous Richard Worley, slaying him and twenty-five other pirates and capturing several vessels. This action saved Charleston from critical attacks by the pirates, although these unsavory parasites continued their activity intermittently for some years along the coast.[3]

The numerous appeals from South Carolina to England for help against the Indians and the pirates, the radical loss of revenue because of the piratical blockade, and the declaration by the colony's proprietors that they were unable to protect the province against future marauders, caused England's Board of Trade in 1715 to call the proprietors before them to ascertain their plans for the colony. This began a series of tortuous negotiations between the crown and the proprietors relative to what compensation would be given for the surrender of the colony's charter. These protracted discussions were hastened in 1716 when the colonial assembly imposed a 10 percent levy upon all imports and exports of the colony in an effort to secure funds for their protection. This levy exasperated the English Board of Trade, and in 1719 the Board repeated their original demand that this be repealed. Thus, the financial resources needed to protect the colony from its enemies were denied to the people, and a confrontation soon came.

On December 21, 1719, the people of the colony met in convention at Charleston, declared that the proprietors had violated their charter, and demanded that the Crown assume control and protection of the province of South Carolina. After a period of provisional control by the Crown, in 1729 the proprietors (with the exception of Lord Carteret, who preferred to retain his one-eighth interest) were compensated for their holdings in South Carolina, including a lump sum for arrears in quit-rents and the assumption by the Crown of all unpaid debts incurred by the proprietors. South Carolina now *de jure* became a royal colony.[4]

Although the loss of early church records has removed the details of many events of this period from the pages of history, it is possible by collateral material to piece together the mournful story of the darkest days of the Charleston church. The internal history of the church was just as tumultuous as conditions were on the outside. The principal problems involved the difficulty of securing stable pastoral leadership, the loss of many leaders by death and removal, a diminishing membership because of the formation of separate churches by some of the arms or branches of the original church, doctrinal controversy and schism, conflict over George W. Whitefield and the First Great Awakening, a deep rift in the membership over the dismissal of the pastor, and a lengthy period of litigation over the church property. These several crises brought "a mournful pause in the hopes of the church," remarked Basil Manly. They will be discussed briefly in chronological order.

Pastoral Leadership

Perhaps the church records are missed most sorely when an effort is made to reconstruct the order and time of the ministers of the church after the death of Screven. The reference in the previous chapter to a minister from England who had assisted Screven briefly before dying, perhaps about 1707, hints that the church at this time, as it did later (and probably earlier also), had written to England and elsewhere for pastoral help. The letter from William Fry and William Sadler to the South Moulton church in England in 1710 suggested that the Charleston church was depending upon part-time pastoral leadership.

Three shadowy figures may be glimpsed as they attempted to lead the church about this time. This first minister from England, identified as a Mr. White by Morgan Edwards, has already been discussed briefly. He may have been the person that Samuel Thomas, a missionary of the Society for the Propagation of the Gospel in Foreign Parts, referred to in 1705 as having recently gone to Carolina from Biddiford, England.[5] In his letter of 1707 to Boston, Screven mourned White's unexpected death.

The second shadowy figure who ministered to the Charleston church was called "Sanford" by Morgan Edwards, evidently relying totally on oral history over a half-century old. This man was supposed to have assisted Screven in the Charleston church and succeeded him as pastor. He evidently was the man mentioned by Francis Le Jau, missionary of the Society for the Propagation of the Gospel, in a letter of August 30, 1712, to the Society in London. Jau said that this man had "arrived in these last Shipps about 6 weeks ago to be a Teacher among the Anabaptists."[6] He accused the preacher of emphasizing the doctrine of predestination in so terrifying a manner that he caused a man who had been "in a Melancholly Condition" for some years past to do himself bodily harm. It seems that the Particular Baptists might have been emphasizing predestination more than the Presbyterians and Congregationalists, the spiritual successors of John Calvin. Jau said toward the close of this self-serving letter that he would endeavor to get more information about the matter and write again, but the records were silent thereafter. One remark by the missionary in this letter is quite interesting. He said that the "whole meeting" of the Baptists had written letters to the melancholy man, which seems to suggest that the entire church had demonstrated a caring spirit in their efforts to help him.

Sanford was also referred to by Commissary Gideon Johnston, who listed the names of Dissenter leaders in Charleston in a letter about 1713 to the Bishop of London. He identified "Mr. Scriven, a Ship Carpenter," as the Anabaptist teacher at Charleston, and "Mr. Sanford, a Tallow Chandler, another Baptist teacher towards the Southward, both of them [Screven and Sanford] extremely ignorant, but this more seemingly modest than the other."[7]

In view of the frequent differences in spelling of proper names at this time, it is difficult to be confident about making identifications. The name "Sanford" or "Sandford" is never found in any will of this province between 1670 and 1760; but the name "Sandiford" is found many times, and one Sandiford was deeply involved in Baptist life. This could not have been the preacher, but quite likely was his son, John Sandiford. John was a brother-in-law of Samuel Screven and an executor of Screven's will. In the town plot of Georgetown, a map dated June 30, 1737, showed the names of the original owners of the various lots. John Sandiford had lots 133-34, William Screven had lots 135-36, and Joshua Peart had lots 137-38.[8] There is no question that the last two were sons of former pastors of the Charleston church, and it is likely that the first (John Sandiford) was the son of preacher "Sanford," the successor of preacher William Screven. When this John Sandiford died after 1748, his executors were James and William Screven and Captain Robert Rivers, all well-known Baptists.[9] Evidently the preacher Sanford (Sandiford) was a strong Particular Baptist, and there was a suggestion in Missionary Jau's letter that the preacher's strong Calvinistic preaching did not please all of the Baptists. This may be an early reflection of the dissatisfaction that was already developing between the Particular and the General Baptists in the Charleston church.

The third rather shadowy figure was the pastor of the church after Sanford. Sanford died about 1717 or 1718, and the scanty traditions named his successor as William Peart (sometimes spelled Pert). Peart was reported by

Morgan Edwards to be a good preacher and a pious man, who had been ordained as a Baptist minister in England and had arrived in the province about the time of Sanford's death. How he learned about the need in Charleston and how long he served as pastor are not clear, but evidently he died before August 8, 1722, when his widow Sarah married Thomas Grimball. There was a tradition that Peart was instrumental in encouraging some of the branches of the Charleston church to begin the erection of houses of worship, but this is uncertain.[10] The only time William Peart's name appeared in any of the wills of this period occurred on July 31, 1720, when he was shown as executor of the will of Mr. Florence Soreney along with Captain Lawrence Dennis and John Sheppard, all Baptists.[11] Morgan Edwards recorded that the preacher had one son, Joshua, who evidently was the man shown with John Sandiford and William Screven as one of the original owners of the lots in Georgetown in 1737. Joshua made his will on April 28, 1741, called himself a joiner of Charleston, and named William Screven and William Elliott as his executors. His witnesses were three well-known Baptists. The will was proved on the following July 4.[12]

After the ministries of White, Sanford, and Peart, collateral records provided more information about the next pastor of the church, Thomas Simmons (sometimes spelled Symmonds or Simmonds). He was English born and educated but migrated to Pennsylvania when his father wanted to apprentice him to the carpenter's trade. Evidently in Pennsylvania, Simmons fell in with the company of young men who were surrendering themselves to the gospel ministry during the period following the organization of the Philadelphia Association in 1707. He first appeared in the records in 1721 as pastor of the Baptist church at Hopewell, New Jersey, where he served two years, then moved to Carolina.[13] In the property litigation during his last years, Simmons said in a sworn petition to the General Assembly that after the death of William Peart he had been asked by the Charleston church to come there from Pennsylvania to become her pastor. He arrived in 1723 with his wife and two children, Thomas and Hannah, and on or about March 20, 1725, was "duly called and chosen by the unanimous Consent and Approbation of the then Members of said Church to be Pastor."[14]

He further said in his petition that he had at that time promptly begun preaching in the original church building of the Charleston church, and that later he occupied a dwelling house that had been built on the church lot. At some time during the ensuing years, his daughter Hannah married Thomas Dale, who exercised considerable influence over his father-in-law. Although Simmons did not die until January 31, 1747, he was engaged in a severe controversy with the Particular Baptist majority of his flock and was suspended from the pastoral office about 1744. He took an active part in several of the explosive confrontations in Charleston Baptist life before his death, and this will be noted hereafter.

Death and Removal of Pioneers

The loss of many of the founding members of the church added to her problems. In the legal litigation of 1744 the statement was made that all of the trustees of 1699 and 1712 were dead. The wills of this period revealed the deaths of many known Baptists: William Adams in 1707, William Chapman in 1712, Thomas Grimball in 1721, Joseph Atwell and Savannah Griffin in 1723, Mary Wyatt and William Skipper (who left fourteen pounds in his will to the poor of the church) in 1724, John Rivers in 1725, Lady Elizabeth Blake (who left fifty pounds for a Baptist parsonage and twenty pounds per year for supporting the Baptist minister) in 1726, Robert Elliott (son of Elizabeth Wetherick) in 1728, Ephraim Mikell and Sarah Barker in 1729, and Thomas Cater and Thomas Ladson (who left the Baptist pastor gifts of ten and twenty pounds, respectively) and Joseph Sealy in 1731. These losses by death continued during the remainder of this period.[15]

The bitter struggle over the Anglican establishment before 1706 may have caused some Baptists to leave the immediate area of controversy, although, of course, they could not get away from the establishment as long as they remained in South Carolina. A cursory examination of the land warrants issued during the five years prior to the Anglican establishment in 1706 showed that about twenty-two known Baptists secured grants of land in various other parts of the province, while in the five years after 1706, no fewer than fifty-four such land warrants were issued to known Baptists, some of them quite substantial and some far from Charleston. Elizabeth Blake alone, for example, secured 3,560 acres of land, mainly in Colleton County, after 1706. William Screven himself, it will be recalled, moved about this time to what is now Georgetown, and his sons Aaron and Robert secured grants for large tracts on the Black River.

Sometimes a group of known Baptists would get grants adjoining one another. For example, on September 4, 1707, Lady Elizabeth Blake, William Baker, Lady Rebecca Axtell (Mrs. Blake's mother), Thomas Kator (Cater), and William Kator (all known Baptists) each secured warrants for five hundred acres of land "on Combee Island." A William Holmes did likewise, and he or his son appeared later among the Baptist ranks.[16] Grants to known Baptists were made to the south as far as what is now Beaufort, to the north in Craven County, and a little later some Charleston Baptists showed up at the Welsh Neck church in the Peedee section. Whether or not the struggle between the Dissenters and the Anglicans caused some Baptists to seek plantations more distant from Charleston cannot be known, but the loss of

Baptist members from Charleston took place whether this was the reason for their moving or not.

The Ashley River Church

Like most other early Baptist churches in America, the Charleston church developed "arms" or "branches" quite early, consisting of new converts or older Baptists who settled away from the city. Although remaining a part of the mother church, these branches would often meet independently for worship at one of the homes in the community. One of the earliest of these branches of the Charleston church was the arm on Ashley River, a few miles to the northwest of Charleston. Several of the pioneers of the Charleston church settled along this river very early and counted themselves a part of the Charleston congregation until 1736. Richard and Sarah Butler conveyed six acres of land located about fourteen miles from Charleston to these Ashley River Baptists on November 22, 1725, and two years later a meetinghouse was erected. The trustees for the land bore familiar names: William Cater, John Bulline, Thomas Inghran, William Elliott, Jr., Robert Booth, John Brown, Samuel Screven, John Raven, and Richard Bedon.[17] Worship was conducted either by ministers coming out from Charleston or the congregation going into Charleston, or occasionally the holding of services at Ashley River by some other qualified person.

About 1733 Isaac Chanler (sometimes spelled Chandler), a mature minister, arrived in Charleston from England. He had been born in Bristol in 1702 and was a sturdy Particular Baptist. Perhaps it was his coming that initiated the move to form a separate church at Ashley River. At any rate, Morgan Edwards said that on May 24, 1736 (although the day cannot be deciphered in the minutes), at a general church meeting in Charleston, the separation came. The minutes said:

> After diverse Debate, it was unanimously agreed by the Churches that henceforth the two _____ Branches of a Church the one Residing in or near Charles Town the other Residing upon Ashley River in this Country _____ should act distinctly _____ by themselves Independent of Each other—that is to say, That ye Minister of Each Branch be maintained _____ by Each Branch where his particular _____ _____ and Reside _____ That Each minister in their Respective places of abode preach Constantly and administer ye Holy ordinances of God's house holy Baptism and ye Supper of ye Lord God without interfering ye one with ye other, and Each Branch manage by Themselves their own Matters Relating _____ to Discipline in all parts thereof.[18]

The constituent members of the church were Isaac Chanler, William Cater, John Bullein, Richard Bedon, Jr., Richard Bedon, Sr., Benjamin Child, John

Shepard, Jr., Charles Barker, Charles Filbin, Francis Shepard, Alexander Shepard, Jacob Bradwell, John Angel, Thomas Ramsey, Sarah Baker, Mary Cater, Susanna Bradwell, Christiana Brown, Ann Maine, Elizabeth Chanler, Elizabeth Bullein, Joyce Griffin, Elizabeth Bedon, Elizabeth Salter, Susanna Baker, Elizabeth Marrian, Mary Shepard, and Ann Peacock.[19] The loss of this large number of faithful Baptists certainly diminished the strength of the mother church in Charleston. It occurred in the same year that the Stono church was constituted from Charleston members, and these two excisions removed many of the older and wealthier members.

The minutes of the Ashley River church revealed that Chanler encountered early difficulties because of his insistence that all converts, immediately after baptism, must receive the imposition of hands "as a means to obtain a fresh Supply of the holy Spirit of grace" before admission into full communion with the church. This practice was followed by some Baptists in both Britain and America and was no longer a test of fellowship in the Philadelphia Association by this time. Chanler had some difficulty convincing the older members of the church that they should submit to this rite after their long experience in the Christian life without it, but the minutes recorded that he was firm about it and that the older members gradually accepted it.

During his thirteen-year ministry at the Ashley River church, Chanler maintained a close relationship with the Charleston church. The minutes of the Ashley River church were tantalizingly brief in mentioning that on June 14, 1742, at a church meeting, "It was concluded by the Church that a Late difference between ye church in Chas. Town & Ashley River . . . should drop." When Thomas Simmons was suspended from the pulpit by the majority of the church at Charleston, Chanler graciously lent his aid to the mother church. The minutes of Ashley River on June 4, 1746, said:

> It was agreed on by the Church that the Church in Charles Town . . . Should have me in Charles Town to Preach there unto them every third Lord's Day which was mentioned and Concluded on without any Limitation of Time. May it Please the Lord to bless my ministrations unto and amongst them for their good and his own glory. Amen and Amen.

It should be said that the minutes were kept by Chanler himself, and his devotional interjections appeared quite frequently in them. Chanler stoutly championed the Particular Baptist convictions of the majority of the Charleston church when controversy arose and gladly welcomed the ministry of George Whitefield, the Calvinistic Methodist, in a time of confrontation. Whitefield called him that "gracious Baptist minister."

Chanler must have been greatly beloved, for several of his congregation remembered him in their wills: Jacob Bradwell with sixty pounds in 1745; John Filben with fifty pounds in 1746; and William Cater with fifty pounds in

1749. During his ministry he published several tracts: *Doctrines of Glorious Grace, Treatise on Original Sin, New Converts, The State of the Church of Christ,* and *A Sermon on Acts 11:23.* In his will, proved on January 5, 1750, (where he spelled his name "Chandler"), he made reference to his four children: Samuel and Isaac under twenty-one years of age, and Ann and Elizabeth under eighteen years of age. He was just forty-eight when he died on November 20, 1749.

In his story of the Charleston church, Basil Manly paid this tribute to Chanler and his contribution to the church during a very critical period in her history:

> Although known to them not longer than about sixteen years, Mr. Chanler had been intimate with the most painfully interesting portions of their history. From his near residence he had been with them in weal and in wo, the firm, enlightened and undeviating friend of truth, and of the cause of Christ. Being distinguished for talents and piety, a good scholar and a sound divine, "a worthy man, and abundant in labors," he stood as a beacon light to the church through that stormy period,—that night of abounding heresy and error: and industriously sought, by the labors of the press, to extend that light beyond his immediate sphere, and into future generations.[20]

Doctrinal Controversy and Schism

Several of the early Charleston Baptist families had secured land warrants near the Stono River about fifteen miles southwest of the town. These Stono Baptists were counted an arm of the Charleston church until 1736. Perhaps with the encouragement of Thomas Simmons, pastor of the Charleston church at the time, Stono Baptists built a thirty-foot-square meetinghouse in 1728 on four acres of land donated by Henry Toomer. Here Simmons occasionally preached and performed pastoral duties, while the Stono group would travel to Charleston for the regular services.

From the earliest organization of the Charleston church, as has been pointed out, there had been both General or Arminian Baptists and Particular or Calvinistic Baptists in the membership. William Elliott, who had donated lot 62 in 1699 for erecting the first Baptist house of worship in Charleston, had been a General Baptist in England before coming to South Carolina. Significantly, Thomas Simmons also testified under oath that he had heard Elliott, Sr., affirm his General Baptist beliefs. It is quite possible that this open and repeated confrontation of his pastor by Elliott, Sr., provides the clue to an understanding of why Thomas Simmons shifted his point of view by the time of the court litigation which arose in 1744. There were undoubtedly other General Baptists in the original Charleston church membership.

As mentioned earlier, it was probably these General Baptists in the

Charleston church that sent the letter to the General Assembly of General Baptists in England in 1702 asking for a minister or books. Doubtless the General Baptist William Elliott, Sr., the wealthiest and most influential member of the church, had written the Assembly to see if they could send a General Baptist minister to replace William Screven. Screven may have moved out to Somerton by 1702 and was often unavailable. He was, in fact, growing old and feeble by this time. Evidently, he was aware of these efforts by William Elliott and the General Baptists, which may account for his great concern that the church should find a *Particular* Baptist preacher immediately. In almost his dying breath he urged the church to get a minister who acknowledged the Particular Baptist confession of 1689. Furthermore, as noted earlier, the strong predestinarian preaching of Mr. Sanford, Screven's successor, did not please some of the church, according to Missionary Jau, which also indicated the presence of a General Baptist party in the church.

A schism took place in late 1736 between the Particular and General Baptist parties in the Charleston church. It was not a friendly separation but a wrenching secession brought about by the doctrinal differences between the two groups. The old records do not entirely agree about the immediate occasion for the final confrontation. Morgan Edwards said that the church at Charleston had copastors, Thomas Simmons for the Particular Baptists and Robert Ingram for the General Baptists, and that their ministries "frequently caused jars in their public administrations to the grief of both parties for a considerable time (vis about 3 years)."[21] On the other hand, a petition presented to the Commons House of Assembly of South Carolina on May 1, 1745, by "Thomas Simmonds, Pastor of the Church of Antipaedo Baptists in Charles Town, and of Francis Gracis, deacon of the said Church," said that long before the time William Elliott had donated the lot for the original church building, the church had contained both Particular and General Baptists and that

> although the two Sects differed upon the Point of the Decrees of God yet they did not think that a sufficient Reason to break the Communion of the said church until the unhappy Differences which of late Years arose in the said Church by some of the Members both of the Calvinist and Arminian Persuasion carrying the peculiar Tenets of their Doctrine to too great a length.[22]

Collateral evidence proves that Edwards was mistaken about the church having copastors for three years. If Robert Ingram had been the General Baptist copastor in Charleston for three years, as stated by Edwards, these years must have been from 1733 to 1736, for the schism took place on November 25, 1736. Ingram could not have been copastor in Charleston during these years. The records of the General Assembly of General Baptists in England showed that Robert Ingram represented the Webstone Baptist Church at the meetings of the Assembly in England on May 31, 1732; on May 16, 1733; on June 5, 1734; on May 28, 1735; and on June 16, 1736.[23] Ingram could not have been in England and copastor in South Carolina at the same time during these years. If he left England for South Carolina after the meeting on June 16, 1736, he could not have been in Charleston very long before the schism on November 25, 1736.

Professor Robert Gardner has published a very important letter from the General Baptist party at Charleston to the General Baptist church at Newport, Rhode Island, dated February 9, 1734/35 (Old Style), which confirms the late coming of Ingram to South Carolina. This letter was signed by William Elliott, Jr., and Joseph Elliott. It is quite enlightening at several points. (1) It asserted that Paul Palmer "who is here with us at this present time" had informed them that the Newport church had "plenty of ministering brethren among you," while the Charleston General Baptists had none. This is the first time that Paul Palmer, the pioneer General Baptist preacher of North Carolina, has been identified as preaching in South Carolina.[24] (2) The General Baptist party in Charleston reported that they had been deeply offended when Palmer was not allowed "to preach once in our meeting house in town though there was to be 4 sermons on ye afores,d 2 days." (3) The General Baptists announced that they were now ready to separate from the Charleston church if they could find a minister of their own opinions. Palmer had told them that John Walton of Rhode Island might be available to send to Charleston, and Elliott and company said that they would be glad to have him. A reply from Newport dated December 3, 1735, reported that Walton preferred to practice law rather than to preach and that no other ministers were available.[25]

This correspondence makes it clear that the General Baptist party had no minister as copastor in Charleston in 1735. The appeal to Newport did not include the name of Robert Ingram. After Newport replied, the Charleston group evidently wrote to the General Assembly in England, and Robert Ingram came to Charleston after June 16, 1736. After the death of Ingram, the same group wrote to the Assembly again in an effort to secure another pastor.[26]

As a result of Ingram's coming, the General Baptist party withdrew on November 25, 1736, and formed a new church at Stono, evidently the focal point of the General Baptists. The following were the constituent members: Robert Ingram, pastor; William Elliott, Sr.; William Elliott, Jr.; Thomas Elliott; Henry Toomer; Richard Butler; Joseph Elliott; Joshua Toomer; George Timmons; Barnard Elliott; John Clifford; Thomas Tew; Thomas Davis; Dorothy Jones; Ann Bonneau; Amerinthia Farr; Mary Toomer, Jr.; Ann Childesy; Francis Elliott; and Elizabeth Elliott (perhaps a sister to Richard Butler). It will be noted that at least eight of the nineteen members were

Elliotts (Amerinthia Farr was an Elliott), and three of them were Toomers.

Upon his death in 1738, William Elliott, Sr., left a secret trust for the church through his three sons (William, Thomas, and Joseph) amounting to ten thousand pounds and a tract of fifteen and three-fourths acres of land on Charleston Neck. It is rather curious that the wills of William Elliott, Sr., and his son Thomas were proved on the same day (November 1, 1738), suggesting that perhaps some accident had claimed both of them. Joseph Elliott died in 1739, while Barnard, the fourth son of William, Sr., lived until November, 1758. The ten thousand pounds and the land willed in trust to the Stono church by Elliott, Sr., were later recovered by the church in a suit filed against William, Jr., after the death of Thomas and Joseph.[27]

The Stono church remained in close contact with the General Assembly of General Baptists in England until almost the time of the church's decease. As has been noted, Robert Ingram came from that body to Stono but died in 1738. The General Assembly, however, followed the practice of including the "Stone" church in South Carolina on its membership roll. In 1737, the year after Ingram went to South Carolina, the minutes showed that a letter had been received from the church, and the Assembly voted "that Bro. Killingworth do draw up an answer to their Letter for their Encouragemt. to Go on in the Ways of Christ."[28] In the Assembly meeting of the following year a letter was received from the church and was answered. The name of the church appeared in the roll of the Assembly churches in 1739, 1740, 1741, and 1742. In 1743 a footnote in the minutes said that the Assembly would no longer include the names of churches which did not send representatives to the annual meetings, and Stono was not shown. However, in 1744 the older practice was reestablished, and Stono was shown again on the roll.

Meanwhile, after the death of Ingram, Henry Heywood (who evidently came from the same town in England as Ingram) agreed to assume the pastorate. He arrived in 1739 and became pastor on May 5, 1740. He was described as being a scholar, "but an oddity in person and conduct." He was very active in pressing the claims of the Stono church in the litigation of the 1740s and in the controversy over George Whitefield, as will be seen shortly. He died on October 29, 1755.[29]

In 1756 the minutes of the General Assembly in England reported a letter from Charles Town, South Carolina, "requesting a Learned and pious Minister might be sent to them for whose Support abt. £70 a Year is appropriated."[30] In 1757 the South Carolina church wrote again to the Assembly saying that she could offer a minister for Stono a salary of one hundred pounds a year and fifty pounds for expenses to make the trip. Grantham Killingworth appealed to the Assembly for someone to volunteer to go.[31] Daniel Wheeler, pastor at Cranbrook, agreed to go, and in 1758

Killingworth advised the Assembly that Wheeler had arrived safely at Stono.[32] In 1759 the Assembly read a letter from Wheeler at "Stone and Charles Town" in South Carolina, and Killingworth was appointed to answer it. A letter was also received in 1761 by the Assembly, and Killingworth again replied. The same occurred in 1762. In 1763 Killingworth read his reply to the Assembly, and it was approved. Daniel Wheeler died in November 1767 with a reputation of being a "good and honest man." It appeared that the Stono church could not find another pastor for a long period. Joseph Pilmoor, a Methodist missionary, reported from Charleston in January, 1773, that he had preached in the General Baptist meetinghouse and that the church had no pastor at that time.

Daniel Dobell, with his preacher father Philip and preacher brother, Benjamin, was quite active in the General Assembly. He succeeded Wheeler as pastor of the Cranbrook church.[33] Philip and Daniel Dobell came to South Carolina and served the Stono church occasionally, but both died in August, 1774.

The church was officially recorded as extinct about January, 1791. On June 11, 1794, Benjamin Dobell (and others) urged that religious correspondence be opened with General Baptists in America, and this was done. None of this correspondence seemed to have been addressed to South Carolina General Baptists. In 1795 and 1797 the famous Dan Taylor (founder of the New Connection General Baptists of England) and John Evans were appointed to correspond with American General Baptists, but the only replies seemed to have come from areas other than South Carolina.

Meanwhile, after the schism of the Stono General Baptists in 1736, Charleston Baptists, under the leadership of Thomas Simmons, faced many problems. Some of the financial difficulties were eased when Lady Elizabeth Blake made provision in her will of September 30, 1725, for fifty pounds toward the building of a parsonage and twenty pounds a year for supporting the minister. Simmons led in the erection of the parsonage and other houses on the back of lot 62. Another of the periodic hurricanes almost destroyed the meetinghouse some time before June 2, 1731, and the congregation was forced to make extensive repairs before it could be used again.[34] Perhaps this expense caused Samuel Screven, one of the sons of the original pastor, to leave one hundred pounds currency for the use of the church in his will of December 3, 1731.

To add to this problem, Simmons began shifting his theological position toward his General Baptist friends and perhaps toward Arianism, an old heresy that subordinated Christ. He was reportedly in his dotage and influenced by his son-in-law Thomas Dale, a close friend to the General Baptist pastor, Henry Heywood. Because the lines between Particular Baptists and General Baptists had been drawn so tightly in the conflict between the parties when the Stono church broke away from Charleston, this attitude by Simmons promptly aroused the hostility of the staunch Particular Baptist majority in the church, as will be noted later. This estrangement was deepened by the antagonistic attitude of Simmons toward George Whitefield, the Calvinistic Methodist (or Anglican) preacher.

Conflict over George Whitefield

The Charleston church shared in the spiritual revival in America known as the First Great Awakening. This remarkable movement seems to have begun with the display of unusual evidences of the convicting power of the Holy Spirit in the congregation of Theodore J. Frelinghuysen in the Raritan Valley of New Jersey about 1726. Frelinghuysen was a Reformed or Calvinistic minister who had apparently been influenced before he came to America by the Pietistic movement of the Lutherans Philip Jacob Spener and August Hermann Francke on the continent. Gilbert Tennent, a Presbyterian neighbor of Frelinghuysen, became an active supporter of the revival and triggered a schism among Presbyterians by his censorious criticisms of his preacher colleagues for their spiritual lethargy. In 1734 Jonathan Edwards, the Congregational pastor at Northampton, Massachusetts, a staid but deeply devout preacher and scholar, experienced a spiritual awakening in his church. "The whole town," he wrote, "seemed to be full of the presence of God." From a human standpoint, these spiritual brush fires would not have been transported to the southern colonies had it not been for the ministry of George Whitefield, one of the colaborers of John and Charles Wesley, the founders of the Methodist movement in England.

George Whitefield was enlisted for preaching in America by John Wesley, who had been serving as an Anglican missionary in 1736 in the new colony of Georgia. In a letter to Whitefield, Wesley spoke of the need for laborers to come to this remote mission field and expressed confidence that God would touch the heart of someone soon. He closed with the words, "What if thou art the man, Mr. Whitefield?" In December 1736, faced with the decision between a "very profitable curacy" in London and the challenge of Wesley, Whitefield chose to turn his life toward America, and he accepted the appointment to Georgia. After a year's ministry in London, where huge crowds hung on every word of this twenty-three-year-old lad, he embarked on the *Whitaker* and arrived in Savannah, Georgia, on May 7, 1738. He determined to found an orphanage in Georgia after the example of A. H. Francke's institution at Halle on the continent. Making this orphanage his headquarters and tirelessly collecting funds for its operation, Whitefield trumpeted the gospel from New England to Georgia for the next three decades. Revival fires were kindled in almost every colony as a result of his ministry. It was indeed a Great Awakening.

Without realizing it, Whitefield greatly influenced the history of the First Baptist Church of Charleston, South Carolina. In one of the church's darkest hours, his preaching helped to sustain her; and in later years, one of his spiritual great-grandsons, Richard Furman, became pastor of the church and brought her to some of her highest achievements. It was a singular Providence that brought Whitefield to Georgia instead of permitting John Wesley to remain there. Wesley preferred to restrict his ministry in Georgia to the Church of England, but Whitefield, having lived in London, had learned to appreciate the worth of Dissenters, including Presbyterians and Baptists. In a letter to a friend from Savannah on January 16, 1740, he said,

> Though I profess myself a minister of the Church of England, I am of a catholic spirit; and, if I see any man who loves the Lord Jesus in sincerity, I am not very solicitous to what outward communion he belongs.[35]

Not only so, but he also differed from Wesley in doctrine, often urging Wesley in his letters to make further study of the doctrines of election and final perseverance. On March 26, 1740, he plainly told Wesley that he was "ten thousand times more convinced, if possible, than when I saw you last" of the truth of the Calvinistic position, although, he said in closing, "you think otherwise."

This was the spirit that Whitefield displayed in Charleston on his many visits there. He preached a dynamic Calvinistic gospel which, of course, appealed strongly to most of the church in Charleston. As would be supposed, Henry Heywood and the General Baptists at Stono were strongly opposed to this type of doctrine. Surprisingly, however, although claiming to be Calvinistic in doctrine, Thomas Simmons, pastor of the Charleston church, was hostile to Whitefield. Simmons himself said that it was this attitude on his part toward Whitefield and his open criticism of a book recommended by Whitefield that brought "the unhappy Difference now subsisting between him and his People."[36]

The willingness of Whitefield to preach for the Dissenters and the indifference which he showed to Anglicanism enraged Commissary Alexander Garden, the Church of England administrative head at Charleston, and in 1740 he ordered Whitefield to come before him to answer charges of ecclesiastical disobedience and irregularity. Whitefield had preached on March 15 at the Baptist meetinghouse in Charleston and had regularly addressed large crowds in the Independent and Baptist meetinghouses. Not unduly alarmed by the Commissary's anger, Whitefield nevertheless came from Savannah to Charleston to face his accuser. He preached on July 7 for Isaac Chanler, "a gracious Baptist minister," as he called him, at the Ashley River church. Two days later, because the crowds were too great to get into the Ashley River church building, Whitefield preached for Chanler to a great throng under the trees near the Baptist meetinghouse. After preaching for about a week while in Charleston for his meeting with Garden, he wrote, "Every day God shews me fresh instances of His love. There are some faithful ministers among the Baptists."[37] In another letter he mentioned preaching to the Baptists in Charleston on August 21, just before leaving for New England in early September, 1740.

This ministry of Whitefield in Charleston came at a time when the Charleston church was facing her darkest days. The forming of a separate church at Ashley River, the schism that brought the General Baptist church at Stono, and the disenchantment of the church with Thomas Simmons for his General Baptist leanings combined to bring the church low. Perhaps it was in about 1740 that the church came "dangerously near to extinction." Morgan Edwards said that one man and two women were the only members remaining and that Whitefield's preaching did much to revive the church.

Dismissal of Thomas Simmons

The controversy over George Whitefield did not subside even after Whitefield had absented himself from Charleston for long periods preaching in England and in other colonies. The Particular Baptists in the Charleston church could not accept the fact that Thomas Simmons, who had been the pastor for about twenty years, had given evidence of General Baptist sympathies despite his claim to be a Particular Baptist in doctrine. Basil Manly said of Simmons that

> though generally esteemed a good man, [he] had surrendered his judgment and feelings too much to the influence of others. This defect in his character had well nigh occasioned the destruction of the Church. In 1744, Dr. Thomas Dale, son-in-law of Mr. Simmons, but a particular friend of Mr. Heywood, the minister of the Arian party [at Stono], caused a misunderstanding and dispute between his father-in-law and the Church. Mr. Simmons was suspended from his pastoral office, by a majority of the Church. But Mr. Francis Gracia, a Deacon, and a few others, forcibly took possession of the place of worship, and introduced him again to the pulpit.[38]

The majority of the Charleston church were unwilling to continue under Simmons' ministry; and about August, 1744, James Fowler, William Brisbane, John Sheppard, and Alexander Sheppard announced that they, John Raven Bedon, Francis Baker, James Nash, Joseph Atwell, and others, would no longer contribute to the church nor attend her services. It was reported that Fowler, Brisbane, and others had sent to Pennsylvania for a Calvinistic pastor for themselves, but evidently this call met with no success at this time.[39]

Litigation over Church Property

It was this break between the church and her pastor that precipitated the first legal litigation over church property among Baptists in America. The deposing of the pastor brought a split in the church, and both the pastor and the majority who suspended him were eager to control the property of the church situated on lot 62 on Church Street in Charleston. Along with this was the fact that the original trust deed of 1699, by which William Elliott, Sr., had conveyed the property to the church, had expired in 1744 without being renewed, and the original trustees were then dead. Consequently, when the majority of the church, who had suspended the pastor, endeavored to take control of the property (including the parsonage where Simmons was living), they found that the title to the property could only be established by an act of the Commons House of Assembly.

So, on January 26, 1745, those members who had ousted Simmons as pastor and who counted themselves as being the true church by reason of their majority number submitted a petition to the Commons House of Assembly. This petition set forth

> that by Indenture made the eighteenth Day of July in the Year of our Lord, one thousand six hundred and ninety-nine, between William Elliott of Berkley County in this Province, Planter, of the one Part, and William Sadler, John Raven, Thomas Bullen, Thomas Graves, and John Elliott all of the said Province, Planters, Trustees for the People of the Antipaedo Baptist Profession in Charles Town, of the other Part, the said William Elliott for divers good Causes and Considerations in the said Indenture mentioned did give, grant, and confirm unto the said Trustees a Town Lot in Charles Town numbered sixty-two with the Appurtenances, to have and to hold the same unto the said Trustees, their Heirs and Assigns, to the only proper Use and Behoof of the said People of the Antipaedo Baptist Profession meeting in Charles Town forever. And in the said Indenture it was declared and agreed by and between all the Parties that in case three of the said Trustees should happen to die then the surviving Trustees should convey the said Town Lot and Premises to three other Trustees, their Heirs and Assigns, for the Use and Benefit of the People of the said Church meeting in Charles Town, and so from Time to Time the two surviving Trustees should continually join with themselves three other Trustees to the Intent that the said Town Lot, Buildings and Premises might have Continuance forever, to and for the Use of the said People of the said Church as a Place of Divine Worship. That a Meeting House for Divine Worship was built many Years ago at the Charge and

Expence of the said Congregation and is now standing on the said Lot, but the said original Trustees being all dead, without having first conveyed the Premises to others agreeable to the true Intent and Meaning of the Donor, the Petitioners are advised that the said Trust is now extinguished by the strict Rules of Law and cannot be revived without the Aid of the Legislature, and therefore to prevent the frustrating of so good and pious a Design humbly praying that Leave may be given them to bring in a Bill for reviving the said Trust and establishing the Premises upon a more solid and lasting Foundation for the Future.[40]

This petition was countered by one from Thomas Simmons (spelle█ Simmonds) and Francis Gracia, representing the minority of the church alleging that Simmons had been unanimously called as pastor of the churc█ on or about March 20, 1725, and that for about twenty years he ha█ maintained possession of the meetinghouse and parsonage on lot 62; tha█ Simmons had been pastor of the church long before Joseph Atwell, Jame█ Fowler, Justinus Stoll, William Brisbane, Nathaniel Gittens, and other█ presenting the original petition had even joined the church; that these five me█ and twelve others actually intended by their petition to turn Simmons out o█ the pastoral charge of the church and use of the parsonage. Simmons said als█ that most of the petitioners had voluntarily withdrawn from communion wit█ the church and had refused to support it. It is clear that he felt that the minority and he constituted the true church, and that the dissenting majorit█ had become schismatics. He closed by asking that the House not allow th█ persons who had cut themselves off from the church to have control o█ management of her property nor force him out of the pastorate withou█ bringing and proving some charge against him for error in doctrine o█ irregularities in conduct.[41]

On March 12, 1745, the Assembly presented a bill for continuing the trus█ of the lot and buildings of the Charleston church, and one week later, at the second reading of this bill, a startling development occurred. By motion█ Elisha Butler and William Butler, both members of the General Baptist churc█ at Stono, were named as two of the trustees of the property. This group had not heretofore been involved in this internal controversy of the Charlesto█ church, and it doubtless came as a great surprise to the Calvinistic majority o█ the church that the Assembly would include people as trustees of the Charleston church who were not members of that church. When their inclu-sion was challenged, the House deliberately voted to keep them as trustees. In addition, by motion at the same time, Francis Gracia was also named as █ trustee of the church. He was the champion of the Simmons faction. This completely unbaptistic and arbitrary action of the House was explained by Leah Townsend as follows:

Rev. George Whitefield had been cited and suspended from the exercise of his priestly office by Commissary Garden, and the more strongly Anglican members of the Commons House evidently seized the chance to embarrass Mr. Whitefield's staunch friends, the rigidly Calvinistic Baptists, by throwing their support to the anti-Whitefield faction of the Charleston Baptist Church in their struggle to retain lot No. 62 for Rev. Mr. Simmons.[42]

This explanation probably accounts for Simmons' stating in the Commons House during this litigation that the difference between him and the majority that evidently was the final straw in bringing Simmons' suspension from office was the reproof which Simmons gave Whitefield.

On April 23, the anti-Simmons majority of the church, represented by Joseph Atwell, James Fowler, William Brisbane, and others, presented another petition protesting the naming of trustees in the bill who were not members of the Charleston church (Elisha and William Butler of the Stono church), since they were not subject to the rules and actions of the church of whose property they would be trustees. Such a situation, said the petition, would produce constant discontent and discord in the Charleston church. Two days later a hearing was held on this petition. Counsel for the petitioners asked that the Charleston church book (in the possession of Simmons) be examined by the House, ostensibly to show that the Butlers were no longer members of the church. After some debate the House voted not to examine the church book. Charles Barker then testified that Elisha and William Butler, two of the trustees named in the proposed bill, were members of the Stono General Baptist congregation which had separated from the Charleston church some years before. Thomas Bullen testified that his father, one of the original trustees of the property, "was of the same Religion with the present Petitioners, and that the said Elisha Butler and William Butler are not of the same Opinion with the Anti Paedo Baptist Congregation in Charles Town, nor Members of that Meeting."[43]

On May 1, in another surprising move, Thomas Simmons and Francis Gracia presented a petition urging that the trustees who were members of the Stono church (Elisha and William Butler) should be included in the group of trustees for the Charleston church, but that Atwell and others "who did cut themselves off from the said Church" should not be named as trustees, especially since Atwell's party would probably force Simmons out of the church and the parsonage if they became trustees of the property. The petition closed by asking that the House name trustees "out of both Persuasions [General and Particular Baptists], and in appointing also an indifferent Person between them to be a Trustee with them."[44]

On May 3, 1745, the Simmons party provided the coup de grace by

producing the church minute book, certified by Henry Heywood, pastor of the
Stono General Baptist church and Thomas Dale, Simmons' son-in-law, in
support of their petition. Evidently this was introduced in behalf of the
General Baptists to show that William Elliott, Sr., had been a General Baptist
when he gave the land to the church originally in 1699. Simmons testified that
he had often heard Elliott, the donor, affirm his General Baptist views which
he had held before coming to South Carolina from England. Then Elliott's son
also testified that his father had always been a General Baptist. The anti-
Simmons majority continued to protest on May 7 and 8 against the naming of
trustees who were not members of the church and not Particular Baptists in
doctrine, but all of their motions were voted down. The bill was engrossed
and signed in the House, was taken to the Council on May 11, and was then
signed on May 25, 1745, by Governor James Glen and William Bull, Jr.,
Speaker of the House. Basil Manly quoted it as reading:

> And forasmuch as it appears by the above recited indenture, that the said
> Town lot, numbered sixty-two, and appertenances, was given to the use
> of the Anti-paedobaptists in general, and for the preventing of any
> disputes that may hereafter arise, it is hereby further enacted and
> declared by the authority aforesaid, that all the Anti-paedobaptists, as
> well those distinguished by the name of General Baptists, as those
> distinguished by the name of Particular Baptists, are entitled to, and shall
> have an equal right in the said lot numbered sixty-two, and the
> appertenances. And each of the said sects shall and lawfully may make
> use of the same for divine service; any law, usage, or custom to the
> contrary, in any wise, notwithstanding.[45]

The trustees were William Screven, John Raven (a minor, with Branfill
Evance to act for him during his minority), and Paul Grimball from the
Particular Baptists; Elisha and William Butler (members of the Stono church
and General Baptists); Francis Gracia (of Thomas Simmons' party); and John
Ladsen (probably the "indifferent party" requested by the Simmons' petition). This, of course, was a blow to the majority Particular Baptist party, for
now not only was it necessary to share the meetinghouse and parsonage on lot
62 with the Simmons-Gracia party, but the General Baptists (who belonged to
another congregation at Stono under the leadership of Henry Heywood) were
also authorized by law to share the property. Manly remarked:

> Mr. Heywood was immediately introduced into the pulpit in town, and
> his popular talents drew around him, for a time, a large congregation.
> "But his doctrines soon disgusted the people, and but few came."[46]

Manly described the immediate response by the church to the loss of the
sole use of her meetinghouse. On June 24, 1745, less than a month after the
unfavorable decision by the provincial legislature, the church observed a day
of prayer and fasting and consideration of what should be done. The leaders

determined to build another meetinghouse, and some familiar names were appointed to carry out this resolution: William Screven, William Brisbane, James Screven, Robert Screven, Thomas Dixon, William Screven, Jr., Nathaniel Bullein, James Brisbane, David Stoll, and Samuel Stillman.[47] The last named is not the outstanding minister Samuel Stillman who served in Charleston and then went to Boston as a pastor, since that Stillman was not converted until 1754 in a revival under Oliver Hart. These committee members were described as being "members of the congregation of Anti-paedo-baptists, meeting in Charleston, holding the doctrine of particular election and final perseverance, and denying Arian, Arminian, and Socinian doctrines." They promptly purchased from Mrs. Martha Fowler for five hundred pounds a "lot of land, bounded to the westward on Church Street, and known in the plat of the town by the number 102," and at least by the following year had built upon it a brick meetinghouse fifty-nine feet by forty-two feet, which, with some enlargement, was later used as the Mariner's Church. At first the Charleston members met every other Sunday in this building and on the other Sundays they used the old church building. They probably continued the use of the old building in order to maintain their claim on the old property. It is interesting to notice that Francis Gracia soon acknowledged his fault and was received back into fellowship with the church.[48]

Another Loss

In the midst of these repeated setbacks, the church soon sustained another loss. It will be remembered that the branch of the church on Edisto Island had scattered, many of the members settling at the Euhaws some forty miles southwest of Charleston. William Fry and Ephraim Mikell had earlier provided leadership for the congregation, but both had apparently died in the late 1720s. Mikell gave two acres of land in 1726, where a meetinghouse was built. The will of Mikell, proved May 3, 1729, provided that the Baptist minister on Edisto Island, should "have residency in my house until Joseph [Mikell's oldest grandson] is of age, or if none is living on said Island, then to one in Charles Town, 100 pounds at interest to be paid yearly."[49] In 1730 the Edisto Island congregation purchased one hundred acres adjoining the church lot, the trustees being Charles Odingsell, Joseph Sealy, Sr., William Elliott, Sr., John Sheppard, and Samuel Screven. Later in their wills, Joseph Sealy and his son left twelve hundred pounds currency to the church, while Ephraim Mikell, Jr., left one hundred pounds.[50]

Perhaps this building activity encouraged the congregation on Edisto Island to look for someone to assist in their services. A twenty-three-year-old man, William Tilly, had come to the Charleston church from Salisbury, England, in 1721 and, under the influence of two early pastors of the church (Peart and

Simmons), had experienced a call to preach. About 1731 he was ordained by the Charleston church. With the deaths of Fry and Mikell, the Edisto Island congregation desired someone to lead their services, although they refused to constitute themselves into a separate church from Charleston. Perhaps a part of the reason for this refusal to separate from the mother church was the fact that the members on Edisto Island were scattering into areas which had no Baptist churches, and they wanted the stabilizing influence of the Charleston church and pastor in their new locations. Some of these Edisto Island Baptists moved to Port Royal Island, Hilton Head Island, and to the Euhaws, an area located at the head of the estuary from Port Royal Sound on the Broad River, which took its name from the Euhaw Indians. Although the meetinghouse on Edisto Island was still used, and another was erected on Hilton Head Island, the Euhaw location became the principal branch of these former Edisto Island Baptists still related to the mother church in Charleston.

Not a great deal is known about the ministry of William Tilly. He seems to have lived on Edisto Island, for in his will all of the executors (Paul, Joshua, and Isaac Grimball, and John Jenkins) were inhabitants of Edisto Island, and Tilly was buried there. When George Whitefield preached in the area in 1740, Tilly, whom Whitefield called a "serious, lively Baptist minister," accompanied Whitefield to Savannah, preached for him on August 10 when Whitefield was ill, and observed the Lord's Supper with Whitefield's congregation. Basil Manly called Tilly "the wise and faithful minister at Edisto Island." He died on April 14, 1744, at the age of forty-six. His young son later became a member of the Charleston church. Isaac Chanler, from the Ashley River church, preached Tilly's funeral, perhaps because Thomas Simmons had been suspended, or soon would be, from the pastorate at Charleston.

After the death of Tilly, the Euhaw congregation continued to relate to the Charleston church as an arm of that body. However, on May 5, 1746, the Euhaw group evidently felt that it was time to form their own separate church, and "under the direction and with the assistance of the Rev. Isaac Chanler, who had occasionally ministered to them, a solemn instrument of union was signed by the members, at Euhaw, May 5, 1746, and they became a distinct body."[51] Manly felt that it was at this time, when Ashley River and Stono had already withdrawn, the property of the church had been distributed in legal litigation, the pastor had been suspended from office, and the Euhaw branch had become a separate body, that the number of communicants had been reduced to three. It seemed, he said, "as if the Lord would 'quench the coal that was left.'"

This was indeed a dark period for the Charleston church. After the suspension of Simmons, the church had no pastor and could find none, despite writing letters to Baptists in Europe, England, and the northern states. The only Baptist minister in this part of the province to whom the church could look for assistance was Isaac Chanler, pastor of the Ashley River church, but calls for his services were so numerous that he could preach to the Charleston congregation only once a month. Even this assistance was removed when Chanler unexpectedly died on November 30, 1749, at the age of forty-eight. Manly wrote that now the church had no visible prospect before her, but of a "famine of hearing the words of the Lord."

Notes

1. Howard, p. 16.
2. Townsend, pp. 61-64.
3. Richard P. Sherman, "Victory Over the Pirates," in *Perspectives*, pp. 27-33.
4. See Charles C. Crittenden, "The Surrender of the Charter of Carolina," in *Perspectives*, pp. 35-42.
5. Townsend, p. 11 n.
6. Original letter in Library of Congress, Fulham Palace MSS, SPG Series A, VII (1711-12).
7. Hirsch, pp. 308-9.
8. SCH&GM, IX:98 ff.
9. Moore, *Wills*, p. 102.
10. Townsend, p. 13.
11. Moore & Simmons, *Wills*, p. 62.
12. Moore, *Wills*, p. 4.
13. A. D. Hillette, ed., *Minutes of the Philadelphia Baptist Association, 1707-1807* (Philadelphia: American Baptist Publication Society, 1851), pp. 17-18.
14. JCHA, February 14, 1745.
15. See Moore & Simmons, *Wills*, passim.
16. Salley, *Warrants*, pp. 207-8.
17. Townsend, p. 33.
18. *Ashley River Baptist Church, Charleston District, South Carolina, Records 1736-1769*. On microfilm at The Southwestern Baptist Theological Seminary, Fort Worth, Texas. These may be the oldest written minutes of a Southern Baptist church.
19. Townsend, p. 33 n.
20. Manly, *Discourse*, p. 29.
21. Edwards, p. 23.
22. JCHA, May 1, 1745.
23. Whitley, *Minutes*, passim.
24. See Paschal, I, pp. 131 ff., 158 ff., and passim, concerning Palmer.
25. See article by Robert G. Gardner, "A Macedonia Call—from Charleston," *Journal of the South Carolina Baptist Historical Society* (Greenville: South Carolina Baptist Historical Society), VI (Nov., 1980): 2-17.
26. Whitley, *Minutes*, II:105-107.
27. For this story, see Townsend, pp. 55-56.
28. Whitley, *Minutes*, II:41.

29. Townsend, p. 56.
30. Whitley, *Minutes*, II:105.
31. Ibid., II:107.
32. Ibid., II:110.
33. Ibid., II:116 ff. See also Index, II:317 for other references.
34. Townsend, p. 14.
35. Tyerman, I:352.
36. Townsend, p. 19.
37. Tyerman, I:401.
38. Manly, *Discourse,* pp. 23-24.
39. JCHA, February 14, 1745.
40. Ibid., January 26, 1745.
41. Ibid., February 14, 1745.
42. Townsend, p. 276.
43. JCHA, April 26, 1745.
44. Ibid., May 1, 1745.
45. Manly, *Discourse,* p. 25.
46. Ibid.
47. Ibid., p. 26.
48. Townsend, p. 20.
49. Moore & Simmons, *Wills,* p. 138.
50. Townsend, p. 37.
51. Manly, *Discourse,* p. 27.

5

Oliver Hart: God's Worthy Instrument

The unexpected death of Isaac Chanler on November 30, 1749, well nigh broke the spirit of the Baptist church in Charleston. The painful division within the church, the dismissal of the pastor, the unjust decision of the legislature in the litigation over church property, and the withdrawal of some of the most faithful members to form the Euhaw congregation had brought the church low. And now Chanler, their only leader, was dead. Since he was pastor of the Ashley River church, he could give only a part of his time to the Charleston flock, but his gracious spirit and leadership had encouraged the church to carry on faithfully while seeking a regular pastor. Basil Manly remarked in his history:

> But, while God's dispensations are mysterious, they are all wise; and while it is the rule of his administration to interpose with seasonable aid in the hour of his people's extremity, he sometimes brings them into the greatest straits, that they may better appreciate and improve the blessings he bestows. The Lord had provided an instrument by which he designed greatly to promote the cause of truth and piety in the province, in the person of the Rev. Oliver Hart; and having selected the Charleston Church as the honored receptacle of such a gift, he prepared them to value it by quenching the only lamp that gleamed through the dark wilderness around. The feelings of the more reflecting part of the church, therefore, can be better imagined than described, when they discovered that *on the very day* on which "devout men carried" Mr. Chanler "to his burial, and made great lamentation over him," *Mr. Hart arrived in the city.*[1]

When Oliver Hart, a "tall, well-proportioned" man of twenty-six years, stepped off the coastwise vessel *St. Andrew* on December 2, 1749, he could not know of the tumultuous times and seasons with which God would match his life in Charleston. In the segment of history allotted to him, he would participate in the convulsions attending the birth of a new nation. Indeed, this was to be a different kind of nation from any that the world had known, for it would be constituted on the principle of separation of church and state and

123

complete liberty of conscience. This was something new under the sun, a achievement judged by competent historians to be the greatest contribution the United States to the science of government. Oliver Hart would be directl related to the French and Indian War that laid the foundations for th Declaration of Independence of 1776 and to the Revolutionary War. Th military operations of this war would drive Hart from the city he was nov entering, would separate him from his wife and family for over eightee months, and would forever sever him from his ministry at Charleston.

Not only so, but in the course of Hart's years at Charleston, his life woul be intertwined with the greatest religious revival America would ever know— the First Great Awakening. There is a direct succession from George White field, the Methodist; to Shubal Stearns, the Separate Baptist; to Danie Marshall, Philip Mulkey, and Joseph Reese, who brought the Separate Baptis gospel to South Carolina; to Richard Furman, the friend and successor o Oliver Hart at Charleston. To Hart must go much of the credit for the promp and effective uniting of the Separate Baptists with the older Regular Baptis in South Carolina.

In addition, at a time when American Baptists were first adoptin denominational structures for benevolent activity, Oliver Hart would becom the most important denominational figure in South Carolina, if not the entir South, in the thirty years of his ministry at Charleston.

So, it was into this kind of destiny that Oliver Hart strode on that cris December day in 1749 as he stepped from the boat at Charleston after nineteen-day trip from Philadelphia. What kind of man was this whom Goo would entrust with such a crucial ministry at this place in a world-shakin time? How would God prepare him for such a task?

"The Lord Will Provide"

Oliver Hart was born in Warminster Township, Bucks County, Pennsylva nia Province, on July 5, 1723, the seventh of six sons and four daughters.[2] His grandfather, John Hart, was an active lay worker in the old Pennepel (Pennepack) church, founded in 1687. In 1702, after the death of the pastor John Hart assisted Samuel Jones, Evan Morgan, and Thomas Griffith in the "public work" of the church for about four years. Oliver Hart was reared i the Baptist home of John and Eleanor (Crispin) Hart in the Southampto community, not far from the Pennepek or Lower Dublin church. On April 3 1741, at the age of seventeen, he was baptized by Jenkin Jones, pastor of the Pennepek church. According to his diary, Hart was baptized at Southampton There was not a separate church at this time at Southampton, but there were enough Baptists living in this community that with the approval of the mothe church, these members often met for services on one Sunday a month in thei own community in the home of Peter Chamberlain or John Morris. Evidentl

Jenkin Jones baptized Hart at Southampton before the separate church was organized and while the members were still a part of the Pennepek church.

Not a great deal has been preserved about the developmental days between Hart's baptism in 1741 and his decision in 1749 to invest his life in South Carolina. He married Sarah Brees on February 25, 1748, a lovely and devout eighteen-year-old, who was to bear him eight children before her death on October 20, 1772. It is known that he worked as a carpenter. On December 31, 1748, he mortgaged fifty acres of land in Warminster for one hundred pounds which he had borrowed from his brother Joseph. He was described in this instrument as a "carpenter, of Warminster," and his wife Sarah signed the mortgage with him.[3]

Also it is evident that young Hart was busy in the life of his church. In 1746 the members of the Pennepek church living at Southampton sent a petition to the mother church asking that they be formed into an independent Baptist church, and Oliver Hart was one of those signing this petition. This action was approved by the Pennepek church. On April 8, 1746, the Southampton Baptist Church was organized with forty-six members. On May 29, 1746, Joshua Potts, "a young man who had been a considerable time on trial," was ordained by Jenkin Jones and Abel Morgan and was called as the first pastor of the Southampton church. A meetinghouse was built on land donated by John Morris.[4] Meanwhile, at almost the same time, members living in the village of Philadelphia, a few miles to the south of Pennepek, also were dismissed by the mother church to organize their own body. Jenkin Jones, pastor at Pennepek for about twenty years, helped in the organization of the new church at Philadelphia, and on May 15, 1746, he resigned at Pennepek to become pastor of the Philadelphia church. It was as pastor of the Philadelphia church that he assisted in the ordination of Joshua Potts at the Southampton church on May 29.[5]

In none of his later writings does Oliver Hart describe when and under what circumstances he surrendered to the work of the ministry. His devout family doubtless was influential in preparing his heart and mind to make this commitment. Too, the 1740s were revival years, and Hart had heard some of the spiritual giants preach—Calvinists like Jonathan Edwards, George Whitefield, and Gilbert Tennent, and eloquent Baptists like Abel Morgan and Benjamin Miller. He lived at the very center of the Philadelphia Association and doubtless had attended many of its sessions during his early years. The presence of so many veteran preachers of Baptist life in these associational meetings could have inspired and encouraged him to consider vocational Christian service. Whatever may have been in the background, there came a day when, like Jacob, he wrestled alone with God in a quiet place, and out of this encounter he emerged as a prince of God who would bear witness to divine power and grace.

On December 20, 1746, about six months after the Southampton church was formed, the church records showed that "Isaac Eaton and Oliver Hart were called to be on trial for the work of the ministry, to exercise at the meetings of preparation or in private meetings that might for that purpose be appointed." Hart preached his first public sermon on February 21, 1748, at the Southampton church, just four days before he married Sarah Brees. Pastor Joshua Potts had suddenly become ill with the measles, and the unusual opportunity came for the young preacher to speak to his own church. How many additional sermons he may have preached during the next eighteen months cannot be identified, but the time for him to forsake his home and to step into the place God had prepared for him was almost at hand.

Although the minutes of the Philadelphia Association did not mention it, the records of the Southampton church showed that Jenkin Jones had received a letter from the church at Charleston in September, 1749, (perhaps written by Francis Gracia), inquiring about the possibility of securing a pastor for their church and that Jones had read this letter before the Philadelphia Association which met on September 19, 1749. The minutes of the association listed Oliver Hart as a messenger for the first time at this meeting, so he likely heard the letter read firsthand. Urged by Jones and other ministers, Hart expressed his willingness to answer the appeal from South Carolina. The Southampton church discussed the matter on October 14, 1749, and four days later, in a solemn service of prayer and fasting, Oliver Hart was ordained. Joshua Potts, his pastor, was assisted by Benjamin Miller and Peter Peterson Van Horn. Because his wife was awaiting the birth of their second child, Hart left her at Southampton and embarked at Philadelphia for Charleston on November 13. He caught his first glimpse of his future home on December 2, 1749, and on that day witnessed the Charleston and Ashley River Baptists sorrowfully bearing the remains of Isaac Chanler to the cemetery. Interpreting the arrival of Hart as a loving providence of God, the Charleston church promptly called him as her pastor, and he accepted on February 16, 1750. For the next thirty years his rich life was woven into the fabric of the First Baptist Church of Charleston, and it marked a new era in the history of the church.

Surely, as Oliver Hart began his work as pastor of the Charleston church, he must have wondered if his preparation and personal resources for this work would be adequate. His preparation seemed rather meager for the task that he was facing. There was a tradition that he had studied with Isaac Eaton, his close friend, who became pastor of the Baptist church at Hopewell, New Jersey in 1748, and later opened an excellent school for young ministers. This seems unlikely. Wood Furman wrote that Hart had only a plain English education as a boy, but that he continued to study diligently as a young preacher, obtaining "a respectable knowledge of the learned language, and an intimate acquaintance with the best authors of our own."[7] Some evidence of his continued study may be glimpsed in his later diaries, correspondence, and sermonic writings. As will be mentioned later, he read widely and retained much of what he studied. He wrote in a clear and legible hand, and his composition was good.

His preparation, however, had been more complete than appears at first glance. The normal method of training for the ministry in that day was through an intensive internship program. Often the young novitiate would move into the home of his pastor, accompany him in his daily ministry, read his books, watch him observe the ordinances, and perhaps even copy his style of sermon preparation and preaching. It is quite probable that this kind of internship was practiced by young Hart between 1741 and 1748 when he married. He was quite close to Jenkin Jones, his pastor, until 1746. This kind of internship would provide him with a considerable amount of spiritual and functional preparation that could never have been found in a classroom.

Furthermore, to a considerable degree, one can glimpse an element of specific preparation for the precise problems that Hart would face at Charleston. After the trying years of controversy and litigation there, the church greatly needed a dynamic leader whose devout and sensitive spirit would bring stability and unity to the church. The lack of Baptist ministers in the South Carolina colony obviously required a pastor who had been reared in an atmosphere that prepared young people to answer the call of God to vocational Christian service. The growing number of Baptist churches in the southern colony demanded someone with an irenic spirit who could develop a larger fellowship on the pattern of the Philadelphia Association. The rise of a new kind of Baptists in the South (the Separate Baptists), as an offshoot of the revivals of George Whitefield, called for a leader possessing infinite patience and a gracious spirit to pull the Separate and the older Regular Baptists together into cooperating rather than competing movements. The growing secularism in Charleston made it vital that all Christian denominations work together in harmony and friendship, and there was need for a man "whose heart was larger than his doctrine." For all of these areas of need, Oliver Hart was God's man. Trained in the midst of the most influential Baptist center in the American colonies, familiar with the work of the Philadelphia Association (the first in America, 1707), and working closely with a deeply spiritual and effective minister like Jenkin Jones, Oliver Hart was especially fitted to wrestle with the very problems that he would meet at Charleston. In addition, he had that personal indispensable resource that J. B. Gambrell called "religious gumption." He faced problems realistically and worked conscientiously to bring solutions. All of these rich endowments in the preparation and character of Oliver Hart were used to the utmost in his long and varied ministry at Charleston.

Yet with all of this preparation, it is probable that had Oliver Hart been able to glimpse the trials he would face in this southern colony, he would hav questioned his ability to endure and make a contribution to the cause c Christ. The simple, uncluttered Charleston of 1700 had disappeared by 175(and a complex and sophisticated society had developed. Planters ha prospered, trade had flourished, and economically Charleston had becom "the most affluent society among the English settlements on the America mainland."[8] This affluence had attached to Charleston the reputation of bein the social capital of the American colonies. The theater, music, dancing social clubs, and glittering balls occupied much of the time and attention c the large upper class. Religion was at a low ebb in general. How often in hi diary and his correspondence with his family, Hart would mourn abou Charleston as a wealthy, sinful, and frivolous city! Political and geographic tensions were becoming evident throughout the colony.

Furthermore, Hart little knew that his thirty-year ministry at Charlesto would be punctuated by two major wars, which would overshadow almost a else in his world for almost half of his service there. Too, he never seeme able to accustom himself to the severe storms that periodically ravaged th area. Early in his diary he mentioned the "great and terrible hurricane" th occurred on September 15, 1752. The wind and waves drove huge vessels i the harbor right up the main streets of the city which was built almost at se level. Hart wrote that his house "was washed down and all I had almos totally destroyed." This was tragic also for the church, for the church book were in his possession, and the loss included these original records of th church. He seemed to have been without a parsonage until December 24 1755, when his diary mentioned that he was moving into one. Many othe storms were described in great detail in his diary, and he always prayed th "sinful" Charleston might be spared.

All of these contributions and trials were still awaiting Oliver Hart as h began his service as pastor in Charleston. His first task, of course, was t serve the church. All of his other contributions developed from this primar base. So, in this chapter an effort will be made to describe his work as pastc and preacher while his extensive ministry beyond the confines of hi congregation will be given attention in the chapter that follows.

The Faithful Pastor

The young Pennsylvania preacher, for the first time displaced from th community where he had been born and spent his early years, soon plante his life securely in Charleston and identified himself with his adopted home Mrs. Sarah Brees Hart and the two children, Seth and Eleanor, arrived i Charleston on July 26, 1750, after a voyage of twenty-eight days. The othe six children of Oliver and Sarah were born in Charleston. Four of their eigl children died in infancy and were buried in the church cemetery adjacent t the meetinghouse. The last of their children, Sarah, was born on October 16, 1772, dying three days later. Her mother died on the next day. The melancholy item inserted into Hart's diary simply said:

> My dear wife, Sarah Hart, departed this life about 3 o'clock on Tuesday morning October ye 20th 1772, aged 42 years, 10 months and 13 days. When married (which was Feb. 25, 1747/8) she was 18 years, 2 months and 18 days old. We lived together 24 years, 7 months and 25 days when death separated us.

On April 5, 1774, after a courtship of about a year, Hart married Anne Maria Sealy Grimball. She was the widow of Charles Grimball, and her parents were William and Sarah Sealy, longtime Baptists of the city. Oliver Hart had two children by Anne. The first, Silas, was born on August 30, 1775, but died three weeks later. The other, William Rogers Hart, was born in Hopewell, New Jersey, on December 13, 1786.

Not only did Oliver Hart marry into an old Charleston family, but his oldest daughter, Eleanor, married Thomas Screven, great-grandson of the first pastor of the church, on March 6, 1770. Hart's son Oliver married Sarah Brockington of South Carolina on November 19, 1778. On January 17, 1784, his second son, John, married Mary, daughter of James and Mary Screven, also descendants of the first pastor. Another rather curious intermingling of the Hart and Screven families was the marriage of Lucretia, sister of Oliver Hart, to William Gilbert of Pennsylvania. Their son Seth married Elizabeth, the great-granddaughter of William Screven, the first pastor.[9] Thus, from many directions, the family of Oliver Hart was united with the family of William Screven and other South Carolina Baptists. It is no wonder that as Oliver Hart buried his children in the Charleston church cemetery and saw his daughter, son, and nephew intermarry with the old Screven family of South Carolina, he developed a sense of identification with the community to which he had come. Even after he was driven out of Charleston by the British in 1780, his correspondence with Richard Furman showed his continuing interest in his "home" and perhaps the possibility of returning there in his last years.[10]

In return, the Charleston church loved Oliver Hart. In a letter to his father in September, 1755, Hart was evidently referring to his congregation when he remarked that they "continue their regard for me, and Love me, Sincerely and fervently; which I endeavor in the best manner I can to return." Some members left him money in their wills. James Fowler bequeathed him two hundred pounds in 1753; Martha D'Harriette provided one hundred pounds and some other gifts in 1758; Ruth Bedon willed him two hundred pounds in 1765.[11] His diary occasionally mentioned gifts from members. On January 1, 1779, he gave thanks for a gift of three hundred dollars from Mr. Hinds, probably Patrick Hinds; while on February 8 of that year he spoke of a gift by letter from "the kind and generous William Mary Lamboll Thomas" of seventy dollars. A striking example of this widespread appreciation for Hart occurred in 1771. His diary said, "March ye 17th 1771 I was robbed of about 30 Pounds currency." Basil Manly wrote that "when this fact was known in town, the gentlemen of other societies made him a present of 730 pounds, which they raised among themselves, without the help of his own people."[12]

Throughout his ministry at Charleston, in the words of Richard Furman, Hart

> took more than ordinary pains to walk humbly and faithfully with God; to live under impression of the love of Christ; to walk in the light of the Divine presence; and to improve all his time and opportunities to the noblest purposes of religion and virtue.[13]

The diary of Hart sometimes leaves the impression that he was a person of little emotional response. His matter-of-fact style in recounting events, sorrows, and losses is probably responsible for this idea. However, it is likely that he was shackled in his utterance by the prevailing view that a man of God must not reveal too much grief or alarm at any loss or tragedy, lest it should be interpreted as a lack of faith in God. Hart rarely grieved or complained in any of his diaries. His correspondence presented another side of him. When his second wife was separated from him because of the Revolutionary War, his letters to her were bathed in deep love and longing devotion. His references to his children always reflected his love for them and pride in their achievements. His letters to his father and brother showed him to be a loving son and brother. Even his diary sometimes hinted at the emotional wrench he felt along the way. When Francis Pelot, his fellow preacher who was probably related to him by marriage, died on November 12, 1774, Hart wrote:

> A greater loss the Baptist interest could not have sustained by the death of any one man in the Province. His family, his church and the neighborhood will feel a sensible and irreparable loss, and as to my own part, I have lost the best friend and counselor I ever was blest with in the world; the most intimate friendship had subsisted betwixt us for about four and twenty years. In all which time I ever found him a faithful friend and gratified to give advice in the most critical cases. . . . To say no more, he was the sincere open, constant and hearty friend, could keep a secret, and in short, few men were ever better qualified for friendship than he. His last illness he bore with much patience and seemed not at all terrified at Death.

Hart must have radiated a warm feeling of comradeship when men like Richard Furman, Edmund Botsford, and other ministers addressed him affectionately as "Father Hart," and shared their problems, joys, and sorrows with him long after he had moved to New Jersey. Botsford, in his correspondence, made no effort to hide his love and esteem for his mentor.[14]

Perhaps the most evident characteristic of Oliver Hart as a good pastor was his sincere commitment and spirituality. An entry in his diary in 1754 read:

> I do this morning feel myself under a sense of my barrenness: Alas! what do I do for God? I am, indeed, employed in his vineyard; but I fear to little purpose. I feel a want of the life and power of religion in *my own heart*. This causes such a languor in all my duties to God. This makes me so poor an improver of time. Alas! I am frequently on my bed, when I ought to be on my knees—to my shame. Sometimes the sun appears in the horizon, and begins his daily course, before I have paid my tribute of praise to God; and perhaps while I am indulging myself in inactive slumbers. O wretched stupidity! Oh, that for time to come, I may be more active for God! and in thy name and strength, to devote myself more unreservedly to thy service, than I have hitherto done. I would resolve to be a better improver of my time than I have heretofore been. To rise earlier in the morning, to be sooner with thee in secret devotion, and Oh that I may be more devout therein! I would be more engaged in my studies. Grant, O Lord! that I may improve more by them. And when I go abroad, enable me better to improve my visits; that I may always leave a savour of divine things behind me. When I go to thy house to speak for thee, may I always go full fraught with things divine, and be enabled faithfully and feelingly to dispense the word of life. I would begin and end every day with thee. Teach me to study thy glory in all I do. And wilt thou be with me also in the night watches; teach me to meditate of thee on my bed; may my sleep be sanctified to me, that I may thereby be fitted for thy service, nor ever desire more than answers this important end. Thus teach me to number my days, that I may apply my heart unto wisdom.[15]

The deep spirituality of Hart was matched by his energetic and conscientious activity as a pastor. His extensive assistance to other churches and his zeal in denominational work were not allowed to interfere with his careful regard for the needs of his congregation. The welfare of his own church was his first concern. His diary reflects a busy program. Regular preaching services were held at the meetinghouse on Sunday mornings and afternoons. On Sunday evenings he lectured in one of the homes on some aspect of doctrine, which evidently laid the foundations for a Religious Society that was formally organized in 1755. He also spoke to this society on Monday, Wednesday, and Friday nights, and occasionally on other nights. He even met for lectures on Wednesday afternoons, but to his patient diary he mourned that so few attended these lectures (and the few were always late) that he was often discouraged.[16]

Oliver Hart's zeal and sincerity made a substantial impact on the people of Charleston. When Edmund Botsford was under severe conviction of sin in

1766, about seven months after arriving in the colony from England, he went from one place of worship to another but could not find a preacher who spoke to his needs. He stayed with a family of very wicked people, and one of the other boarders, himself a scoffer, noted Botsford's distressed condition and said:

> There is but one minister in this place, who can be of any service to you, but he, I am told, is a Baptist; all the rest of the ministers deserve not the name. I would advise you to go and hear him.

After some delay, Botsford went to hear the man, Oliver Hart, and soon was converted. Hart's reputation for religious integrity caused this wicked man to point Botsford to the Baptist church in Charleston to find relief from his conviction of sin.[17]

One brief glimpse of Hart's regular worship service has been preserved. Botsford wrote in his journal that on the last Sunday in August, 1766, he attended the services of the Baptist church in Charleston. After seating himself in a convenient place, he waited for the services to begin.

> Presently the minister came; though I did not like his dress, there was something in his countenance which pleased me. He began worship by prayer; I was pleased with it. After singing, the venerable man of God took his text from Acts xiii.26; 'Men and brethren, children of the stock of Abraham, and whosoever among you feareth God; to you is the word of this salvation sent.' To describe the exercise of my mind under this sermon would be impossible. However, upon the whole, I concluded it was possible there might be salvation for me, even for me. I then determined, that, in future, I would attend worship in this place. I do not remember, that, when able to go, I ever once omitted attending, while I lived in Charleston. Indeed, I would not have omitted one sermon for all the riches in the world.[18]

The description of Hart by Botsford in 1766 as a "venerable man of God" might suggest that Hart (who had just become forty-three years of age) had matured early. However, this language was quite common to describe preachers in their forties in that day. Richard Furman provided a description of Hart.

> In his person, he was somewhat tall, well-proportioned and of a graceful appearance; of an active, vigorous constitution, before it had been impaired by close application to his studies and by his abundant labours. His countenance was open and manly, his voice clear, harmonious and commanding; the powers of his mind were strong and capacious, and enriched by a fund of useful knowledge; his taste was elegant and refined.[19]

It should be added that Oliver Hart wore a gown and bands when he preached.

This was not uncommon among Baptist preachers in England and America. It was this "dress" that Botsford did not like. It is quite possible that Richard Furman was attracted to this type of preaching attire from his association with Oliver Hart. Furman wore a gown and bands in his preaching at Charleston until the time of his death. He certainly did not get this idea from Joseph Reese, the Separate Baptist under whom he was converted and began his preaching.

Not only did Hart possess that inner spirituality and active commitment to the task that drew his people to him, but as well he displayed a rational good will toward all groups. The only friction of record within the church occurred about 1763 when Nicholas Bedgegood, a gifted man whom Hart had befriended and helped to ordain, endeavored to supplant Hart as pastor, doubtless with the encouragement of some of the members. This effort failed, although Wood Furman remarked that a few members left the church because of it.[20] Hart never referred to this confrontation in his diary.

This same kind of irenic spirit was displayed toward the General Baptists in Charleston and Stono. It will be recalled that following the litigation of 1745, it was ordered that the Particular Baptist majority of the church must share the original church building on lot 62 of Church Street with the General Baptists of Stono. The Charleston church then erected the house of worship "near the bridge at the south end of Church Street," which later came to be called the Mariner's Church, and the congregation met alternately in the two buildings. It is possible that this practice was begun in order to maintain a legal claim to the original church property. However, after the coming of Hart, an agreement was reached between the Particular Baptists and the General group on October 9, 1758, by which the General Baptists were given sole use of the old church building on lot 62, while the Particular Baptists acquired sole use of the parsonage situated on the same property. This seems to have ended the continuing confrontation between the two groups, and there is no indication of any further friction between them during the remainder of Hart's ministry in Charleston.

Hart's goodwill toward other Baptist groups may be glimpsed also in his relations with the Welsh Neck Baptist Church, far to the north of Charleston. These Baptists had come from the Welsh Tract Baptist Church in Delaware and settled on the Pee Dee River. It is an interesting fact that Jenkin Jones, who baptized Oliver Hart, was one of the early pastors of this Welsh Tract church. Whether this influenced Hart or not, his attitude toward the Particular Baptists in the Pee Dee section to the north was one of cordiality. He often preached at Welsh Neck and invited her ministers to preach at Charleston for him. When without a pastor, the Welsh Neck church tried to secure Hart. He also assisted in the services of many of the branches of the Welsh Neck church.[21]

Mention has already been made of a new kind of Baptists flowing into South Carolina about 1759-60. The Separate Baptist movement in the South stemmed from the work of Shubal Stearns and Daniel Marshall, who were converted from Congregationalism in Connecticut by the preaching of George Whitefield. Both subsequently became Baptists and in late 1755 organized the Separate Baptist church at Sandy Creek, North Carolina. The name "Separate" was probably derived from their separation from Congregationalism and differentiated them from the older Regular Baptists who had not developed from the Whitefield revival. Many of the older Regular Baptists looked upon Separates with disdain and suspicion because they were "noisy" in their religious meetings, displayed emotion and physical enthusiasm in their preaching and witnessing, and permitted women to take part in their public services. In doctrine the Separate Baptists were probably mildly Calvinistic.[22]

This Separate Baptist movement swept into South Carolina about 1760 when Philip Mulkey crossed the border from North Carolina and established the Broad River church. Daniel Marshall brought a second group to the area in 1760. On December 13, 1762, Mulkey led a group to form the Fairforest church, which became a mother church with many branches. One important daughter church was formed at High Hills of Santee in 1772, not far from the present town of Stateburg. In "this wicked wicked" neighborhood, Joseph Reese (or Rees), a convert of Philip Mulkey, alarmed many brazen sinners by his bold preaching. One of the converts of Reese was young Richard Furman, whose father had moved to South Carolina from New York when Richard was yet an infant.

From the beginning of the Separate Baptist movement in South Carolina, Oliver Hart cordially welcomed them, despite the antagonism displayed against them by many of the old Regular Baptist ministers. His diary often identified one whom he met as a "Separate Baptist," but never was a word of disparagement included. He had Abraham Marshall, Joseph Reese, Philip Mulkey, and other Separates come to Charleston and preach in his church on many occasions, making every effort to break down the prejudices existing between the Separates and the Regulars. Hart should probably be given credit for bringing Richard Furman into that larger fellowship that later swallowed up all distinctions between the Separates and the Regulars. Furman embodied the best qualities of both the groups. He always revered Oliver Hart and regularly addressed him as "Father Hart" in respect and appreciation.

This friendly spirit of Oliver Hart extended to denominations other than Baptists. William Hutson and John Joachim Zubly, pastors of the Independent churches in Charleston and Wappetaw, often preached in the Baptist church for Hart. Hart also worked closely with William Tennent, another Independent pastor, preaching a memorial sermon when Tennent died in 1777. Even Rector Richard Clarke, the Anglican minister in Charleston, knew the warmth of Hart's friendship. Hart made reference in his diary to conducting a funeral on October 27, 1754, when he buried a child "in the Church Burying Ground and Spoke Extempore, perhaps the first instance of this Nature that ever was known in this Province." Rector Clarke was ill and evidently asked Hart to conduct the service. Hart revelled in the "Catholick Spirit" of Clarke who "gave me free Liberty to speak in my Own way." He then exclaimed,

> Oh that all Bigotry was rooted out of the Earth; then would there subsist a greater Harmony between persons of all persuasions, than what does; it is Indeed a pity that our little outward Differences Should cause Such a Shyness between us.[23]

This spirit was also displayed when Joseph Pilmoor, one of the first Methodist missionaries sent to America by Wesley, arrived in Charleston in January 1773. Pilmoor seemed to anticipate a good reception from the General Baptists because they, like him, were Arminian in theology, but he evidently was greatly surprised at the welcome accorded him by the Calvinistic Baptist Oliver Hart. In his journal he reported preaching twice to large crowds in the Particular Baptist church and found Hart to be not only sensible "but truly evangelical and very devout."[24]

This friendly attitude toward other denominations did not mean that Hart was not totally Baptist in his doctrinal views. He provided a rather interesting illustration of this when he was fleeing from the British armies. On July 9, 1780, at the Mossy Brick meeting in Virginia, a Presbyterian community, two Presbyterian elders were impressed by his biblical preaching and invited him to speak for them at their Stone Meeting House on the following Sunday. His diary showed that he preached to the Presbyterians there on July 16, 23, and 30. On August 3 he had a service for the purpose of immersing a Captain John Stephenson, a convert from the Presbyterians. Hart said in his diary that after his companion Edmund Botsford had preached, he arose and took the text from Mark 16:16 "from which Text I endeavored to prove that Believers are the only proper Subjects of Baptism, and that Dipping is the Mode of Administration." He then commented, perhaps naively, "How the People felt, I don't know, being all Professed Presbyterians, except my Brother, Mr. Botsford, and myself." He then immersed Stephenson, "a Man of good Character and Member of the Presbyterian Church." He soon learned how the Presbyterians felt. On August 18 he was informed by Botsford that the Presbyterians had sent a young Presbyterian minister to preach at Stone and that all invitations to the Baptist ministers to preach there had been canceled. Later, the Presbyterian pastor at Mossy Creek apologized to Hart for not inviting him to preach but said that the Presbyterians did not want a Baptist preaching in their churches any more. Hart noted in his diary, "Bigotry seems to be a Part of some Men's Religion. What they may gain by it I cannot tell."

The Effective Preacher

The Charleston church heard pungent and powerful preaching when her pastor was in the pulpit. Richard Furman described Hart's preaching in the following words:

> His sermons were peculiarly serious, containing a happy assemblage of doctrinal and practical truths, set in an engaging light, and enforced with convincing arguments. For the discussion of doctrinal truths he was more especially eminent, to which also he was prepared by an intimate acquaintance with the Sacred Scriptures, and an extensive reading of the most valuable, both of ancient and modern authors. His eloquence, at least in the middle stages of life, was not of the most popular kind, but perspicuous, manly and flowing,—such as afforded pleasure to persons of true taste, and edification to the serious hearer.[25]

Furman also said that Hart was a "fixed Calvinist, and a consistent, liberal Baptist," and that

> Christ Jesus, and Him crucified, in the perfection of his righteousness, the merit of his death, the prevalence of his intercession, and efficacy of his grace, was the foundation of his hope, the source of his joy, and the delightful theme of his preaching.[26]

As a general statement of Hart's ability as a preacher, Basil Manly wrote:

> Mr. Hart's preaching attracted considerable attention in Charleston, and his character, universal respect. Had he possessed a less spiritual mind, he would have found enough food for self gratulation in the general approbation with which he was received by all ranks. But this did not satisfy him. While his great end in life was the glory of God, he viewed the salvation of sinners as a principal means of promoting it. He longed for the souls of men; and was jealous over them and himself, with a godly jealousy, lest by any means he should run in vain.[27]

Between 1773 and 1794, Hart kept a careful record of which texts he used and where he preached. A few of his sermons and sermon outlines have survived. During the last twenty-two years of his ministry, he preached about 1,552 sermons, averaging (with a substantial drop-off in his last five years due to illness) over 70 sermons a year. From his diaries and what is known of his preaching between 1750 and 1773, it is estimated that he must have preached almost 1,600 sermons in these twenty-three years, or a total of about 3,200 sermons in his forty-five years of ministry from 1750 until his death.

A study of his record of texts used between 1773 and 1794 is revealing. He used texts from thirty-two of the thirty-nine books of the Old Testament. He never preached from Leviticus, Ruth, 1 Kings, 1 Chronicles, Ezra, Obadiah, and Nahum. He preached only once from Joshua, Nehemiah, Habakkuk, and

Zephaniah. His favorite Old Testament book was Psalms, from which he preached 120 times. Isaiah followed with 114 texts, while Song of Solomon (38) and Proverbs (30) completed the list of Old Testament books from which he preached more than 14 times.

In the New Testament, Hart used texts from twenty-four of the twenty-seven books between 1773 and 1794. Only Philemon, 2 John, and 3 John were not included. His favorite New Testament books were John (133 texts), Matthew (66), Romans (65), Luke (62), Hebrews (52), 2 Corinthians (51), 1 Corinthians (46), and Revelation (43). He preached about twice as much from the New Testament as from the Old.

Hart's diary showed that he would use the same texts more than once, a practice which preachers still continue. It appears that he used Luke 13:24 more than any other text between 1773 and 1794, with fourteen sermons preached from this statement of Jesus: "Strive to enter in at the strait gate: for many, I say unto you, will seek to enter in, and shall not be able." He loved 1 Corinthians 3:11: "For other foundation can no man lay than that which is laid, which is Jesus Christ," using this text ten times. He also preached ten times from Romans 8:1: "There is therefore now no condemnation to them which are in Christ Jesus, who walk not after the flesh, but after the Spirit." In nine sermons he sounded the warning from 1 Peter 4:18: "And if the righteous scarcely be saved, where shall the ungodly and the sinner appear?" On eight occasions he used Colossians 3:4: "When Christ, who is our life, shall appear, then shall ye also appear with him in glory."

This use of texts more than one time does not necessarily mean that Hart simply repeated the same sermon each time. For example, on October 20, 1755, Hart took 2 Timothy 1:9 as a text but used only the first clause: "Who hath saved us." On October 20, 1757, he chose the same verse for his sermon, but this time he used the second portion of the text: "and called us with an holy calling, not according to our works, but according to his own purpose and grace, which was given us in Christ Jesus before the world began." Similarly, on July 13, 1755, he preached the morning message from 1 Timothy 2:5: "For there is one God, and one mediator between God and men, the man Christ Jesus." He used the same text on June 5, 1763, and while there is some repetition, it is evident from the extant notes that the second sermon was a completely fresh effort, taking a somewhat different approach and using new material not involved in the earlier sermon. The lack of numerous extant sermons or outlines makes it impossible to judge if Hart reworked and took a new tack in every case when he used older texts, but it is quite evident from the two examples that remain that he did not simply use old notes from former sermons to preach again on a text previously used. As a matter of fact, when he preached at Hopewell, New Jersey, on November 5, 1780, in view of a call, he used Romans 1:15 for his text. Evidently he did not choose to use an old effective sermon for this important occasion but preached a new one.

Although there is no information on how Oliver Hart developed his methodology in the preparation of his sermons, he evidently followed in general the plan used by those preachers in Pennsylvania whom he had heard and admired. From the few extant sermons and outlines, it appears that he generally would give a short paraphrase or explanation of the text he had chosen and magnify the doctrine that it taught. Then in a series of propositions he would deduce certain truths from the text. Finally, he would apply the text and his propositions to the congregation.

An example may be seen in his sermon on Sunday morning, June 5, 1763. His text was 1 Timothy 2:5: "For there is one God, and one mediator between God and men, the man Christ Jesus." Hart opened by noting that reason teaches the existence of God and nature declares him; that all men should worship his infinite perfection. "But how He is to be worshipped, in an acceptable Manner, by fallen, sinful Men; is a Point beyond the utmost Stretch of human Reason to determine; without the assistance of Divine-Revelation." Then, in an eloquent passage, Hart moved to his subject:

> Here the Heathens have ever been plunged, not being able to find out by what means they should pacifie an offended Deity. Hence they have been driven to ye most extravagant Practices, of macerating their Bodies; cutting them with Lancets; offering human Sacrifices; and causing even their own Children to be lost in ye Fire, as the most likely Victims to appease their angry Gods. Awful Indications these, of the depravity of human nature! Wo what monstrous & horrid Practices doth Ignorance drive the Sons of Adam. But wherewith shall we come before the Lord,—and worship the Almighty's Acceptance? Will the Lord be pleased with a thousand Rams or ten thousand Rivers of Oyl? Shall we offer our Firstborn, the Fruit of our Body for the sin of our Soul? Such Sacrifices would utterly be condemned. Blessed be God, we are not left to grovel by the dim light of Nature. But we have a more sure Word of Prophecy whereunto we shall do well, that we take Heed. God has put into our Hands the clearest Revelation of Grace, which discovers unto Him, as a reconciled Father and a kind Friend! Here we have a Saviour proposed. An advocate to plead our Cause. A Mediator who has attoned for our guilt and brought in an everlasting Righteousness. *For (as) there is one God, so there is one mediator between God & Man, the Man Christ.*

After carefully explaining the nature of God as trinity in unity, and the person of Christ as both divine and human, Hart laid down two propositions. The first showed what a mediator supposes; namely, (1) a quarrel subsisting between persons—God and man; (2) a very wide breach that cannot be accommodated without the interposition of some third person; (3) a necessity that the breach should be healed, the differences removed, and the parties reconciled; and (4) a probability that the contending parties can be reconciled. The second proposition discussed how Christ executed that office as mediator. He was (1) chosen and set apart to that office; (2) willing to engage in that work; (3) a lover of peace and desirous of producing it; (4) a person of greatest sagacity, profoundest wisdom, deepest penetration, integrity, and uprightness; (5) frequently faced with many difficulties in his work of mediation; (6) often opposed by strangely obstinate persons unwilling to comply with any honorable terms of reconciliation; (7) possessed of most cogent and powerful arguments and winning and engaging motives to bring men to terms of reconciliation; (8) willing to act the most merciful and tender part, and yet adhere to the strictest rules of justice; and (9) made sole judge of all spiritual matters, and will pass the definitive and determinative sentence, from which there is no appeal. Hart then closed his sermon with the application of his text and propositions. There were six of these. (1) We may see the love of God in providing and accepting a mediator. (2) We may see the love of Christ in taking upon himself the office of a mediator. (3) What wretched ignorance and horrid impiety are those guilty of who address anyone else as mediator between God and man. (4) How inexcusable are those who make a mediator of their own works. (5) How God should be blessed for revealing this glorious mediator. (6) Let all seek God through the merits of this mediator.

All of the extant sermons of Hart show this type of treatment of texts and his earnest and skillful application to the needs of his hearers. His own view of the ministry can be glimpsed in an ordination sermon based on 1 Timothy 4:16. From his listing of sermons, he apparently used this same text in his sermon at the ordination of Edmund Botsford in Savannah, Georgia, on March 14, 1773, and at that of Joseph Cook on April 27, 1776, at the High Hills of Santee church. However, the context of the sermon showed that he was speaking to two young men at their ordination, so undoubtedly the extant sermon was the one referred to in his diary on February 26, 1759, when he "assisted Rev. Mr. Francis Pelot and John Stevens in the ordination of Nicholas Bridgegood (Bedgegood) and Samuel Stillman to the work of the ministry." Hart's notes on this sermon were rather full, although he would occasionally insert an isolated word to jog his memory about some statement that he would plan to phrase when the time came. From his text in 1 Timothy 4:16, he spoke to the two young ministers from his experience of about nine years as pastor of the Charleston church and at the advanced age of thirty-five years. His message spelled out the implications of the text: "Take heed unto [yourselves]. . . . " He called the two to a recognition of the solemn work that would be theirs: one which had engaged all the zeal of the prophets, apostles, evangelists, and preachers of righteousness in every age; one which called for the death of Jesus Christ, the son of God; one which made them fellow-workers with God himself. His first emphasis was that they should take heed to themselves with reference to their own salvation. By self-examination they should constantly remember their own interest in Christ and the work of grace in their own souls.

> You cannot be qualified to deal with wounded spirits, unless you have been sensible of your own wounds. It is not possible you should, in a suitable Manner, direct Sinners to Christ, without an actual Closure with him yourselves.

They should be lively and active in the constant exercise of every Christian grace and virtue. With a strong faith, a firm hope, a fervent love, and a sincere repentance, they should imitate Christ. More is expected of them than of other Christians. His second emphasis was that they should take heed to themselves relative to their personal conduct. They will live in the midst of a censorious world. They must be wise in their walk, grave but not sullen, cheerful but not light and vain. They must learn to reprove, visit sick and dying persons, and use every opportunity to witness. Hart's third emphasis was upon their training. Here he said:

> You have acted a Wise Part, in that you have carefully, and industriously acquir'd some good degrees of useful Learning.
>
> Labor to improve your stock, to build upon the Foundation laid, and to make your knowledge of the learned Languages, and liberal arts, and Sciences, as copious, and extensive as you can. Learning is an excellent Handmaid to Grace, and when apply'd to the Service of the Sanctuary may answer great and good Purposes. But above all Things you are to apply to the Study of the holy Scriptures, of the Old and New Testaments. Here you have that more sure Word of Prophecy, whereunto you will do well that you take heed. This is able to make us wise to salvation, and to furnish the Man of God for every good Work. The Work of the Ministry, to which you have been separated, is a good Work. O study to shew yourselves approved unto God, Workman who need not be ashamed, rightly dividing the Word of Truth.

Hart then urged that in choosing their sermons, the new ministers should "feel your Subject from the Lord, and labour if possible to have the matter well digested in your own Breasts before you deliver it to others." He recommended that "A plain and simple stile, seems best to comport with the Simplicity of the Gospel, but let it not be low, or groveling—However plain, it ought to be manly & striking." Advance nothing, he exhorted, "but what you can confirm wth a 'Thus saith the Lord.'" Christ and his gospel should be their delightful theme, the sum and substance of all of their discourses. "A little dry Morality, however refin'd will never feed the minds of your Hearers."

In his fourth main section, Hart urged the novitiates to take heed to their doctrine. It should be the doctrine of the Scriptures, of Christ, of godliness.

> In the general you will insist much upon the two following Topics, namely, our Apostacy from God, and our Redemption by Jesus Christ, which will very naturally lead you to take notice of the Transactions of God in Eternity, with reference to your Salvation.

The persons for whom God's salvation has been given "are a certain, select number, out of the Race of Mankind, who are redeemed by his Blood, justified by his Righteousness, called by the inscrutable operations of his Spirit, sanctified by his Grace, and finally glorified." Hart then magnified other doctrines that they should preach, summarizing them by saying: Whatever you find in the sacred oracles of God, you are to preach with the greatest plainness, earnestness, and faithfulness, persevering in them at the cost of life itself. He showed his Baptist convictions by noting that in observing the ordinances, they should "point out the proper Subjects and mode of administration."

He exhorted with the remainder of the text: In doing these things you will both save yourselves and them that hear you. Hart remarked that this did not mean that these works saved them; but, as Gill (an English Baptist preacher) had taught, by taking heed to himself and his doctrine the minister "saves himself from the Pollutions of the world, from the errors & heresies of false Teachers, from the Blood of all men, & from all just Blame in his Ministry." Those who hear the faithful minister will also be saved from erroneous principles and immoral practices, and, through the gospel, to an eternal salvation.

Hart then gave an inspiring charge to "these our two young friends."

> When the Lord Jesus Christ, the Great Shepherd, and Bishop of Souls, ascended up on high, leading Captivity captive, he received Gifts for Men, and set some in the Church, first apostles, then prophets, Teachers, and the like, who were design'd for education of the Body, and the building up of the Saints in love, that God the Lord might dwell amongst them. Neither did the Ministry of the Word terminate with those primitive ages of the Church, for it is according to the divine appointment if there should be a standing Gospel Ministry in the world, even to the end of it.

A personal note ended what must have been a most impressive message. As Hart helped set apart Nicholas Bedgegood and Samuel Stillman, his own sensitive heart was touched by the truths that he was probing.

> But oh, how unequal am I to the Task? I am this Day conscious of my own weakness & defects! How then shall I impose a Charge, in which I have conducted so unworthily myself? But, I would not depreciate the Grace of God, for it is by his Grace that I am what I am, and I trust that

his Grace bestowed upon me hath not been altogether in Vain. Oh blessed be God, some here present (and among them one however of those now set apart to the great work) are the Fruit of my Labours, the Seals of my Ministry, my Joy & Crown. And however I am sensible of very great Degrees of Weakness, and unworthiness, yet I am not altogether without an inward testimony of some degree of Faithfulness, Sincerity.

It was probably inevitable that such stirring preaching would attract those beyond his congregation. His diary indicated that his preaching ministry reached far beyond Charleston. He traveled a great deal for one reason or another, and everywhere he went he preached. Friends and strangers alike became his congregation wherever he might stop for the night. Typical of many journeys was his trip to Philadelphia in 1756 to seek a missionary for the Charleston Association. He left Charleston on January 19, 1756, and did not return until November 4 of that year. For almost a year he preached throughout Pennsylvania and New Jersey. After his return home, he wrote his father at Warminster, Pennsylvania, on March 10, 1757, to say:

I would fain be made Instrumental in bringing many Souls home to Jesus Christ. I believe the Lord hath owned my poor Labours while in Pennsylvania, and the Jerseys: I have received several Letters, giving me some encouraging Accounts of Something being done by Such an Unworthy Instrument while there; may all the Praise be to him to whom alone it is due.

In his prime years, Hart was called upon many times to deliver sermons on various special occasions. Some of these were put into print. These included his sermon on the death of the Reverend William Tennent, *The Character of a Truly Great Man Delineated and his Death Deplored as Public Loss,* delivered August 18, 1777, at Charleston, South Carolina; a sermon, *Dancing Exploded,* delivered in Charleston on March 22, 1778; a sermon, *A Humble Attempt to Repair the Christian Temple,* delivered before the Philadelphia Association on October 21, 1783; a sermon, *America's Remembrancer with Respect to her Blessedness and Duty,* delivered on Thanksgiving Day, November 26, 1789, at Hopewell, New Jersey; a sermon, *A Gospel Church Portrayed and her Orderly Service Pointed Out,* delivered before the Philadelphia Association on October 4, 1791; a Circular Letter of the Philadelphia Association titled "Christ's Mediatorial Character," printed in the minutes of 1782; Circular Letters of the Charleston Association in 1775, 1777, 1778, and 1779, printed in the minutes for each year; and a portion of the Circular Letter of Bethel Association of South Carolina, printed in the minutes for 1792.[28]

Thus, although denied a substantial formal education as a young man, Oliver Hart developed excellent study habits for himself and became a champion of ministerial education throughout his entire ministry. Rhode

Island College awarded him the honorary Master of Arts degree in 1769. His activity in providing an opportunity for young ministers to secure literary and theological training will be discussed in the following chapter.

The Prospering Church

With this quality of pastoral commitment and preaching, it is no wonder that the Charleston church made good progress in the thirty-year period of Oliver Hart's ministry. The statistics of the church for this period have disappeared entirely, and the Charleston Association did not seem to have an interest in recording numbers until after the visit of Morgan Edwards, the historian, to the association in 1772. The associational records showed that in 1775 the Charleston church had baptized three, bringing her membership to seventy-four. Occasional and incomplete records from then until 1780, when Hart was forced to flee from the British armies, indicated that the church membership probably remained at about this level during the remainder of Hart's pastorate. It is quite possible that the revolutionary times had brought a decline from a larger membership in the earlier years of Hart's service in Charleston, for Morgan Edwards spoke of a membership of about two hundred communicants after the years of litigation.[29]

From a financial point of view, the Hart years at the church brought considerable prosperity. As will be mentioned later, by 1772 the church had accumulated about 15,000 pounds through legacies and gifts of several sorts, which yielded the handsome annual income of 1,430 pounds.[30]

There are only hints of the events in the life of the church before 1780, apart from the activities of the pastor. From his diary and collateral information, it is known that the year 1754 was a fruitful one for Hart and the church. A moving revival swept the church in the summer of that year, which was particularly effective in reaching young people. It was in this revival that Samuel Stillman, who would become the distinguished and beloved pastor of the First Baptist Church, Boston, Massachusetts, for over forty years, was converted. This conversion may have led directly to the development by Oliver Hart of an organized program for ministerial education through his Religious Society. Perhaps stirred by the moving of God's Spirit in his own church, Hart preached on nearby James Island, and on October 10, 1754, an entry in his diary described how he had baptized ten persons and fervently made intercession for them: "Take them O Lord; take them into thy peculiar Care and keep them as ye apple of thine Eye."[31]

In September, 1755, Hart wrote to his father and mentioned that the church was at peace and had "considerable additions, of Souls." He also referred to the revival that had occurred during the previous summer.

Another glimpse of his church comes from an entry in his diary for November 8, 1769. As he left the church to visit his son in Virginia, he remarked that his soul was refreshed before he set out on the journey because

Miss S. C——r had been won to the Lord Jesus Christ on the previous day. Hart also said that before leaving he had committed his people to the Lord "and left them under the Care of the Reverend Mr. Smith." This was none other than Hezekiah Smith, who served as Brigade Chaplain in the American army during the Revolution, a friend of George Washington and General Horatio Gates, and longtime outstanding pastor of the Baptist church at Haverhill, Massachusetts. He was fourteen years younger than Oliver Hart. He had been baptized by John Gano, was a pupil of Isaac Eaton, and graduated from Princeton with James Manning, a close friend of Hart. After graduating in September 1762, Smith began a preaching tour throughout the southern provinces, partly to recover his health. According to Smith's diary, he came to Oliver Hart's home on Thursday, February 17, 1763, preached twice for him on the following Sunday, and then spent the week with Hart. On this trip Smith laid foundations for securing pledges later on to Rhode Island College, which was chartered in 1764. He visited Thomas Screven in Charleston and John Screven of James Island, who later made pledges of fifty and ten pounds, respectively.[32] He also spent the night at the home of James Brisbane in Charleston, who later pledged twenty pounds to the college. Smith preached acceptably to the Cashaway church for some time, and on Monday, September 19, 1763, he recorded that "I wrote my confession," and on the following day he was ordained by Oliver Hart, John Stephens, Francis Pelot, and Nicholas Bedgegood to the work of the ministry. After spending about fifteen months in the South, Smith took ship to New York. His diary showed that on Thursday, October 12, 1769, he sailed again for Charleston, arriving there on October 20. He went directly to Hart's home and spent the next eight months in South Carolina and Georgia. It was on this occasion that he served as supply pastor of the Charleston church during all of Hart's absence from November 8, 1769, until February 2, 1770. He returned to New York on April 30, 1770, having secured pledges of more than 3,700 pounds for Rhode Island College.[33]

The Charleston church was generous in her assistance to God's workers and in supporting denominational benevolences. Edmund Botsford is an example of the former. In about 1767 he had "indented himself" for three-and-a-half years to a very wicked man in order that he might learn the trade of carpenter. However, the man became intolerable. Even the food provided Botsford was so poor in quality that he could hardly eat it. One of the church members, hearing of the situation, brought Botsford to his own home every evening for a wholesome meal. Then Botsford, in a confrontation with his wicked employer, was able to secure his release from the indenture. He began to feel that God had delivered him in order to use him in the gospel ministry. When Oliver Hart heard of this, he invited Botsford to speak before the church to determine if the young man had gifts in this direction. When Botsford had spoken, it became evident that he should be encouraged in his commitment to preaching. The church then arranged for him to pursue a course of study, one member providing his instruction and his board, while another supplied him with clothing.[34] In denominational projects, the Charleston church was at the forefront of all benevolent movements, whether the support of Rhode Island College, associational missions, or ministerial education.

As will be noted in the next chapter, Hart was busy during these thirty years on matters affecting his denomination and his country. His diary showed that he was away from Charleston a great deal. No doubt there were complaints about his long absences, and his family must have wished that he would remain at home more often. A brief survey of the record that he kept of his sermons indicated that he missed one of the regular Sunday morning or afternoon services either because he was away, had a guest preacher, or was ill, on at least six occasions in November and December 1773, thirty-seven times in 1774, sixty-one times in 1775 (for a part of which time he had fled to Euhaw to escape the British threat), fifty-seven times in 1776, twenty-two times in 1777, twenty-eight times in 1778, and fifty-one times in 1779 (with much illness this year). On February 11, 1780, he began his flight from Charleston because of the British. Between 1773 and 1780, he used the following preachers to fill his pulpit, either at a morning service or an afternoon service or both: John Gano (2 times), Edmund Matthews (10), Francis Pelot (3), Edmund Botsford (11), John Joachim Zubly (3), _____ Piercy (7), _____ Richards (2), Joseph Cook (4), Abraham Marshall (1), _____ Edmonds (4), Joshua Lewis (1), Philip Mulkey (1), Elhanon Winchester (16), _____ Hill (23), _____ Copon (2), _____ Newton, perhaps John (1), Richard Furman (5), _____ Casson (6), _____ Rogers, perhaps William (1), _____ Cowan, perhaps John (1), _____ Patten (1), Joseph Reese (1), and _____ Coe (1). Some of these supply preachers cannot be identified, but the very fact that twenty-three different preachers were available at various times to fill the pulpit suggests the contrast with the situation in 1749 when no preacher could be found in the province to supply the church.

Evidently the financial condition of the church was excellent during all of the time Oliver Hart was pastor. Morgan Edwards noted the substantial legacies of the church which, with the rent from the pews and the like, provided a good salary for the pastor.

Despite his many absences from the pulpit, Hart was recognized as a faithful preacher and effective pastor. If there were complaints about his many absences on denominational matters or otherwise, they were never recorded anywhere. His people knew that whether absent or present Hart would never neglect his active witness for Christ. The principal reason for these absences from his own congregation was his ceaseless concern about other facets of the kingdom of God which demanded his attention. That story will be told in the following chapter.

Notes

1. Manly, *Discourse,* p. 11.

2. Loulie Latimer Owens, *Oliver Hart 1723-1795, A Biography* (Greenville: The South Carolina Baptist Historical Society, 1966), p. 31.

3. Ibid., p. 7.

4. Ibid.

5. Gillette, pp. 12, 20-21.

6. Manly, *Discourse,* p. 32.

7. Wood Furman, comp., *A History of the Charleston Association of Baptist Churches in the State of South-Carolina* (Charleston: J. Hoff, 1811), p. 77.

8. M. Eugene Sirmans, "The Colony at Mid-Century," in *Perspectives,* p. 55.

9. See H. A. Tupper, ed., *Two Centuries of the First Baptist Church of South Carolina, 1683-1883* (Baltimore: R. H. Woodward and Company, 1889), pp. 21 ff for these records.

10. Owens, *Hart,* p. 22.

11. Townsend, p. 25 n.

12. Manly, *Discourse,* p. 34 n.

13. William B. Sprague, *Annals of the American Baptist Pulpit* (New York: Robert Carter & Brothers, 1860), p. 49.

14. Charles D. Mallary, *Memoirs of Elder Edmund Botsford* (Charleston: W. Riley, 1832), pp. 31, 71.

15. Manly, *Discourse,* pp. 34-35.

16. Townsend, p. 21.

17. Mallary, *Botsford,* pp. 28-30.

18. Ibid., p. 30.

19. Sprague, p. 49.

20. W. Furman, pp. 76-77.

21. Townsend, pp. 63 ff.

22. See William L. Lumpkin, *Baptist Foundations in the South* (Nashville: Broadman Press, 1961), for the best story of the Separate Baptist movement.

23. Townsend, p. 22.

24. Ibid., pp. 23-24.

25. Sprague, p. 49.

26. Ibid.

27. Manly, *Discourse,* pp. 33-34.

28. Owens, *Hart,* pp. 37-38.

29. Edwards, p. 20.

30. Manly, *Discourse,* pp. 45-46.

31. Townsend, p. 22.

32. Guild, p. 38 n.

33. Ibid., pp. 33-39, 133.

34. Mallary, *Botsford,* pp. 35-37.

6

The Denominational Stalwart

In the midst of a turbulent world, Oliver Hart not only carried on his pastoral and preaching duties conscientiously at the Charleston church but laid broad foundations for a cooperative denominationalism in South Carolina. He was the pioneer denominational leader in the South and vitally concerned with the growth and development of other Baptist churches. He sensed that in winning people to Christ he had fulfilled only part of the Great Commission. Baptists as a denomination should share the responsibility of "teaching them to observe all things" after they had become disciples and been baptized. Of course, there were other Baptists in this era who glimpsed the larger denominational fellowship involving the communion of the saints, but it was Hart who first initiated the movement in the South to put this grand design into structured form. He was the architect of the first Baptist association in the South, the second in America.

The time was ripe for this larger concept. Baptists in the South were beginning to multiply rapidly, particularly as a result of the First Great Awakening and its offshoot, the Separate Baptist movement. As an example of this rapid growth, it may be noted that in 1740, before the awakening had affected the South, there were only about eight functioning Baptist churches—four in South Carolina, two in Virginia, and two in North Carolina.[1] These eight churches probably had no more than three to four hundred members in them. By 1790, when somewhat accurate figures can be determined, the four churches in South Carolina had increased to 67, with 91 ministers, and 3,878 members. In Virginia there were 204 churches, 262 ministers, and 20,443 Baptists; while in North Carolina there were 94 churches, 154 ministers, and 7,503 Baptists. In addition, where there had probably been no Baptist churches in 1740, Baptists in Maryland had organized 12 churches, with 11 ministers and 776 members; Georgia Baptists had 42 churches, with 72 ministers and 3,211 members; Kentucky Baptists had 42 churches, with 61 ministers and 3,105 members; and Tennessee Baptists had 18 churches, with 21 ministers and 889 Baptists. Population in the South had multiplied by 1790: Maryland numbered 319,728 people;

Virginia, 748,308; North Carolina, 393,751; South Carolina, 249,073; Georgia, 82,548; Kentucky, 73,677; and Tennessee, 35,691.[2]

One unexpected result of this denominational thrust was a change in the image of Baptists. Along with other leaders, Hart helped alter this image. In the earlier years Baptists had been looked upon as sectarian subversives. It was even whispered that if they were able to gain enough adherents, they would massacre the population and seize control of the government. By their patriotic spirit, adherence to the principles of religious liberty for all, and orderly conduct, they earned the respect of their contemporaries. Wesley M. Gewehr judged that the social status of Baptists by the close of the American Revolution was equal to that of any other religious group.[3]

At a time, then, when structural patterns were being developed for a burgeoning denomination, Oliver Hart made significant contributions during the important years between 1750 and 1780. His activity may be glimpsed in an expanding ministry to other churches, the organization of the first Baptist association in the South, the missionary thrust, enlisting new leaders, ministerial training, and the struggle for political and religious liberty.

An Expanding Ministry

With the death of Isaac Chanler of the Ashley River church just before the coming of Oliver Hart to Charleston, the only Particular Baptist minister in the Low Country area of South Carolina was removed. In fact, the only other Particular Baptist minister in the entire colony was probably Phillip James, pastor of the Welsh Neck Baptist Church in the far north. Henry Heywood was pastor of the dwindling General Baptist church at Stono.

A few months after becoming pastor of the Charleston church, Hart entered in his diary that John Stephens had arrived from Philadelphia on May 12, 1750. Stephens was born on Staten Island, New York, and had organized a small Baptist church at Horseneck, Connecticut, after his ordination in 1747. It seems probable that his coming was initiated by Hart.[4] The minutes of the Ashley River Baptist Church noted that on May 28, 1750, the church met to counsel about getting a pastor and at that time called John Stephens. He was offered a salary of four hundred dollars a year. On June 1, the minutes continued, Stephens was inducted into the pastoral office with the preaching of Oliver Hart.

The Euhaw church also had been without a regular pastor since the death of William Tilly in 1744. Isaac Chanler, Oliver Hart, and John Stephens had assisted the church by intermittent preaching, conducting funerals and weddings, and similar pastoral ministries, even after the Euhaw church had become a separate congregation on May 5, 1746. Perhaps the church had thought that one of the two young men whom she licensed on May 18, 1746, might soon become her pastor. One of these later turned away from a religious vocation. The other was Francis Pelot, a well-educated Swiss Calvinist who had come to America with his family on October 28, 1734, settling at Purrysburgh, South Carolina. John Sealy employed Pelot as tutor for his children, and on May 12, 1741, the tutor married Martha Sealy. This probably related him to Oliver Hart by marriage. On August 1, 1744, he was baptized by Isaac Chanler and, as indicated, having given evidence by 1746 of spiritual gifts, he was licensed by the Euhaw church. In his diary for November 12, 1774, Hart remarked:

> Thus he continued as a candidate (resisting, through modesty and self diffidence many solicitations to ordination) until at last, he was overcome (as he himself often acknowledged) by the arguments of one whom he ever honored with his friendship and esteem. And on Monday Jan. ye 13th 1752 he was solemnly ordained or set apart to the Ministry at Euhaw by the Rev. John Stephens and Oliver Hart. The latter preached his ordination sermon from Matt. 10:16: "Behold, I send you forth as sheep in the midst of wolves. Be ye therefore wise as serpents and harmless as doves." Many attended the solemnity and in general they were much affected. He now took upon him the pastoral charge of the church, and in that capacity acted a faithful part, as long as he lived.

The Charleston Association

It is evident that Hart was not only thinking of assisting Ashley River and Euhaw, daughter churches of Charleston, by helping them secure pastoral leadership, but also had specifically in mind the uniting of these congregations and Welsh Neck into an associational relationship such as he had observed during his formative years in the Philadelphia Association.[5] The early existence of this desire by Hart is given credence by the fact that at the time Hart took steps to organize the Charleston Association in October, 1751, neither Francis Pelot of the Euhaw church nor Joshua Edwards of the Welsh Neck church had yet been ordained. It appeared that Hart could hardly wait to initiate the Charleston Association.

Since there was but one associational body in America at this time, and many American Baptists opposed the organization of any denominational structure that might interfere with the traditional independence of each local congregation, it might be well to include here a brief word about the adoption by Baptists of this type of body.

The earliest Baptist churches in Great Britain, while maintaining the autonomy of the local bodies, gave evidence of their desire to have a larger fellowship that included sister Baptist churches. The pattern for the structure of such larger fellowship seems to have come from the experience of British Baptists in military service during the civil war from 1642 to 1649 between the king, Charles I, and parliament. "Associations" were formed to facilitate the war effort, and in Cromwell's parliamentary army, in particular, regiments sent representatives to these associations to discuss policy and action.[6] When Baptists stationed in the army in Ireland in 1653 were disbanded, this kind of structure was utilized by widely separated Baptist congregations there who desired fellowship and concert of action with other Baptist churches. The name "association" was adopted from the army structure for the body that was formed for this fellowship.

Doubtless through the influence of Elias Keach, pastor of the Pennepek church in Pennsylvania, which was organized in 1688 by British Baptist immigrants, American Baptist churches in 1707 formed the first association in America. The minutes of the Pennepek church in 1707 said that

> it was concluded by the several congregations of our judgment, to make choice of some particular brethren, such as they thought most capable in every congregation, and these to meet at the yearly meeting to consult about such things as were wanting in the churches, and to set them in order.[7]

The Philadelphia Association met regularly each year thereafter. It is likely that Oliver Hart began attending these meetings shortly after 1741 and continued until 1749.[8] In that year, the association prepared an essay on its nature and powers. Oliver Hart was one of the twenty-nine messengers of the Philadelphia Association who signed this essay in 1749. When he went to South Carolina about three months later, he evidently carried a copy of it with him. As soon as Ashley River had secured John Stephens as pastor, and even before Euhaw had called Francis Pelot, Hart initiated an effort to unite these Low Country churches, including his own, with the Welsh Neck church in the Pee Dee section into an associational relationship. Perhaps relating to the initiation of this associational work by Hart, a curious remnant, consisting of sixteen small pages of notes in the handwriting of Oliver Hart, was found among his papers. The first and last sections of the notes are missing. In fact, the remaining final page of these notes is tattered and mutilated as though it had been kept or filed for a long period of time. No date of any kind is found in the notes. The notes discuss the organization of an association. Only the last two paragraphs of the first general head remain, which outline the nature, business, and power of an association. Only a small portion of the second general head remains, which names the advantages of an association.

A study of these notes indicated several things. First, the message of these notes was delivered orally. In introducing the second general head, Hart said, "And now having spoken something of the Nature, Business & Power of an Associa.n, I shall. . . . " Also, at times Hart inserted a word or an incomplete sentence as he often did in his other sermon notes, designed to remind him of an idea that he would develop further when he delivered the message. Too, throughout these notes there was a conversational tone and an occasional hortatory interjection that would not be found in casual notes or a formal paper of some kind.

A second conclusion from the reading of these notes is that they must have been prepared during the early ministry of Oliver Hart in the context of sharing preliminary ideas with others. There was a tentativeness in Hart's approach to some of the matters discussed that could not have appeared later in his life after he had taken a central place in the work of the Charleston Association from the very beginning. For example, under the heading of the business of an association, the third subhead discussed how the association should deal with those persons who called themselves preachers but actually, from the evidence of their lives and false doctrines, were not God's preachers. In these notes Hart said:

> I shall not prescribe Measures to be prosecuted in this affair, for, without being chargeable w.th false Humility I may say, I doubt not but yt your Wisdom will direct to more suitable means than I could point out.

Finally, there was no place for this kind of message in the known ministry of Oliver Hart unless it was delivered to the initial group that he addressed on October 21, 1751, when he was urging the formation of an associational body. A review of all of his extant sermons, the record of his preaching from 1773 to 1794, his circular letters and addresses at meetings of the Charleston, Bethel, and Philadelphia associations, and his numerous diaries fail to disclose any occasion when such an address as this was made or was relevant. It is true, of course, that there is an absence of material covering long periods of time during the 1750s and 1760s, but his diaries, skimpy at times, give no indication of any occasion during these years where such a message would be appropriate. This would be true particularly in view of some of the tentative ideas expressed in the notes.

This evidence strongly suggests that the fragment of notes by Oliver Hart were probably used by him in 1751 when he urged his compatriots to organize the Charleston Association. If this is true, these notes represent a valuable and sentimental historical monument in the history of Baptists in the South.

Whether these were actually his notes for it or not, Oliver Hart made some sort of appeal for the formation of an association to the messengers from Ashley River, Welsh Neck, and Charleston when they met on October 21, 1751. Euhaw messengers were prevented from attending this first meeting, evidently by swollen rivers.[9] Wood Furman described the initial organization as follows:

> The object of the Union was declared to be the promotion of the Redeemer's kingdom, by the maintenance of love and fellowship, and by mutual consultations for the peace and welfare of the churches. The

independency of the churches was asserted, and the powers of the Association restricted to those of a Council of Advice. It was agreed to meet again in Charleston, Nov. 1752. At that time the delegates from Euhaw attended, and the proceedings of the first meeting were ratified. The instrument of Union bears the following signatures: John Stephens, Oliver Hart, Francis Pelot, John Brown, Joshua Edwards, Ministers: James Fowler, William Screven, Richard Bedon, Charles Barker, Benjamin Parmenter, Thomas Harrison, Phillip Douglass, and John Mikell, Messengers.[10]

It is interesting to notice that two of the preachers were not ordained until 1752 (Pelot and Edwards). Edwards was probably counted as a licentiate minister in the 1751 meeting, and Pelot was not there. Edwards was the oldest among them at age forty-seven; Brown was thirty-seven; Stephens was probably about thirty to thirty-two; Pelot was thirty-one; and Hart was the youngest at twenty-eight. Brown and Edwards were from Welsh Neck, the former being pastor in 1751; Stephens was pastor at Ashley River; Pelot was pastor at Euhaw; and Hart, of course, was pastor at Charleston.

Of the eight lay messengers present, two were members of the Charleston church (Fowler and Screven); two were from the Ashley River church (Bedon and Barker); three were from the Euhaw church (Parmenter, Harrison, and Mikell); and one was from the Welsh Neck church (Douglass). All of them were active Baptist leaders.

The relationship between the new association and the Charleston church continued to be quite close. During the remainder of Hart's pastorate, its meetings were so regularly held at Charleston that it took the name "Charleston Association." According to Wood Furman, between its organization in 1751 and the flight of Oliver Hart in 1780, the association met at Charleston for its first twenty-six sessions, then met once at High Hills of Santee in 1778, but returned to Charleston in 1779. The fall of Charleston to the British army in 1780 caused the association to meet elsewhere after the war until 1786.[11] Hart served as its moderator in 1759, 1764, 1769, 1773, 1775, and 1778. He was its first clerk in 1752, serving for the first six years, then named again as clerk in 1777. He brought the sermon at the associational meeting in 1755, 1758, 1762, and 1769. Although not its moderator during the first seven years, he, like John Calvin in Geneva under similar circumstances, was influential in shaping its thought and activity, as will be noted shortly.

In 1767 the Charleston Association adopted the confession of faith published by the London Assembly of 1689.[12] Oliver Hart and Francis Pelot were requested to draw up a system of discipline similar to the *Short Treatise of Church Discipline* adopted by the Philadelphia Association in 1743. In the introduction to their *Summary of Church-Discipline,* Hart and Pelot said that the Charleston Association needed this new publication since the *Short Treatise* was out of print, was not as concise as the *Summary,* and contained things that "appear to us exceptionable." They expressed their indebtedness both to the *Short Treatise* and to John Gill's *Exposition* and *Body of Divinity.* As indicated heretofore, they leaned heavily on Gill's *Body of Divinity.*

The *Summary* was presented to the Charleston Association in 1772. Perhaps in recognition of his first visit to the association, the body asked the distinguished scholar and historian Morgan Edwards, along with David Williams, a scholarly friend of Hart, to "assist the compilers in revising it." The association adopted the *Summary* in the following year, and published it along with their confession of faith.[13] Wood Furman remarked that this confession and the *Summary* were "printed under the inspection of Mr. Hart."

Hart also played a principal role in the uniting of the older Regular Baptists, as represented by the Charleston Association, with the burgeoning Separate Baptist movement which swept into South Carolina about 1759 or 1760. As mentioned before, the Separates had organized the Sandy Creek Association in North Carolina in 1758. Evidently Philip Mulkey, Separate Baptist pastor at the Fairforest church in South Carolina, was interested in the possibility of pulling the Regulars and Separates together in associational fellowship, for in 1762 he sent several queries to the Charleston Association relative to this matter. Oliver Hart was appointed by the association to answer these queries, and later he and Evan Pugh were delegated to attend one of the Sandy Creek Association's meetings to endeavor to effect union. Hart's diary indicated that he was at Sandy Creek several times, but just when he attended the association is uncertain. The minutes of the Sandy Creek Association for this period were destroyed by fire in 1816.[14]

In 1770 the Sandy Creek Association divided, South Carolina Separate Baptists forming the Congaree Association on December 26, 1771. In the following year, after a visit from Morgan Edwards, the Congaree Association began correspondence with the Philadelphia Association, and in 1773 Daniel Marshall, Joseph Reese, and Samuel Newton attended the Charleston Association meeting. Wood Furman said:

> The Association testified their desire of union by proposing liberal terms, which allowed their brethren the observance of their peculiarities, reserving to themselves the right of friendly discussion on the points of difference. But the Separates would be satisfied with nothing short of the Regulars coming fully into their views. So the desirable object was not then accomplished.[15]

However, through the friendly attitudes of Regulars like Hart, Evan Pugh, and Edmund Botsford and of Separates like Daniel Marshall, Joseph Reese, and others, all prejudices were broken down. Distinctions between the two groups began to disappear without formal action.

Additional friendly ties were developed also with other associations during this period. In 1774 John Gano attended the Charleston Association as a messenger from the Philadelphia Association, and he, Oliver Hart, and Francis Pelot were appointed by the Charleston Association to address "the Baptist Associations throughout America in favour of a plan of contribution for augmenting the funds of Rhode-Island College." In the following year correspondence was begun with the Ketocton Association of Virginia organized in 1766, and with the Warren Association of Rhode Island organized in 1767. The struggle of Massachusetts Baptists for religious liberty was discussed, and plans were made to send offerings to Isaac Backus to assist in this cause. Oliver Hart played an active part in these interassociational movements. In 1779, the last meeting of the association before Charleston fell to the British, he, Evan Pugh, Edmund Botsford, and Richard Furman were named as a standing committee

> to transact business of emergency during the recess of the Association; particularly to treat with government on behalf of the Churches; to correspond with other Associations, to detect impostors, and recommend travelling Ministers of good character.[16]

Thus, through her pastor, Oliver Hart, the church at Charleston extended her ministry into the entire colony of South Carolina and beyond by the organization of the Charleston Association, the first in the South.

The Missionary Flame

Although a project of the Charleston Association, another ministry initiated by Oliver Hart and the Charleston church was so sweeping in its significance and influence that it must be mentioned under a separate head. The Charleston church sent a query to the meeting of the Charleston Association in early November, 1755, which in effect urged that the gospel be preached to destitute people in the interior settlements of South Carolina and neighboring provinces. Why would Oliver Hart and his church urge the Charleston Association to become involved in a mission, as it later turned out, in North Carolina when the back country of their own province was being populated by many people, some of them Baptists? How, indeed, did Oliver Hart and the Charleston church even know about the need in the neighboring province of North Carolina? The answers to these questions can be given with reasonable certainty.

The sequence of events that led to the action of the Charleston Association in November, 1755, can be traced from the records. The "fertile and pleasant banks" of the Yadkin River in North Carolina with "as rich a soil . . . as any in this western world can afford" had brought many settlers as early as 1753 or 1754 to what is now Davidson County, North Carolina.[17] Among these settlers were Baptists who belonged to the Scotch Plains Baptist Church in New Jersey, whose pastor since 1747 had been Benjamin Miller.[18] Miller evidently migrated to North Carolina with some of his church members no later than September 3, 1755, and probably as early as 1754.[19] This area became known as the Jersey Settlement. George W. Paschal felt that Miller had come to North Carolina with his migrating church members to help them establish a church or perhaps an arm of the Scotch Plains church.[20] Miller's preaching in the Jersey Settlement resulted in the conversion of Presbyterians in that area to Baptist views.

But Miller was not alone in this Yadkin mission work. A young minister named John Gano joined him for a season. Gano was born in 1727 into the home of a devout French Huguenot family. His great-grandfather Francis Gerneaux had escaped from France after the revocation of the Edict of Nantes in 1685. John Gano followed the family's Presbyterian faith until Benjamin Miller, pastor at Scotch Plains, won him to Baptist views.[21] At Miller's funeral, Gano said, "Never did I esteem a ministering brother so much as I did Mr. Miller." Through Benjamin Miller, Gano had learned about the work at the Jersey Settlement on the Yadkin and was persuaded to begin a missionary tour of the South in 1754 after his ordination in May. On this journey Gano stopped at the Jersey Settlement and spent some time with his mentor, Benjamin Miller.[22] He went directly from here to Charleston, where he preached for Oliver Hart in the Charleston church. Gano's journal described the inner feelings of this novitiate in Charleston:

> When I arose to speak, the sight of so brilliant an audience, among whom were twelve ministers, and one of whom was Mr. Whitefield, for a moment brought the fear of man upon me; but, blessed be the Lord, I was soon relieved from this embarrassment; the thought passed my mind, I had none to fear and obey but the Lord.[23]

These were sturdy words for a twenty-seven-year-old in the presence of many veteran preachers of the gospel. Who can doubt that while at Charleston Gano enthusiastically described to Oliver Hart the great ministry he had just witnessed on the Yadkin by Benjamin Miller? Gano had returned to Philadelphia for the association meeting on October 7, 1755, when the Philadelphia Association voted that one brother from New Jersey and one from Pennsylvania should visit North Carolina at the expense of the association. It has generally been felt that they were appointed in an effort to "Calvinize" the General Baptist churches in North Carolina, but the fact that a New Jersey minister was specified as one of the two appointees suggests that the association knew about the work on the Yadkin by Benjamin Miller, the

New Jersey pastor. Miller, along with Peter P. Vanhorn of Pennsylvania, was appointed "to visit North Carolina."

On November 13, 1755, at least one week before the party of Shubal Stearns and Daniel Marshall left Opekon, Virginia, to migrate to North Carolina and begin the Separate Baptist movement at Sandy Creek, the Charleston Association met, and Oliver Hart presented the query from his church about securing a missionary to labor among the destitute people "in the interior settlements of this and neighboring States (then provinces)."[24] It must be more than coincidental that the instructions of the association sent Gano to mission work in the neighboring province of North Carolina when its own back country was needy. The recent visit of Hart with Gano in Charleston, the fact that when Hart was asked to find someone suitable for this work he promptly sought out John Gano, and the willingness of Gano to leave good prospects in the North to accept an appointment to the Yadkin mission field all suggest that Hart had learned about the Yadkin field from Gano, had brought the query to the association with the Yadkin field in mind, and had determined to get Gano as the missionary to serve there. In his diary Hart wrote:

> On Saturday morning Jan. ye 19th 1756 embarked on board the Sloop *Fancy,* Capt. Barnes commander, for Philadelphia. Had a good passage and arrived there the Saturday following. Returned from Philadelphia by land Thursday Nov. 4, 1756.

After this stay of about nine months in Philadelphia and vicinity (where he preached constantly while visiting his relatives), Hart returned home just nine days before the meeting of the Charleston Association in his church. John Gano was in attendance, while John Stephens was moderator and Hart the clerk. "The Association requested Gano to visit the Yadkin first and afterwards to bestow his labours wherever Providence should seem to direct."[25] John Gano went to the Yadkin and evidently worked there for about eight months, then returned to New Jersey to become pastor of the Morristown church.[26] In 1757 the Charleston Association praised his work, evidently all done at the Jersey Settlement on the Yadkin.

> He devoted himself to the work; it afforded ample scope for his distinguished piety, eloquence and fortitude; and his ministrations were crowned with remarkable success. Many embraced and professed the Gospel.[27]

It is not inappropriate to add that Gano continued to serve the Yadkin church after his appointment by the Charleston Association had ended. He had returned to his church at Morristown, New Jersey, but the Yadkin group sent two messengers to induce Gano's church to give him up to their service. The Morristown church refused, but finally told Gano to follow the Lord's leading in the matter. Gano returned to the Jersey Settlement to serve for about two years until he was forced to leave by the war with the Cherokee Indians. The church at the Jersey Settlement joined the Charleston Association in 1759.[28] However, she soon disbanded, probably because of the Indian menace, and her successor was not organized until 1784.[29]

This missionary thrust of the Charleston Association marks it, along with the Philadelphia Association, as a pioneer in the beginning of associational missions.

Enlisting New Leaders

When Oliver Hart came to Charleston in 1749, the province had been without suitable ministers for the church. As pointed out relative to the Charleston Association story, Oliver Hart promptly moved to secure ministers for the Ashley River and Euhaw churches who, with the cooperation of the Welsh Neck church in the Pee Dee section, joined with Charleston in organizing the first association in the South. But Hart had been reared in an atmosphere that bred preachers. In an ordination sermon on February 26, 1759, he bared his soul to say that the grace of God had not been bestowed on him altogether in vain, for

> some here present (and among them one however of those now set apart
> to the great work) are the Fruit of my Labours, the Seals of my Ministry,
> my Joy & Crown.

Hart looked upon this aspect of his ministry as an "inward testimony of some degree of Faithfulness, Sincerity."

It cannot be determined how much Hart and the Charleston church had to do with calling out some of the preachers whom they helped. In the case of Francis Pelot, already mentioned, there can be no doubt that Oliver Hart personally exerted great influence upon securing him for Kingdom service. From the time of his ordination on February 13, 1752, until his death in 1774, Pelot was pastor of the Euhaw church and a close confidant of Oliver Hart. Indeed, Hart wrote in his diary, "As to my own part, I have lost the best friend and counselor I ever was blest with in the world; the most intimate friendship had existed betwixt us for about four and twenty years."

Another important minister coming under the influence of Hart was Samuel Stillman, born February 27, 1737, in Philadelphia, who came to Charleston in 1748. Converted in 1754 during the stirring revival in the Charleston church, he was baptized by Oliver Hart and immediately began studying with him for ministerial service. On February 17, 1758, he preached his first sermon and on February 26, 1759, along with Nicholas Bedgegood, was ordained by Hart, Pelot, and John Stephens, promptly becoming pastor of the church on James Island, near Charleston. Because of his health, Stillman removed to New Jersey two years later. After brief pastorates in New Jersey and Massachusetts, he became pastor of the First Baptist Church, Boston, on January 9, 1765, where he performed a distinguished service for forty-two years. Widely renowned and honored as pastor and preacher, he died on March 12, 1807. Through him, Hart's ministry was prolonged and expanded.

Another young minister greatly influenced by Hart was Nicholas Bedgegood, ordained at the same time Stillman was set apart on February 26, 1759, by Hart, Pelot, and Stephens. Bedgegood had been an Anglican before coming to Georgia but through his reading became convinced of the need for believer's baptism. On July 19, 1757, at the age of twenty-six, he was baptized at the Charleston church and ordained two years later. He soon went to the Welsh Neck church as pastor and, except for a brief stay at Charleston in 1763 and two years with the church on James Island in 1765-67, remained at Welsh Neck until his death in 1774. It appears that the spiritual gifts of Bedgegood were impressive, for about 1763, while he was briefly serving as assistant to Oliver Hart at Charleston, an effort was made to supplant Hart with Bedgegood at the Charleston church. This movement failed, and Hart never mentioned the incident in his diary.

Evan Pugh was in the circle of Hart's influence. Pugh was born in Pennsylvania on April 2, 1729, and was converted from Quaker views to those of the Baptists in 1754 in North Carolina. He moved to Welsh Neck, South Carolina, in 1762, studying there for the ministry, and then moved to Charleston to work and study with Oliver Hart, Francis Pelot, and others. On November 22, 1764, at the Euhaw church, he was ordained by Hart, Pelot and Stephens. On January 4, 1766, he became pastor of the Welsh Neck church; two years later he went to the Cashaway church, where he served until his death on December 16, 1802.

Another outstanding Baptist minister felt the warmth of Hart's assistance. Hezekiah Smith has been mentioned previously. Soon after graduating from Princeton, he toured the South in 1763-64 and spent much of his time with Hart at Charleston. On September 20, 1763, he was ordained by Hart, Stephens, Pelot, and Bedgegood. Later, in 1769-70, he supplied the Charleston church for about three months during Hart's absence. Smith became the distinguished pastor at Haverhill, Massachusetts, and a brigade chaplain during the Revolution.[30]

Edmund Matthews, a native of Bristol, England, was converted in America under the preaching of Philip Mulkey, the Separate Baptist. In 1767 he was received into the Charleston church, and on November 8 of that year was licensed to preach. On February 8, 1770, he was ordained at Charleston and soon began serving the congregation on Hilton Head Island.

A much larger area of assistance was provided by Oliver Hart in the calling out of Edmund Botsford. Arriving in Charleston from England on January 28, 1766, at age twenty-one, Botsford was converted under the preaching of

Oliver Hart on November 1, 1766. With the encouragement of Hart and the church, Botsford began making preparation for the gospel ministry. David Williams, who had come to Charleston to live with Hart on January 14, 1756, and later became an active and faithful member of the church, aided Botsford in his pilgrimage. Hart instructed Botsford in theological and pastoral studies. Hart and Pelot assisted in his ordination on March 14, 1773. He had already proved his commitment by preaching quite effectively at the Tuckaseeking branch of the Euhaw church in Georgia after being licensed to preach at Charleston on February 24, 1771. On November 28, 1773, Botsford became pastor of the New Savannah church in Georgia, which was organized by Hart and Pelot. The church later became known as the Botsford's Old Meeting-house.[31] Botsford accompanied Hart in the flight from the British in 1780; he returned to become pastor at Welsh Neck (1782) and at Georgetown (1796). He was a regular correspondent with Oliver Hart during Hart's lifetime, and continued his correspondence with Richard Furman until dying in 1819.

Another minister whom Oliver Hart had a hand in helping was Joseph Cook. In conference with Richard Furman and Hart, Cook became a Baptist and was baptized by Furman in 1776. Hart then assisted Furman in the ordination of Cook at the High Hills of Santee church. Cook promptly joined the Charleston church, and in 1778 became pastor at Euhaw as successor to Francis Pelot.

Another pivotal figure touched by the ubiquitous Oliver Hart was Joseph Reese, reared as an Anglican and noted for his youthful enjoyment of nonreligious pleasures. He was brought to Baptist views by Philip Mulkey, the Separate Baptist, about 1763 in South Carolina. Impressed with a call to preach, Reese compensated for his lack of background and training by an indomitable courage and enthusiasm in presenting the gospel. In February 1768 Reese was ordained to the ministry by Oliver Hart and Evan Pugh, serving faithfully at the Congaree church for many years.

The most impressive influence of Oliver Hart probably was in his relationship with Richard Furman, his successor at the Charleston church. Hart had met Furman at the High Hills church at the "Big Meeting" there on December 31, 1773. Furman was then eighteen years of age, had been converted two years before under the preaching of Joseph Reese whom Hart had helped ordain, and had been licensed to preach in 1773. He had not yet been ordained, but was an eloquent and precocious preacher of the gospel. In the protracted meeting at the High Hills church, Oliver Hart preached in the forenoon Sunday service on January 2, 1774, from Colossians 2:6: "As ye have therefore received Christ Jesus the Lord, so walk ye in him." At the afternoon service, evidently for the first time, Hart heard this lad, barely turned eighteen, deliver the sermon, bringing a "time of refreshing to the People of God." From that day until Hart's death in 1795, Furman and Hart were intimate friends, to the benefit of both of them. Furman always thereafter referred to Hart as "Father Hart."

Other young ministers touched by the ministry of Hart stand in the shadows. In his diary Hart said that on March 25, 1777, he assisted Joseph Cook in the ordination of Lewis Richardson to the work of the ministry "in my Meeting House Charles Town." Basil Manly mentioned in his history that in 1779 a young minister by the name of John Newton belonged to the church at Charleston.[32] This was evidently the minister shown in the Charleston Association minutes for 1778 and 1779 as representing the Charleston church with Oliver Hart.[33] Newton had an interesting background. Born August 7, 1732, at Kent, Pennsylvania, he became a Baptist in 1752 and was baptized by Joshua Potts of Southampton, who had assisted in the ordination of Oliver Hart. Under the influence of the Separate Baptists in North Carolina during a decade there, he felt a call to the ministry. In 1765 he moved to South Carolina and in February 1768 was ordained at the Congaree church by two Regular Baptist pastors, Oliver Hart and Evan Pugh. For this "irregular" ordination the Sandy Creek Separate Baptist Association instructed the Congaree church to silence him. However, after the Sandy Creek Association divided in 1771 and the Congaree Church helped form the Congaree Baptist Association of South Carolina on December 26, 1771, Newton assisted Joseph Reese at several of the branches of the church. It is not known when he joined the Charleston church. He later moved to Georgia and died there in 1791.[34]

It is also clear that the Charleston church was supplied by many ministers: some were Regular Baptists; some, Separate Baptists; some, out-of-state Baptist ministers; some, Independent pastors; and some that cannot be identified. Certainly a part of the human agency for calling out many of these ministers was the busy pastor of the Charleston church.

Ministerial Education

There can be little doubt that Oliver Hart's important ministry of calling out young people to the service of Christ led him unerringly to the concomitant need for ministerial training. Perhaps the conversion and Christian commitment of Samuel Stillman in 1754 was the catalyst that brought Hart to take steps for the education of the ministry. As this gifted young lad studied theological materials and pastoral methods in Hart's home or at the church, it must have occurred to the pastor that there was a vital need for a more systematic and better organized method of assisting young men who were just surrendering to the ministry. In pursuit of this grand goal, Hart developed the Baptist Religious Society at Charleston in 1755 "which had for its purpose the collection of a library, the discussion of religious subjects and especially the fostering of ministerial education." To it is reckoned the honor of being the first religious partnership among Baptists in America in the interest of ministerial education.[35]

At the meeting of the Charleston Association in 1757, the following query from the Charleston church was presented: "Whether there could not be some method concluded upon, to furnish, with suitable degree of learning, those among us who appear to have promising gifts for the ministry?" Oliver Hart, the clerk of the association, doubtless handed the query to the chairman, Francis Pelot, who found the messengers favorable to undertaking ministerial training as a part of their task, and pledges for the enterprise were promptly taken. The Charleston church pledged 60 pounds; Ashley River, 40 pounds; Euhaw, 20 pounds; Lunch's Creek, 5 pounds; Cashaway, 5 pounds; and Catfish, 3 pounds. This total of 133 pounds was placed in the hands of a committee consisting of Hart, Pelot, and John Stephens. Hart was named the treasurer of the fund.

The influence of Oliver Hart and his enthusiasm for this project were quite evident. After the messengers left the association, they began to have second thoughts about what they had done. They developed the same resistance that later faced Richard Furman when he endeavored to incorporate the association for the purpose of carrying on this educational task. As summarized by Basil Manly in 1828, the question involved the nature of an association.

> From its very purpose and constitution an association of Baptist churches was regarded as merely and only an advisory council: it was held necessary to declare in express terms not only that it was not intended to interfere with the independence of the churches, but that it would exercise no powers whatever, either spiritual or secular, except such as might be inseparable from a council of advice. Hence it was composed only of delegates from churches agreeing in doctrine, discipline and sentiment; and, to preserve its entirely spiritual character in this aspect so as to retain the confidence of the churches, many were unwilling to see its deliberations complicated or distracted with any affairs, however important, aside from those purely spiritual concerns committed to its charge.[36]

A second objection involved the attitude of the Separate Baptists, who

> not only took no part in the formation of a fund for the education of ministers, but even looked with suspicion and distrust upon the efforts of others in this direction as savoring of the hierarchy, which, in Virginia, had been so oppressive and odious to them.

Finally, the difference between an independent, voluntary society for a specific benevolence like ministerial education and an association made up of "delegates from churches limited to purely spiritual matters, and to an advisory power alone" was emphasized, indicating that the two should not be intermingled.[37]

For these reasons, the majority of the churches related to the Charleston Association did not continue to support the associational venture for ministerial training. As a result, Hart's Religious Society became the principal organized agency for assisting young ministerial students. The South Carolina *Gazette* of June 23, 1757, advertised the opening of a private school by William Mason in the Baptist meetinghouse. Students would be taught "reading, writing, and arithmetic, vulgar and decimal, and the extraction of roots," and to keep books and similar commercial skills. Whether this was in any way related to Hart's program for young ministers is not known, but the very presence of this school in the church building suggested Hart's interest in all types of education.

The Religious Society belonged peculiarly to Oliver Hart and the Charleston church. When Hart fled from the British in 1780, the Society lost its vitality. It is significant that when the Society dissolved about 1814, its funds passed to the Charleston church. Among those helped by this fund during what Cook called "the Oliver Hart Age of Education and Benevolence" were Samuel Stillman, Evan Pugh, Edmund Botsford, Edmund Mathews, and perhaps Hezekiah Smith.

Political and Religious Liberty

Until the middle of the eighteenth century, the American colonies of Britain were related closely to the mother country and participated in her political and military adventures. They played a part in King William's War with the French (1697), Queen Anne's War with France and Spain (1713), and King George's War with Spain (1748). In these conflicts the colonies were only peripherally involved, although South Carolina, as mentioned previously, was harrassed by the Spanish and French forces.

During the thirty-year ministry of Oliver Hart in Charleston, however, the old American colonial world was overturned in the course of two related wars that finally brought political and religious liberty to a new nation. The French and Indian War, beginning in 1754, just three years after Hart began his work in Charleston, virtually became a conflict between Britain and France over the North American continent.

Oliver Hart's correspondence and diary reflected this war. In a letter to his father in September 1755, Hart closed on a doleful note:

> We are in daily expectation of a new Governour, and, as it is expected that a War will shortly commence between the English and French, we are a building of Walls, and forts round the Town; O may ye Lord of Hosts be our Defense! We have had a very Wet, and fruitful Season. The planters, or farmers here go much upon Indico, which proves a very profitable Comodity; if peace was to Continue, in all probability this would be the

richest province upon the Continent by far; Oh that it may be rich in good Works.

Hart made no mention of the war in his letter to his father dated March 10, 1757, but his diary for Sunday, July 17, 1757, mentioned that he had preached to Colonel Boquet's regiment of soldiers in Nightingale's pasture. In a letter to his brother dated July 17, 1761, Hart wrote:

> Our Army have had an engagement with the Indians, in which the latter have been worsted, but I fear are not humbled. Particulars, it is like you will have in your paper.

After many defeats, the British (and the Americans) were finally able to pull out the victory, and with the stroke of a pen in 1763 the future of the world was changed. In the Treaty of Paris practically all of the French possessions in North America were given to Great Britain. Subsequently, this meant that the colonists would not have to fight two powers for control in America. It also resulted in securing France as an ally against Britain, and she played a significant role in winning the war for independence. Not only so, but the French and Indian War had brought British officials to the colonies where, for the first time, they saw the extent of anti-British activity. The British Navigation Acts and other laws were being ignored or bypassed, and it was plain that the colonials were reluctant to place the interests of the mother country above their own. Incensed, Great Britain determined to force the Americans to bear a part of the great costs the war had entailed and to tighten royal control. A rash of regulatory laws was passed to this end, culminating in the Stamp Act of 1765. Charleston was the scene of riots as the people protested the sale of stamps, and mobs forced entrance into houses suspected of having the hated stamps. When this act was finally repealed, there was "great and prolonged celebration" in the streets of Charleston.[38]

Another phase of the confrontation began with the new cabinet of Lord Townshend and the levy of external duties in 1767. An ominous note was sounded with the Boston Massacre of 1770. The Tea Act, passed as a boon to the British East Indies Company, was the final blow. Ships arriving in Charleston with the tea in late 1773 and 1774 met open hostility. The tea was placed in a warehouse and left unused for years. It finally was sold by the colony to help defray expenses of the Revolutionary War. The "Intolerable Acts," in response to these activities, brought the First Continental Congress in 1774 and the outbreak of fighting in the following year. South Carolina set up a provincial government in 1774 and in 1776 drove out the royal governor.

On April 19, 1775, the "shot heard around the world" was fired at Lexington, Massachusetts, following the midnight ride of Paul Revere and others. Hart's diary noted that he had learned about this on May 8 when

"Capt. Allen brought the news of the commencement of hostilities by the King's troops at Lexington on ye 19th April."

Hart rarely confided his inner thoughts and motives to his diary. When he wrote on May 27, 1775, that he "Left Home this Aftn. in Order to pay a Visit as a Supply to the 1st Baptist Church in the City of New York," it was obvious that he was not going to travel that distance simply to preach at the relatively small church of his friend, John Gano. Hart knew that the First Continental Congress had met on September 5, 1774, at Philadelphia, and a second time on May 10, 1775, in the same city. South Carolina had sent five representatives to the Congress, and they and the colony approved the action of the body and had arranged for a provincial congress early in 1775. He also knew that George Washington had been named commander-in-chief of the intercolonial military forces and probably was familiar with the tense situation in Massachusetts following Lexington and Concord. He wanted to go to New York to observe the situation for himself and talk with his family and friends in the North. Hart stopped briefly at Scotch Plains, New Jersey, to preach for Peter P. Vanhorn, then took ship again for New York. He preached in New York in the afternoon service on June 1 but did not feel the freedom that he desired. On the following afternoon he walked to the city green and viewed two companies of light infantry and horses as they paraded, and "they made a brilliant appearance, but seemed not so perfect in their Discipline." During the week he visited the old fort, the docks, shipyards, probably thinking about the defense of the city if war came. New York City actually did become the funnel point for British troops in their northern campaign. On Thursday, June 5, he preached at the New York church and exulted in his diary: "Blessed be God my Tongue was set at Liberty this Evening in Preaching for the first Time since I came to the city. O that my Visit may be of some use." On June 8 he preached three times in the New York church, with much freedom in the morning, "set at Liberty" in the afternoon, but "in ye Evening was somewhat strained." He left New York on the following day, stopping to visit with Vanhorn at Scotch Plains, and arrived at Charleston about 5:00 PM on June 11.

Hart did not remain at home for very long. In June, 1775, after the battle of Lexington and Concord, the South Carolina provincial congress met and created a thirteen-member Council of Safety, who prepared a test oath known as the "Association," by which signers pledged themselves to defend the colonial cause, even by arms if necessary. Eager to win some of the traditionally Tory population of the northern and western frontiers of the colony, the Council named the Honorable William Henry Drayton and William Tennent, pastor of the Independent Church in Charleston, to visit the large number of Tories who lived in the vicinity of the Saluda and the Broad rivers. Three days later on July 26, 1775, Oliver Hart, who had just returned from New York, was addressed by Henry Laurens, President of the Council of Safety, as follows:

> The Council of Safety having had it represented to them that your presence in the western and northern frontiers of this colony may be of great service by explaining to the inhabitants, in a proper and true light, the nature of the present dispute unhappily subsisting between Great Britain and the American colonies, have ordered me to request you will join the Rev. Mr. Tennent, and the Hon. William Henry Drayton, Esq., who are going into those parts of the colony, and who have particular directions from the Council on this head, which these gentlemen will lay before you for your further information. Your compliance will be esteemed by the Council of Safety as an instance of your zeal and in the public service, when the aid of every freeman and lover of constitutional liberty is loudly called for.[39]

Both Tennent and Drayton were members of the Council of Safety, and evidently the request for Hart to accompany them grew out of the fact that there were many Baptists in the western and northern frontiers of the colony.

In his diary Hart said succinctly:

> On Monday July 31, I set off for the frontiers of this province, being appointed by the council of safety to accompany the Honorable William Henry Drayton and the Rev. William Tennent to try to reconcile a number of the inhabitants, who are disaffected to Government.

Hart recorded the events of this trip in some detail until his return on September 6. Since his wife, whom he called Nancy, was awaiting the birth of their first child, he wrote to her every few days. He made his way up to the home of Joseph Reese, pastor of the Congaree church, and preached for him on August 6 to a good congregation. Reese agreed with the colonial sentiments expressed by Hart and consented to accompany him on part of his journey. On the following day, they joined with Drayton and Tennent at Congaree Store, near the present town of West Columbia. The three principals agreed to meet ten days later at the home of Colonel Thomas Fletchall, one of the most important Tories of the area. Hart traveled northwestward between the Saluda and Broad rivers through the present Richland, Newberry, and Laurens counties. Increasing crowds provided audiences to hear the colonial side of the story, and many signed the association.

On August 17 the confrontation took place at Fletchall's house, located by the falls of Fairforest Creek, near the present town of Union. Fletchall and his followers would not sign the association, but the Colonel did agree to call a muster of his troops four days hence at Ford's, near the present town of Enoree. During the meeting with Fletchall, Hart spent the nights with Philip

Mulkey, pastor of the Fairforest Baptist Church. Despite all of Hart's efforts, Mulkey continued to reflect Tory sentiments. On August 21 came the most enjoyable part of the journey for the colonial advocates: a barbecue at Captain Wofford's house on Tyger River not far from the present town of Spartanburg. Many of the large number signed the association. On August 23 the muster called by Colonel Fletchall at Ford's brought about 270 men together. After a near violent confrontation, some signed the association while others were sympathetic without signing. After this meeting, Hart made his way back toward Charleston. Riding forty or more miles a day, he returned home about 4:00 PM on September 6, 1775.[40]

On November 29, the provincial congress of South Carolina passed a resolution of appreciation for the services of the two preachers, which read:

> That the thanks of the Congress are due to the Reverend Mr. Tennent and also to the Reverend Mr. Hart, for the important public services by them respectively rendered to this colony in their late progress into the back country.[41]

Harvey T. Cook (*A Biography of Richard Furman*) must have been in error in believing that Richard Furman, young pastor at the High Hills of Santee church, accompanied Hart on this journey.[42] The detailed diary of Hart would surely have mentioned the presence of Furman. Evidently Furman had made some other trip, perhaps with Hart, into the back country, giving rise to Cook's story.

While Hart was away on this trip, Nancy Hart gave birth to their first child, Silas, on August 30 about 7:00 PM. The child died on September 21 while Hart was unfortunately away again, this time visiting his daughter Nelly who was seriously ill at the home of her husband Thomas Screven. Hart grieved that he was away at both the birth and death of the son, "a heavy tryal to my dear Nancy."

On Friday, October 6, 1775, Hart and his family loaded their household furniture on the schooner of Captain John Knight and began a circuitous journey to Euhaw (where Joseph Cook was pastor) to escape the threatening British ships that had been moving into the harbor of Charleston for several months. Fearing that an attack on the city was imminent, they determined to go southwest to stay with the widow of Francis Pelot at Euhaw, a less likely target of the British. Adverse tides and winds greatly slowed them, but finally on October 14 they unloaded their furniture at Mrs. Pelot's house in Euhaw. They remained there until August 3, 1776, although from his sermon records Hart seemed to have returned occasionally to Charleston for the Sunday services.

In June, 1776, the British attacked Charleston, but were driven off by General William Moultrie. In his diary, Hart mentioned that on June 28 "the famous Battle of Sullivan Island was fought, when God appeared for me, and defeated our enemies." His diary also noted that "On Thursday July ye 4 the thirteen united colonies of North America were declared free and independent states by the continental congress." A few days after returning to Charleston, Hart's son John was commissioned as second lieutenant in the Second Regiment under the command of General Moultrie.

While Hart was at Euhaw, the South Carolina colony, on March 19, 1776, "broke off the British yoke and established a new form of Government upon a free and generous plan, our rulers being chosen from among ourselves." Hart, along with Elhanan Winchester, pastor of the Welsh Neck Baptist Church, addressed a letter on March 30, 1776, to Henry Laurens, who had been named vice-president of South Carolina under the new government, congratulating him and expressing confidence in the cause of liberty. "We hope to see liberty sit regent on the throne and flourish more than ever under the administration of such worthy patriots."[43] Laurens replied with a gracious letter.

The new constitution, however, did not alter the religious situation. Baptists and other Dissenters were still required to support the Anglican Church by taxation, and the net result of the new constitution was the transfer of ecclesiastical power from England to Charleston. The Welsh Neck church had already spoken out on this matter. At the church meeting on March 8, the pastor, Elhanan Winchester, had proposed

> that as the Association did not meet in Charleston this year on account of the troubles there; there might be a meeting of the Churches in this Province, at the High Hills of Santee on the Wednesday night before the last Sunday in April next, in order to choose delegates to attend the Continental Association, which he judged very expedient and necessary at this session, in order to obtain our liberties, and freedom from religious tyranny or ecclesiastical oppressions; which the Church unanimously agreed to: and chose two messengers vis brethren Abel Wilds and Thomas Evans to the provincial Association at the same time and place mentioned.[44]

So, as suggested, a conference of the ministers of all dissenting denominations was called to meet at the High Hills church for discussion of the best methods of putting pressure upon the Commons House of Assembly to bring religious liberty to the new state. A large group responded, and plans were made to ask the Assembly to face the question of religious liberty. Among other things, a petition was prepared for submission to the Assembly, meeting on January 11, 1777. The petition said in part:

> That there never shall be any establishment of any one denomination or sect of Protestants by way of preference to another in this State. That no Protestant inhabitant of this State, shall by law, be obliged to pay towards the maintenance and support of a religious worship that he does not

freely join in or has not voluntarily engaged to support, nor to be denied the enjoyment of any civil right merely on account of his religious principles, but that all Protestants demeaning themselves peaceably under the government established under the constitution shall enjoy free and equal privileges, both religious and civil.[45]

In behalf of the Dissenters, William Tennent, pastor of the Independent Church in Charleston, spoke eloquently at the Assembly in favor of disestablishment and urged the Assembly to approve the petition. Thousands of Dissenters of many denominations in the state had signed the petition, which Tennent said represented the views of seventy-nine dissenting churches (thirty-eight Presbyterian, twenty-eight Baptist, eight Lutheran, and five unclassified). Even Church of England members had signed the petition.[46] Despite strong efforts to amend the petition to allow all denominations to be supported by public taxes, the Assembly passed the original petition, thus eliminating any type of church establishment in South Carolina.

On February 5, 1777, the Charleston Association adopted a circular letter, evidently composed principally by Oliver Hart, clerk of the body, which addressed the churches concerning both civil and religious liberty. It read in part:

> We are happy in being able to say that there is not one in this Association but heartily joins in the measures taken by America in general and this State in particular, to secure our liberties. Secondly, we heartily congratulate you on the prospect of obtaining universal religious liberty in this State; an event which must cause every generous mind to rejoice; as by that every one may sit down under his own vine and under his own fig tree, and none to make him afraid i.e. every person may enjoy ease, liberty and property, without molestation or interruption. The terms which we understand are proposed by the House of Assembly, to be complied with, by all who desire the protection of the State are reasonable and easy, and we recommend to you to conform thereto, as it will be of singular advantage in many instances.[47]

One week later Oliver Hart wrote to Richard Furman, as follows:

> We now have a bright prospect that we shall obtain religious liberty, in its full extent, in this State, it cannot fail if we dissenters will be careful to attend the next session of Assembly. The point is not carried altogether according to the mode of our petition, nevertheless, all that was asked is granted, and more too; for according to the plan proposed, every congregation in the State, may upon application to the House of Assembly, become an incorporated body, to be known in law, and so entitled to all the immunities and privileges of the State.[48]

An interesting sidelight was provided in the closing section of Hart's letter to Furman. Hart used this occasion to urge unity between the Regular Baptists and the High Hills and Congaree churches. His letter of February 12 to Furman said:

> The enclosed copy of the Minutes will inform you of what was done. One paragraph you will find respecting your church. I hope we shall have your Voice and influence for the junction there proposed. We have now no Prospect of association with the churches on the Frontier (the Separates). If you and the Congarees will come into the Plan it will be strengthening of us all. I am much of the Opinion, it would be much to the Advantage of the Baptist Interest, in this State; and the more so on account of our new Constitution, which will necessarily render us more conspicuous to the State; and I see no reason why we should appear in the most diminutive Light to that State, by which we expect to be protected, and from which we expect all our Privileges, civil and religious. I am more for this juncture, because I fear some of the Baptists on the Frontiers will be deemed unfriendly to the Government. Therefore let all of us who are willing to stand up in Support of our happy Constitution unite together in one band; we shall Thereby be the more respectable in the eyes of the Government.[49]

The paragraph about Furman's church in the minutes of the Charleston Association read:

> Appointed Rev. Evan Pugh to draw up a letter to the Congaree and High Hills Churches, inviting them to join this Association, as it appears to us that it would be for the Glory of God, and the Interest of Religion.[50]

The fact that Furman and the High Hills church promptly accepted the invitation reveals that he identified himself with the Regular Baptists of the Charleston Association even though he was converted under a Separate Baptist. Joseph Reese and the Congaree church, on the other hand, did not respond to this invitation. The Congaree church did not join the Charleston Association until several years after the death of Reese.

The adoption of the petition on January 11, 1777, by the Assembly eliminated the Anglican establishment that had been observed since 1706. This meant that no longer would Baptists and other dissenting denominations be forced to pay taxes to support the Anglican ministers and build Anglican churches. Under the new government, all denominations were permitted to organize churches and incorporate them for the purpose of recovering legacies and holding property. Before this time, all such secular concerns had to be handled through trustees by dissenting churches. The only restriction to incorporation was subscription to five religious articles, as follows: (1) There is one Eternal God and a future state of rewards and punishments. (2) God is to be publicly worshiped. (3) The Christian religion is the true religion. (4) The Holy Scriptures of the Old and New Testaments are divinely inspired and are the rule of faith and practice. (5) It is lawful, and the duty of every man being thereunto lawfully called, to bear witness to the truth. It is evident that this subscription was a definite limitation on liberty of conscience, for not only Jews and unbelievers but many other sectarian groups would find it difficult to subscribe to these doctrines. At any rate, feeling that the incorporation of the church would bring benefits in addition to formal recognition, the Charleston church petitioned the authorities, subscribed to the five religious articles, and on March 19, 1778, secured a charter of incorporation.[51] Because the war by this time had concentrated around Charleston, the church continued to utilize trustees for secular concerns for some years.

Meanwhile, the war was growing in intensity. In his diary Hart noted that on November 7, 1777, it had been confirmed that General John Burgoyne's army had surrendered to General Horatio Gates at Saratoga, New York, on October 17, 1777. Hart could hardly restrain his jubilant pen.

> This grand event . . . is scarce paralleled in History and will shine in the annals of America to the latest ages. It calls for Thankfulness to the Lord of Hosts from every true friend to his country.

He also rejoiced that on May 26, Charleston had heard that France had acknowledged America's independence and had "entered into a treaty of amity and commerce with our plenipotentiaries." On July 22, 1777, Hart had a long section in his diary about the execution of a soldier for desertion and described in some detail how he had prayed three times with him just before the soldier was shot. Hart mentioned that he had worn his gown and bands on this sad occasion.

On March 24, 1778, Oliver Hart wrote his brother Joseph in Warminster, Pennsylvania. The letter condemned in strong terms the conduct of British armies—"Their Cause is unjust, and their Measures Diabolical." There was also a description of the fire which destroyed about one-fourth of Charleston on January 15. The Baptist meetinghouse caught fire three times but, like the parsonage, escaped destruction.

Hart wrote his brother again on July 5, 1778, evidently having received by Henry Laurens his brother's letter from New York. The story told by his brother had kindled the anger of Hart, who wrote:

> This Affair comes nearer Home than any Thing that happened during the War. Perhaps you may judge by your own Feelings, of the Indignation and Resentment, which fired my Breast, on reading the Account. I could think of nothing but Retaliation, and almost felt a Disposition to have them treated like Agag. Surely some signal Judgement awaits those bloody Butchers.

He sang joyfully as he contemplated the victory of the war:

> With Joy I often look forward and contemplate the rising Glories of this Continent; its Inhabitants nourished by the most free, generous and perfect Form of Government ever modeled; and cherished by the best of Rulers, chosen by ourselves whose Interest and Inclination will conspire to make the ruled happy. When Peace, like the swelling Tide, shall flow over the Mountains and cover the whole Land. When Religion, freed from its Shackles—Learning and Virtue, encouraged and promoted, shall spread far and wide. Wisdom and Knowledge shall increase, and every Pesant be qualified for a Senator. Every Man shall sit down peaceably under his own Vine, and under his own Figtree;-and the Trade, Favour and Protection of America will be courted by all Nations under Heaven.

On September 10 he wrote Joseph again, continuing the theme of the barbarity of the British soldiers.

The war was brought closer to Charleston in the winter of 1778. British General William Howe was replaced by General Henry Clinton, who sent forces in December, 1778, to capture Savannah, Georgia. The move was successful, and the British occupied most of Georgia during the remainder of the war. Oliver Hart wrote to his brother on January 14, 1779, describing in some detail the confusion brought by the southern campaign of the British.

> It now appears probable that our Southern States will, for a Time, be the Seat of War. The Enemy are already in Possession of Georgia. They landed about 3000 troops there on ye 29:th Ult. The few continental Troops we had there, aided by some of the Militia, endeavoured to obstruct their March to Savannah Town, but were obliged soon to retreat, with some Loss, some say about 3 to 400 men; but as yet we have no Return of the Killed, wounded and missing. . . . The Enemy, on their entering Savannah, fell into the Possession of a great Quantity continental Stores of Provision; together with Household Furniture &c. &c. . . .
>
> Comodore Hyde Parker and Lieu.t Col: Archibald Campbell, have issued a Proclamation, inviting all who are Friends to the royal Government, in N. and S. Carolina and Georgia, to repair to the royal Standard, at Head Quaters, in Savannah, without Loss of Time; promising Pardon and the most ample Protection. How this Proclamation may operate on the Minds of the People, I cannot say; but probably the infatuated Tories (who are too numerous in every State) will repair to the royal Standard, in Hopes of possessing their Neighbours Estates, by and by; to accomplish which, they would cut their Neighbours Throats.
>
> It is not long since a Number of Augustine Plunderers, made a Descent upon Georgia, ravaging, sacking and burning every Thing in their Way. Not only private Houses, but even the House of God was reduced to Ashes. A spacious, elegant Meeting House, in St. John's Parish, was burnt to the Ground. General Screven, a brave Commander of the

Militia, being too adventurous, was first wounded, and then barbarously fired upon, while on the Ground, calling for Quarter; he languished of his Wounds (seven in Number) a few Days, and died, much lamented; leaving a Widow (since dead also) and four Children. Gen. Screven was an own Brother to my Soninlaw, Mr. Thomas Screven.

The Inhabitants of this State are generally in Motion; the Militia from all Quarters are draughted, to guard the Sea Coasts, and be ready for Action, in Case of Emergency. God knows what will be the Event of these Things. If He is on our Side, all will end well.

Hart wrote his brother again on February 16, 1779, vividly describing beleaguered Charleston:

The Enemy, since their Landing at Savannah, have been reinforced by a Party from Augustine; and a Number of the Tories in Georgia have also joined them. About 15 to 1600 have marched up Savannah River, as high as Augusta, near which Place it is thought they intend to cross over into this State, with an Expectation of being joined by a great number of disaffected Inhabitants on our Frontiers; and from thence, it is not very improbable, they may intend a Push for Charlestown. Do you ask, what are we about all this while? I answer, we have been buying and selling, and preying on each other like Vultures. I wish we may not, in the End, have bartered away the State, and purchased to ourselves Ignomy and Distress, in the highest Degree. Many blame our late President for being too tardy in his Operations. Be this as it may, we are in such a Situation that unless Providence kindly and remarkably interposes on our Behalf, we are an undone People.

. . . Our Country is all Confusion. We have now a worthy Governor, John Rutledge, of proved, and approved, Integrity and Abilities. This affords us a Gleam of Hope in our present gloomy State. Our Assembly are about making the governor a Dictator, which shows what Confidence we place in Him. I hope and believe He will not abuse his Trust; but it is delegating very great Power to an Individual. After all, nothing can save us but the Interposition of the great Governor of the Universe; in Him may we place all our Confidence and may He mercifully condescend to help a sinful People.

Hart wrote an account to his brother again on May 3, 1779, which showed the ever-tightening circle around Charleston.

My last informed you that the Enemy were in Possession of Georgia, a Party of them have now crossed Savannah River and encamped in this State. What farther Designs they have in Contemplation is hard to say; some suppose they intend to make a bold Push for Charles Town; others think that having gleaned Georgia, they have come over for Plunder. Be this as it may, they now occupy the ground where Genl. Lincoln lately had his Head Quarters. . . . Hitherto the two Armies seem to have been playing Cat-in-Pan. In all Probability they will e'er long play a more decisive Game. I expect shortly to hear of some bloody Work. . . .

My son John has been for some time desirous of coming to Action; as He is now with our Army at the Southward, He will probably be gratified; May God shield him in the Day of Battle.

Glad should I be to see a Period to the present Contest, upon honourable Terms to America, not otherwise. We now feel the Effects of War in the Purchase of every Article of Life. Upon an average we pay eight hundred per cent advance upon Marketing, Liquor and Dry Goods; which makes it hard upon the poorer Sort, who have no resources.

Oliver Hart reported again about the peril of Charleston in a letter to his brother on July 18, 1779, saying:

Soon after Genl. Lincoln's Attack on their Lines, and this Attack on our Gallies the Enemy thought proper to retreat; they passed over Wadmalaw, and crossed North Edisto River over to Edisto Island; from hence they passed over some smaller Islands, and it is said Part of them are now at Beaufort, and Part of them at Savannah in Georgia. The Plunder they have carried off with them is immense, but they have failed the grand Object, namely the taking of Charles Town; God having once more prepared for us in a remarkable Manner, which we ought never to forget.

. . . I am persuaded these Plunderers never had the Pleasure of ravaging so opulent a Country before; and the Havoc they have made is not to be described. Great Numbers of Women and Children have been left without a 2.nd Shift of Clothes. The furniture which they could not carry off they wantonly broke, burnt, and destroyed. They have, however, taken away with them some Thousands of Negroes, with a great quantity of Plate, Jewels and all Kinds of Treasure. They give out that they will have Cha.s Town yet, but I trust Omnipotence will still defend us.

Another letter on December 11, 1779, from Hart to his brother, breathed an optimistic note, although reporting a rumor that the British were sending large reinforcements to the Savannah area from New York City. This was the last word from Charleston by Oliver Hart in his extant correspondence, but his skimpy diary of the period continued the story. Rumors had persisted throughout the fall that American General Lincoln would attack the British force at Savannah. The encounter took place in October, 1779, and Hart reported in his diary that Count Pulaski had received a mortal wound in the fight. With some pride, Hart said, "My son John had the command of a company, was in the thickest danger, the bullets falling all around him like hail, but God in mercy spared his life."

Hart's ministry in South Carolina was coming to a close. On February 11, 1780, the British fleet appeared off Stono bar. Hart became ill with fever which persisted over a week, and his doctor suggested that he go into the country for recuperation. On February 16 he and his wife took ship to the home of Thomas Screven, his daughter's husband, in Saint Thomas Parish. While there, Hart received word on Sunday, April 15, that British troops were marching toward them. At noon Hart

> took Leave of my dear Wife, and the Family (the most affecting Parting I ever experienced) and set off, I know not whither, in Company with Mr. Hamilton. In ye Evening we arrived at Anderson's Ferry, Santee where we lodged.

After Charleston fell on May 12, Hart was joined by Edmund Botsford, also wanted by the British for his patriotic activities, and they fled to the home of Hart's brother near Augusta, Virginia. Here Hart and Botsford preached for some time, and Hart even considered the possibility of settling here. He finally decided against this because of problems involved in moving his family to this place. Preaching constantly, he slowly made his way up the coast toward his place of birth.

On December 16, 1780, he accepted the call of the Baptist church at Hopewell, New Jersey, and remained as her pastor until his death in 1795. He kept up a constant correspondence with Edmund Botsford, Richard Furman, and others in the Charleston church. When the church invited him to return as pastor at the close of the Revolutionary War, he felt that he could not do so. He wrote Furman that he would come to the meeting of the Charleston Association in 1788. Leaving home on September 2, he began the overland trip to Charleston with several friends to assist him along the way. He got as far as his brother's home in Virginia on September 14, where he remained until September 25. Not being well and having trouble with the horses and sulky, Hart decided to abort the trip and returned to his home at Hopewell. After a difficult journey of almost a month, most of the time alone, he arrived at Hopewell about noon on October 23. Later Furman wrote him of the disappointment all had felt at the association meeting when they did not see their old friend. When Hart died on December 31, 1795, both Furman and William Rogers of Philadelphia preached memorial sermons which were later published.

By 1780 the Charleston church was without a pastor. For long periods, because of the war, the congregation had seen little of the Hart family as they fled here and there from the enemy. The funds of the church also had been almost totally depleted. Before the war, according to a statement made after April 27, 1780, by Colonel Thomas Screven, the acting trustee, and certified by Major Benjamin Smith and Mr. Thomas Smith, the church had been relatively prosperous under the ministry of Hart. The church had accumulated almost 15,000 pounds through various gifts, and this sum in 1772 yielded an annual income of 1,430 pounds. However, by various losses during the war and particularly by the depreciation of paper currency, all funds of the church by 1780 amounted to approximately 445 pounds. Since the government was in great fiscal difficulty because of the war, the church donated all of the remainder of her funds (about 332 pounds) to the public treasury. Basil Manly remarked, "I suppose it was again refunded to them in due time; but of this we have no account."[52]

Services at the church were discontinued for several years after the flight of Hart. The British seized the Baptist meetinghouse and used it as a storehouse for salt beef and other provisions. The old original church building on lot 62, which was owned conjointly with the General Baptists (although used only by the General Baptists by agreement), was used to store forage.

So, by 1780 the Charleston church had been laid waste. Her pastor had been driven away, her place of worship seized by the enemy, her members scattered, and her resources depleted. The war was going badly. Only God knew what the future would bring.

Notes

1. Baker, *Southern Baptist Convention,* pp. 39-40.
2. See ibid., chap. 5.
3. Wesley M. Gewehr, *The Great Awakening in Virginia, 1740-1790* (Durham, N.C.: Duke University Press, 1930), p. 116.
4. Owens, *Hart,* p. 10.
5. W. Furman, p. 8.
6. For a summary of this, see Robert G. Torbet, *A History of the Baptists,* 3rd ed., 8th print. (Valley Forge: Judson Press, 1973), pp. 43 ff.
7. Gillette, p. 25.
8. He was an elected messenger only in the last named year, however.
9. Owens, *Hart,* p. 10.
10. W. Furman, pp. 8-9.
11. Ibid., table pp. 52-53.
12. Ibid., p. 12.
13. *A Confession of Faith . . .* [and] *A Summary of Church-Discipline . . .* (Charleston: David Bruce for the Charleston Baptist Association, 1774).
14. George W. Purefoy, *A History of the Sandy Creek Baptist Association* (New York: Sheldon & Co., 1859), p. 74.
15. W. Furman, p. 14.
16. Ibid., p. 17.
17. Henry Sheets, *A History of the Liberty Baptist Association* (Raleigh, N.C.: Edwards & Broughton Printing Co., 1907), p. 71.
18. Gillette, p. 22.
19. Sheets, p. 73.
20. Paschal, I:266.

21. Sprague, pp. 62 ff.
22. Sheets, p. 74.
23. Sprague, p. 63.
24. W. Furman, p. 10.
25. Ibid.
26. Sprague, p. 63.
27. W. Furman, p. 11.
28. Ibid., p. 55.
29. Sheets, pp. 76-77. See Garland A. Hendricks, *Saints and Sinners at Jersey Baptist Settlement* (Thomasville, 1964), chaps. 1-3.
30. See Guild for details of Smith's life.
31. Mallary, *Botsford,* pp. 45 ff.
32. Manly, *Discourse,* p. 44.
33. Townsend, p. 30.
34. Ibid., pp. 143-44.
35. Harvey T. Cook, *Education in South Carolina under Baptist Control* (Greenville: n.p., 1912), p. 11.
36. Ibid., p. 13.
37. For this discussion, see ibid., pp. 13-15.
38. Robert H. Woody, "Christopher Gadsden and the Stamp Act," in *Perspectives,* p. 70.
39. Harvey T. Cook, *A Biography of Richard Furman* (Greenville, S.C.: Baptist Courier Job Rooms, 1913), p. 50.
40. This summary is taken from the excellent article by Loulie Latimer Owens, "Oliver Hart and the American Revolution," ed. J. Glenwood Clayton, *Journal of the South Carolina Baptist Historical Society* (Greenville: South Carolina Baptist Historical Society, 1975-), I:2-30.
41. Cook, *Furman,* p. 50.
42. Ibid., pp. 51-52.
43. Ibid., p. 52.
44. Townsend, p. 277.
45. Cook, *Furman,* pp. 54-55.
46. Ibid., pp. 58, 63.
47. Ibid., p. 56.
48. Ibid.
49. Ibid., p. 57.
50. *Minutes,* Charleston Baptist Association, 1777, p. 2.
51. Manly, *Discourse,* p. 44.
52. Ibid., pp. 45-46.

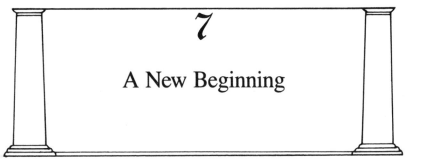

7

A New Beginning

Charleston Baptists experienced the full measure of humiliation and suffering in the war for independence. British Generals Clinton and Cornwallis united their forces in Savannah, and a frontal attack overwhelmed Charleston on May 12, 1780. The city remained in enemy hands for about two years. After the fall of Charleston, the British armies began to enlarge their hold on South Carolina. American General Horatio Gates engaged the British at Camden but was defeated. Harried by heroic patriot leaders like Isaac Shelby, John Sevier, Andrew Pickens, Francis Marion, Thomas Sumter, and Daniel Morgan, Cornwallis slowly moved northward. General Nathanael Greene, who had assumed command of the American forces in the South, outfoxed Cornwallis and mauled his army at Guilford Court House on March 15, 1781. In April, with reinforcements, Cornwallis started north again, hoping to attack Lafayette at Richmond, Virginia; but instead, fearing entrapment, Cornwallis retreated to Yorktown on the coast, where he hoped British ships would aid him. However, the French fleet controlled the waters around Yorktown, and soon General Washington closed the trap. Cornwallis surrendered on October 19, 1781. The war was practically over, although the peace treaty was not formally signed at Paris until September 3, 1783.

Of the suffering endured by the Charleston church at this time, Basil Manly remarked:

> But all their privations and losses might well be borne, in view of the unspeakable blessings, both civil and religious, which the Revolution had gained. The price it had cost was immense; and this church seems to have paid their full share; yet all was forgotten in the grateful sentiments which the dawn of liberty inspired. Their place of worship, long desecrated by the possession and vile use of the enemy, they yet venerated more than ever; because it was now nearly associated with the triumph of civil and religious freedom—with the complete establishment of those principles of entire toleration, the glory of this country, for which the Baptists had been the first to contend, and for which the founders of this very church had suffered.[1]

177

Massive Problems of Independence

The end of military operations did not solve the acute political, economic, and social problems the new independent states faced. There were serious disagreements among them about the kind of political union they wanted to form. The resolution of Richard Henry Lee at the Second Continental Congress on June 7, 1775, had not only asserted that the colonies "are and of right ought to be free and independent states," but also urged that a plan of confederation be adopted. By July, 1778, the Congress had adopted a plan and sent it to the various states for ratification. After three years, the Articles of Confederation became the bond that provided a form of government for the united states. Meanwhile, the Continental Congress had followed this pattern of government during the remainder of the war. But this Confederation was born in an atmosphere of reaction to the authoritarian and coercive rule of Great Britain when the states were uneasy about forming a central government that might usurp the liberties of the people in the states. The manifest weaknesses of the central government under these Articles of Confederation made diplomatic relations with the great powers of Europe almost impossible. Exclusion from favorable trade relations with other nations foisted a deepening economic depression on America after the war. Even bumper crops were of little value without a market. Unhappy farmers in Massachusetts, the victims of lost markets and imminent foreclosures on their farms, threatened anarchy and rebellion. Clearly a more perfect union was needed.

The new constitution prepared at a convention in 1787 remedied many of these weaknesses. Under its provisions, George Washington was elected the first president of the Republic in 1789. The Bill of Rights adopted in 1791 provided additional guarantees of the liberties of the people. The new nation now specifically granted religious liberty and affirmed the separation of church and state. Although the form of government under the new constitution of 1789 solved some of the immediate problems experienced under the Articles of Confederation, it would take centuries for the principles and relationships involved in this constitution to be hammered out.

One particularly vexing problem inherited by the new nation from colonial days was the political, moral, and economic question of Negro slavery. It had begun in America in 1619 when a Dutch ship brought Africans to the Virginia colony for involuntary servitude. The colony protested, but Great Britain forced the initial acceptance of this institution because of its potential economic value. In a relatively short time, however, the profits from the slave trade and the ability of southern planters to use large numbers of unskilled laborers on large plantations in a warm climate mollified the early American hostility to human slavery. At the height of the system, it should be observed, however, that two-thirds of the white families in the South owned no slaves a all. No section of the seaboard states was blameless in this melancholy story. Theodore D. Weld, one of the leading northern abolitionists of the nineteenth century, asserted that the slavery system was maintained by the political, financial, and commercial power of the North.[2] Northern merchants sought the high profits that came from sending their ships to African ports to import the black people and providing finances for southern planters to purchase them, but the greed of the southern planters encouraged and helped prolong this evil.

Charleston, of course, shared in all of the massive problems facing the nation after the war. As a part of the southern culture, the city was a participant in the slavery system. The Baptist church at Charleston had experienced a serious problem with slavery as early as 1711, as has already been mentioned. When a member of the church punished his slave according to the provisions of the provincial law, other members of the church protested the cruelty involved. The church sought advice from a Baptist church and an association in England and were advised not to destroy the peace of the church by condemning the severity of the master who had acted according to law.[3] Oliver Hart made several references in his diary that indicated his involvement with this system, but before his death he had spoken against it.[4] As a matter of fact, the church at Charleston was active in its efforts to win Negroes to Christ. In later years, the Negroes constituted a majority of the church members.[5]

Stirring the Coals

The flood of war and violence in Charleston did not destroy the Baptist church there. Exactly how the initial recovery took place is not clear, but it is possible that Edmund Botsford, who had fled to Virginia from Welsh Neck after the defeat of General Gates at Camden, was the first to return to Charleston to preach. After the surrender of Cornwallis, Botsford and his family, who had suffered great losses during the war, felt that it was safe to return to South Carolina. About January 1, 1782, he and his family arrived at Welsh Neck, where he had evidently served as interim pastor before the war. He was promptly called as regular pastor of the church, and from this base he was able to minister at Charleston also.

The Charleston Association met with the Welsh Neck church in October 1782 where "ministers were appointed to visit the destitute Churches." Whether Botsford was one of those appointed to help Charleston at this time is not known, but he probably was. Botsford said that he visited Charleston in 1783 and "searched out a few of the male members, and engaged them to fit up the house of worship; after which, he preached several discourses to a pretty numerous congregation."[6] This sounded as if the church had not begun to function until Botsford arrived.

However, a surprising number of details of this period have been preserved. Evidently about this time Richard Furman, the young pastor at the High Hills of Santee who had fled from the British armies in 1780, also ministered to the Charleston church. He had returned to his own church at High Hills in 1782, and he might have been in contact with the Charleston church before Botsford came. It is known that on a visit by Furman to Charleston in early April, 1783, the trustees of the church (Patrick Hinds, John Gourley, and Thomas Screven) requested Furman to write Oliver Hart in behalf of the church and invite him to return as pastor. Furman wrote the letter to Hart on April 14, but on June 26 Hart replied, declining the invitation because of

> the providential direction he had received to Hopewell, New Jersey—the strength of mutual attachments—the pleasing prospects of the church he then served—his own better health—his opinion that a younger and more active man was necessary for them—and his comparative want of success during the latter part of his residence in Charleston.[7]

The energy of the church seems to have been restored rather quickly, even though a pastor was not secured for several years thereafter. The regular house of worship used before the war was cleaned, and temporary seats and a pulpit were installed. The parsonage was rented out for fifty pounds, and a committee was named on June 20, 1783, to investigate the status of the church property on Edisto Island. The title to this property was held by the Charleston church after Edisto Baptists had removed to Euhaw to form the church there. The Revolutionary War had so dispersed the Euhaw church that none of them claimed the Edisto Island rents which the Euhaw church had been receiving since the formation of the church there. On December 15, 1783, the Charleston church directed Thomas Screven, one of the Charleston trustees, to lease the Edisto Island lands, and on March 5, 1784, Screven reported that he had done so.[8] The titles and the rent collected evidently were surrendered in 1787 to the trustees of the revived Euhaw church.[9]

On March 8, 1784, according to Manly, the number of trustees was increased, and the following were in this office during this time and for a few years later, being authorized to transact all business without consulting the church except in new or very important cases: Thomas Screven, Patrick Hinds, John Gourlay, John Hamilton, Thomas Rivers, Jeremiah Brown, Charles McDonald, John Hart, and John Michael. Probably John Hart was named later than 1784, since he was not converted and baptized until February 7, 1786. There is also a problem with the dating of Thomas Screven. Also on March 8, 1784, the trustees endeavored to secure Richard Furman as pastor of the Charleston church, but he felt constrained to remain at the High Hills of Santee church at that time.

On February 19, 1785, the trustees of the Charleston church petitioned the legislature in an effort to recover the property of the Ashley River Baptist Church which had become extinct during the revolutionary war. Probably Richard Furman, with his knowledge of surveying and land values, had pointed out that Baptists would lose such property if some interested party did not seek to secure it. The petition was without success. Wood Furman reported that the property had been "seized by an individual, and converted to his own use."[10] Probably the property had been claimed by the heirs of Richard Butler, who had given the land for the erection of a Baptist church, and the deed likely included a reversionary clause.[11]

That these efforts to recover Baptist property were not selfishly motivated is suggested by the fact that when the Methodists desired to begin their work in Charleston and wanted a place for the famous Francis Asbury to preach, the Charleston church (which had a legal interest in the old property on lot 62) gladly allowed them to use the old church building there, since the General Baptists had ceased to use it.[12] After the Methodists had finished using the building and it was again vacant and unused, the church petitioned the legislature on February 16, 1786, to secure possession of the property. This in effect meant the reversing of the decision of 1745 that had allowed title to the property to be vested in both the General and Particular Baptists in Charleston and Stono. The petition of 1786 asserted that there was no longer a General Baptist Society existing in Charleston, although a group of General Baptists challenged this by filing a counter-petition opposing the change. In 1787 the court awarded the property solely to the Particular Baptists. A later court decision revealed that the General Baptists had become extinct about 1791.[13]

Edmund Botsford visited Charleston again in 1784, and he met "with some success." During his third visit to Charleston in early 1785, he wrote Oliver Hart on March 30 to say that he had been there for six Sundays and expected to stay two more; that he had already baptized two and expected to immerse others before leaving Charleston. He continued:

> There is a pretty good work begun. I have preached 41 sermons, go from house to house, and blessed be God, sweet times we have. I have time to write but a few lines; indeed I have hardly enjoyed an hour to myself since I have been in town. Numbers of blacks come to see me, and some whites; and many I must go and see. I doubt not that if there were a minister settled here, there would soon be a flourishing Church. Who would have thought that your poor son Botsford would have been owned as an instrument to bring souls to the Charleston Church? I find the heart is the same in Charleston, as in the country. Crowds attend public meetings, which are held three times on Lord's days, and on Wednesday evenings; every other evening we have meetings at private houses, in which I have introduced praying for those poor distressed souls who ask.[14]

Botsford later wrote Hart that he had returned to Welsh Neck on April 16, 1785, and said concerning his Charleston visit:

> In town I baptized 5 whites and 6 blacks, administered the communion twice, preached 61 sermons, and had I been at liberty would have taken up my abode in Charleston.[15]

In this letter to Hart he mentioned that he could talk bravely like this from his study at Pee Dee, but, "when I stand up in town before three or four hundred people, I sometimes quake again." This sounded as if he had been preaching in Charleston to rather substantial crowds.

When the Charleston Association met in October, 1785, at the High Hills of Santee church, the Charleston church requested that the association provide supply preachers for them until the church could find a pastor. The association then requested Richard Furman to assist the church in December; Joshua Palmer, in February; Edmund Botsford, in March; Evan Pugh, in May; and Joseph Cook, in July. These men, along with Joshua Lewis, James Fowler and Joseph Redding, seem to have performed this service faithfully.[16] A brief word should be said about each of these.

Furman and Botsford, of course, had already extended this assistance taking the time from their churches at High Hills of Santee and Welsh Neck to do so. Joshua Palmer, an English immigrant, was probably itinerating at this time, although he soon moved to Lynches Creek.[17] Evan Pugh, who had been a student under Oliver Hart and Frances Pelot in the Religious Society, was preaching at and around Cashaway, about twenty miles south of the Welsh Neck church, but was no doubt happy to be able to repay in part his debt to the Charleston church. Joseph Cook, ordained by Richard Furman and Oliver Hart at High Hills, was pastor at Euhaw and was able doubtless to make the short journey to Charleston without great inconvenience.[18] Joshua Lewis was at this time pastor at Cheraw Hill church, about fifteen miles north of the Welsh Neck church on the Pee Dee River. He was an Englishman, described as being of portly mien, pleasant countenance, fine voice, and marked ability. He had met Hart and Pelot while living at Coosawhatchie, where he was ordained and preached.[19] James Fowler at this time probably was pastor of the Sandy River church, about 150 miles northwest of Charleston, although he might not have settled there yet after the war.[20] Joseph Redding helped constitute the Turkey Creek church, about 160 miles northwest of Charleston on the Saluda River on January 29, 1785, but may have assisted at Charleston before going there as pastor on May 7, 1785.[21]

After Richard Furman declined the call to Charleston in 1784, the church wrote Oliver Hart at Hopewell again asking him to reconsider returning to Charleston. After delay and considerable ambivalence on the part of Hart, he urged the church to ask Richard Furman again to become her pastor. In his letter of August 2, 1785, Hart wrote that she should use every means to secure this "prize of inestimable worth." At the same time, Hart wrote Furman urging him to accept the call. Furman agonized about this move. He ministered again in Charleston in December, 1785, as requested by the association, baptizing eleven not long after Edmund Botsford had baptized six in that city. Furman wrote Botsford on January 31, 1786, to say "I remain in great perplexity about moving to Charleston." In an undated letter recently discovered by Sara Walls in the Mary Furman Maxwell collection, the Charleston church urged the High Hills congregation to "resign him entirely to the will of God" and agree for Furman to come to Charleston. This letter probably should be dated shortly after the one from Botsford to Hart early in 1786 which said, "Mr. Furman has not yet concluded to settle in town, but I believe he will ere long."

Meanwhile, Furman continued to assist the Charleston church. On February 7, 1786, he wrote Oliver Hart in New Jersey rejoicing that among about thirty candidates he had baptized on that day was Hart's son, Captain John Hart, along with John's wife.[22] Botsford was unrestrained in his happiness as he wrote Hart about this on February 24:

> I received accounts from town that Capt. Hart and wife, and some others have been baptized. I heartily congratulate my honored father. Whatever you may have known, we all knew J. to have been the wildest of Mr. Hart's children. God's name be praised. Husband and wife! May God enable them to walk like Zacharias and Elizabeth. . . . Why, all heaven rang with the news. Remember, it is the conversion of the son of a man I regard above all men on earth.[23]

Among the thirty candidates baptized by Furman were two young men who later became preachers. One was Peter Bainbridge, a mature young man of twenty-two, who later moved to New York. The other was a twelve-year-old lad with a great heritage. He was Charles O. Screven, great-grandson of the original preacher of the church and son of General James Screven, the Revolutionary War hero who was slain in an engagement in Liberty County, Georgia. Charles surrendered to preach in 1802 after completing Brown University (formerly Rhode Island College, to which his family had made liberal gifts). In 1803 he was ordained at Charleston by Richard Furman and spent his entire ministry in the area of Sunbury, Liberty County, Georgia, where he did a monumental work.[24]

Finally during the time the church was without a pastor, the trustees moved with faith to repair and enlarge the meetinghouse.

> Since the peace, they had borne a principal part of the expenses of the church themselves; but now a general effort became necessary. The prospects of the congregation were such as to render more room

desirable. To effect this, the front part of the building was extended several feet toward the street; three galleries were erected and vestry rooms prepared; a baptistery was built, (for, before that, the ordinance was administered in a font situated in our present church yard,) a new pulpit was erected, and the situation of it changed, from what had been the end of the house, to what became the end after the alterations.[25]

The Charleston community bore a part of the expenses of these alterations, contributing over $2,300. The debt was not finally retired until about 1790, when this was achieved after an assessment on the use of the pews equal to half the amount of the annual rent and by the active subscription efforts of John Hart, formerly the "wildest son" of Oliver Hart, but now a dependable and faithful stalwart of the church.

While these alterations were being made to the meetinghouse, the Charleston church moved back to the old building on lot 62 for their worship services, the General Baptists having discontinued their services there during the war and not having made any effort to resume them. The Charleston church understood that the General Baptist party formerly using this old building had become extinct.[26]

The Inestimable Prize: Richard Furman

The repeated appeals by the Charleston church and the urging of Oliver Hart made it increasingly evident to Richard Furman that he must find God's will about whether to accept the city pastorate or remain with his beloved church at High Hills of Santee. He shrank from leaving the High Hills church without a shepherd. When Peter Bainbridge surrendered to preach and was licensed by the Charleston church, Furman felt that perhaps this rather mature young man might be able to serve the flock at High Hills. He indicated this in letters to the Charleston church and to Edmund Botsford. Finally, however, he realized that his first responsibility was to follow God's calling for himself and to trust God to provide a pastor for the High Hills church. So he notified the Charleston church that after presiding as moderator at the session of the Charleston Association which would meet at the High Hills church in November, 1787, he would move to the Charleston field. His acceptance on October 18, 1787, was reckoned as the beginning of his pastorate in Charleston. Who was this young preacher, barely thirty-two years of age, who was already counted as first among equals in the Charleston Association and the man whom the Charleston church first approached to be their pastor after Oliver Hart had decided not to return to South Carolina?

The statistics of Richard Furman's life are familiar. He was born on October 9, 1755, at Esopus, New York, on the Hudson River, the youngest son of Wood and Rachel (Brodhead) Furman. In the spring of 1756 he was taken to

South Carolina by his mother, his father having preceded them. Their abode there was first on an extensive tract in the region known as the High Hills of Santee in central South Carolina on the Wateree River. Shortly, however, Wood Furman moved his family to Saint Thomas Parish on the coast, then to Daniel's Island on the Cooper River near Charleston. In May, 1770, the family moved back to the High Hills and settled on the land which they had occupied about fifteen years earlier.

Their son Richard was thus brought to the scene of the most memorable days of his young life. His rapid growth and development in other ways could not compare with his spiritual change. He had been sprinkled as a baby and reared in a God-fearing home but had never experienced an immediate confrontation with God. When the Furman family moved to the High Hills area, God provided this time of confrontation. Cook described how the central situation, the quantity of fertile land, the proximity of a navigable river, and the healthfulness of the climate and environment had caused many people to emigrate to the vicinity of what was called the High Hills of Santee, probably from the French word for "health." For the most part, the early settlers were nonreligious, addicted to sports and social gaiety, and were mainly illiterate.[27] Into this spiritually barren country God sent a rugged preacher, a veritable John the Baptist, whose name was Joseph Reese. Ordained by Oliver Hart and Evan Pugh in 1768, Reese had preached in places destitute of the gospel. In none of these places was the gospel more needed than at the High Hills when he came about 1769. He had been preceded in the same year by Jeremiah Dargan, whose preaching efforts in "this wicked wicked" neighborhood resulted only in enraging the people. Undeterred, Reese preached vigorously in the community, winning and baptizing several. Joseph Howard, one of his converts, donated a four-acre tract of land for the building of a meetinghouse for all denominations, and in 1770 a community church building was erected. It soon became a Baptist church. Just at the time the Furman family moved into the community, a revival was taking place in this building under the preaching of Reese.

To this small house, measuring but twenty-four by thirty feet, the Furmans came to hear Reese after October, 1771. Young Richard had already received serious religious impressions during his early home life, where the Bible was a familiar book. Under the pungent exhortations of Reese, young Richard was brought to realize that Christianity was not simply receiving a church sacrament but was a personal confrontation with God. His orderly mind recognized the significance of the doctrines of sin, divine provision, and free grace. Urged by Reese to accept Christ by faith and be baptized, he resisted. Experiencing the sense of anxiety and lostness that theologians call "conviction of sin," Furman went to a quiet place in the woods and in a moment of surrender prostrated himself before God. Soon he returned to tell the preache that God was dealing with him and that he wanted to present himself "as sinner willing to accept the free grace of the Gospel."

Then a dramatic scene occurred. Before the assembly of the people, Rees began to question young Furman after the pattern followed by many Baptist of this period. At first somewhat haltingly, then with increasing freedom Furman divulged the new convictions of his soul. One of the hearers was hi gentle mother. The first witnessing of her sixteen-year-old son brought he and several others of the congregation to the place of surrender. They were a: baptized by Joseph Reese. Little did Reese know that the greatest hour of hi ministry had just occurred. The vast blessings of the fruitful life of Richar Furman flowed from that moment, and this untrained but zealous preacher c God shared in its glory. Other important converts from the preaching c Joseph Reese here were medical doctor Joseph Howard, deacon Thomas Neal and another faithful minister, Lewis Collins.

Young Furman had a brief time of depression and doubt so very familiar t those who have stood for a moment on the mountaintop and then must retur to the everyday affairs of life. A deepened faith and increased strength came however, as he moved upward from contemplating the terrors of judgmer presented in the gospel story and grasped firmly the grace of God in providin the free gift of salvation to those who trust in Christ.

This was a period of intellectual maturity as well as spiritual growth. H had been a precocious child. Before he was old enough to hold the famil Bible in his lap, he had opened it on a stool before him and begged his famil to teach him to read it. His gifted father and mother influenced him greatly Wood Furman had been a merchant, a teacher, and a surveyor. After movin to High Hills he became a local magistrate and Judge of Probate.

> With the help of his parents, but mostly by his own diligent study, in due
> time Furman learned acceptably mathematics, physical sciences, Latin,
> Greek, Hebrew, French, German, metaphysics, logic, history, English
> grammar, and classical literature. His remarkable memory equipped him
> to recite in middle life lengthy selections of poetry which he had learned
> as a lad.[28]

The inquisitive and retentive mind of young Richard made him a participar in every noble discipline that he contacted. From his father he acquired a excellent knowledge of surveying, which he later used to assist his neighbor in safeguarding their land claims against fraud. It is likely that young Furma also used this general background of knowledge when he assisted th Charleston church after the revolutionary war in her efforts to retrieve Baptis church property whose title was imperiled by the confusion of the war.

Another important field for blessing others was begun by young Furman a this time in his acquaintance with Joseph Howard, the pious and skille

redical doctor at High Hills, who instilled in Furman a desire to study
natomy and learn enough medicine to be able to minister to the sick when no
hysician was available.

> A quick perception, a habit of accurate observation and reflection, an
> acquaintance with the treatment adopted by reputable practioners, while
> in attendance on the sick occasionally brought under his inspection;
> together with deep felt concern for the happiness of his fellowmen on
> whose life such momentous consequences depend, incited and enabled
> him to serve his friends and others when laboring under disease. With
> this view he kept constantly a considerable supply of medicine suited to
> the more common disorders and gratuitously administered them when a
> physican could not be procured. This early habit prepared him for more
> eminent services in the same line afterwards.[29]

This was also a period of rapid physical maturing for Richard Furman. He
ad inherited a strong physical constitution, and strengthened his body by
utdoor activities, particularly in hunting wild game after moving to the
ertile and somewhat isolated area of the High Hills of Santee. His biographer
ommented that Furman had an unusually rapid physical growth and that by
he time he had reached the age of sixteen, the boy had the physical
ppearance and stature of a mature man.

In the period between his conversion and the beginning of the revolutionary
var, Richard Furman continued to enlarge his understanding of his task and to
efine his natural gifts through study and voluntary Christian service. The
icriptures and doctrinal books were studied assiduously, interspersed with
ong hours of prayer and Christian meditation. He was a witness of his faith
rom the very time he was converted. Servants, relatives, and friends learned
rom his lips how the Lord had dealt with him. He found much pleasure
ittending the worship services in the home of Joseph Howard, the dedicated
nedical man. The High Hills congregation remained a branch of the
Congaree church until January 4, 1772, when it was formed into an
ndependent body. Visiting ministers knew that after they had preached at this
nfant church, they could call upon young Furman to exhort the congregation
o faithfulness in the Christian walk. It was to be expected that young people
of Furman's own age, reflecting the peer opposition that defies logic, would
ry to disrupt his service or amuse themselves by mimicking Furman in his
preaching or exhorting. He ignored this ridicule. The unruly parties gradually
urned to other outlets for their amusement and developed respect for the
earnest young man.

Another trial for young Furman was the outspoken desire of his father that
he gifted lad should choose law as a life work. As the boy began to spend
much time in preaching here and there and needed conveyance to more distant
areas, the father gained an opportunity to discuss life goals with his son. For a

time the father did not attend his son's preaching services, perhaps feeling that after a time this zeal for preaching would abate and the boy would be amenable to the study of law. However, young Furman never wavered from his conviction that God had called him to preach. After his father finally heard his son preach, he evidently realized that God had indeed laid hands on the lad and never again was there a word of objection. Many years later a distinguished jurist heard Richard Furman command logic and eloquence in presenting arguments from the pulpit on a religious theme, and remarked, "That is a first-rate lawyer spoiled." But Furman was needed for a higher court than the jurist served.

Gradually the fame of the "boy-evangelist" spread. He preached before and after his ordination through much of the middle region of the state, principally from the Congaree and Santee rivers on the west to the Pee Dee river on the northeast. He visited Georgetown and even Charleston in the lower country.

The High Hills church licensed Richard Furman to preach in 1773 when he was seventeen or eighteen years old. He had already been serving that congregation since April, 1772. In his diary, Oliver Hart mentioned what was evidently his initial introduction to young Furman. A protracted meeting at the High Hills was held from December, 1773, into early 1774. Hart preached from Colossians 2:6 in the morning service on January 2, 1774, and in the afternoon, Richard Furman spoke. From their later relationship, there can be little doubt that Hart was greatly impressed with this young preacher from the first time he met him. In 1774, the outstanding evangelist John Gano stopped at the High Hills. He was a messenger in that year from the Philadelphia Association to the Charleston Association meeting in February, and probably after their associational gathering he and Furman made a preaching trip to Georgia. Furman was delighted with "the vigorous intellect, the ready eloquence, scriptural knowledge, evangelical simplicity and fervid devotion" of Gano, now a mature man of forty-seven years. Doubtless on this trip to Georgia, Furman also met Daniel and Abraham Marshall and Edmund Botsford. He and Botsford began a warm friendship that endured until the latter was claimed by death in 1819.

Despite his youth, in 1774 the High Hills church called for the ordination of Richard Furman. He had displayed unusual maturity for an eighteen-year old, having preached at the church for about two years. He was an uncommonly serious young man in his deportment and preaching and could point to many fruits of his brief ministry. On May 16, 1774, he was set apart to Christian ministry by Evan Pugh and Joseph Reese. One must feel a sense of significant symbolism in his ordination by these two men. Pugh had a Regular Baptist background (although he may have been converted to Baptist views by the Separates of North Carolina), while Reese was a disciple of

Phillip Mulkey, the pioneer Separate Baptist of South Carolina. Oliver Hart had helped ordain both of these men, and they represented the vanguard of a new breed in South Carolina, uniting the strengths of both the Regulars and the Separates. Richard Furman was the finest example of this union. He assumed the High Hills pastorate in November, 1774. Evidently Furman waited until he was married to accept the church's call.

The High Hills church now began to grow "in numbers and in grace." Furman's own sister, Mrs. Sarah Haynesworth, soon had a bright conversion under his ministry. Just a month before Richard Furman's death fifty-one years later, she wrote to her brother a loving letter manifesting her warm faith and assurance.[30] Also about this time Furman baptized Stephen Nixon, who surrendered to preach and in 1802 became pastor of the Congaree church. As mentioned, the first months after his ordination also brought a joyous occasion to young Furman. In November, 1774, he married Elizabeth Haynesworth, whose brother had previously married Furman's only sister, Sarah.

It was probably about this time that Furman became acquainted with Timothy Dargan, who was called late in life to preach the gospel. During the next several years he and Dargan, a man "of most amiable temper and uncommon piety," traveled together on preaching trips. Furman probably learned from this older man (who died in 1783) how to witness in a gracious and effective manner. H. A. Tupper mentioned one trip the two made to Virginia, which was probably the early home of Dargan. On this trip they faced many difficulties.

> Creeks and rivers without bridges, wide spaces traversed only by bridle-paths, places of accommodation at remote distances, the absence of houses of worship, and other impediments made the work hard.[31]

An experience of Furman has been preserved describing how he first preached at Camden, a settlement on Wateree River some distance from the High Hills. He had been invited by interested people to preach at the Camden courthouse. A substantial group stood outside waiting for Furman's arrival, since the doors of the building were locked. When the sheriff refused to allow them to use the building because Furman was not an Anglican minister, some of the crowd wanted to force open the door and enter, but Furman took them to a nearby spot and captured them in the open air by his eloquent preaching. He was not again refused the use of the courthouse.[32]

Richard Furman played an active part in the revolutionary war. Doubtless he, like most American Baptists, took the colonial side not only because of the civil implications, but also with the hope that civil liberty would bring with it complete religious liberty. Non-Anglicans in South Carolina were still taxed for the Anglican establishment in that state. Familiar with the existence

of the large body of Tories in the up-country between the Broad and Salud
rivers, where he had preached extensively, Furman was not greatly surprise
in November, 1775, when word came that some of them were plotting to assi
the invasion of a British army into the area. Furman appealed to the Tories in
long letter in early November, 1775, to consider the justice of the coloni
cause and not to take up arms against the colonial effort for liberty. Colone
(later General) Richard Richardson accidently stumbled upon a copy of th
letter written by twenty-year-old Furman. He was impressed by its logic an
spirit and had it published. Copies were scattered in advance of his army as h
moved into the backcountry, and the letter was credited with forwarding th
American cause.[33] Not only so, but young Furman volunteered for militar
service and even marched to Charleston with a volunteer company con
manded by his brother, Captain Josiah Furman. However, Governor Rutledg
suggested that he return to the High Hills where he could do more good fc
the American cause in enlisting the support of the people.

As mentioned heretofore, Cook recorded a story of how Richard Furma
and Oliver Hart made a journey to the interior settlements in an effort to wi
these communities to support the colonial cause. On one occasion, Coo
noted, the leaders in a Tory community planned to seize the two Bapti
preachers and deliver them to the British. They made the mistake of fir
allowing them to address the large audience which had gathered. The
sincerity and logic convinced many of the listeners of the justice of th
colonial cause, and the plans to seize the preachers for the British wei
abandoned.[34] Evidently this story came from some occasion other than Hart
trip to the backcountry with Drayton and Tennent.

Events moved rapidly in 1776. When the provisional government of Sout
Carolina was initially formed on March 26, Baptists and other Dissente
deplored the omission of any action to secure relief from the discriminator
religious establishment of the Anglican church. In April, a "Continenta
Association" was called to meet in that month at the Baptist meetinghouse a
the High Hills of Santee, where leaders from all dissenting denomination
could consider the best means of amending the March constitution so as t
provide religious liberty for all. As discussed in the previous chapter, th
Dissenters' petition growing out of this meeting was approved on January 1
1777, by the Assembly, and religious liberty was finally restored in Sout
Carolina after over seventy years under the Anglican establishment.

Early in the following month the Charleston Association met in its annu
session, and on February 5, 1777, adopted a circular letter which rejoiced i
the formation of the new government in South Carolina and in the provisio
made for religious liberty. The association appointed Evan Pugh to dra
letters to the Congaree and the High Hills churches, not yet members of th
Charleston Association, inviting them to "unite together in one bond" i

support of the new state constitution with its guarantees for religious liberty. Oliver Hart wrote Furman on February 12 and personally urged Furman to give consideration to this. Hart's letter probably influenced Furman and the High Hills church in their decision, for in the following year (1778) the church united with the Charleston Association. The welcome given to the High Hills church may be glimpsed by the fact that in October of that year the Charleston Association met in its formal session with the High Hills church, for the first time in its history assembling away from Charleston.

By coincidence, Richard Furman had the opportunity to minister to William Tennent, the eloquent pastor of the Congregational or Independent church in Charleston, who had performed good service in urging the South Carolina Assembly of January, 1777, to approve the religious liberty petition of the Dissenters in South Carolina. Tennent had gone to New Jersey to bring back his widowed mother and, while returning to Charleston, became ill near the High Hills. He died there on the evening of August 11, 1777. Furman waited by Tennent's bed during his last illness and later wrote Mrs. Tennent a description of the calm assurance which her husband had displayed in his last moments.

This widespread activity of Richard Furman in the early years of the American Revolution caught the attention of the Welsh Neck Baptist Church. Not unexpectedly, the minutes of the church for November 1, 1777, expressed the desire to call Furman as pastor of the church, but at the next business meeting it was agreed that the church should not call him "as there is no possibility of obtaining him."[35]

After Charleston fell on May 12, 1780, Furman and his wife and their two children were forced to seek safety behind the American lines in North Carolina near the Virginia border. In Virginia he made the acquaintance of Patrick Henry, the distinguished patriotic leader, and the two formed friendly ties. In appreciation for the preaching of Furman, whose services he attended regularly, Patrick Henry presented Furman with a classical work on rhetoric. Except for several short visits to the High Hills, Furman remained principally in North Carolina where he ministered to the soldiers and preached in the churches.

A very popular story about these revolutionary war experiences of Furman surfaced in 1814. As the preacher was passing through Washington, DC, returning from the organizational meeting of the General Missionary Convention in Philadelphia, he happened to meet an acquaintance who was in the company of James Monroe, then in the Cabinet of President James Madison and later to become president himself from 1816 to 1824. Furman was introduced to Monroe, who had heard of the flight of Furman from the British troops and the steadfast loyalty he had exhibited in the cause of American liberty. At Monroe's insistence, Furman preached before Congress, counting in his audience President Madison, the entire Cabinet, foreign ambassadors and other distinguished visitors. From various reports, it appears that hi message was eloquent and effective.[36]

In 1782, after hostilities had practically ceased in South Carolina, Furma returned to his beloved church at the High Hills. Now a mature twenty-seve years of age, he plunged into his work and study with a new zeal. Coo described how he helped his neighbors to survey their lands and doubtless t secure their titles after the confusion of the war. He continued to stud anatomy and to learn from Joseph Howard about medical treatment. H revealed his intense interest in education even this early in his life by assistin General Thomas Sumter and others in forming a library society and helpin organize a literary school at Stateburg, called Claremont Academy. Thi school had a Female Department and provided instruction in English mathematics, and the classical languages. The school closed in 1788, the yea after Furman left the High Hills church.[37]

An interesting anecdote about Furman also suggests his early interest i education. In 1785 the Charleston Association began a fraternal relationshi with the young Georgia Association. The Georgia representatives, Sila Mercer and Peter Smith, came to the High Hills church in that year to atten the annual session of the Charleston Association in early October. Mercer wa already well known for his piety and his leadership among Georgia Baptists He preached the associational sermon at the High Hills church on thi occasion. Georgia Baptists were in the midst of a controversy over th propriety of education for the ministry. Silas Mercer reflected the negativ attitude toward education in his interview with Furman at this meeting believing it to be unfriendly to religion.

> In the interview, however, he was fully convinced of its utility, and became not only an indefatigable student, but a zealous promoter of learning during the remainder of his life. Silas Mercer was the father of Jesse Mercer, and the patronymic is now indissolubly joined with higher education. Little did the young pastor at the Hills foresee the widespread and long-continued influence, in a great State like Georgia and beyond it, of those seed-thoughts which he was planting in the mind of Silas Mercer.[38]

This persuading of Silas Mercer to reverse his stand on a very controversia topic of Georgia Baptists also reflects the maturity of Furman, who was abl to speak with convincing logic to a man who was over ten years older than h and was known for following his convictions.[39]

The principal task of Furman, of course, was his work as pastor of the Hig Hills church. There had been no regular preaching in the area since 178 because of the war, and Furman was welcomed back with rejoicing an thanksgiving. In addition to his stated ministry at the High Hills, Furma continued his practice of carrying the gospel to the surrounding neighborhoods. Through his influence, principally after the war, branches of the High Hills church were formed at the Upper Fork of Lynches Creek (Flat Creek), Ebenezer (Jeffreys Creek), Second Lynches Creek, Bethel (Black River), Swift Creek, Camden, and Calvary.[40]

As has already been indicated, Furman was also active after 1782 in helping the Charleston church whose pastor had been gone since 1780. The appointment calendar of young Furman must have been completely filled every day in his unwearied activity of occupying his own pulpit, ministering to the flock at the High Hills, establishing over half-a-dozen branches of his church and supplying their needs, helping the Charleston church get a new start, serving three times as moderator of the Charleston Association in this period, preaching its sermon in 1786, and serving as a member of the important standing committee of the Charleston Association since 1779, not to speak of the extensive amount of studying and personal involvement in learning situations described by his biographer.

The busy pastor also shared in the losses common to preacher and people alike. In February, 1783, his father died at the High Hills, and since it was impracticable to secure another minister to officiate at the funeral, "it became his mournful duty to address a numerous and affected audience on the solemn occasion." In 1785, his infant son died, and in June, 1787, his wife Elizabeth was taken after a long illness. "The bereaved husband performed at her funeral the same sad office which had devolved on him at his father's."

The year 1787 was one of decision for Richard Furman. For at least three years he had been wrestling with the entreaties of the Charleston church for him to become their pastor. Although Oliver Hart had given ample reasons for not returning to the Charleston church, later correspondence between him and Furman suggested that Hart really had not put out of his mind the idea that he might return to his old pastorate. Perhaps it was this ambivalence on the part of Hart, plus the fact that Furman loved the High Hills church and was reluctant to leave her without a pastor, that made Furman's decision so difficult for him. Too, in the nearby cemetery was the fresh grave of his beloved companion, near those of his father and his infant son. Perhaps another factor that deterred him was the growing accpetance of his ministry at the High Hills. The church had substantially increased in size, so much so that the house of worship was often too small to accommodate the large congregation that had gathered. Furman finally became convinced, however, that he must answer the call of Charleston. So after the Charleston Association had adjourned its session at the High Hills, at which he presided as moderator, he held his farewell service in the High Hills church.

> His pathetic and solemn farewell discourse is still remembered [wrote his
> son Wood Furman]. On the day of his departure, his house was filled with

affectionate and weeping friends of whom after exhortation and praying
he took a tender adieu, accompanied by his mother and children.[41]

This was the kind of man who moved to Charleston as pastor in November
1787. He was mature beyond his thirty-two years. Indeed, one of the
outstanding indicators of the gifts of Richard Furman was his early matura
tion—physically, intellectually, and spiritually. His ability to sway individu
als and audiences seems not to have developed slowly and by degrees, but
like his body, resembled that of a mature person when he was but sixteen. Hi
powerful preaching was impressive even as a youth. Churches and pastor
usually were reluctant to ordain an eighteen-year-old, but Furman was matur
in every way at that age. His brilliant letter to the Tories, which had a telling
effect on their attitude toward the revolutionary war, was written when
Furman was barely twenty. In his diary, Oliver Hart remarked that on
"Saturday April ye 27 (1776) I assisted Rev. Richard Furman in ordaining Mi
Joseph Cook to the work of office of the Gospel of Ministry, at the High Hill
of Santee." Here was the fifty-one-year-old veteran pastor of the most
important church in South Carolina describing how he had assisted a twenty
year-old lad in the ordination of a twenty-six-year-old man. Neither Hart no
Cook seemed to feel that there was anything extraordinary about the
youthfulness of the High Hills pastor. On February 12, 1777, Hart addressed
a cordial and important letter to young Furman, and there is no hint of
condescension as he wrote his twenty-two-year-old fellow pastor.[42] Hi
maturity was such that all of his older friends seem to have been totally
oblivious to his youthfulness.

It should be added, however, that the new Charleston pastor never gave the
impression of being overly impressed with his own remarkable gifts. He wa
fond of company and often found himself overrun with friendly visitors
Although usually reserved in his demeanor, he would sometimes let his humo
and affability slip out on social occasions. After he had moved to Charlesto
and lived in the small parsonage which stood in the midst of the cemetery o
lot 62, he was wont to say to someone visiting him, "We live in a grave yard
it is true, but not so gloomy a place as might be imagined."

The church at Charleston rejoiced to secure this "inestimable prize." H
would lead her in the golden years of her history.

As he came to Charleston, the appearance of Furman was striking. He wa
about six feet in height and heavyset without being obese. His hair and eye
were dark. His large, open face, even in modern portraits, reveals a ma
without guile. His voice was clear and strong, and he articulated distinctly a
he spoke.

His dress, to the last like that of the older men of Charleston of that day,
was the costume of the Revolutionary times.—coat with pockets in the

skirts opening outwardly under a lapel, waistcoat reaching the hips, knee-
breeches and long stockings, the latter protected in foul weather or on a
journey by the high-topped boots.[43]

When preaching, Furman wore a gown and bands, perhaps copying his older
friend and predecessor at Charleston, Oliver Hart.

His preaching style was simple. His text was generally followed in the
outline of his message. His introduction emphasized the relevance of the text,
and was usually followed by three points and the application (called
"improvement"). He spoke extemporaneously, but was remarkably adept in
eliminating the repetition and redundancy that extemporaneous speakers often
develop.[44] William Bullein Johnson, later president of the General Missionary
Convention and of the Southern Baptist Convention, remembered how he as a
boy had heard the distinguished preacher in the pulpit. In every way, Johnson
said, Furman "was more solemn and imposing" than any other man he had
ever seen. "In the service of the sacred desk, such was the appropriate
solemnity of his manner, that the audience *felt* themselves to be in the
presence of a man of God."[45] Johnson went on to say,

> I remember hearing him, more than forty years ago, preach from the
> text,—"I am set for the defense of the Gospel"—it was truly a masterly
> effort. Never shall I forget his solemn, impressive countenance, his
> dignified manner, his clear statements of the Gospel doctrine and
> precepts, his unanswerable arguments in support of the Gospel's claim to
> a Divine origin, the lofty sentiments that he poured forth, the immovable
> firmness with which he maintained his position, and the commanding
> eloquence with which he enforced the whole argument.[46]

A young woman who had been in Furman's congregation from her
childhood, although she had heard some of the outstanding preachers of
North and South, placed Furman at the very top of her favorite preachers.

> Dr. Furman had a manner peculiar to himself; his voice excelled in
> melody; grace of action he possessed in an eminent degree. He lived and
> preached for eternity. He had power to move the affections and to warm
> the heart; and how many are now reaping the benefit of his prayers! To
> sound judgment and the exalted piety were added a sweetness and
> vivacity of manner which rendered him a charming companion.[47]

Along with his succinct, informative preaching style, Furman's lofty pulpit
presence and sober eloquence seemed to captivate his audience. His biographer remarked,

> Combining efforts of intellect, memory, judgment, personal advantages
> of figure, countenance and voice, he was in preaching peculiarly
> impressive; at once exemplifying the benevolent spirit of the gospel and
> inculcating its precepts with energy that commanded the respect of all.

> His delivery was animated but never vociferous. It was his special aim,
> by exhibiting divine truth in its simplicity and importance, to enlighten
> the understanding, to quicken the conscience, and produce the genuine
> effects of repentance and faith.[48]

Contemporaries of Furman always remembered his superlative gift of communication. There is a strong temptation to insert into the story a generous sampling of his uplifting and penetrating sermons. It is likely that the words of his sermons, however, would fail to capture the impact of the whole personality of Furman as he focused all of his intellectual, spiritual, and emotional gifts into the charged atmosphere of a worship service or a huge inspirational gathering. William B. Johnson sensed this holistic effect when he spoke of one of Furman's sermons, remarking that the great preacher was in "one of his tenderest frames, & seemed to reign over all hearts with irresistible influence."[49] A similar example involved his sermon before the distinguished delegates who met to organize the General Missionary Convention at Philadelphia on May 21, 1814. The program had been incomplete until the group had gathered for the organizational meeting, when it suddenly occurred to them that no one had been asked to prepare a sermon for the occasion. Belatedly, the leaders asked Furman to preach. He took for his text the promise of Christ in Matthew 28:20, "And, lo, I am with you alway, *even unto the end of the world.*" His simple outline gave no hint of his powerful call for all Baptists to unite in the proposed work of the new body. His closing appeal was masterful.

> Let the wise and good employ their counsels; the minister of Christ, who
> is qualified for the sacred service, offer himself for the work; the man of
> wealth and generosity, who values the glory of Immanuel and the
> salvation of souls more than gold, bring of his treasure in proportion as
> God has bestowed on him; yea, let all, even the pious widow, bring the
> mite that can be spared; and let all who fear and love God, unite in the
> prayer of faith before the throne of Grace; and unceasingly say, "Thy
> Kingdom come." And O! let it never be forgotten, that the Son of God
> hath said: "Lo, I am with you alway, even to the end of the world."
> Amen and Amen.[50]

No wonder the august body called for its publication with the documents of the Convention.

Furman's contemporaries spoke often of his ability as a counselor. Basil Manly, his successor as pastor at Charleston, once remarked about Furman "He was the wisest man I ever knew." To the sick and dying he seemed to have special unction.

> He appeared to know all the avenues of the heart, to perceive, at once,
> the very hinge on which turned the whole burden of grief, and to meet the
> more common possibilities of human woe with some seasonable relief.

> On such occasions, there was something in his manner which partook of a divine eloquence; when standing by the couch of the afflicted, he pointed to scenes of future rest, and spoke a word in season for the honor of God and the merciful designs of his discipline.[51]

When Furman presided over a meeting at the church or in some denominational body, he showed an intimate knowledge of parliamentary rules and conducted the service with ease, propriety, and dignity. "Indeed, his very appearance preserved order."

His writing style was excellent. When the Honorable Charles S. Todd, American ambassador to Russia and other nations, was asked to prepare a biographical sketch of John Gano, the distinguished pastor, evangelist, and chaplain, for use in Sprague's *Annals of the American Baptist Pulpit* in 1856, Todd responded by requesting that a eulogy of Gano prepared by Richard Furman fifty years earlier be substituted for his own effort. The beautiful pen portrait of Gano by Furman revealed the insight, the eloquence, and the orderly mind of the Charleston pastor. After a description of Gano's person (both when Gano was young and in later years) and educational training, Furman characterized his friend's spirit, nature, ministry, doctrines, patriotism, and closing years in a brief but glowing description that wasted not a single word. Some excerpts from this writing reveal the facile pen of Furman.

> His mind was formed for social intercourse and for friendship. Such was his unaffected humility, candour, and good-will to men, that few, if any, have enjoyed more satisfaction in the company of their friends, or have, in return, afforded them, by their conversation, a higher degree of pleasure and moral improvement. . . .
>
> As a minister of Christ, he shone like a star of the first magnitude in the American Churches, and moved in a widely extended field of action. . . . He was not deficient in doctrinal discussion, or what rhetoricians style the demonstrative character of a discourse; but he excelled in the pathetic,—in pungent, forcible addresses to the heart and conscience. The careless and irreverent were suddenly arrested, and stood awed before him; and the insensible were made to feel, while he asserted and maintained the honor of his God, explained the meaning of the Divine Law,—showing its purity and justice,—exposed the sinner's guilt— proved him to be miserable, ruined and inexcusable, and called him in unfeigned, immediate repentance. . . .
>
> He lived to a good old age; served his generation according to the will of God; saw his posterity multiplying around him; his country independent, free and happy; the Church of Christ, for which he felt and laboured, advancing. And thus he closed his eyes in peace; his heart expanding with the sublime hope of immortality and heavenly bliss.[52]

This preeminent pastor and eloquent preacher influenced Baptist life at many points. Far beyond the sound of his voice in the Charleston pulpit, he wa heard in the councils and programs of English and American Baptists; an being dead he yet speaketh. That story will be sketched in the followin chapter.

Notes

1. Manly, *Discourse,* p. 46.
2. Gilbert H. Barnes, *The Anti-Slavery Impulse, 1830-1844* (New York: Appleton Century-Crofts, 1933), p. 163.
3. Original of letters in Backus Collection, Newton, Massachusetts. Reprinted i the *Journal of Southern History,* November 1963, XXIX, No. 4, pp. 495-97.
4. Owens, *Hart,* p. 29.
5. Townsend, p. 29.
6. Mallary, *Botsford,* p. 63.
7. Manly, *Discourse,* p. 47.
8. Ibid., pp. 47-48.
9. Ibid., p. 47 n.
10. W. Furman, p. 61.
11. Joe M. King, *A History of South Carolina Baptists* (Columbia: R. L. Brya Company, 1964), p. 25.
12. Manly, *Discourse,* p. 50.
13. Henry A. M. Smith, "The Baronies of South Carolina," in SCH&GM, XV pp. 158-61.
14. Mallary, *Botsford,* pp. 63-64.
15. Ibid., p. 64.
16. Manly, *Discourse,* pp. 49-59.
17. Townsend, p. 227.
18. Ibid., p. 41.
19. Ibid., p. 48.
20. Ibid., p. 141 and 141 n.
21. Ibid., pp. 182-83.
22. Furman to Hart, February 7, 1786.
23. Mallary, *Botsford,* p. 66.
24. Manly, *Discourse,* pp. 65-70.
25. Ibid., p. 51.
26. Cook, *Furman,* p. 19.
27. Ibid., p. 4.
28. King, p. 21.
29. Cook, *Furman,* pp. 14-15.
30. Ibid., pp. 47-48.
31. Tupper, p. 134.
32. Cook, *Furman,* pp. 9-10.
33. For copy of this letter by Furman, see Loulie Latimer Owens, "Richar

Furman's 'Address on Liberty,'" in *Journal of the South Carolina Baptist Historical Society* (Greenville, S.C.: South Carolina Baptist Historical Society), XX, vol. 2, Nov. 1976, pp. 10-19.

34. Cook, *Furman,* pp. 51-52.

35. *Minutes,* Welsh Neck Baptist Church, 1738-1841, p. 22.

36. Cook, *Furman,* pp. 72-73.

37. Townsend, p. 285 n.

38. Tupper, p. 142.

39. C. D. Mallary, *Memoirs of Elder Jesse Mercer* (New York: John Gray, 1844), pp. 12-13.

40. Townsend, p. 153.

41. Cook, *Furman,* p. 19.

42. Ibid., pp. 56-57.

43. Tupper, p. 147.

44. Referred to in Charles G. Sommers, *Memoir of the Rev. John Stanford, D.D.; Late Chaplain to the Humane and Criminal Institutions in the City of New York* (New York: Swords, Stanford and Company, 1835), pp. 413 ff.

45. Sprague, p. 164.

46. Ibid.

47. Tupper, pp. 298-99.

48. Cook, *Furman,* pp. 8-9.

49. Sprague, p. 164.

50. Vail, pp. 389-93.

51. Cook, *Furman,* pp. 8-9.

52. Sprague, pp. 66-67.

Richard Furman

A Baptist Young People's Union banquet, July 2, 1925; setting is the Lecture Room.

Interior and exterior view of First Baptist Church circa 1909-11

Interior of sanctuary showing chancel area, 1982

Interior view of sanctuary made from pulpit area, 1982

Henry Erban pipe organ built circa 1845; photo made in 1982

Church beach house on Folly Beach

Church pastorium, 53 Church Street

48 Meeting Street Building—used for classrooms and offices

Dr. John A. Hamrick

John A. Hamrick Activities Building

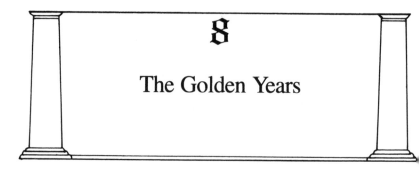

8

The Golden Years

Some of the pivotal events in American and world history occurred during the four decades almost spanned by the ministry of Richard Furman at Charleston from 1787 to 1825. Furman's extant writings reflect his knowledge of, and in some cases, participation in historic events in South Carolina, America, and the world.

Three years after his arrival in Charleston as pastor, Furman was called upon to assist in the constitutional development of his own state. The Legislature had called for the election of a convention to form a new constitution for the state and to determine the place to locate the permanent seat of the capital. Furman, along with several other clergymen of different denominations, was elected as a member of this convention.[1] He was requested to preach before the body, a task which he performed well. He showed himself to be an advocate of conciliation and mutual concessions in disagreements between delegates from the upper and the lower parts of the state, who were already showing sectional tendencies. He took an active part in the discussions over whether ministers should be excluded from seats in the Legislature because of their religious vocation. He felt that ministers owed it to their fellow citizens and the state to contribute to the support and defense of the state by serving as members of the Legislature. His efforts, however, were defeated by a quick-witted opponent of the measure.

> His allusion in debate to the intelligence and influence of the clergy as an argument for their eligibility, gave an adroit opponent occasion to pay him a compliment at the expense of his cause, and to point out the danger which he said might be apprehended from the influence of such a body of men, possessed of the eloquence and ability exhibited by this advocate.[2]

Furman was more successful in initiating legislation to abolish some surviving remnants of the former Anglican establishment.

The national constitutional convention had met shortly before Furman accepted the Charleston pastorate, but it required two years for the necessary number of states to ratify the new instrument. This involved a considerable

206

amount of discussion, since the new proposed constitution was not simply a
revision of the old Articles of Confederation under which the nation had
united after securing independence. The new instrument of government
cautiously shifted more power from the states to the central government,
providing a system of checks and balances designed to control the possible
abuse of power by any branch of government. South Carolina approved the
new constitution on May 23, 1788. However, before giving approval, Virginia
(probably influenced by Baptists in that state) exacted a solemn promise that a
Bill of Rights would be promptly adopted in order to safeguard by specific
statement some of the fundamental liberties of the people. The final
ratification of the new constitution was a victory for the Federalists—the
name given to those favoring the division of sovereignty between the states
and the central government. Leah Townsend classified Richard Furman (as
well as Henry Holcombe and Evan Pugh) as having Federalist sympathies.[3]
As one reads the eloquent eulogy delivered by Furman on the death of
Alexander Hamilton, as well as the strong political support accorded Charles
Cotesworth Pinckney, he would find it difficult to disagree with Leah
Townsend's evaluation.

Furman was aware of national and world events. His relationship with
leaders of the New American nation went far beyond preaching eulogies about
their achievements. He pondered the significance of the French Revolution
and the rise of Napoleon Bonaparte, the Louisiana Purchase of 1803, the
second war with England in 1812, the cession of Florida to the United States,
the era of good feeling under the presidency of his friend James Monroe, the
financial panic of 1819, and the Missouri Compromise of 1820. He sensed the
world-shaking importance of the invention of the cotton gin in 1793 by Eli
Whitney, the Yankee schoolmaster. He could not have failed to notice that
with this technological development the production of cotton by the southern
states jumped from two million pounds in 1791 to eighty million pounds by
1811; that short-staple cotton could now be grown profitably in the uplands;
and that the institution of Negro slavery, which had been dying in the
eighteenth century because it had become economically unprofitable, was
now resuscitated.

In addition to his involvement with state and national matters, Richard
Furman regularly performed many civic and patriotic duties. He was the
favorite orator for the Cincinnati and the American Revolution societies.
These were well-known patriotic bodies growing out of the revolutionary war.
The Cincinnati Society was founded in June, 1783, shortly before the
disbanding of the Continental army. It was named after Cincinnatus, the
famous Roman soldier-turned-farmer, in view of the approaching discharge of
the Continental officers from the army to return to civil life. Its principal
object was the raising of funds for widows and children of those who fell in

the war. George Washington was its first national president followed by Alexander Hamilton. Membership was limited to former officers in the revolutionary war and their descendants. Branches of this society, as well as the kindred American Revolution Society, were formed in the various states, much like the Daughters of the American Revolution organization later.

On the anniversary of George Washington's birth following his death in 1799, the American Revolution Society asked Furman, one of their members, to preach a commemorative sermon on the character and contributions of the first American president. He charmed a large and appreciative audience with this message. On July 4, 1802, Furman preached a patriotic sermon before the two societies concerning the responsibilities involved in the new political liberty the nation had won. Hymns sung on this occasion were composed by the versatile preacher. Similarly, when Alexander Hamilton was slain in a duel with Aaron Burr on July 11, 1804, the two societies asked Furman to deliver a eulogy on Hamilton. He took the occasion to condemn the practice of dueling. This message was printed and widely circulated. As one reads it many generations later, he is impressed with the earnest and scholarly eloquence of the preacher.

His civic activities were many: the founding of a society in 1795 at Charleston to encourage emigration of "virtuous citizens" from other countries; delivering an eloquent oration at the Charleston Orphan House in 1796; providing leadership to succor Charleston citizens when a succession of destructive fires swept the city in 1796; treating many patients (with remarkable success) during the yellow fever epidemic of 1796; and maintaining close friendship and active political support of Charles Cotesworth Pinckney.

However, it must not be overlooked that Richard Furman was first of all a man of religion. While sensitive to government, politics, economics, wars, and trade, his central concern was the relationship of men and women to God. He was much more impressed with the beginning of the modern foreign mission movement under William Carey and the Kettering band in 1792, for example, than with Bonaparte, the Louisiana Purchase, or the cotton gin. So, the principal thrust of this chapter will include Furman's pastoral ministry; his larger stewardship in forwarding ministerial education, local, and world missions; his splendid denominational leadership in the work of the local association, the formation and structure of the first national Baptist body for benevolent causes, and the development of the first Baptist state convention in the nation; his completion of a new house of worship for the Charleston church; and his last days and death.

With his mother and two children (Rachel and Wood), the new Charleston pastor moved into the parsonage at Charleston in early November, 1787.

Evidently his mother lived with them until after Furman remarried on May 5, 1789. The second wife was Dorothea Maria Burn, a gracious and talented Charleston girl. She was a remarkable woman, called "Dolly" by her devoted husband and "Mama" by her children and stepchildren. Richard Furman loved his home and his family, and, as Loulie Latimer Owens has pointed out, the children in their extant letters showed almost a reverence for him. A few days after the father's death, one of the children wrote to an absent member of the family, "O my brother, in the midst of all our grief should we not feel the debt of gratitude we owe to our heavenly father for granting us such an earthly parent!"

His gifted wife possessed considerable business acumen, assuming oversight of shipments of cotton from Furman's High Hills plantation and the return of the wagons loaded with salt and bagging. She was a deeply religious person, and the church rejoiced when she presented herself to be baptized by her husband in May, 1793.

In addition to becoming a loving parent to Rachel and Wood, her stepchildren, Dolly Furman bore her husband thirteen children, two of whom died in infancy. John Gano I was born in 1793, after Richard B. and Samuel, but lived only two years. The other children were Josiah Brodhead, Charles Manning, Maria Dorthea, Henry Hart, Sarah Susannah, John Gano II, Thomas Fuller, James Clement, Anne Eliza, and William Brantly. All of the surviving children were an honor to their parents; some were outstanding. Wood Furman became a teacher of the classics and wrote the *History of the Charleston Baptist Association* (1811). Richard B. Furman became a medical doctor and active Christian worker. Samuel and Josiah B. Furman were effective preachers. Charles M. Furman became an outstanding businessman. The most prolific writer of all the Furmans (including her father) was Sarah Susannah Furman, known as Susan. It is probable that she was the author of the biography of her father edited by H. T. Cook. John Gano Furman II was a creative writer and poet, trained for law, but he died at twenty-four. James Clement Furman was doubtless the best known of the children, giving fifty-five years of sacrificial service to the school that bears his father's name.[4]

Furman's mother was also a constant joy to him. She moved back to the High Hills plantation after her son remarried on May 5, 1789, but they remained close. One can catch the loving and humorous note in his letter to her on October 9, 1792, when he mentioned his astonishment at the "very good natured mistake" which must have been made when Rhode Island College conferred on him the honorary Master's degree. This school awarded him the honorary Doctor of Divinity degree in 1800, as did the state university of South Carolina in 1807. In his correspondence with his mother, he addressed her as "Honored Mother" and took delight in pleasing her. She died in October, 1794. Five months later, another blow came in the loss of his son. He wrote his sister to say,

> God has been pleased to make another Breach upon us in the death of our dear little John Gano, who was taken from our embraces the 24th of February, after suffering a severe and painful trial with the Rash, Fever and Measles.[5]

Two unrelated and seemingly incidental events occurred not long after Furman moved to Charleston. They speak eloquently of the gracious spirit of the new pastor. Edmund Botsford wrote into his journal that in 1788 he had "visited the city again, preached fifty-four sermons, and received presents from his kind friends which, at home, would have cost him nearly *one hundred and eighty dollars.*"[6] Only one person would have been in a position to provide Botsford a pulpit for fifty-four sermons. Undoubtedly Richard Furman had invited his old preacher friend to return to the church for this rather lengthy preaching ministry so that the people might have an opportunity to express their appreciation to Botsford in a substantial way for his effective assistance to the church while she was without regular pastoral leadership.

The other incident concerned Oliver Hart, the former pastor. Evidently Mrs. Hart, now transplanted from her beloved Charleston to Hopewell, New Jersey, missed the familiar environs of her early home and her children by her first husband. The correspondence between her and Oliver Hart after he had fled to New Jersey to escape the British, while she remained in Charleston for many months, revealed her great reluctance to leave Charleston. After going to Hopewell she must have continued to reflect on the joys of her Charleston home. Whatever may have been the triggering cause, Furman received word that Oliver Hart might desire to return to the Charleston church as pastor. Despite the fact that he had new babies in his home by his second wife and that the church had tripled in size since Hart left in 1780, Furman wrote a gracious letter on August 27, 1790, which said in part:

> I feel willing to obey the call of providence and should it appear to be the will of the ever blessed God you should return and be settled here, I should without reluctance seek some other place as my field of duty in the gospel service. It gives me sorrow to think that at your advanced period of life you should be straitened, besides the anxiety suffered by Mrs. Hart removed as she is from her children and relatives. Let me entreat you, dear sir, to use freedom with me and let me know your real sentiment.[7]

Oliver Hart, now within five years of the close of a long life and not in good health, recognized that he was not physically able to carry on the activities of the growing Charleston pastorate. Furman never lost his deep regard for Hart and upon learning of Hart's death in late 1795, he preached a beautiful sermon at Charleston on February 7, 1796, using the title, "Rewards of Grace Conferred on Christ's Faithful People."

Furman's Pastoral Ministry

From his busy pastoral service at High Hills, Richard Furman moved to an equally demanding ministry in Charleston. In a letter to Oliver Hart on July 21, 1788, he said,

> As I was determined to make full proof of my ministry at the High Hills before I left that place; for upwards of twelve months before my departure, I undertook personal visitation through an extent of near thirty miles, as well as frequent preaching, together with society meetings held in different places as a means to promote Christian knowledge and experience. An attendance to these prevented my paying any attention, almost to the common concerns of life.
>
> And since I have been in Charleston I have till within a fortnight preached twice on the Lord's day and an evening in the week besides; which with visiting, the cares of a family, making, repairing, etc., and some calls into the country, leave me very little time to spare. The fifteenth day of June was a twelve months, since I lost the companion of my life which in a variety of respects has been the means of opening the avenues of pain to my heart.[8]

It would be expected, of course, that the sermons of the grave and eloquent pastor of the Baptist church in Charleston would attract many listeners, especially since his patriotic character had been demonstrated so widely during the recent war. It is likely that some in the Charleston church who heard this outstanding preacher deliver an impressive address from the pulpit might have wondered if such a dignified and solemn orator would unbend enough to be a real pastor to the flock. They had no reason for uneasiness. Furman had a pastor's heart. He exhibited in his pastoral ministry a winsome charm and personal empathy with the people that causes any pastor to be loved. The formal portrait of him that appears in many books may have been the way he looked as he took his text in the pulpit, but when he walked with his people in their times of need or of joy, his speech was gracious and his heart was warm. One of the young women who grew up in the Charleston church, Mrs. Eliza Yoer Tupper, set down fond recollections of her pastor. Her mother, she said, was the last person baptized in the baptistry which then was located on the old church lot 62 on Church Street. This occurred on October 28, 1798. Her father, Samuel Yoer, was the first person to be immersed in the new baptistry on February 3, 1799, located in what became known as the

Mariner's church. Eliza then recalled her own baptism by the same pastor:

> As I stepped down into the water, my dear pastor whispered in my ear,
> "My dear child, how happy your sainted father would have been could he
> have witnessed this scene." He baptized me as "Elizabeth."

When Furman visited her home after the birth of her child, she never forgot
how he

> made a solemn dedicatory prayer for our household, not forgetting baby
> Samuel Yoer. He fervently asked God's blessings on our child that he
> might be like the child Samuel in the Bible, and also like his sainted
> grandfather, whose name he bears.[9]

From Elizabeth's pen also came a description of some of the other pastoral
ministries of Richard Furman. She related how he preached three sermons on
Sunday and one on Thursday night. In addition, he would regularly attend a
social gathering at the house of a member, during which he would read from
some good author to those who were present.

> Dr. Furman read from Bunyan's "Holy War," and we children laughed at
> some of the incidents in that wonderful book, and we were glad to be able
> to say, when gently reproved, "We saw *mother* laugh."

In Furman's early years at Charleston, the Sunday School movement had not
yet been developed, but he would hold quarterly seasons to quiz anywhere
from sixty to one hundred children over the material in Keach's Baptist
Catechism.

> The girls standing at the south of the pulpit, the boys, meeting them in
> the centre, to the north, Dr. Furman would in his majestic, winning
> manner, walk down the pulpit steps and with book in hand, commence
> asking questions, beginning with the little ones (very small, indeed,
> some were, but well taught and drilled at home.) We had to memorize the
> whole book, for none knew which questions would fall to them. I think I
> hear at this very moment the dear voice of our pastor, saying, "A little
> louder, my child," and then the trembling sweet voice would be raised a
> little too loud. It was a marvel to visitors on these occasions, the
> wonderful self-possession and accuracy manifested by the whole class.
> . . . What a pity that such a course of instruction has been abandoned.[10]

The first Sunday School was organized in July, 1816, in the school room of
Wood Furman, the pastor's son. Robert Missildine was the first superintendent. The Sunday School was soon moved to the church building, but there are
no specific records of the attendance and organization during the remainder of
Richard Furman's pastorate.

A part of the pastoral ministry of Furman involved the large black
membership of his church. On January 11, 1795, Bishop Francis Asbury of

the Methodist church attended a service at the Baptist church and commented on the excellent sermon of Furman. He remarked that there were probably no more than 70 white hearers in this service. Leah Townsend judged that since the church had over 240 members at this time, most of them probably were Negroes.[11] However, in another discussion she noted that the records listed only 63 black members by 1800.[12] Probably the black membership grew rapidly at about the turn of the century. On January 28, 1830, Abram Rogers, who had been a member of the church before Furman became pastor, said that black members multiplied after the conversion of Peter Wood, a leader among them, who died in April, 1809. Rogers said that before the work of Wood the black members numbered no more than a dozen.[13] The minutes of the Charleston Association in 1827, shortly after the close of Furman's pastorate, showed that the church had 862 members, of whom 697 were Negroes and 165 were whites.

Furman himself reflected the attitude of his culture on the question of the rightness of Negro slavery. Although in the early 1800s he had written that this system was undoubtedly an evil, he later became its defender from the Scriptures. At the time of his death he owned over two dozen slaves. He was kind to them and used every effort to assist them in their bondage, but his relation to them was one of paternalism.[14] At the bicentennial anniversary of the church in 1882, one of the addresses concerned the ministry of the Charleston church to the Negroes, evidently prepared by H. A. Tupper. He recalled sitting in the church for worship services with "the immense crowd of negroes in the north gallery." He made reference to the Negro Sunday School "superintended from its origin to its conclusion by members of the writer's family." The use of the catechism, especially for the children, was a part of the training of Negro members. Tupper closed with the general statement:

> But never will the time come when negroes shall have truer friends and more devoted laborers for their religious welfare than was the Old First Church, with regard to which it shall be said of many a rejoicing African in the other world: "This and that man was born in her." Yea, is it not true that in the two hundred years of this church its colored children greatly exceeded the number of whites born of her by the Spirit of God? And is this not a fact worthy of prominent and grateful record, that the greatest harvesting of souls in this vineyard of the Lord, from William Screven to Edwin T. Winkler, was among the sons and daughters of Ethiopia?"[15]

Not only did the Charleston church find Richard Furman to be an oustanding preacher and a warmhearted pastor, but as well the people learned that he was an excellent administrator. It has already been mentioned that the church had secured sole title to lot 62 where the original church building and the parsonage stood. This property would become the location of the permanent church edifice which was erected later during the pastorate of Furman.

It will be recalled that before the incorporation of the church under the provisions of the charter obtained in 1778, all temporal matters were handled through trustees elected by the church. Furman felt that the interests of the church would be better served by functioning under the provisions of the church's charter of incorporation. Accordingly, a committee was named consisting of Thomas Screven, William Inglesby, Thomas Rivers, E. North, Isham Williams, John McIver, and the pastor to prepare a constitution and bylaws amenable to the charter of 1778. On August 21, 1791, the church voted to accept this constitution, and with amendments agreed to on April 2, 1824, this instrument has provided the permanent principles under which the incorporated church at Charleston has continued to operate.[16]

The excellence of Furman as an administrator may be glimpsed also in his financial leadership of the church. The rather substantial permanent fund of the church had been lost during the revolutionary war. Working with his leaders, Furman continued the plan of renting pews for worship services of the church, not only to church members but to nonchurch members who desired them. Although this practice is unusual in a Baptist church of the twentieth century, it was not uncommon in the eighteenth century. Furman explained in 1822 to the young state convention in South Carolina how the system worked. The church would rent a pew at the rate of from about $10.00 to $60.00 per year, depending upon the desirability of the pew's location. Free pews were provided for the poor and for strangers. Through the income derived from pew rents, the church could calculate in advance approximately how much support the minister could expect from this source. The system had its advantages. An entire family could be assured of sitting together where the parents could supervise the attendance and conduct of the children, and if a friend of the pewholder happened to visit, he would be assured of a good seat for the services. Although Furman did not mention it, another advantage of this arrangement would be that the preacher could easily tell which ones of his flock were not attending regularly. Furman felt that pew renting would encourage the erecting of more spacious houses of worship, which would tend to forward the work of Christ and make it more convenient to accommodate larger numbers for the observance of the ordinances.[17]

The effectiveness of Furman as a preacher, pastor, and church administrator is reflected in the records of the church. Certainly, his success in the work of the local congregation was fundamental to all of the other achievements of Richard Furman. This was his first responsibility. Had his church not prospered, the Charleston pastor would not have been so uniformly renowned in other areas of work. Most of the growth of the Charleston church during the

Furman years came through regular day-by-day and year-by-year development, not through sporadic and sudden bursts of activity. It is true that there were occasional seasons of widespread revival. A post-war revival reached its climax in 1789 after the spiritual depression of the Revolution, and Furman baptized thirty-one in the Charleston church.[18] The Second Great Awakening in Kentucky and Tennessee occurred in the opening years of the nineteenth century, and some of its enthusiasm spread to the east coast. Furman himself, hearing of the unusual emotional manifestations in some of these meetings, rode to one such revival at the Waxhaws near the North Carolina border on May 21, 1802, about 170 miles from Charleston. He wrote an extended account of the meeting where he estimated that from three to four thousand people had assembled. It appeared from his description that he was not overwhelmed by what he saw, but he reported in a balanced and restrained way both the good and the "incidental evils" that he witnessed.[19] Another period of revival occurred in the church during 1822-23, and many young people were converted at this time including Furman's second son, Richard.[20]

However, it must be apparent from the records that the church moved forward principally by the regular and faithful ministries of the pastor, not from the occasional revival seasons. It is true that Furman baptized thirty-one in the revival of 1789, but he had baptized twenty-five in 1788; he baptized twenty-six in the revival of 1804, but he baptized twenty-nine, twenty-two, thirty-seven, thirty-eight, and forty-eight in the next five years, respectively; in his last revival period, he baptized thirty-eight in 1822 and forty-three in 1823, but he had baptized an average of almost forty-four per year for the previous ten years in the church. While the revival seasons of 1789, 1804, and 1822-23 doubtless were significant periods in the church, the in-between years were quite as fruitful.

For the first time in the history of the church, a record of the members making up the corporation was preserved for the years 1793-1800.[21] They were listed as follows: Thomas Rivers, Ichabod Atwell, Thomas Screven, Thomas Ross, John Hart, Charles McDonald, Richard Furman, Benjamin Baker, George Yoer, Samuel Rivers, Charles Screven, Joseph Johnson, David Adams, Anne Brown, Margaret McCartey, Susanna North, _____ Rivers, Mary Seymour, _____ Gourlay, Esther Smith, Ann Hart, Mary Anne McIver, Sarah Johnson, Amarinthe Screvin, Mary Screvin, Beatrix Thomson, _____ Poyas, Margaret Theadcraft, Martha Inglesby, _____ Rouse, Elizabeth Gilbert, _____ Langford, Esther Bellamy, _____ Goodwin, _____ Lawrence, Mary Adams, _____ Boucheneau, _____ Ross, Elizabeth Calvert, Henrietta Roberts, Sarah Henning, _____ Henning, _____ Bonnote, Elizabeth Stuart, Dorothea M. Furman, Eleanor Beaty, Rachel Furman, Grace Cain, Mehitable Blackwell, Grace Hampton, Arabella Evanse, Sarah Clarke, Elizabeth Nichols, Ann Rivers, Katherine Prisgar,

1818	44	7	0	0	0	11	680
1819	35	7	1	1	0	13	707
1820	39	4	13	3	4	14	724
1821	45	0	1	0	0	12	757
1822	38	4	6	2	0	7	751
1823	43	4	3	2	3	20	776
1824	19	4	6	2	3	14	780
1825	15	6	0	3	4	14	780[22]

The rapid and continuous growth of the church during the ministry of Richard Furman created increasing pressure to erect a new and larger building for worship. The church had been meeting in the building known as the "Mariner's church" since 1748 after the litigation in the legislature over the original lot 62. A petition from the Charleston church to the legislature on February 14, 1787, resulted in the awarding of this property to the church, totally excluding all claims to its use by other groups. This was the spot where William Screven and the original company erected the first Baptist meeting-house in the South about eighty-seven years earlier. During his thirty-eight-year pastorate at Charleston, Furman baptized 1,077 people, and the church membership roll grew from 178 to 780. It is no wonder that the members clamored for larger quarters.

As early as 1805, the pastor presented the church with a lot in Saint Paul's parish (Colleton county), valued at $1,000 at the time, indicating that when the church was ready to build a new meetinghouse, this lot should be sold and the proceeds applied to that purpose. In 1807, William M. Turner donated a lot in Hempstead for the benefit of this same object. When the Religious Society formed in 1755 by Oliver Hart became extinct in 1810, its funds were transferred to the church in accordance with the original provisions of the society's founders. From these and other gifts the church received about $7,000. This amount was increased to more than $20,000 when friends in the congregation and in other denominations circulated a subscription paper in 1815 and from the proceeds of the sale later on of the old church building.

Thus, on October 22, 1817, the church named a building committee composed of William Rouse, George Gibbs, Tristram Tupper, Richard B. Furman, and James Nolan. After several delays, work was begun on the new building on old lot 62, a spot rich in the history of the church. On September 19, 1819, in a solemn service, the pastor laid the cornerstone containing valuable historical documents at a point under the southeast corner of the new edifice. The last service in the building which had housed the church for seventy-seven years was held on Sunday, January 13, 1822.

> In the evening, Dr. Furman, deeply penetrated with the varied reflections which the occasion inspired, and scarcely able to command himself, took

leave of the consecrated spot, with sobbing and many tears; the feeling of the flock were scarcely less intense than his own; and the place of their pasture was now literally a Bochim, a place of weeping.[23]

On the following Thursday (January 17, 1822), the new edifice was opened for worship with a sermon by the pastor. He chose the appropriate text, "But Jehovah said unto David my father, Whereas it was in thy heart to build a house for my name, thou didst well that it was in thy heart" (ASV). This new place of worship was designed by South Carolinian Robert Mills, the distinguished American architect and outstanding benefactor, and exhibited

the best specimen of correct taste in architecture of the modern buildings in the city. It is purely Greek in its style, simply grand in its proportions and beautiful in its detail.

The plan is of the temple form divided into four parts—the portico, vestibule, nave and vestry rooms. The whole length of the building is 110 feet, and breadth, 60 feet. The facade presents a portico of four massive colums of the highest proportions of the Doric, surmounted by a pediment. Behind the main wall rises an attic story squared up to the height of the roof and crowned by a cupola or belfry. The side walls of the building are opened by the requisite apertures for windows and doors, and a full cornice runs around the whole.[24]

The move of the church to the new building marked the occasion for "the most extensive revival of religion during the ministry of Dr. Furman in Charleston." Many young people were converted during this revival, the pastor himself evidently leading all of the services. Several young men were ordained to the ministry during this period. Robert Missildine had come to Charleston from England and evidently was active in Sunday School and church life. He had been employed for home mission work and had displayed gifts for preaching. On July 23, 1821, he shared with the Charleston church his desire to become a minister and on that day was licensed. In May, 1823, at the request of the church, he was ordained as an evangelist. This action was taken because Missildine had not yet been called as pastor by a church, and this practice was not uncommon among Baptist churches of that time. In November, 1823, he became pastor of the Bethel church in Sumter district.

Cyrus Pitt Grosvenor had come to Charleston as an Independent minister from Massachusetts to raise funds for Amherst College. During this revival he made the decision that the immersion of believers was the only proper baptism. On May 18, 1823, Furman baptized him, and he united with the Charleston church. Another young man, Daniel Sheppard, had come to South Carolina from New Jersey, and he joined the church by letter during this revival. The two were ordained as "evangelists" by Furman and W. T. Brantly, the latter evidently still at the Beaufort church. It is one of the ironies of history that two of the outstanding abolitionists of the next generation were related to the Charleston church. It is known that Cyrus P. Grosvenor was a member, and William H. Brisbane assisted in ordinations at the church and may have been a member. Brisbane will be mentioned in the following chapter, since he was related to the church during the ministry of Basil Manly. Grosvenor became pastor of the Georgetown church after his ordination, but returned to New England to serve as pastor at Salem, Massachusetts. Here he identified himself as a militant abolitionist by 1833.[25]

The Larger Stewardship

In his address at the sesquicentennial of the church in 1832, Basil Manly remarked that while Richard Furman was very conscientious in fulfilling the pastoral needs of his congregation, "yet he was not insensible to the claims of missionary labor," and that he served a church "that seconded the enlarged desires and liberal views of his own mind."[26] This larger stewardship beyond the local pastoral ministry was a part of Furman's concern even before he accepted the call of the Charleston church in 1787. It can be glimpsed after his move to Charleston in his effective leadership in behalf of ministerial education, in his zeal for local or domestic missions, and in his interest in the early modern foreign mission movement.

Equipping for Ministry.—The concern of Furman for the education of the ministry has already been mentioned. As he began his work in Charleston he learned that interest had declined in the support of the Religious Society which Oliver Hart had organized to aid young ministers with their education. It had not functioned since Hart fled in 1780 to escape the British army. Furman had already called for the involvement of the Charleston Association in ministerial education while he was pastor at High Hills in 1785. He renewed this call after moving to Charleston, and the story of his successful effort will be told in connection with the Charleston Association shortly.

Continuing a Territorial Ministry.—The same type of territorial ministry that Furman had exercised while at High Hills was developed at Charleston. Not long after settling there, Furman received an appeal from some of his congregation residing at Georgetown, about sixty miles northeast of Charleston. Baptists had lived in this area for many years. The first pastor of the Charleston church, William Screven, had retired and died here in 1713. His son, Elisha Screven, laid out the site of what is now Georgetown, and specifically reserved an acre of land on lot 228 as a site for a Baptist meetinghouse and burial ground. Little is known about the settling of a church there until after William Cuttino was converted under the ministry of Oliver Hart in 1767. Later, in 1780, on his flight from the British who had taken Charleston, Hart was welcomed at Cuttino's home in Georgetown before moving northward. On July 21, 1788, Furman wrote to Hart in Hopewell, New Jersey, saying that he had preached twice in Georgetown that spring and on the last visit had baptized Mrs. Cuttino and her oldest son and had administered the Lord's Supper to twelve communicants. Six other applicants had been received before Furman left Georgetown.[27]

Desirous of securing a pastor for the Georgetown congregation, Furman wrote to James Manning, president of Rhode Island College, and John Rippon, editor of the *Baptist Annual Register* in London, inquiring about someone to minister at Georgetown. Manning recommended John Waldo, a licentiate and teacher, who came to Georgetown and temporarily served the congregation while teaching school. Rippon read Furman's letter at a meeting of ministers in London. This group quickly mentioned that William Staughton, a young minister twenty-three years of age, had expressed a deep desire to serve in America. Staughton had been converted at Birmingham, England, six years before; had studied at the Baptist Theological School in Bristol; and, despite his youth, had acquired a reputation for being an outstanding preacher and a "star in the denomination." Indeed, he had declined a call to the important Northampton Baptist Church because of his desire to preach in America. He arrived in Charleston in October, 1793. He assisted Furman in the organization of the Georgetown church in June, 1794, with thirty-six members. He was soon married to Maria Hanson by Furman and became pastor of the Georgetown church. After about two years, Staughton moved to New York, where he began an illustrious ministry in the northeast.[28]

In another instance of local missionary activity, Richard Furman was called upon in 1795 by some of his members who had moved to Savannah, Georgia, to assist them in the formation of a church there. There was no Baptist meetinghouse in Savannah, but because of the esteem for Furman by the Presbyterian and Episcopal pastors in Savannah, he was invited to preach in their houses of worship. On Sunday and weekday evenings he preached to large audiences. A Baptist church was organized there on November 26, 1800, and Henry Holcombe became her pastor.[29] An interesting experience occurred in Savannah several years later. In January, 1804, Furman went there as a messenger of the Charleston Association to the Savannah River Association, which had been formed in 1802. While there he assisted in the ordination of Joseph Clary, who had surrendered to the ministry after serving as a distinguished federal judge for Georgia. Later in the spring, Clary preached to overflow crowds in Furman's church at Charleston. This experience was repeated two years later on a second visit by Clary to Charleston.[30]

How much Furman had to do with the organization of the Beaufort church on January 27, 1804, is uncertain. This congregation had long been an arm of the Euhaw church, and over 150 members (18 of them whites) had been present to constitute the new body. Furman preached the sermon, "made the surrendering prayer, and pronounced the newly constituted body a regularly formed church of Christ." His protege, Joseph Bullein Cook, became the pastor.[31]

Although it did not result in the formation of a new church, Furman endangered his health in an effort to assist the church at Wassamaw in 1802-1803. This congregation was without a pastor, and Furman rode the thirty miles there to preach to them on weekdays, while carrying on his own services at Charleston on Sundays. While this ministry considerably strengthened the church at Wassamaw, the drain on Furman's health caused by exposure and exhaustion put him to bed with fever in June, 1803, after preaching there for three successive days and braving inclement weather on the journey.

Other local missionary efforts of Furman are hinted at but not described in the records. Basil Manly said that the gathering of the Goose Creek and Mount Olivet churches in 1812 followed "in a measure" Furman's activity.[32] Additional labors of this sort probably were not recorded or the records were not retained.

Answering the Foreign Mission Call.—The inauguration of the modern foreign mission movement under William Carey about 1792 immediately enlisted Richard Furman in the cause of foreign missions. In fact, even before the challenging appeal of Carey at the Northampton Association in that auspicious 10:00 o'clock sermon on May 31, 1792, Furman had been in correspondence with Samuel Pearce of Birmingham, John Sutcliff of Olney, and John Ryland of Northampton, who had ordained Carey and who, with Carey and Andrew Fuller, would soon constitute the Immortal Five to launch the foreign mission enterprise from Kettering in early October, 1792. Harvey T. Cook underscored Furman's interest in this project.

> The early ministrations of Mr. John Thomas in India, the formation of the Baptist Missionary Society in England, its sending out of Dr. Carey and his coadjutors, the consequent formation of the London Society and the zeal and harmony which it exhibited took strong hold of his affection, and engaged his earnest wishes, hopes and prayers.[33]

As a matter of fact, Richard Furman was involved in the context out of which the foreign mission work of William Carey developed. During the first two decades of the eighteenth century, England was stirred by the challenge of engaging in intercessory prayer for world missions. In 1746, the appeal for continued prayer for this cause was made in Boston, and Jonathan Edwards, the Congregationalist theologian and pastor, was deeply moved. In 1748, he published an appeal for worldwide Concert of Prayer for missionary work, which was reprinted again and again during the next century.[34] Alert to engage the Charleston church in such a significant movement, Furman set aside the first Tuesdays in January, April, July, and October for his church to observe this Quarterly Concert of Prayer for world missions. The exact date of the inauguration of this program has not been recorded, but by 1795 this observance was recommended to the churches of the Charleston Association. After 1810, the Charleston church observed a Monthly Concert of Prayer on the first Monday evening of each month after the pattern of the Nottingham Association in Great Britain, who had initiated this monthly movement on June 3, 1784.[35]

After the organization of the English Baptist missionary society, Furman took an active interest in the movement. In 1805-1806, with others, he was successful in securing generous offerings of funds for assisting the English missionaries Carey, Marshman, and Ward in translating the Scriptures into Indian dialects.

A significant offshoot of Furman's interest in missions occurred in 1807. In that year he visited Edisto Island, about forty miles south of Charleston, and by his preaching was able to win several whites and a large number of Negroes. Probably among his converts at this time was Mrs. Hephzibah Jenkins Townsend, although the time is not certain. She was the child of a revolutionary war officer, Captain Daniel Jenkins, and his frail young wife, Hephzibah Frampton Jenkins. When the father was imprisoned by the British in Charleston, the dying mother entrusted her baby to two faithful slaves known only as Jack and Jean. They were told to take the child to Edisto Island and give her to the Townsend family for safekeeping. The six-day journey from Charleston to Edisto Island through the marsh creeks in order to avoid detection by the enemy must have worked some mysterious alchemic change in the baby, for after Hephzibah Jenkins Townsend came to her maturity she never lost her concern for black people. The Townsends were Presbyterians, but their adopted daughter became a Baptist, probably during the services of Richard Furman on the island in 1807. It seems certain that she had become a Baptist at least by this time and rather regularly attended the preaching services of Furman, accompanied by eight of her black friends who poled the dugout boats to Charleston from the island at high tide. Inspired by the missionary sermons of her pastor, she determined to have a personal share in this enterprise. Building a large tabby oven from crushed oyster shells, she began baking golden brown gingerbread in long pans. With this start, she sent a note to some of her women friends in the neighborhood to stop for a visit at Bleak Hall, her lovely home. Over tea, she discussed the need for mission support with them, pointing out that there were many ways to raise funds. Hephzibah then led them to the huge oven which at that very time was gracing the entire neighborhood with the fragrant odor of fresh-baked bread. To the astonished women she explained how her pastor had spoken of Miss Mary Webb of Boston and the organization of a "mite society" for missions. By selling this bread, Hephzibah concluded, money could be raised for missions, and she noted that each woman had particular talents that could be so utilized. The other women were enthusiastic and shared ideas as to how they might earn money for missions.

Thus was born, at least by 1811, the Wadmalaw and Edisto Female Mite Society, the first organized mission society by women in South Carolina. In 1812, the society gave $122.50 to the mission fund of Charleston Association. Inspired by the work of Hephzibah Townsend, the women of South Carolina organized mite societies all across the state.[36]

It should be added that Hephzibah Townsend revived the old Baptist church which the Charleston church had established on Edisto Island in 1730. With the assistance of her Charleston pastor, she secured title to the land, and he helped dedicate a church building there in 1818. The building was later given to the black congregation and became the meetinghouse of the Negro Edisto Island Baptist Church, which in 1980 is vigorously alive.

The Denominational Architect

Richard Furman utilized the denominational bodies that existed in his day and, beyond that, became one of the chief architects of new structures for denominational cooperation. Furman lived most of his life at a time when denominational organizations beyond the local churches and associations were unknown. Conditioned by his long relationship with the Charleston Association and unfettered by inhibitions about the dangers which many thought were inherent in additional denominational structures, Furman's orderly mind quickly conceived of additional patterns for denominational bodies that could be utilized for tasks beyond the scope of Baptist churches and associations. He had been immunized from provincialism by his wide contacts with leaders of all denominations and by his correspondence with Baptist leadership in all parts of the world. Although the physical labor involved in letter writing was distasteful to him, he faithfully engaged in correspondence with leaders among Baptists in the North and in England. He was recognized as the principal Baptist leader in denominational affairs in South Carolina. For example, when Rippon's *Baptist Annual Register* was published in 1791, an advertisement in the minutes of the Charleston Association informed those interested in securing this work to contact Furman of Charleston. Out of this context he became one of the leaders in the resuscitation of the Charleston Association (which had suspended its meetings because of the revolutionary war), in the formation of the first national benevolent body in 1814, and in the organization of the first state body in the United States in 1821. He brought to each of these bodies the zeal and insights he had reflected since his first pastorate at High Hills of Santee.

The Charleston Association.—It will be recalled that in 1779, just before the revolutionary war engulfed South Carolina, the Charleston Association had named a special committee to manage their affairs in the emergency they were facing, and Richard Furman was a member of this group. There is no record of the meeting of this committee during the trauma of the war, but in 1783, at the first meeting of the association after the conflict had subsided, this committee was again named and Furman became its head. With the withdrawal of Oliver Hart, Furman was thrust into the role of the principal leader in the association after the war. He dominated the Charleston Association from this time until his death in 1825. His name appeared as moderator, secretary, preacher of the associational sermons, and writer of the annual Circular Letters to the churches much more than any other person. He was named regularly to correspond for the association with similar bodies elsewhere, and headed special committees to aid the Philadelphia Association in publishing religious information and to help Rhode Island College.

The existence of this special *ad interim* committee to handle the affairs of the association and the emergence of Furman as the leader of the association prepared the way for the events of the next several years as Furman endeavored to involve the association in the movement to forward ministerial education. It is an interesting commentary on Furman's initiative and continuing efforts for the education of young ministers that when he died in 1825, one of his protégés, Joseph B. Cook, delivered a moving eulogy before the association describing Furman as their "beloved father in the Gospel" and singled out the program for ministerial education of the association as the outstanding achievement of Furman through the association. The events of this period confirm this evaluation of Furman's contribution. In 1785, even before he had become pastor at Charleston, Furman wrote Hart that he had "snatched a few minutes just before the meeting [of the Charleston Association] and drew up the plan" which he submitted to the association suggesting that the body be incorporated under the laws of the state in order that it might hold funds and annuities for use in assisting young ministers in their education.[37] The attendance at the associational meeting in 1786 was so small that no action was taken, but Furman wrote the annual Circular Letter advocating the plan.[38] When the suggestion for incorporating the association was renewed in 1787, Edmund Botsford, a close friend of Furman, objected strenuously. Botsford's biographer wrote:

> It was the desire of some to raise an Association fund, the proceeds of which should be expended in the education of indigent, pious young men, called of God to the gospel ministry; and that this fund might be secured and managed to the best advantage, it was proposed that the Association should apply to the Legislature for an act of incorporation. Mr. Botsford, with others, was much opposed to this latter scheme. He contended, that the Association was purely and strictly an advisory council, that this important feature should be sacredly guarded; but that it

would be destroyed by investing the body with corporate powers, and therefore he was obliged to oppose the measure. He did not probably take a proper view of the subject; but it was by no means surprising that our pious fathers should have exercised a severe and rigid jealousy over the rights of the churches, in these early days, and that they should at first have looked with dread upon many measures, which at present, are regarded as not only harmless, but useful and necessary.[39]

In a letter to Oliver Hart, Botsford confessed that he had "considerable mercury in his constitution" and expressed deep regret if he had been intemperate in his opposition. The favoring of such denominational concentration of authority by both Hart and Furman speaks of their centralizing ecclesiology and confidence in denominational structures.

Although Botsford later wrote Furman that he would "forbear speaking and writing anything about it," Furman felt it expedient not to press for incorporation of the associational body. Instead, in 1789 Furman prepared a plan by which churches in the association would have a "charity" sermon preached once a year by their pastor, followed by a collection for ministerial education and, significantly, for any other religious and public uses the church might wish for these funds. Furman evidently was anticipating what later developed: that the association would foster other denominational benevolences in addition to ministerial education. These funds would be entrusted to the association, and a committee of the body, made up of one member from each church in the association, would control the expenditure of the money. This same committee would examine candidates for ministerial assistance and guide them in their educational pursuits for ministry. Furman said that specific rules for the work of this committee would be submitted later and requested that this committee, rather than the association, be incorporated under the laws of the state for collecting and disbursing these funds. When the rules were presented to the association in 1791, it is interesting to note that they provided authority for the committee also to take possession of any "glebes or other property" which belonged to the churches related to the association which were or would become extinct and liable to revert to the public or become private property.[40] Botsford raised no objection to this plan, but Evan Pugh, another influential leader of the association, expressed his disagreement. However, Furman was able to win him over, and the association approved all of the proposals of the committee.[41] That Furman was not insensitive to the autonomy of Baptist churches may be seen from the fact that the independence of the churches in both spiritual and temporal matters was vigorously asserted in his plan.

In 1792, Furman prepared a petition for the state legislature to incorporate the General Committee for the Charleston Baptist Association Fund. He was elected its first president and served in that capacity until his death in 1825.

During this time at least thirty young men were helped, either wholly or in part, from the fund, including such leaders as Joseph Bullein Cook, whom Furman encouraged and inspired; Jesse Mercer, the Georgia stalwart; John M Roberts, the gifted scholar and educator; and William T. Brantly, eloquent pastor at Philadelphia and Charleston, who would preach the funeral sermon for Furman. The treasurer of the committee from its beginning until his death in 1804 was Charleston member Thomas Screven, son-in-law of Oliver Har and great-grandson of William Screven. Furman led his church in the liberal support of this educational ministry through the association.

> Its liberality was perennial and in the end the sum total exceeded the amount given by the remainder of the Association. This long period of its history stands out without a parallel in all Baptist history in intermittent giving to the cause of education.[42]

Cook also remarked that the white members of the church averaged about two dollars per member for thirty-six consecutive years for this cause, in addition to providing a larger sum per member for missions during the last ten years o Furman's ministry. After assisting several dozen men, the fund still had a surplus in 1825 of $7,791.86.[43] Year by year Furman reported his activities to the association, but he could not summarize the extensive correspondence and activity that engaged his energy and time as he provided funds and attempted to arrange internships for young ministerial students. Joe M. King judged that many outstanding Baptist schools in many states, including Mercer in Georgia Furman in South Carolina, and The Southern Baptist Theological Seminary were the direct products of "the keen educational concern of Richard Furman."[44]

A significant development in the ministry of this General Committee of the Charleston Association must not be overlooked. In 1800, the Charleston church sent a query to the association and asked:

> Is there not at this time, a call in providence for our churches to make the most serious exertions, in union with other Christians of various denominations, to send the gospel among the heathen; or to such people who, though living in countries where the gospel revelation is known, do not enjoy a standing ministry, and the regular administration of divine ordinances among them?[45]

Doubtless this bold call for the association to enter actively into domestic and foreign missions developed from Furman's knowledge of missionary activity by several Christian denominations in the North, the result partly of Carey's foreign mission emphasis and partly from the Second Great Awakening in New England. The Charleston Association responded by employing John Rooker to preach among the Catawba Indians in York and Lancaster district of South Carolina. He began this ministry in 1803 and served under the auspices of the General Committee of the association until 1817 when "from the diminution of the tribes, their being so entirely surrounded by the habitations and churches of the whites, and their own wandering habits," the mission was discontinued. In addition to the missionary work accomplished, this domestic mission program was important because it revealed the denominational thrust of Furman's thinking. This program was administered by the only incorporated body of South Carolina Baptists, the General Committee of the Charleston Association. This meant that the General Committee was conceived as more than a structure for ministerial education; it now received and disbursed funds for a second benevolence, domestic missions. The final step—the assignment of foreign missions to this denominational multibenevolent committee—would soon come.

The General Missionary Convention.—Having utilized the Charleston Association's structure for forwarding ministerial education and domestic missions, Furman was ideally prepared for the next large step: the organization of a national body to stir all American Baptists to those larger ministries which were beyond the capabilities of local churches and even associations. From experience Furman knew the value of the larger fellowship. In addition to working with English Baptists in their foreign mission enterprise, he had entered vigorously into the international movement for the circulation of religious tracts and the Scriptures. Soon after Joseph Hughes, the British Baptist minister at Battersea, had helped initiate the interdenominational Religious Tract Society in 1799, Furman and Isaac Keith, the Congregationalist pastor in Charleston, organized a similar body in Charleston, and Furman was its president for many years thereafter. When the British and Foreign Bible Society was formed in 1804, Furman was also active in organizing the Charleston Bible Society in 1804 and served as its vice-president during the remainder of his life.

Furman was loved and respected by ministers of other denominations. Typical of his larger ministry was his support for John Johnson, a Methodist missionary sent to America in 1791 to superintend the Bethesda Orphanage in Georgia. Furman invited Johnson to preach in the church at Charleston, and for about a year this Methodist and his wife were guests in the homes of the Baptist congregation. When Johnson left, Furman provided letters of commendation to leaders in the northern states, which opened many doors for the missionary. Furman's church also gave Johnson a "handsome sum of money" to assist him in returning to England in 1793.[46]

So, as a man prepared, Furman was ready for the momentous events of 1813. God was moving American Baptists to participate in the foreign mission enterprise. Not only Furman but many American leaders in the North had been corresponding with the English missionaries, such men as William Rogers and William Staughton of Philadelphia and Thomas Baldwin of

Boston. A curious providence occurred in the opening years of the nineteenth century. It appeared to be a severe blow to the missionary cause, but instead turned out to the forwarding of the movement. The British East India Company resented the work of William Carey and others in India, feeling that the Christianizing of the masses in India would hurt their secular enterprise. The company decided to refuse passage to missionaries on any of their ships from England to India. However, the missionary society in England began to send the missionaries by other ships to America, where they were transferred to ships going to India. In the process, it was sometimes necessary for these dedicated missionaries to wait many weeks before a ship from America to India could be boarded. During this time, they lived in the homes of American Baptists, sharing with them their own commitment to world missions. This orientation of American Baptists to missionary work continued for about ten years before American Baptists were faced with the question of initiating their own program of foreign missions. In addition, American Baptist leaders like Furman and others had been encouraging their people to contribute funds and provide assistance to these and other missionaries.[47]

By 1813 the fullness of time had come. Adoniram and Ann Hasseltine Judson and Luther Rice had been converted to Baptist views as they sailed to India under the auspices of another denomination. Knowing that they would encounter Carey and other Baptists, they had studied their Greek New Testaments and read all of the literature on the subject of baptism to buttress their own views, but instead they became Baptists themselves. The three were immersed by William Ward, the English Baptist missionary in India.[48] After correspondence with Baptist leaders in America, offering their services as Baptist missionaries, the Judsons and Rice agreed that Rice should return to America to help raise funds for the foreign mission enterprise.

Upon his return to America, Luther Rice consulted first with northern Baptist leaders who encouraged him to appeal for funds in a tour of both northern and southern Baptist churches. In early November, 1813, Rice attended the meeting of the Charleston Association at the Welsh Neck church. He was received with great affection, and a committee headed by Richard Furman heartily commended his work. This committee suggested that the incorporated General Committee of the association, which already had been conducting the work of ministerial education for twenty-two years and domestic missions for eleven years, now add foreign missions to its supervision. This was approved, and for the first time Luther Rice, a new Baptist convert, saw an example of a single Baptist denominational body formally structured to carry on multiple benevolences. It was the Southern Baptist Convention in microcosm over thirty years before the organization of that body. There can be little doubt that William Bullein Johnson, the "father" of the Southern Baptist Convention's constitution in 1845 who was in attendance at this meeting, learned his ecclesiological ideas here. It is not surprising that while Rice was traveling in the South he developed the idea for a representative national body for the support of foreign missions, although as yet he had given no indication of any interest in ministerial education.[49]

A call was issued for those interested in foreign missions to meet in Philadelphia on May 18, 1814. Furman desired to participate in this meeting, but he felt that his busy schedule at his church would make it impossible. The church, however, overruled him, providing both funds and a leave of absence for the pastor to take this trip. The war with Great Britain prevented Furman from making the journey by sea, so in company with Judge Matthias B. Tallmadge of New York (who often spent the winters in Charleston for his health) he traveled overland to Philadelphia.

At the meeting on May 18 he joined thirty-two others who had responded to the call. It was a select group. From the older South came five messengers: Furman from South Carolina, William B. Johnson from Georgia, Robert B. Semple and Jacob Grigg from Virginia, and J. A. Randalson from North Carolina. Eight were there from Pennsylvania: William Rogers, "the most widely known and highly honored Baptist in the middle states"; Henry Holcombe, pastor of the First Baptist Church, Philadelphia; William Staughton, Philadelphia pastor; Joseph Mathias, moderator of the Philadelphia Association at this time; William White, gifted author and pastor of the Second Baptist Church in Philadelphia; John P. Peckworth, pastor of the Third Baptist Church, Philadelphia; Silas Hough, pastor at Montgomery, Pennsylvania; and Horatio Gates Jones, pastor near Roxborough, Pennsylvania. Eight messengers came from New Jersey: Burgiss Allison, the distinguished educator; Henry Smalley, pastor at Cohansie; Richard Proudfoot, pastor and educator; William Boswell, pastor of First Baptist Church, Trenton; Isaiah Stratton, pastor at Pemberton; Stephen C. Ustick, deacon of Burlington; and two other laymen—John Sisty and Matthew Randall. Five messengers are identified with New York: Judge Matthias B. Tallmadge of Poughkeepsie; and John Williams, pastor of the Olive Street Baptist Church, New York City, with three of his lay members—Thomas Hewitt, Edward Probyn, and Nathanael Smith. Lucius Bolles, the young zealous pastor of the First Baptist Church, Salem, and Thomas Baldwin, "the most prolific Baptist writer of his time in America" from the First Baptist Church, Boston, attended from Massachusetts. Lewis Richards, pastor of the First Baptist Church, Baltimore, and Thomas Brooke, also a pastor from Baltimore, represented Maryland at the convention. Stephen Gano, pastor of the First Baptist Church, Providence, Rhode Island, and David Dodge, pastor from Wilmington, Delaware, completed the list of messengers. These were the principal Baptist leaders in America. Vail commented that "the Convention did not count much, but it weighed immensely."[50]

From this distinguished group of outstanding Baptist leaders, one stood out distinctly, according to Vail, who said,

> In 1814, at fifty-four years of age, when he appeared in Philadelphia, Doctor Furman was, viewed in every light, perhaps the foremost Baptist in America; and as the embodiment of all castes of mission sentiment and all forms of mission endeavor and all collateral forms of benevolence none surpassed him.[51]

The important place held by Furman in this Convention was indicated by the fact that on Saturday, May 21, the minutes of the Convention requested that the sermon preached in an earlier meeting by Furman "with special reference to the purpose and work of the Convention, and as in some sense its forerunner and guide" be published. In his reminiscences, W. B. Johnson said that no provision had been made for a convention sermon, so Furman had been asked to preach at the last minute. The structure and lofty tone of the sermon, written by Furman for publication after its delivery, gave direction and tone to the opening sessions of the meeting.[52]

At the first meeting Furman became president, and Thomas Baldwin was elected secretary. The extensive discussions involved in the adoption of a constitution brought into focus the conflicting views of the members concerning the nature and functions of a general body. There was a difference of opinion among American Baptists at this point, and the difficulties that surfaced in the committee of fifteen to prepare a constitution may be traced, in part at least, to this ecclesiological disagreement.

As early as 1755, according to Vail, the task of carrying on a domestic mission program was begun in the Philadelphia Association.[53] Other associations followed suit. However, after the formation of a *missionary society* by William Carey and his Kettering confreres, American Baptists began to look with favor upon this method of doing benevolent work. There were five distinct differences between the *associational plan* and the *society plan* for doing mission work. The associational plan was geographically based, while the society plan was financially based. The associational plan provided for fostering many kinds of benevolent work in one body (involving all of the benevolent activity of the association), while the society plan fostered but one benevolence for each separate society. The associational plan was directly related to the churches, as messengers from these bodies made up the membership of the association, while the society plan was essentially based on individuals who had one vote for a stated amount of money contributed. The associational plan related all of the benevolences to one another in a denominational cooperative effort, while the society plan was benevolence-centered and was in a sense antidenominational. The associational plan involved an interdependence in benevolent work because of a denominational emphasis, while the society plan involved the formation of independent and autonomous bodies.[54]

Historically, the associational plan was used for mission work by American Baptists from 1755 to about 1800. However, between 1800 and 1814, when these leaders met at Philadelphia to discuss the organization of a national body for foreign missions, American Baptists had shifted almost all of their mission work from the associations to separate societies. Vail felt that this rapid adoption of the society plan occurred because American Baptists were sensitive about the possibility that associations might begin wielding too much authority over the churches related to them.[55]

Thus, in 1814 when the thirty-three leaders met at Philadelphia to discuss the form of the general body for which they were preparing a constitution, some favored the more concentrated associational plan for organizing a foreign mission body while others preferred the more independent society plan. W. W. Barnes felt that the southern brethren favored the former, the northern brethren the latter.[56]

After the original committee of fifteen which had been named to prepare a constitution were not able to agree on the form it should take, a new committee of five consisting of Furman, Baldwin, Gano, Semple, and White was appointed. This committee's constitution, which was adopted by the messengers after being considered *seriatim,* provided for the formation of a society with a financial basis which would promote only one benevolence, foreign missions. This General Missionary Convention, as it was named, would meet every three years to transact necessary business, hence the name given to it in popular conversation, the Triennial Convention. A board of twenty-one commissioners was named to transact necessary business during the recess of the Triennial Convention. Their duty was

> to employ Missionaries, and, if necessary, to take measures for the improvement of their qualifications; to fix on the field of their labors, and the compensation to be allowed them for their services; to superintend their conduct, and dismiss them, should their services be disapproved; to publish accounts, from time to time, of the Board's Transactions, and an annual Address to the public; to call a special meeting of the Convention on any extraordinary occasion; and, in general, to conduct the executive part of the missionary concern.[57]

On May 24, the Tuesday following the opening of the meeting on the previous Wednesday, the board of the convention met. Furman was elected its president, but he felt that he must decline the office because of his great distance from Boston, the proposed seat of the board. On the following day, the board named Luther Rice as its first missionary, requesting him to remain in America until he could "excite the public mind more generally" in missionary endeavors. Adoniram Judson in India was named a missionary, and $1,000 was transmitted to him for his support.[58]

Before describing the remainder of the events making up this first meeting, it should be said that the foreign mission thrust of this Triennial Convention was splendid. By 1845 the body reported missionaries working with eight major Indian groups in North America; in France, Germany, Denmark, and Greece in the European field; in one African field; and in Burma, Siam, China, Assam, and India in the Asiatic field. The total program by 1845 involved 17 missions; 130 mission stations and outstations; 109 missionaries and assistant missionaries, of whom 42 were preachers; 123 native preachers and assistants; 79 churches, 2,593 baptisms in the previous year, and more than 5,000 church members; and 1,350 students in 56 schools.[59]

The convention requested Furman, Baldwin, and Staughton to "prepare an address on the subject of foreign missions and the general interests of the Baptist denomination, to be circulated among the constituents of this Convention and throughout the Union." When this address was published, it was signed by Richard Furman as president of the convention, and attested by Thomas Baldwin, secretary.[60] A curious question was raised by Baron Stow fifty years later. He said that from internal evidence he thought that this address was written by William Staughton. Albert L. Vail said that no one was sure concerning its authorship, but that he thought that Staughton, as "Corresponding Secretary" might have written it.[61] While this is not a crucial matter, it must be said that this address sounds much more like the writing of Furman than of Staughton. Also, it bore the name of Furman, the secretary who attested it was not Staughton but Baldwin, and it is most certainly the ecclesiology of Furman after the pattern of the General Committee of the Charleston Association. If Staughton wrote it, he reflected Furman's mind exactly at this time. Perhaps his early experience in the Charleston Association gave him this orientation, although he did not mention that in his correspondence with England in 1813.[62]

Regardless of the authorship, this address reflected exactly the ecclesiological thinking of Furman. It said:

> The efforts of the present Convention have been directed chiefly to the establishment of a foreign mission; but, it is expected that when the general concert of their brethren, and sufficient contributions to a common fund shall furnish them with proper instruction and adequate means, the promotion of the interests of the churches at home, will enter into the deliberations of future meetings.

Regarding ministerial education, the address said:

> It is deeply to be regretted that no more attention is paid to the improvement of the minds of pious youth who are called to the gospel

ministry. While this is neglected, the cause of God must suffer. . . . Other denominations are directing their attention with signal ardour to the instruction of their youth for this purpose. They are assisting them to peruse the sacred writings in their original languages, and supplying other aids for pulpit services, which, through the grace of the Holy Spirit, may become eminently sanctified for the general good. While we avow our belief that a refined or liberal education is not an indispensable qualification for ministerial service, let us never lose sight of its real importance, but labour to help our young men by our contributions, by the origination of education Societies, and if possible, by a general theological seminary, where some, at least, may obtain all the advantage, which learning and mature studies can afford, to qualify for acting the part of men who are set for the defence of the gospel.[63]

This address involved a gospel of denominational cooperation in a multi-benevolent body, one whose pattern was the General Committee of the Charleston Association and a pattern reproduced again in the state convention of South Carolina in 1821 and the Southern Baptist Convention in 1845. As far as can be determined, this address by the committee of Furman, Staughton, and Baldwin was the only suggestion at this time concerning the expansion of the foreign mission society into a general denominational body that would promote ministerial education and domestic missions in addition to the foreign missions.

After the General Missionary Convention had adjourned, Furman visited Esopus, New York, and slept in the house where he had been born fifty-eight years before. He then briefly stopped at most of the important cities of the Northeast before turning southward toward his home. The story of his preaching before Congress at the request of James Monroe developed from his visit in Washington at this time. This trip represented his longest absence from his church in the thirty-eight years of his ministry at Charleston.

Between the meeting of 1814 and the second triennial session in 1817, Furman was caught in the cross fire between Luther Rice and some members of the board. As early as June 26, 1815, Henry Holcombe and William Rogers of Philadephia wrote Furman a long letter of criticism about Luther Rice.[64] Without reviewing the charges and counischarges, it should be noted that Furman met with Rice in Charleston in the winter of 1816 and acquainted him with these developments. Rice wrote to Furman on March 20, 1817, referring to this meeting, and answered some of the charges they had discussed. Unfortunately, strong parties supporting Rice and those opposing him were already forming. The circumstances were such that Furman could do nothing to prevent controversy. He expressed this concern in a letter to Edmund Botsford on January 24, 1817, when he wrote about the upcoming meeting of the Convention a few months hence:

> I think it will be an important meeting in its consequences as well as its
> nature: either for forwarding the mission and giving rise to other
> undertakings highly interesting to our churches, and the cause of God; or
> else of laying a foundation for discord and discouragement among the
> Baptist churches respecting schemes of concert and publick utility. I fear
> that at Philadelphia there is a source of evil which is likely to spread its
> baneful influence far. In fact I fear that Satan has taken some of our
> brethren there in a snare, in a manner that they are not sensible of, and
> that their views and feelings respecting some particular things, excite
> them to say and do, what is directly contrary to the best interest of
> religion, and their own true renown, and Dr. Holcombe has now
> published a pamphlet against the Philadelphia Association; and churches
> are likely to form into parties.[65]

In a letter to Judge Matthias Tallmadge, Furman identified some of Rice's
bitter antagonists as the evil he was referring to in his letter to Botsford.[66]

At the meeting of the Convention in 1817, Furman continued to wield
much influence. After considerable hesitation the convention agreed to
extend its powers "to embrace home missions and plans for the encouragement of education."[67] After the close of the Convention, John Mason Peck
and James E. Welch were set apart as home missionaries, but this program
was discontinued at the meeting of the Convention in 1820.

Approving plans "for the encouragement of education" seemed to suggest
that the convention would develop this aspect of the work rather slowly. In his
presidential address in 1817, Furman presented a plan for the promotion of
ministerial education quite similar to the one he had advocated to the
Charleston Association twenty-six years earlier. He suggested that the
churches have "charity sermons" each year, followed by an offering. These
funds would be brought to the Triennial Convention, who would set up a
General Committee much like the one operating in the Charleston Association. When sufficient funds were available, the board could establish a
theological seminary at some convenient and central location where Baptist
ministerial students might be taught by pious and learned professors. In June,
1817, Furman's plan was approved by a committee of the board. From this
time until the meeting of the Triennial Convention in 1820, there developed a
critical division among the leaders of the board of the convention. Most of
them were favorable to the establishment of a seminary, but disagreement
came over when and how it should be begun. Without waiting for approval at
the 1820 meeting of the convention, the board leaped into action. The
Philadelphia Education Society, formed in 1812 by Baptists in the Middle
States, and the New York Education Society, which was organized about the
same time by New York and New Jersey Baptists, had been conducting a
small seminary since 1813 under the aegis of William Staughton, the
scholarly Philadelphia pastor. In August, 1818, representatives of both

societies met in New York and expressed their willingness to cooperate in a seminary of the General Convention. The Convention's board voted that the Philadelphia seminary would be assumed as the official seminary of the Convention. Staughton and Irah Chase were named as teachers, and plans were laid to raise money for the project. It was stated that the institution would be simply theological, not a school for literary and classical training. However, on their own initiative, Luther Rice, Obadiah B. Brown (pastor in Washington), Spencer H. Cone, and Enoch Reynolds purchased a plot of land containing 46½ acres about a mile north of the White House in Washington. The cost was $6,000, and the four men opened a subscription paper to purchase the lot "for the use of a college, and of a Theological institution, under the direction of the General Missionary Convention of the Baptist Denomination in the United States."[68]

Furman watched these developments with considerable concern. He lamented the great haste and unauthorized major decisions that were bringing confusion to the movement. He felt that opening a seminary, employing a faculty, granting coordinate status for the educational societies with the convention, buying land for two schools in Washington, and similar initiatives which were taken without informing the constituency and securing the approval of the General Convention were serious mistakes that could bring financial trials and vitiate the entire program of ministerial education. On April 12, 1818, a document protesting the activity of the board was approved by "the Special Committee of the Baptist Churches united in the Charleston Association." In this document prepared by Furman, he specifically asserted that the plan he had laid before the General Convention in his presidential address of 1817 had been in operation for nearly thirty years in the Charleston Association, and that the same mature and deliberate decisions that brought success to the Charleston program would likewise insure the success of the General Convention's efforts.[69]

When this protest and similar remonstrances from other important leaders were received by the convention's board, they decided to postpone further activity until the meeting of the General Convention in 1820. At the convention meeting in 1820, Rice reported that he and his friends had purchased the large tract of land in Washington and that a building to accommodate eighty to one hundred students was already in the process of being erected. In a burst of enthusiasm the convention gave its approval to this Washington venture, voting that two institutions be developed there: one for the education of gospel ministers and another for literary and related disciplines. Furman was not reelected to the presidency of the convention, not because he opposed the plan which he had introduced in 1817 but because he felt that the precipitate action of the board was unwise. The school, known as Columbian College, was chartered in February, 1821. By that time it had a five-story building measuring 117 by 47 feet, which provided living quarters for one hundred students, adequate classrooms, and a small chapel. Things looked bright for its success.

Unfortunately, however, Furman's warnings about moving too rapidly were correct. A series of circumstances ultimately proved to be fatal to Columbian College. The most important of these critical factors were the controversy over Rice personally and his method of making collections; the financial panic of 1819 and the depression that followed during the 1820s; the strong surge of antimissionism that included opposition to any human educational efforts; and the fragmenting of the leadership of the board. Thomas Baldwin, probably the most influential northern Baptist leader, had seconded Furman's protest about running ahead of the convention and the constituency in the opening of the college. Yet it is a tribute to the spirit of the two men that the rejection of their leadership did not embitter them nor lessen their efforts for the success of Columbian College. When the constitution of the new state convention in South Carolina asserted its interest in ministerial education in 1821, it reflected this spirit by Furman in Article III which said:

> In what relates to education, and particularly to the gratuitous education of indigent, pious young men, designed for the gospel ministry, the organization and support of a seminary of learning in this state, under the care of the convention, and on a plan of accordance with that at Washington (Columbian College), under the patronage of the general convention, as stated in the preceding rule, shall be considered as a primary object.

Again, in the address to the constituency in South Carolina, also prepared subsequent to the 1820 meeting of the General Convention, it was pointed out that under the care of the state convention a respectable academy might be formed so that the students might be prepared to enter into the Washington school where the "general interests of the whole denomination, in the United States, are designed to be concentrated."[70] Furman's death in 1825 removed him from any additional relationship to the struggles of Columbian College, but as indicated, he maintained his concern for the school to the very last.

Many historians point to the educational impulse of 1817 in the General Convention as the beginning of an educational awakening among American Baptists that led to the founding of such well-known Baptist schools as those at Hamilton, New York; Waterville, Maine; Washington DC; Georgetown, Kentucky; Newton, Massachusetts; Richmond, Virginia; Wake Forest, North Carolina; Greenville, South Carolina; and Macon, Georgia.[71] Naturally these historians endeavor to identify the person responsible for the educational thrust of 1817. There is enough honor to memorialize all of the leaders of the General Missionary Convention of 1817 for this educational thrust. Some have singled out Luther Rice for specific leadership; some have named Furman.

If any one person must be named, it can assuredly be none other than the pastor of the Charleston church. He was advocating ministerial education by denominational bodies before many of the leaders at the 1817 meeting were born or had attained maturity. He provided the pattern in his plan for the General Committee of the Charleston Association in 1791 that probably called the attention of Luther Rice to Baptist ministerial education for the first time in 1813. The Address to the Public by a committee of the General Convention in 1814, whether Furman's composition or that of someone else, bore his name and reflected his longtime interests. He presented the plan for the national body's involvement in ministerial education in 1817. His distinguished character and leadership moved the General Convention in the direction of making it a multibenevolent body by including ministerial education and domestic missions in its structure. When his influence was removed, the General Convention promptly resumed its character as a foreign mission society only. This does not denigrate Luther Rice, who was employed by the Convention after being a Baptist for only about a year. Rice was a gifted and dedicated Baptist leader whose enthusiasm and lack of experience in Baptist life led him to make occasional errors in judgment, but his shining commitment to the cause of Christ can never be sullied. As far as can be known, he initially developed his interest in ministerial education through his contacts with Furman and perhaps others no earlier than 1813 when he attended the Charleston Association.

South Carolina Baptist Convention.—In addition to his assistance in resuscitating the first Baptist association in the South after the revolutionary war and in forming the first general body for benevolent work by American Baptists in 1814, Richard Furman played a principal part in the organization of the first Baptist state convention in America in 1821. W. B. Johnson called him the "founder and father" of the body. It is to this third denominational structure that Furman gave himself wholeheartedly in the closing days of his life.

As Joe M. King has pointed out, the several associations of South Carolina had corresponded with one another by letter and fraternal messengers before 1821 but had never engaged in a cooperative undertaking. Like most Baptists they felt no need to organize simply for the sake of fellowship. Their ecclesiology magnified the autonomy of the local churches, and the multi-plication of denominational structures which might threaten that local autonomy was usually viewed with suspicion. No better example of this can be found than in the difficulties encountered by leaders in South Carolina in the 1820s as they attempted to organize the first Baptist state convention. It is true that Massachusetts Baptists had organized the Massachusetts Baptist Missionary Society in 1802, which some have viewed as the first Baptist state convention in America since this society was later incorporated into a state convention. However, the fact that this Massachusetts society was not a state body before 1821 needs little argument. In fact, when the editor of the *American Baptist Magazine* of Boston published in 1822 an account of the formation of the South Carolina state body, he wrote:

> We cannot but remark, that our brethren in the South have in this as in many other cases, presented us an example most worthy of imitation. . . . Our Associations unite our churches; why should not a Convention unite our associations? . . .
>
> We here publish the constitutional principles of the body to which we have alluded. We intreat our ministering brethren especially, to give them a thoughtful perusal. Let each one, wherever he may reside, ask himself, why might not a general convention be established in *this* state as well as in South Carolina? It may cost us some labor to arrange its first organization. But would not the beneficial effects upon the churches of Christ in ten years, amply compensate a whole life of labor. We do hope that this subject may be agitated at all of our Associations, that the collective wisdom of our teachers and brethren may be brought to bear upon so important a subject.[72]

Associations had been gaining general acceptance among Baptists by the time of the revolutionary war, although there were still many examples among both northern and southern Baptists of strong churches refusing to unite with associations. The opposition of Edmund Botsford and Evan Pugh to developments in the Charleston Association is an example of the suspicion of many brethren about associational authority.

The first proposals for the organization of a state body in South Carolina, as would be anticipated, brought much negative response for many years. At the meeting of the Charleston Association in November, 1819, the High Hills and Charleston churches proposed the formation of a state body which would forward the educational and missionary causes in South Carolina. Richard Furman, John M. Roberts, and J. B. Cook, the latter two the beneficiaries of the Charleston education fund, were appointed to prepare a plan for the proposed body and an address to other South Carolina associations urging them to cooperate in the project.[73] It was reported in the following year that the other associations had not responded favorably, although some of them had referred the matter to their affiliating churches for consideration. The Charleston Association then voted to send a thousand copies of Furman's address on this subject to churches in other associations in South Carolina, emphasizing the boon such a body would provide for ministerial aid, the establishment of a theological school, the promotion of the Sunday School, and all areas of home and foreign missions.

The response to these efforts was considerably less than desired. The association called for a meeting of representatives from the various associations in South Carolina, but only nine "delegates" met at Columbia on December 4, 1821. From the Charleston Association came Furman, William Dossey, Joseph B. Cook, William B. Johnson, Richard M. Todd, and Lee Compere; from the Edgefield Association came John Landrum and Colonel Abner Blocker; and from the Savannah River Association came Thomas Gillison. Four other undelegated ministers (evidently one Mason, William Pauling, Basil Manly, and Michael W. Crestman) were invited to seats at the meeting. Blocker and Gillison were laymen. Undaunted by the small representation, the group determined to organize the state body. Richard Furman delivered a brief address, and by motion

> it was agreed that the Delegates now met do form themselves agreeably to their appointment, into a regular body under the character of the Baptist State Convention in South Carolina, whereupon Richard Furman was elected President, & Abner Blocker, Secretary.[74]

Furman headed one committee, along with W. B. Johnson and John Landrum, to prepare a constitution and another committee to prepare an address to the associations of the state. Neither committee had the necessary time to complete its task at this session, but the constitutional principles prepared by the committee were adopted by the body and the substance of the address to the associations was approved.

According to the constitutional principles, the new body would provide a bond of union to exploit all of the energies of the denomination for the promotion of missions, the establishment of Sunday schools, and Christian education. The total independence of the churches was specifically attested. Representation was to be based on associations and those "from other religious bodies of the Baptist connexion."

At the convention in 1822 the same committee was asked to complete the formal draft of the constitution following the principles approved in 1821. The new document was adopted in 1822 and provided for cooperation with the General Missionary Convention in missionary and educational work. A board of ten members was elected to conduct the business of the body between sessions of the convention. Furman was elected first president of the state body and held this office until his death in 1825.[75] As pointed out, Furman and his group were careful to emphasize that this new state convention did not intend to undercut the missionary and educational activities of the General Missionary Convention.[76]

At the meeting of the state convention in Edgefield in November, 1823,

Jesse Mercer and W. T. Brantly from Georgia conferred with a South Carolina committee concerning the possibility of providing joint support by Baptists in both states for a common educational institution. These efforts were not successful at this time. Richard Furman died in the fall of 1825, and his leadership in this enterprise was gone. His contributions to the cause of ministerial education led directly to the school that is called by his name, as will be mentioned in the following chapter.

Furman's Last Years

Born with a strong constitution and reared in an environment that encouraged vigorous outdoor activities, Richard Furman enjoyed relatively good physical health to the last decade of his life. He was busy about his duties until almost the time of his death, when, like a soldier pillowing his head on his weapons in the place of battle, he took his departure. Cook remarked:

> As he approached the termination of his course, his exertions far from being intermitted, seemed to acquire new vigor and embraced a wider range. The numerous institutions, which by various means were aiming at the promotion of religion, occupied much of his time. His pastoral duties were attended to with a minuteness and fidelity which indicated his great solicitude for the spiritual welfare of his flock, and an ample course of public preaching was still upheld. He also made stated visits to Edisto Island where was a branch of his church, which had been furnished with a commodious place of worship through the generosity of one of its female members.[77]

The visits to Edisto Island which were mentioned by Cook involved the work of Hepzibah Townsend who, as related earlier, provided a house of worship there. Furman dedicated the building on May 23, 1818, but Mrs. Townsend was so devoted to her pastor that she continued as a member of the Charleston church until after his death.

These last years, so filled with Christian ministry, also brought personal joys and sorrows to the venerable pastor. In 1822, he baptized his son Richard, who later became a distinguished physician. In December, 1824, he baptized his son Samuel, and soon rejoiced to learn that this spiritual but rather reserved son had become a minister. In 1823, while at the High Hills, he baptized the grandson of Joseph Howard, the medical doctor who had encouraged him in former years, and also baptized the granddaughter of Oliver Hart, the daughter of Furman's late deacon Thomas Screven.

There were sorrows also. His wife's mother died in early October, 1817. His youngest child, William Brantly Furman, died in March, 1819, and his beloved Dolly followed a few days thereafter. Her death was a heavy blow. His close friend, Edmund Botsford, was taken on Christmas Day, 1819. In the funeral message, Furman said, "I have lost my most particular friend on earth."[78] His text was Revelation 2:10, and he titled it, "The Crown of Life Promised to the Truly Faithful." It was later published. In November, 1822, Furman was called to High Hills for the funeral service of his oldest grandson, W. F. Baker, and in the following November performed a similar service for his longtime companion, Evander McIver, a deacon friend who had attended meetings of the Charleston Association with Furman for over forty-five years. These numerous deaths in his family and from the inner circle of his friends doubtless reminded the preacher that he too was approaching the completion of his work.

There was much sickness and death in Charleston in the summer of 1824. The medical skill and spiritual ministry of Furman brought calls from many ill people, and he would often spend an entire night in the sickroom. While attending the meeting of the Charleston Association in the fall of 1824, he displayed painful and disturbing symptoms of mortal illness. He prepared his last circular letter for this gathering, appropriately magnifying the deity of Christ. It was to be his last appearance at the Charleston Association after forty-six years of faithful attendance.

In December, 1824, he attended the fourth session of the South Carolina state body meeting at Coosawhatchie, where he preached the introductory sermon from 1 Corinthians 3:10, not realizing that it summed up his own life. One more significant meeting awaited him. In February, 1824, President James Monroe had invited the aged Marquis de Lafayette, the distinguished French patriot who had risked his life for the American cause during the revolutionary war, to visit the United States. Lafayette arrived in New York on August 16, 1824. On his leisurely tour down the east coast and then to the West, he was greeted by great multitudes of people at every stop. He arrived at Charleston in the spring of 1825. Although Furman was not well, at the urgent request of half-a-hundred ministers in and around Charleston, he addressed the distinguished visitor and the large assembly that had gathered. With eloquence and insight, Furman spoke well for the people of South Carolina.

It is not known when he delivered his last sermon, but in the funeral address, William T. Brantly said that Furman had used the text, "And Enoch walked with God: and he was not; for God took him." The description of Furman's exhaustion after completing this sermon suggests that it must have been delivered in the latter part of the summer of 1825. The faithful pastor had overdone in the epidemic of the previous year when he had tried to minister to both the physical and spiritual needs of his flock. His biographer remarked that this "excessive labor, watching and anxiety broke his constitution and shortened his life." In July, he received a final letter from his sister, who had become a Christian because of his testimony over fifty years before. She cheered him with promises from the Scriptures. He probably did not learn that his friend Charles C. Pinckney had died a few days before he did.

His daughter Susan was nearby during the last days. In a long letter she described his suffering, his patience, his earnest testimony to non-Christian friends at his bedside, and his bright faith. On August 25, 1825, he asked for the reading of the twenty-third Psalm, and while hearing it he slipped away to the Celestial City.

From any point of view it is most difficult to evaluate the life and ministry of Richard Furman as he served the Charleston church. One cannot fail to mention his widespread influence upon young ministers through supervising the educational activities of the Charleston Association for a generation. Furman University, which had its beginning at Edgefield on January 15, 1827, was the lengthened shadow of the man. How much Richard Furman had to do with the initial impulse that led to the entire national educational thrust among Baptists of his generation and the next must be judged by the impartial historian, but without question his influence and example were substantial. There is a temptation to record his direct influence on outstanding individuals whom he helped mold, like William Bullein Johnson who himself became such a dominant figure in Southern Baptist life, but that task would be almost endless. Even his personal warmth penetrated those about him. When Basil Manly addressed the church in 1832 on her sesquicentennial anniversary, he was composed and in command of the occasion until he came to the description of Furman's death. He later wrote in his diary:

> In the conclusion of the last discourse, Speaking of the death of Dr. Furman, my revered Father and Friend, my feelings quite overcame me—I had not the power of utterance—I sobbed out a few of the last words, and was constrained to take my Seat & recover before I could conclude the Service with prayer.[79]

Eulogies were delivered everywhere in Baptist Zion when this great man fell, but his life exceeded all of them in eloquence.

Notes

1. Letter of Richard Furman to Oliver Hart dated May 1, 1790. These letters are on microfilm secured from the Historical Commission, Southern Baptist Convention, Nashville, Tennessee.

2. Cook, *Furman*, p. 21.

3. Townsend, p. 279.

4. I am indebted to Loulie Latimer Owens for the use of her unpublished study, *The Family of Richard Furman* (np, nd, 11 pages) for this résumé.

5. Cook, *Furman*, p. 45.

6. Mallary, *Botsford*, p. 67.

7. Cook, *Furman,* pp. 41-42.

8. Ibid., p. 41.

9. Tupper, pp. 295-96.

10. Ibid., pp. 300-301.

11. Townsend, p. 29.

12. Ibid., p. 257.

13. *Diary of Basil Manly.* Manly Collection of Manuscripts 1798-1930. On microfilm in the Library, Southwestern Baptist Theological Seminary, Fort Worth, Texas.

14. For the best discussion of this, see Loulie L. Owens, *Saints of Clay* (Columbia: R. L. Bryan Company, 1971), pp. 68-88.

15. Tupper, pp. 315 ff.

16. Manly, *Discourse,* p. 54.

17. King, pp. 232 ff.

18. Townsend, p. 296.

19. Baker, *Source Book,* pp. 49-51. See also King, pp. 151-55.

20. Cook, *Furman,* p. 34.

21. In Townsend, pp. 30-31.

22. From records of the Charleston Association year by year.

23. Manly, *Discourse,* p. 62.

24. Tupper, pp. 305-306.

25. Baker, *Relations,* pp. 40 passim.

26. Manly, *Discourse,* p. 56.

27. Cook, *Furman,* p. 41.

28. Sprague, pp. 335-36.

29. Cook, *Furman,* p. 24; see also Sprague, pp. 216-17.

30. Cook, p. 27.

31. Townsend, pp. 46-47.

32. Manly, *Discourse,* p. 56.

33. Cook, *Furman,* p. 29.

34. For this summary, see Stephen Neill, *A History of Christian Missions* (New York: McGraw-Hill, 1964), pp. 239-40.

35. Manly, *Discourse,* p. 58.

36. This story is charmingly told by Loulie Latimer Owens, *Banners in the Wind* (Columbia: The Woman's Missionary Union of South Carolina, 1950), pp. 1-10.

37. Furman to Hart, January 26, 1786, and *Minutes,* Charleston Association, 1785, p. 1.

38. *Minutes,* Charleston Association, 1786, p. 4.

39. Mallary, *Botsford,* pp. 67-68.

40. *Minutes,* Charleston Association, 1791, p. 2.

41. Furman to Hart, November 29, 1791, and *Minutes,* Charleston Association, 1791, p. 2.

42. Cook, *Education,* p. 20.

43. *Minutes,* Charleston Association, 1825, p. 11.

44. King, p. 24.

45. Manly, *Discourse,* p. 59.

46. Cook, *Furman,* pp. 23-24.

47. Albert L. Vail, *The Morning Hour of American Baptist Missions* (Philadelphia: American Baptist Publication Society, 1907), pp. 238 ff.

48. Baker, *Source Book,* pp. 53-59.

49. James B. Taylor, *Memoir of Rev. Luther Rice* (Baltimore: Armstrong and Berry, 1841), pp. 146 ff.

50. Vail, p. 310. Judge Tallmadge was listed in the minutes as being from South Carolina, but his permanent home and work were in New York.

51. Ibid., p. 316.

52. Ibid., pp. 389-93.

53. Ibid., pp. 62 ff.

54. For a fuller discussion of these two methodologies, see Robert A. Baker, *Relations Between Northern and Southern Baptists* (Fort Worth: n.p.), 2nd ed., 1948, pp, 10 ff. Also see Robert A. Baker, *The Southern Baptist Convention and Its People* (Nashville: Broadman, 1974), pp. 94-101.

55. Vail, pp. 150-51.

56. W. W. Barnes, *The Southern Baptist Convention 1845-1953* (Nashville: Broadman Press, 1954), pp. 8 ff.

57. Baker, *Source Book,* p. 63.

58. Ibid., pp. 63-64.

59. Baker, *Convention,* pp. 112-13.

60. Baker, *Source Book,* p. 65.

61. Vail, p. 402.

62. See Barnes, *Convention,* p. 8.

63. Baker, *Source Book,* p. 65.

64. Cook, *Furman,* pp. 93 ff.

65. Cook, *Furman,* p. 99. For the best summary of this controversy, see Evelyn Wingo Thompson, *Luther Rice: Believer in Tomorrow* (Nashville: Broadman Press, 1967), pp. 152-74.

66. Furman to Matthias Tallmadge, July 17, 1816.

67. Baker, *Source Book,* p. 67.

68. Taylor, *Rice,* p. 189.

69. Cook, *Furman,* pp. 106 ff.

70. *Minutes,* South Carolina Baptist Convention, 1821.

71. Cook, *Education,* pp. 33-34.

72. Baker, *Source Book,* pp. 76-77. See also Baker, *Convention,* p. 313.

73. *Minutes,* Charleston Association, 1819, p. 1.

74. Ibid., 1821, p. 1.

75. For an excellent discussion of the constitution and W. B. Johnson's address to the churches in behalf of the state body, see King, pp. 172-77.

76. Furman to Basil Manly, May 9, 1824.

77. Cook, *Furman,* p. 35.

78. Mallary, *Botsford,* p. 217.

79. *Diary of Basil Manly.* Manly Collection of Manuscripts 1798-1930.

9

Changing the Guard

Richard Furman was gone. Most of the members of the Charleston church had known no pastor other than Furman. The loss of this distinguished man and denominational leader occurred at a critical time. A bitter sectional confrontation was developing in the United States that would divide several religious denominations and ultimately would flame into civil war. South Carolina was involved in both the religious and civil aspects of this confrontation. The two pastors of the First Baptist Church in Charleston during the period from 1826 to 1845 were Basil Manly (1826-37) and William T. Brantly (1837-45).

Basil Manly: The Versatile Man

In the sesquicentennial edition of the *Alabama Baptist* on December 6, 1973, marking that anniversary of the Alabama Baptist State Convention, Jonathan Lindsey wrote a brief sketch of Basil Manly, calling him the "Protean Man." Indeed he was. The church could have turned to many gifted ministers well known in her own state, like William B. Johnson, Richard Fuller, W. T. Brantly, J. L. Reynolds, or others, but she could not have secured a more versatile pastor than Basil Manly. Perhaps one reason she did turn to Manly to succeed Richard Furman was that Furman himself "on the eve of his departure" suggested him as a competent successor.[1]

Basil Manly was born near Pittsboro, Chatham County, North Carolina, on January 29, 1798. He was baptized on August 26, 1816, by Robert T. Daniel, pastor of the Rock Spring Baptist Church. In 1818, while seeking to determine his life's work, he conferred with William T. Brantly, the thirty-one-year-old pastor of the Baptist Church at Beaufort, South Carolina, who influenced him toward the ministry. He was licensed on April 25, 1818, by the Rock Spring church after exercising his gifts among them. The license was signed by Robert T. Daniel and Robert Ward, deacon. Manly mentioned in his diary that on October 26, 1818, he was named clerk of the Sandy Creek Baptist Association of North Carolina, and that upon his return from that session he made his first attempt to exhort publicly at an evening meeting in the home of William Marsh in the Hickory Mountain region.[2]

He soon left for Beaufort, South Carolina, where he studied for a year with Brantly. It may have been Brantly's influence that caused Manly to be received as a beneficiary of what Manly called the "Southern Education Society" in its meeting at Coosawhatchie on May 17, 1818. He preached his first sermon in the Beaufort church on May 19, 1818, on the text in Colossians 4:2: "Continue steadfastly in prayer, watching therein with thanksgiving" (ASV). Manly never forgot the helpful and impressive assistance of W. T. Brantly as a teacher and pastor. He loved him with "affectionate reverence," and remarked that he owed more to Brantly in the formation of his habits as a student and preacher than to any other person.[3] Manly's father became able to help him with school expenses, so Manly left the patronage of the education society in June, 1819. He entered South Carolina College as a junior in December, 1819. On December 3, 1821, he received his B.A. degree and delivered the valedictory oration.

On January 24, 1822, Manly preached at Edgefield Village in the South Carolina back country. On February 2, 1822, he joined the Little Stephens Creek Baptist Church in Edgefield County, probably for the purpose of being ordained. On March 10, 1822, under the leadership of John Landrum and Enoch Breazeale, with "fasting, prayer, and laying on of hands of the Presbytery," he was set apart for ministry by this church. His ordination certificate has been preserved.

He became the first pastor of the Edgefield Village church, which was constituted in April, 1823, serving this congregation until March 19, 1826. During this period he married Sarah Rudulf on December 24, 1824. They had five children, of whom Basil Manly, Jr., and Charles Manly became outstanding educators. It must be mentioned that while Basil Manly, Sr, wrote revealing diaries, letters, sermons, and other material that delight the historian, it was Sarah who carefully preserved them for posterity.

Manly later estimated that in his four years as pastor at Edgefield Village he had baptized about three hundred persons. He also had gained the reputation of being an eloquent and scholarly leader, and following the recommendation of Richard Furman just before his death, Basil Manly was called as pastor of the Charleston church. He had also been invited to preach at this time for the Baptist church in Augusta, Georgia, by W. T. Brantly, who was preparing to accept the pastorate of the First Baptist Church, Philadelphia, but Manly chose rather to turn to Charleston. On Sunday, March 26, 1826, he preached his first Lord's Day sermon as her new pastor.

The Good Undershepherd.—Manly's ministry at Charleston was a boon to the church and to himself as well. He matured greatly in the eleven years that he served this church. In his early correspondence with the church relative to his coming, he had indicated his uneasiness about his age and "attainments" in following a minister like Richard Furman, who had sown rich seed among them during these many years "with such pious faithfulness and tender assiduity." However, Manly's gifts were many, and the opportunity afforded in the Charleston pastorate quickly gave them visibility. E. T. Winkler remarked that Manly was an admirable choice for this post,

> for the slender and fragile youth had already taken position among the most effective preachers of the South. His natural qualities, his fluent music of speech, his elevation and force of character, his engaging tenderness and simplicity of heart, his peculiar cast of piety which seemed to blend the zeal of Peter with the love of John, gave fresh life to his discourses.[4]

Manly was indeed a "slender and fragile youth." In different parts of his diary he mentioned that he had weighed 127 pounds when he married in 1824, 141 pounds on February 18, 1830, and 161 pounds on April 3, 1832. His portrait was painted on February 9, 1831, by a Mr. Rand of Boston, at the request of two brethren in the church. This portrait hangs in the president's mansion at the University of Alabama, Tuscaloosa. It shows him in an academic robe that sets off his youthful, handsome countenance, his black eyes and hair, and his long, graceful fingers. There is a mark of aristocracy in his appearance, perhaps a family trait shared by his older brother Charles, who became governor of North Carolina, and his younger brother Matthias, who became a justice of the Supreme Court of North Carolina.

Manly was the right man to succeed Richard Furman. His pastoral ministry at the church was of high quality. He radiated much of the same warmth that his predecessor had displayed. Evidently Manly continued the children's catechetical services, or perhaps the following incident grew out of one of the Sunday School special days in the church. O. F. Gregory, another distinguished product of the Charleston church, remarked in an address in 1882:

> One of the then little ones of six or seven remembers Dr. Basil Manly, Sr., putting his hand on her head, and praying that "Jesus, who loved little children, would take her in his arms, and bless her;" and she distinctly remembers how bitterly disappointed she was that Jesus did not do it, then and there.[5]

There was a transparent genuineness about Manly that attracted others to him. He spoke in his diary about his joy at the birth of his third son, John Waldo Manly, on April 8, 1830. The child was not well in early November when the father needed to attend the meeting of the Charleston Association. In later years, Manly described how he and his wife had prayed about whether he should attend or not, and both finally felt that he ought to go on to the meeting. His diary simply said that on November 4, 1830, he left for the associational meeting and on November 6, while he was away, the child died and was buried. Upon his return he preached on the following Sunday from the text in Genesis

43:14, "If I be bereaved of my children, I am bereaved," in which he declared his faith in God despite the personal sorrow and loss. In attendance at this service was Mrs. Ker Boyce who, with her husband, had been reared in the Presbyterian church. Ker Boyce was a wealthy banker and entrepreneur. Manly wrote in his diary in May, 1831, that he had visited Mrs. Boyce at her request and had learned that his sermon after the death of his son had greatly blessed her. She was converted to Baptist views, and although her husband never became a member of the Charleston church, he served as president of the board of trustees and was a generous supporter of the Baptist congregation. His distinguished Baptist son, James P. Boyce, was a lad in the Charleston church while Manly served her, and he had a clear recollection of the pastor. He wrote many years later:

> Indeed, I do not know how a people could be more attached to a pastor than they were to Mr. Manly. He made himself accessible to all, manifested deep interest in their welfare, readily advised them according to his best judgment, and above all showed a cordial sympathy with their joys and sorrows. Especially was this true in spiritual matters. No one ever understood better how to console a suffering soul, or dealt with it more tenderly. And his people loved him with a depth of devotion seldom equalled. Nor was this confined to the members of the church. The presence of no one conferred more pleasure upon any family. The little children felt him to be their own, and spoke of him as such. And he loved them, and never forgot the word of kind exhortation, or admonition, or sympathy, suited to their case. The elders found in his genial intercourse a true copy of that of his Master, who mingled with men everywhere, entering into the ordinary social festivities of life, yet ever ready to utter the warning words of wisdom or counsel. It was his peculiar *forte* to say a word in season, and from his lips things unseasonable from other would be acceptable, because of the way in which he spoke them. . . . After a lapse of more than thirty years I can yet feel the weight of his hand, resting in gentleness and love upon my head. I can recall the words of fatherly tenderness, with which he sought to guide my childish steps. I can see his beloved form in the study, in the house in King Street. I can again behold him in our own family circle. I can remember the very spot in the house, where the bands which he was accustomed to wear with his gowns were laid on a certain Thanksgiving Day on which he dined with us. I can call to mind his conversations with my mother, to whose salvation had been blessed a sermon preached on the Sunday after the death of one of his children upon the text, "If I be bereaved of my children, I am bereaved." And once more come to me the words of sympathy which he spake while he wept with her family over her dead body, and ministered to them as it was laid in the grave."[6]

No description of Basil Manly would be complete without a reference to his sense of humor. With all his splendid gifts, he kept his ego firmly under control at all times. His diary often lamented that he was not pleased with this or that sermon or that he had found it a struggle to preach on some occasion. Alas, what preacher has not known days when the wheels of the gospel chariot have turned slowly or with difficulty! The Charleston pastor was saved by his humor and the ability to smile at himself. His letters were filled with nuances that speak of a private joke on himself, or occasionally he mounted a full-blown assault on his own dignity. In a letter to his wife several years after leaving the Charleston pastorate, the distinguished president of the University of Alabama described how he had gone to Enon, near Huntsville, Alabama, for a preaching service. The floor of the old brick meetinghouse was covered several inches deep with wheat straw, and a few benches were scattered about. He mounted the crude pulpit to preach.

> The book board was low, and only about 3 inches wide—no room to lay my notes. However, I recollected the injunction in my text [Neither give place to the Devil] and went doggedly to work. When about to take my text, an old man, very deaf, father of Bro. Sandige, mounted the pulpit along side of me, and stuck his ear as close to my mouth as he well could. This finished the business of preaching. The Devil had place, preacher, and all, for that time. I drew up my glasses, took my notes, read from them as well as I could, and brought matters to a conclusion, as well as I was able. It will not surprise me greatly, should I ever find out that one particle of good was done. What made the matter worse, the Old man Sandige was very restless—listening a while, very close to me,—then groaning lugubriously in deep disappointment, showing that he did not hear, he would turn away. Presently he would renew the effort, and seek to put his face down to read my notes. These I kept pretty close to myself knowing that I had no resource if they failed. Thus, between the old man on one side, and the "old boy" on the other, I had a wretched time of it.[7]

The diaries of Basil Manly provide many details of the active church program at Charleston. Regularly he recorded days spent in prayer and fasting for God's work. "Experience meetings" were described, usually held after a revival had resulted in the addition of new Christians to the church. At regular intervals a "committee to examine candidates for the communion service" would be appointed to guard the celebration of the Lord's Supper. Manly spoke of his regular missionary sermons. Always on his calendar was a sermon on ministerial education followed by an offering. The regular meetings of the corporation were described, as well as special meetings of that group. For example, on February 28, 1831, the church was offered an organ for use in the worship services. The church voted fifty-one to twelve to accept it. However, on March 3 the corporation was assembled to discuss whether females should be allowed to vote on this matter. Manly gravely said that, according to the

Scriptures, he felt that it was not best to allow females to vote on such matters as discipline and the like, but that they probably should have a voice in voting on the organ.

The Sunday School was active during this period. From occasional records it appears that William Riley was superintendent from 1823 to 1827, then assumed that office again in 1831. Teachers in sixteen classes in 1833 were Jane Hands, A. C. Smith, Jane Cameron, M. W. Hussar, Ellen G. Moore, Robert Brodie, Jane Thompson, J. L. Reynolds, Caroline O'Hara, Charles H. Lanneau, Margaret Burch, Emily Brown, a Miss Bartlett, John Graddick, Matilda Hard, Ezekiel Rice, Marie Cooper, and Eliza Lawrence. Other teachers named in 1833 were William Holmes, Irma Cameron, Jane Thompson, Susan Moore, and Ann Lawrence. Benjamin F. Smith was librarian of the school. Interesting comments are often penned into the record. For example, on July 24, 1831, it was noted that there was "received from children through Robert Brodie $30.87 to pay for educating Burmah girls to be called Dorothea Maria Furman." The figures show that in 1831 the school numbered about 100 to 120 pupils; in 1832 it had increased to 140 to 160 pupils; in 1833, down to 130 to 150 pupils; in 1834, 150 to 160 pupils; and in 1835, 160 to 180 pupils.[8]

The church enjoyed many seasons of protracted meetings, utilizing some of the finest preachers, Baptist and non-Baptist. In early April, 1831, for example, Manly spoke in his diary of a four-day meeting when a large number of Baptist preachers held forth in morning, afternoon, and evening services. This was followed shortly thereafter by an interdenominational meeting of the same sort. Also, individual ministers were often invited for revival services in the church. Richard Fuller, for instance, began a revival on March 23, 1835, and spent a week preaching mornings and evenings to large congregations.

During the ministry of Manly, he and the church took an active part in licensing and ordaining many ministers. On April 15, 1832, James C. Furman and Isaac Nicholes were ordained as evangelists, and both soon appeared in the records of the Charleston Association. On January 15, 1833, Manly went to Beaufort, South Carolina, to assist in the ordination of Richard Fuller. E. T. Winkler described how some of the outstanding pulpit orators of the land addressed the congregation on this occasion. With masterful eloquence they thundered the judgment of God upon sin and sinners with all the fearful pictures of the Book of Revelation. The people were terrified. For the final message, Manly spoke with unction from 1 Corinthians 6:20 and with anguish mentioned a more fearful judgment: to look upon the Christ whom they had denied or rebuffed. As he spoke the people wept openly, and the word was given everywhere: "None can compare with Manly as a preacher."[9]

On July 8, 1833, Joseph B. Furman was licensed, and was ordained on November 11, 1833. On Christmas Day, 1836, J. L. Reynolds was ordained, and on April 23, 1837, W. E. Bailey, principal of Furman Academy, was licensed to preach. On November 6, 1831, Manly took part in "one of the most moving, interesting services I ever attended." One week earlier, Manly had received a letter from Lucius Bolles, corresponding secretary of the Board of Foreign Missions, of the Triennial Convention in Boston, suggesting that either his church or that of C. D. Mallary in Augusta, Georgia, should set apart Thomas Simons, whom the Board had recently appointed as a missionary to Burma. After an exchange of correspondence, it was agreed that the ordination should take place at Augusta. The service opened with the reading of the Scriptures by Jabez P. Marshall. Manly delivered the ordination sermon from Acts 22:21. C. D. Mallary questioned the candidate, and Joseph B. Cook led the ordination prayer. Jesse Mercer delivered the charge to the candidate, the Bible was presented by Jesse Hartwell, and Luther Rice gave the right hand of fellowship and pronounced the benediction. A hymn prepared by Mallary closed the service. What a host of distinguished names on an historic occasion!

The busy pastor of Charleston also recorded his preaching activity on Edisto Island, at Georgetown, and elsewhere for churches without pastors. Touching personal ministries sometimes were mentioned. In early 1832, for example, he led in an effort to provide funds for the care and education of the two deaf and dumb children of William Holmes, a Sunday School teacher of the Charleston church.

With this gifted and conscientious man as pastor, the church grew at a rapid rate. There seem to be a few mathematical discrepancies in the reports shown in the associational records, but the following table represents accurately their reports:

Year	Bap-tized	Letter	Re-stored	Dis-missed	Ex-cluded	Dead	Whites	Blacks	Total
1826	69	6	0	3	1	16			835
1827	43	5	4	2	6	17	165	697	862
1828	57	9	2	3	11	18	191	707	898
1829	67	?	?	12	3	15	195	753	944
1830	117	9	2	4	3	14	235	814	1049
1831	63	8	2	10	8	21	245	840	1085
1832	46	7	2	15	4	17	253	851	1104
1833	108	122	4	28	4	28	258	1020	1278
1834	44	20	1	8	11	21	259	1044	1303
1835	106	16	3	15	6	26	307	1068	1375
1836	44	14	4	29	2	19	296	1091	1387
1837	50	6	3	22	8	19	280	1117	1397[10]

From this table it can be determined that Manly baptized 814 persons at Charleston between 1826 and 1837 (not including, of course, hundreds of others he baptized at Edisto, Georgetown, and elsewhere). Membership at

Charleston increased from 835 in 1826 to 1,397 in 1837, the latter figure including 1,117 blacks and 280 whites. The membership was composed of 697 blacks and 165 whites in 1827 (the first year the associational statistics made this racial distinction during Manly's pastorate). Of the additions between 1827 and 1837, 420 were blacks and 169 were whites. The percentage of white members in the church in 1827 was 19.14, which increased to 20 percent by 1837. The large number of additions by letter in 1833 evidently consisted principally of blacks, according to the breakdown in the chart. A surprising statistic was the number of deaths, totaling 231, or an average of almost 20 deaths each year. This exceeded the number received in the church by letter during the same period. In fact, the number who died, were lettered out, or were excluded (449) far exceeded the number of additions by letter and restoration (about 269). The number of white members gained in some years was quite low: only four in 1829, ten in 1831, eight in 1832, five in 1833, one in 1834, and losses of eleven in 1836 and sixteen in 1837. This, of course, meant a corresponding loss of income, for the black members at this time had few funds of their own. However, the church had no financial problems during Manly's pastorate. In his diary on April 7, 1830, he mentioned that the church was now prospering, the usual income being between $300 and $400 more than the expenses (probably each year). Pew rents still provided part of the income of the church.

Denominational Activity.—Like his predecessors, Basil Manly maintained an active program beyond the regular calls of his pastoral ministry in Charleston. He participated extensively in the affairs of the Charleston Association, the South Carolina Baptist State Convention, and the Baptist national benevolent societies.

Manly enjoyed the meetings of the Charleston Association. His diaries reflected "a lively and refreshing time" more than once, and a close acquaintance with the work of the body. He was one of the principal members of several committees appointed to visit churches which were having internal troubles. On March 26, 1830, for example, at the request of the association he and Daniel Sheppard visited the church on Edisto Island, where the pastor and people had a disagreement and confrontation. The two representatives from the association conferred privately with the pastor, who agreed to resign if the church so desired; later on he did so. Similarly on June 20, 1835, Manly described in his diary a visit to the Georgetown church to settle a difficulty in the church. This kind of ministry for the association speaks of the confidence that the churches had in Manly's judgment and goodwill.

He was active also in the educational and missionary programs of the Charleston Association, often acting as spokesman and leader for the association in the meetings of the state body for the benefit of ministerial and classical education. So intertwined were the efforts of the association with those of the churches and the state body in this educational thrust that it is difficult to determine from Manly's diary which of these bodies he was representing in some of his activity.

He recorded a human touch in his diary in 1833. On November 8 of that year he returned from the Charleston Association and confided to his ubiquitous diary that he had been elected moderator of the association in the place of Joseph B. Cook who had died. He wrote:

> This is the first time I have ever been called to preside over so public a deliberative assembly of Christians. Just 15 years ago I made my first appearance in the Charleston Association as a visitor. Little did I then think that in the same body at the same place just 15 years after, it would fall to me to preside over the assembly.

The associational reports showed the Charleston church to be the largest contributor in the association to the several benevolent objects—foreign missions, domestic missions, and education. In 1835, for example, the church gave $401.25 to these objects, while the association as a whole gave but $679.79; in 1837 the church gave $211.25 of $658.84 raised by the entire association. It is interesting that in the 1835 gifts, the association recorded that $44.37 was collected at the Monthly Concert of Prayer by the Charleston church to provide medicine for Burma, while $60.00 was collected after the Sunday School sermon to be used in the education of a Burmese youth to be called "Richard Furman."[11]

The work of the state convention absorbed much of Manly's time. He was a visitor at the initial meeting in 1821, and in 1822 he was shown as one of the agents of the new body. In 1823, he assisted in influencing the Saluda Association to request and receive membership in the convention, but this association left the state relationship in the following year. Manly did not assume the principal leadership in the state body, probably because William B. Johnson, a gifted South Carolina veteran preacher sixteen years older than Manly, was named president of the body when Richard Furman died in 1825 and continued in that office until 1854. This does not mean that Manly's abilities were not recognized and utilized. He served on practically every important committee of the Convention during his entire ministry at Charleston, particularly in the efforts to found what became Furman University. Joe M. King remarked that in the critical years after 1830 "only the toil and personal sacrifice of Jesse Hartwell, Basil Manly, and one or two others kept it alive." Manly's diary speaks of how he took journeys "west of the Santee" to raise funds for the struggling educational institution.[12]

The number and quality of South Carolina Baptist leaders at this time may be glimpsed in the naming of the first board of trustees for Furman Theological Institution after it was moved to Fairfield in 1835. This board consisted of

Jonathan Davis, Abraham D. Jones, Iveson L. Brookes, James C. Furman, John B. O'Neall, John K. M'Iver, Josiah B. Furman, M. T. Mendenhall, William B. Johnson, Basil Manly, Henry Bailey, Amaziah Rice, Richard Fuller, Nathan L. Griffin, John W. Lewis, Nicholas W. Hodges, Darling Peeples, Samson H. Butler, Alexander J. Lawson, Jennings O'Bannon, John O. Balfour, Zebulon Rudolph, Sr., James Mobley, Joseph Grisham, Charles M. Furman, and Thomas Blackwood.[13] It would be difficult to name such an able group of religious leaders from any other state in the nation during this period.

The original General Missionary Convention of 1814 had, since 1826, become strictly a foreign mission society. Baptists organized a tract society in 1824 and a home mission society in 1832.[14] These societies met every three years in a given city. Every year each society would have a public meeting of their official board (called the Executive Committee by some of the societies). These were attended by interested friends and were known as the anniversaries.

It is difficult to determine from Manly's diaries exactly how many of the meetings of the national benevolent societies he attended. The records of the societies themselves indicate that he attended the General Missionary Convention when it met at Philadelphia in 1829 where he was elected to a three-year term on the Board of Managers for Foreign Missions. He evidently did not attend the triennial meeting in 1832, but was named as the alternate preacher for the meeting in 1835. The list of contributions in 1832 showed that he had raised funds for the foreign mission body amounting to over $1,850 in connection with the sending of Thomas Simons to Burma, as mentioned previously. Manly was not shown as being present at the anniversaries of 1833 and 1834, nor at the triennial meeting in 1835 at Richmond. He was present on April 27, 1836, at the anniversary of the foreign mission body in Hartford, Connecticut, where he was named one of the vice-presidents of the convention and served on one of the committees. Also in that year he attended the American Baptist Home Mission Society, which had been organized in 1832, and was named to the executive committee of the body for 1836.[15] Manly did not attend the anniversaries in 1837, his last year at the Charleston church.

Although not a regular attendant at the national benevolent meetings, Manly was active in their councils and work. His diaries and correspondence reflected his involvement, for example, with the struggle of Columbian College to retire its large indebtedness. In his letters of April 11, 1837, and July 16, 1827, addressed to Luther Rice, Manly spoke very plainly to Rice and mentioned that some of the leaders from the North had been conferring with him on the financial problems of Columbian College.

It will be recalled also that Manly corresponded with Secretary Lucius Bolles of the Baptist Board for Foreign Missions concerning the ordination of Thomas Simons and later assisted in that service. The Charleston pastor became well acquainted with all of the leaders in the North. At various times his correspondence included personal letters from such northern leaders as Heman Lincoln, the treasurer of the General Convention, and Francis Wayland, president of Brown University and the chief denominational figure of the North. This friendly relationship continued until after the separation between Baptists North and South in the areas of foreign and home missions in 1845.

In addition to his pastoral and denominational duties, Manly was involved with an unbelievable number of interdenominational benevolent projects: the American Tract Society, the Orphans House, the Educational and Missionary Society, the Society for Sacred Music, the Literary and Philosophical Society, the Monthly Concert of Prayer, and the Charleston Bible Society, to name some of them.

The Scholarly Historian.—One aspect of Manly's ministry at Charleston endeared him to all church historians. He recognized the importance of history, and his scrupulous care in providing a permanent record of almost everything he said or did, made him a historian's delight. For example, on March 30, 1826, he recorded his first wedding at Charleston in which he united William Vance and Susan Dart at the home of E. M. Adams, receiving an honorarium of $20.00. During his almost twelve years at the Charleston church he recorded 136 marriages, identifying the date, place, and fee for each. Four of these couples were marked "coloured." He was quite conscious of the fact that one day someone would pore over his numerous papers and diaries.[16]

On January 28, 1830, he wrote in his diary about a visit with Abram Rogers, who had been a member of the Charleston church before Richard Furman came as pastor in 1787. Rogers described the trials of the church during the revolutionary war, involving the loss of the church's records and resources during the military operations. Rogers also told Manly that the Charleston church did not have many Negroes in her membership until Richard Furman won and enlisted Peter Wood, after which the church began to gain many Blacks and continued to do so after Wood's death. From 1830 on, Manly seems to have devoted a considerable amount of time in trying to reconstruct the history of the Charleston church. This research may have inspired Manly to initiate a move to have a sesquicentennial celebration of the founding of the church. At a church meeting on February 8, 1830, the church appointed a committee composed of Manly, William Inglesby, and Roger Heriot to look into the preparation of a history. The committee was asked also to inquire of the Furman family about a memoir of Richard Furman. Evidently the Furman family was planning to prepare the story of their progenitor, for in his messages later on, Manly asserted that he would not attempt to describe Richard Furman's pastorate because another hand was preparing that story.[17]

Manly noted in his diary that on February 10, 1830, he spent the entire Wednesday morning gathering information on the history of the church from William Inglesby. When Manly went to Georgetown on February 14, 1830, he located the grave of William Screven and sought more information about the early days of the Charleston church. On February 24, 1830, Thomas Screven brought Manly a box of books and mentioned that they might have some historical value. Manly found that they had belonged to Oliver Hart, the maternal grandfather of Thomas Screven. Manly listed seventeen of these books that he decided to keep. Among them were Wood Furman's history of the Charleston Association, and another book, apparently a commentary, which had inscribed in it the signatures of William Peart, Isaac Chandler, and Francis Pelot. Those books that Manly did not keep were sent to the library of Furman Academy.

In early March, 1830, Manly spent many hours at the Charleston public library recording a number of items about the church's history. Perhaps one offshoot of this increased historical interest occurred on April 7, 1830, when the corporation of the church endeavored to secure the chandelier "now suspended from the ceiling of the Mariners' church" which was given to the original church by the mother of Governor Joseph Blake during the early years of the eighteenth century.

On May 3, 1830, William Inglesby brought to Manly a box containing books and papers of the late Colonel Thomas Screven. Manly did not mention whether any of the books were of historical value, but on the following day he sent two boxes of books to Furman Academy.

It appears that Manly was busy for at least a full year composing his address for the celebration of the church's sesquicentennial. On September 23 and 30, 1832, almost exactly 150 years after the founding of the Kittery church which was transferred to Charleston, Manly read his story in two Sunday morning services. He made the following entry in his diary:

> Sept. 30. I this morning finished what I had last Sabbath begun A Sermon on the history of the Charleston Baptist Church from the formation in *1682*.—This being the 150th Anniversary of the Church, the Corporation requested me to preach the Sermon. . . . The *reading* occupied on Both occasions *nearly 3 hours*.[18]

There was a curious development in the events surrounding this historical address that revealed clearly the sensitive nature of Basil Manly. In early October two years later, Manly was asked by a member of the church to publish a sermon that had been highly appreciated. Only then did Manly whisper to his diary (and evidently to no one else) that he had been greatly disappointed that the corporation had not requested him to publish the historical address on which he had spent so much time and effort. He recorded that he had at the request of the corporation prepared the address

> with immense research and labour & delivered on two successive Sundays. This service was the more valuable to the congregation because

no effort had heretofore been made to collect what few remnants had survived the *Fire*, The flood, and the hand of the British Army during the Revolution—and because if the work was not done by me, no other man living (or that ever would live except the heir of my *papers*) would ever accomplish the work with any tolerable Satisfaction or completeness.— And from the fact that I had been particularly requested to attend to this duty by a resolution recorded on their minutes I had considered the sermon worthy of some *acknowledgment*, at least, from the great pains & labour it had caused me, who was the only one in the world that could do it, & who had plenty of business to engage my time without this. Yet, it is to this hour a fact that no mention has ever been made of the subject on any Corporation Meeting. No Vote of thanks—not even the fact attested that the service was performed: & for all that appears on the books of the Corporation, the future historian will never know whether it was done or not.—I did not wish the sermons published; if so, I could easily have published them myself—But I at least think that the service should have been respectfully acknowledged.

Whatever contingency may hereafter arise, while things remain at their present footing, I can never so far forget myself as to grant anything for publication to the call of the congregation, however unanimous or urgent. I do not know that any circumstances would now arise which would induce me to yield *even the Sermons in question* to the request of the Corporation.[19]

Thank God the "Sermons in question" were subsequently published and preserved for later generations![20]

Resignation and Removal to Alabama.—A series of events prepared the mind and heart of Basil Manly to leave the pastorate at Charleston and accept the presidency of the University of Alabama. The death of Jonathan Maxcy, president of the South Carolina College, probably was the first of several events that moved Manly to the area of academia. On March 10, 1835, Manly's beloved teacher, W. T. Brantly, completed a short visit with his former pupil. Brantly, the outstanding pastor of the First Baptist Church, Philadelphia, Pennsylvania, and a denominational stalwart in the national benevolent societies, told Manly at this time that the rigorous climate in Philadelphia was compounding his health problems and expressed a desire to move back to the South. Manly recorded that he had recommended Brantly to the trustees of South Carolina College to succeed Maxcy as president of the school and that Brantly had indicated a willingness to accept the post. Later, on August 21, 1835, the trustees of the college approached Manly about accepting the professorship of Sacred Literature and Evidences of Christianity. After lengthy correspondence with many friends about the advisability of moving to the classroom, Manly, although elected to the post, wrote on December 7, 1835, to the church that he had not made a decision about accepting it. On February 5, 1836, a committee from the church presented him with a long resolution urging him to remain as pastor.

In an unusual church service on March 13, 1836, Manly called W. B. Johnson to the chair at the evening hour, and various preachers of the Charleston Association presented the pros and cons about Manly's leaving the church to become professor. About 11:00 PM, after a season of prayer, Manly announced that he had doubts about leaving the church, so he was declining the professorship.

On May 10, 1836, while attending the anniversaries of the benevolent societies in the North, Manly addressed a letter to President Alva Woods of the University of Alabama who had written him about becoming a professor there. After considerable correspondence about the professorship, Manly learned that Woods was resigning and that he was now being considered for president. On July 13, 1837, Manly noted in his diary that he had been awarded the honorary Doctor of Divinity degree by the University of North Carolina, and he wrote President Swain at that school on that day expressing his appreciation. On August 22, 1837, he was notified that he had been elected president of the Alabama school, and on August 30 he accepted the new task. In a letter on the following day to Richard Fuller, he listed some reasons for making the move. Among these things, he told Fuller that he had been having difficulty with his throat for the past two or three years and that in his preaching the previous winter he had been free of pain in his throat only a few weeks. On August 31, 1837, the church wrote him a tender letter accepting his resignation, and Manly confided to his diary that he was deeply grieved to leave the people. His last service was held on November 2, 1837.

It should be added that this man went on to a distinguished career as president of the University of Alabama. He was a prime mover, as will be noted, in the separation of northern and southern Baptists in 1845. In Alabama he helped promote the Hospital for the Insane and was active in the organization of the Alabama Historical Society. He resigned as president of the university after eighteen years of effective service. After four years as pastor of the Wentworth Street Baptist Church in Charleston and two years at Montgomery, Alabama, he returned to Tuscaloosa for two years before suffering a stroke in 1864. He retired to the home of his son Basil, Jr., at Greenville, South Carolina, where the young Southern Baptist Theological Seminary was located, and his son was a teacher. He had played a leading part in the founding of this first southwide seminary. W. W. Barnes credited Manly with being the first to suggest such a southwide theological school. He died in his seventieth year on December 21, 1868, at Greenville. Outstanding preacher, beloved pastor, creative and effective denominational leader, careful historian, hymn writer, and university president—a versatile man indeed—

Basil Manly served the Charleston church well during a critical period in her history.

The Eloquent Brantly

The successor to Manly at the Charleston church was his teacher and counselor, William Theophilus Brantly, large in heart, body, and mind. Brantly was well known to the Charleston church, having been pastor at Beaufort, South Carolina, for eight years and at Augusta, Georgia, for seven years, and had gained national distinction as pastor of the First Baptist Church, Philadelphia, for eleven years. He had preached the funeral sermon for Richard Furman in 1825, and evidently had appeared before the church on other occasions while his protege, Basil Manly, was pastor. H. A. Tupper hinted that perhaps Richard Fuller, "always the counselor of this church," had a part in the coming of Brantly to Charleston. It is likely, however, that Basil Manly was the chief human instrument for suggesting Brantly to this church as pastor. Both Brantly and Manly had been born in Chatham County, North Carolina, the former being eleven years older. Both had spent their early years on North Carolina farms. In the widespread revival in 1802, young Brantly, at age fifteen, experienced severe conviction of sin under the preaching of George Pope. He immediately began to exhort both privately and publicly, and many testified that the earnest words of "that young man," poured out after the completion of the regular sermon, had turned them toward God. He was soon licensed to preach, and his fine voice and pleasing appearance brought him a wide hearing. It speaks of his good judgment that despite this early success, he recognized the need for education. He enrolled in South Carolina College at Columbia under the outstanding educator Jonathan Maxcy, graduating with distinction in 1808. He was financially assisted by the General Committee of the Charleston Association in these educational pursuits. Surely, not only George Pope through winning Brantly to Christ, but Oliver Hart and Richard Furman also added new stars to their crowns in glory because the Charleston education fund, which Hart and Furman had struggled so valiantly to nurture, made it possible for W. T. Brantly to get his training under its auspices. He became the key link that brought Basil Manly to South Carolina and helped mold the life of Richard Fuller and perhaps that of James P. Boyce by his teaching.

Basil Manly related how Brantly had returned to Chatham County in 1808 to visit loved ones and had preached at the Old Fork Baptist Church. Manly, as a ten-year old lad, was impressed by the youthful preacher and when struggling to find the will of God for his life, sought Brantly's counsel.

After teaching school at Camden, South Carolina, for about a year, Brantly moved to Augusta, Georgia, in 1809 to become head of Richmond Academy there. In the same year, he was ordained to the ministry and married Annie McDonald Martin, by whom he had four children. In Augusta, Brantly found no Baptist church, so he began preaching each Sunday at the Academy's meetinghouse. In 1811 he received a call from the struggling church at Beaufort, South Carolina: "If you will come and minister to us in spirituals, we will minister to you in temporals." He accepted this pastorate and, in addition, taught at Beaufort College. Basil Manly mentioned that about 1817 Brantly returned to his native soil in Chatham County, and here "made an impression on multitudes of those who had known him from his childhood, which will never be forgotten."[21]

In 1818, while at Beaufort, South Carolina, Brantly's wife died, and in the following year he married Margaret Joyner, who bore him ten children. During this period he also contributed articles to the *American Baptist Magazine* under the pseudonym *Theophilus*. These articles greatly enhanced his reputation as a scholarly and gifted preacher and writer.

In 1819, Brantly returned to Richmond Academy in Augusta, Georgia, where he also led the Baptist Praying Society of Augusta in the organization of a church and the building of a meetinghouse, which was dedicated on May 6, 1821. It is interesting that almost exactly twenty-four years from that day, his son William T. Brantly, Jr., was pastor of this church when the Southern Baptist Convention was organized here. The father made his mark in Georgia Baptist life while serving at the academy and the church between 1819 and 1826. His zeal for service was such that sometimes he did not count the cost to himself and even to his family. Most certainly this prince of the pulpit was not a "hireling" preacher. William Cathcart said of him,

> His service as preacher and pastor, like many of the earlier Baptist ministers in the South, he unwisely for the people, but generously, gave for nothing.[22]

Richard Fuller noticed this same unworldly trait in his old teacher during a visit to Philadelphia in 1835. He reported,

> He took me with him to Philadelphia to hold a meeting in his church. His worldly affairs were, at this period, somewhat embarrassed, and he was greatly perplexed as to his duty in reference to a call from Georgia.[23]

Brantly took an active part in the organization of the Georgia Baptist state body in 1822 and in promoting missions and ministerial education. Manly recorded an experience of Brantly during this time that speaks of the consummate skill and outstanding gifts of the Georgia pastor and teacher.

> While residing in Augusta, between 1819 and 1826, he was one of a Committee, sent by the Georgia Association to another Body of the same kind, to labour "to restore common views and feelings between the two Associations on the subject of Missions, and perhaps other points of

difference." On this errand, after explaining himself with great patience and kindness to his brethren, the Association took the mortifying and repulsive ground of refusing to receive him, and the other messengers of the Georgia Association. He submitted to this discourtesy in a quiet humour. The public feeling of the congregation, however, required that he should preach on the Sabbath. In presence of the Body that had rejected him, on the day before, he rose and announced his text,—Job xxxvi.2. "Suffer me a little, and I will show that I have yet to speak on God's behalf." From this starting point, he poured forth the Divine message of grace to guilty men, in a strain so grand, subduing and attractive, that, though no visible manifestation of Deity was given, the Almighty answered not out of the whirlwind, the stricken multitude could scarcely have been more affected and overwhelmed, had such really been the case. By an action not uncommon among the Southern Churches, while he was yet speaking, he came down from the platform, and nearly the whole assembly rushed involuntarily to meet him. Down they fell upon their knees, many at once asking him to pray for them, while the big tears in profusion coursed down his manly face. Such was the sequel of prayer and love which followed the rejection of his mission on the day before.[24]

In 1826, Brantly answered the call of the First Baptist Church, Philadelphia, to become her pastor. Until 1837, Brantly served this church with distinction, baptizing six hundred persons into the fellowship of the church and assisting in the formation of the Norristown church. He also carried on a writing ministry, contributing to several periodicals and publishing a volume of sermons. At the same time, he was active in the Baptist national benevolent societies for home and foreign missions and the distribution of tracts. In 1827, the *Columbian Star*, a Baptist paper begun by Luther Rice and others about 1822, was moved from Washington, DC, to Philadelphia, and Brantly became its editor. In May, 1832, Brantly wrote to Jesse Mercer of Georgia with a suggestion that the paper be moved to some central point to serve "Carolina, Georgia, and Alabama." Mercer accepted the suggestion, and the paper, which had been renamed the *Christian Index*, began its first issue in Georgia on September 14, 1833, at Washington, Georgia, with Mercer as its editor and proprietor.[25]

In recognition of his contributions through his church and numerous benevolent activities, Brantly was awarded the Doctor of Divinity degree in 1831 by Brown University, Providence, Rhode Island.

By 1835 Brantly's health had declined perceptibly, and he began to think about moving from Philadelphia to the more temperate climate farther south. His visit to Basil Manly in 1835, relative to the presidency of South Carolina College after the death of Jonathan Maxcy, has been mentioned. In 1837, after the resignation of Manly, the Charleston church called Brantly as pastor, and he evidently came either in December of that year or early in the following year.

As he accepted this significant post, Brantly still retained much of the eloquence and preaching power that were remembered so well by Manly, Richard Fuller, and James P. Boyce. He was a man of deep piety, and his spiritual preaching showed that despite the bustle and toil of endless duties that crowded him in every one of his pastorates, he always found time for private prayer and devotions. He gloried in the pulpit ministry. Richard Fuller described Brantly's princely qualities and powerful preaching and wrote:

> You wish me to say what struck me most in Dr. Brantly's preaching. I reply, the grandeur of his conceptions, and his earnest love of truth. No one could have sat under his ministry without recalling sermons, in which his mind seemed to soar quite beyond the verge of time, and in high and rapt communion, to mingle with eternity. But it was not on such occasions only that the grandeur of his intellect appeared. His thoughts and illustrations could elevate and shed a consecration over the most common topics; and I have admired the nobleness of his imagination, as much when he was enforcing some familiar duty, as when expatiating on the glories of the Deity, or bewailing the doom of the lost, or lapping the soul in all the blessedness of Paradise.[26]

In all his laborious and conscientious ministry, in which he was never satisfied with one responsibility, Brantly displayed that gift, honed by necessity, of rapidly grasping the central truth in a scriptural text. With little time for immediate preparation, he was able, from his earlier thorough study and reading as well as from sheer ability, to draw forth from his vast store of knowledge the supporting and adorning materials and illustrations that refreshed the people and communicated truth. Manly emphasized this, saying:

> That which struck me most, however, was the readiness with which he could turn the whole vigour of his thoughts on any subject at will, together with his power of comprehension and analysis. Being often in his study when he was preparing for the pulpit, he has seemed to me to make a sermon, complete, in a time not much longer than it has required to write this paragraph. I have then gone with him to church, and heard him preach those sermons, the skeletons of which I took down, and have preserved to this time; and on every review of them, they surprise me by the justness of their distribution, and the rich veins of well elaborated thought to which they lead. Imagery and illustration he had very aptly at command. . . . On one occasion, when preparing a sermon for the afternoon, the bell struck, denoting the hour of service. "Ah," said he, smiling, as he rose from his paper on which he had hastily dashed off a dozen lines in large misshapen letters,—my sermon is like a half formed insect on the banks of the Nile,—part out, part in." I walked with him to

the house of worship, and never heard him more fully in command of his subject, or of the minds and feelings of his audience.[27]

The new pastor was markedly different from both Richard Furman and Basil Manly. His predecessors in their preaching were sometimes moved to deep emotion and even tears during the course of their sermons. Manly's preaching was often called "pathetic" (full of pathos) and "pitiful" (full of pity). Brantly's preaching, on the other hand, was "modelled after the classic authors; perhaps, for some years, it had a little too close resemblance to the rotound and sonorous Latin," said Manly. H. A. Tupper called Brantly's funeral sermon for Richard Furman, "a masterpiece of spiritual analysis, Gospel exposition and Ciceronian eloquence." But *pathos* and *emotion* were words rarely applied to Brantly's sermons. Tupper, Fuller, and Manly went out of their way to indicate that Brantly really was a "tender hearted man," but then each proceeded to characterize him as one who could be hard to approach and rarely showed emotion in his preaching.[28] Tupper remarked:

> But he was formed in a mould of such physical and intellectual and spiritual grandeur that he inevitably towered above many of the amenities and conventionalities of society, and appeared to some to be vested with an atmosphere of inapproachable majesty. In college he always seemed to me like Jupiter giving brain-birth to full-armed Minerva, and in the pulpit like the incomparable Paul magnified into three-fold physical greatness.[29]

This contrast in preaching style with the former pastors was accentuated by a different pastoral image. Manly had magnified pastoral visitation, but Brantly practically discontinued it. For one thing, he was too busy. After coming to Charleston, Brantly was named president of the College of Charleston, a position for which his background and scholarly bent of mind fully qualified him. When the board of trustees of the college advised Brantly that the presidency was a full-time position, suggesting that he resign as pastor of the church, he replied that "he had accepted the pastorship of the church with the distinct understanding that he might teach also: and on this reply the implied condition of the resolution was waived by the trustees."[30] Thus, Brantly had two full-time positions. It is likely that neither the church nor the college was completely happy with this situation. It also was a great drain on the strength of the man, however gifted he was.

But, as Tupper noted, even if Brantly had had the time,

> it would have been impossible for him to have done the pastoral work that Dr. Manly did; for Dr. Manly was endowed with a matchless genius for impressing himself and the gospel on the social circle.[31]

Brantly, then, was not only too busy to carry on pastoral visitation; he was not gifted in this area.

God made him so, and the church learned so thoroughly the lesson that a Brantly could be a Manly no more than a Manly could be a Brantly, that one of the churches that came out of this body limited the obligation of pastoral ministries by the people's obligation to request such visitation.[32]

Brantly introduced other changes into the church. Gowns and bands, worn by Hart, Furman, and Manly in the pulpit, were eliminated. The old image of the worship services was altered.

The sounding board over the pulpit, regarded as a sacred thing, was taken down; the south gallery was fitted up for white attendants, and the cross aisles leading to side doors were built up with pews, while the Sunday-school was removed from the church to the newly-built lecture-room, and during a vacation of the pastor the pulpit was supplied by Rev. William Wightman, afterwards the Methodist Episcopal Bishop of South Carolina.[33]

Actually, the revamping of the church was not a new idea. Manly had discussed it with the corporation on April 7, 1830, but the proposition evidently had opposition and was laid on the table, never to be taken off. Relative to the pulpit supply of Wightman, Manly had been quite willing to share his fellowship and pulpit with ministers of other denominations, but evidently Brantly's interdenominational concepts were more liberal than those of Manly. While Brantly was a Baptist by conviction, the church under his leadership "stood under a banner broad enough to cover in Christian fellowship all who hold the truth as it is in Jesus."[34]

With these rather marked differences in church life under Manly and under Brantly, it is not surprising that some members were restless and finally in 1841 were formed into the Second or Wentworth Street Baptist Church.[35] It is interesting that Richard Fuller, in a letter of April 2, 1848, remarked that

as a Pastor and a man, Dr. Brantly was not known in Charleston. It would be painful to allude to circumstances which rendered his removal there a misfortune to him, and retrenched his influence in that city.[36]

Doubtless Fuller was referring to the excision of a group to form the new church. However, it must be said that H. A. Tupper viewed this event as a blessing in the experience of the church, although at that time it seemed unfortunate. Tupper said that this "colonization" was "promoted, if not originated, by Dr. Brantly, and accomplished by a formal action of the church." When the cornerstone of the Wentworth Street church was laid, Thomas Curtis said:

As a second church of the same faith and order, we come forth to fulfil the resolution of the first. We were sent out with solemn pledges of its countenance and support, and are of them in our principles and our history.[37]

Despite the loss of members in this excision and the contrast with Manly's leadership, the Charleston church moved forward during the ministry of Brantly. The following chart has been taken from the records of the Charleston Association between 1838 and 1844.

Year	Baptized	Letter	Restored	Dismissed	Excluded	Dead	Whites	Blacks	Total
1838	17	5	4	12	8	18	278	1107	1385
1839	19	11	1	16	0	4	272	1124	1396
1840	38	15			7	11	288	1143	1431
1841	53	14	5	92	3	19			1344
1842	35	26	6	21	3	9			1378
1843	53	14	5	16	10	20			1410
1844	75	21	6	21	13	11			1461

This chart shows that Brantly got off to a slow start in 1838 and 1839, perhaps caused by the immediate strain on the pastor of holding two vocational responsibilities at the same time. A net loss of twelve members occurred in 1837, and a net gain of only eleven took place in 1838. Baptisms totaled but seventeen and nineteen in these years, respectively. However, from 1840 to 1844, baptisms averaged almost fifty-one each year. Apart from the large loss by letter in 1841 when the new church was formed, the gains were impressive.

With the double burden of the church and the college, it is not surprising that Brantly's health did not improve with his move to the South. Overwork and poor health probably made it difficult for Brantly to assume active leadership in the association, the state body, and the national benevolent societies between 1838 and 1844. This does not mean that he did not participate in these areas, but his overcrowded calendar and health problems were weighty deterrents to additional tasks. When Mercer University looked to him as president in 1839, he felt obliged to decline.

On July 13, 1844, as he was preparing to hear the recitation of his class in the college, he suffered a severe stroke. Bedfast, he remained in Charleston until February, 1845. A tender story comes from these last difficult days for the great preacher. His son John was converted while a student in the College of Charleston. During a summer vacation, evidently in 1839, young John visited with relatives in Georgia and made a profession of faith in a service there. His father immediately baptized him in the Oconee River near Milledgeville. In 1844, while visiting his father in the sick room, John determined to enter the ministry. The "last official act" his father performed at the Charleston church was the signing of the license for his son to preach. John became a distinguished minister and educator, as did his half-brother, William, Jr.[38]

The stricken Charleston pastor was moved to Augusta, Georgia, in February, 1845, and died there on March 28. On May 18, 1845, Richard Fuller preached a funeral discourse at the Charleston church from the text, "But I hold not my life of any account as dear unto myself, so that I may accomplish my course, and the ministry which I have received from the Lord Jesus, to testify the gospel of the grace of God" (Acts 20:24, ASV). Tupper said that he could never forget the "superlative eulogy" which Fuller delivered on that occasion.

> Many an heart cried out that night with the eloquent orator, "My father, my father, the chariot of Israel and the horsemen thereof."[39]

The Approaching Storm

A few weeks after the death of William T. Brantly and only twenty years after that of Richard Furman, Baptists in the North and South separated in the work of foreign and home missions. That story must be reserved for another chapter, but the critical years preceding the schism occurred during the pastorates of Basil Manly and W. T. Brantly. One must look carefully at the events of these years in order to understand what took place on May 8-10, 1845, when Southern Baptists organized their own general body for the promotion of foreign and home missions. Brantly took little active part in this confrontation, but Manly, having moved to the presidency of the University of Alabama, became one of the chief actors in the drama.

The two decades between 1825 and 1845 were critical in American Baptist life. Gone were the comparatively simplistic and uncluttered days of Oliver Hart. The war for American independence was revolutionary indeed! Four factors combined thereafter to beget a complex and violent change in every part of American life. One was the unresolved question of ultimate political sovereignty under the national constitution of 1789. As early as 1798, the Virginia and Kentucky Resolutions asserted the view that the federal constitution was a compact among sovereign states and that the individual states retained the right to make the final judgment on the actions of the central government. This was not simply the position of the South in the early years under the constitution. The Hartford Convention of 1814-15, for example, insisted that sovereign states had the right to secede from the compact even during a time of war with England. Georgia actually nullified a federal decision in 1830-31 in the case of the Cherokee Indians. Several of the northern states nullified *de facto* the Fugitive Slave Law of 1850 by passing Personal Liberty laws.

Opposition to this conception of the constitution developed rather rapidly, particularly among those states which learned to utilize the federal machinery to their economic and political advantage. The bold spirit of Chief Justice

John Marshall greatly enhanced the authority of the federal judiciary. As Woodrow Wilson pointed out, the sectional antagonism over these conflicting views developed because the South had stood still upon the basis of her old principles while the North had undergone fundamental changes.[40]

This ideological conflict approached a confrontation in the 1830s. The most celebrated case involving this principle occurred in South Carolina. Resisting the encroachment of federal authority, leaders asserted that the proposed federal law to impose a protective tariff was unconstitutional. Undeterred, Congress passed the act in 1832. South Carolina called a state convention to meet on November 19, 1832, which adopted an ordinance nullifying this federal act as not binding upon South Carolina. Basil Manly, the pastor of the Charleston church, was asked to become a member of this state convention, but he declined on the ground that his vocational task would not permit him to enter into this political controversy.[41] Prompt and stern action by President Andrew Jackson terminated the nullification movement, but this conflict kept South Carolina in turmoil for several years and deepened the sectional breach.

The second factor entering into this struggle was the growing sectional antagonism involving economic interests but critically affecting the political balance. The industrialization of the northeastern states fixed their economic interests in manufacturing, processing, and commercial enterprises. The western areas of the new nation had retained farming as their principal occupation. The production of cotton provided the chief economic interest of the South Atlantic region. Each of these three sections of the nation was conscious of the importance of political clout as a means of forwarding its own particular interests.

This growing sectionalism involved a third factor that led to ultimate confrontation. A climatic and geographic determinism funneled the institution of Negro slavery into the South. The climate and small farm areas of New England initially precluded for that area any profitable use of unskilled labor on a large scale. Huge plantations in the warmer climate of the South, on the other hand, could use this labor in the growing and processing of cotton. Southern planters overcame their original aversion to this institution and utilized the slaves in this way. Although over two-thirds of the white families in the South owned no slaves at all at the height of the system, the entire southern culture was permeated by it either directly or collaterally. This institution, involving as it did sensitive moral and religious issues, exacerbated the economic and political sectionalism into a deeply personal and emotional encounter.

The fourth factor, curiously enough, was an invention by a Yankee schoolmaster, Eli Whitney. His cotton gin in 1793 was the catalyst that ultimately brought civil war. The cotton gin made possible the profitable cultivation of short-staple cotton which could be grown in the interior states. This led directly to the extension of the cotton-growing area from the South Atlantic region to the newly-settled South Central states. In turn, this brought increased migration to the interior states, including Negro slaves, for the cultivation of the cotton. With this spread of cotton and slavery to the Southwest and the rapid migration of people into this area, particularly after the extinguishing of the Indian titles to the land there between 1812 and 1830, the new states from this section which were admitted to the Union threatened to shift political domination in the Congress to the southern block of cotton-growing states. Had it not been for this political aspect, as Marcus Lee Hansen has noted, a military confrontation would not have occurred.[42] It appeared, as Justin H. Smith remarked, that with the introduction of cotton and slavery into the western territories, the South, through political domination, would be able to trample upon the rights of the Northeast, ruin the protective tariff, hurt the shipping business, and imperil the Union.[43]

Thus, the volatile secular melange that brought schism to several religious denominations and ultimately civil war to the nation, developed partly from confrontation over constitutional interpretations; from accelerated sectional rivalries; from the presence of a malignant sectional issue (Negro slavery) which deeply stirred an emotional response to religious, moral, social, economic, and political factors; and from the uncompromising political realities involved in the growing strength of the southern cotton block. In the case of the Baptist separation, there were additional factors, as will be discussed hereafter.

The Charleston church, of course, was a part of the culture of the South and reflected the southern point of view. It is curious that two strong abolitionist leaders had been related to the Charleston church: one was a northern transplant, Cyrus P. Grosvenor, who has been mentioned heretofore; the other was William H. Brisbane, the descendant of an old South Carolina family. Brisbane was born in Charleston about 1806 and educated in South Carolina except for attendance at a military school in Middleton, Connecticut, from 1817 to 1821. He surrendered to preach, probably about this time, but it is not known where he was ordained. He was a slaveholder and did not question the system until November, 1833, when an antislavery pamphlet set him to thinking about the rightness of slavery. He later published several essays in the *Charleston Mercury* endeavoring to vindicate slavery on biblical grounds. On September 26, 1834, Brisbane wrote to Basil Manly from Beaufort to secure Manly's support for the publication of a new Baptist paper in Charleston. Manly was favorable and the South Carolina Baptist Convention in 1834 approved the publication of the *Southern Baptist*. The first issue appeared on January 1, 1835. In that year the state convention again expressed appreciation for the paper and its editor, Brisbane. Manly's diary showed Brisbane assisting in several ordinations at the Charleston church during this time. In July, 1835, the editor read a copy of Francis Wayland's discussion concerning slavery, which produced "a powerful effect." He became convinced of the wrongness of slavery, and in the spring of 1836 resigned as editor of the paper and subsequently moved to Cincinnati, Ohio, and freed his slaves. His last twenty years were spent as pastor of small churches in Wisconsin. He died on April 5, 1887.[44] Before his death he was a militant abolitionist and became a *cause célèbre* in the antislavery movement.[45]

Baptist newspapers show almost exactly when slavery became a divisive movement among American Baptists. In 1832, the American Baptist Home Mission Society was organized, and several northern leaders who later became strong abolitionists asserted that they could all work together for home missions at that time. However, on the last day of 1833, British Baptists (who had just been successful in stamping out slavery in the British Empire by legislation) addressed American Baptists about eliminating slavery in the United States. On September 1, 1834, Corresponding Secretary Lucius Bolles replied for the General Convention, asserting their fellowship with the southern brethren and refusing to "array brother against brother, church against church, and association against association in a contest about slavery."[46] However, on May 26-27, 1835, a large group of Baptist ministers condemned this reply and pledged "to labor in the use of weapons not carnal, but mighty through God to the overthrow of this as well as every other work of wickedness."[47] Officers of the Baptist national home and foreign mission bodies in the North moved rather rapidly toward the abolitionist side. An effort was made at the triennial meetings in Baltimore in 1841 to maintain the unity of the national bodies, but the newspaper controversies in 1842 and 1843 revealed the uncompromising attitudes of Baptists North and South. Most Baptist abolitionists separated in 1843 from the Baptist national mission societies. Georgia Baptists developed a test case in August, 1844, asking the Home Mission Society to appoint a known slaveholder as a missionary. The Society declined to consider a test case, which was consonant with the policy adopted at the triennial session in 1841. The final confrontation came in November, 1844, when the Alabama Baptist State Convention sent a series of resolutions to the General Convention demanding the distinct avowal that slaveholders were equally eligible with nonslaveholders for appointment by the convention. In the following month, Alabama was informed that the convention would not appoint a slaveholder as missionary. This brought the call from Virginia for a southern Baptist consultative convention to discuss how they could carry on domestic and foreign mission programs in the South in the light of the refusal of the societies to appoint them as missionaries.

W. T. Brantly, pastor at Charleston from 1837 to 1845, did not play an active role in these several confrontations, perhaps because he had been pastor at Philadelphia for many years and also because of his health. He was critically ill for the year preceding the separation. However, Basil Manly, Brantly's predecessor at Charleston, was a leading figure in this confrontation. There is evidence in Manly's correspondence that he prepared the Alabama Resolutions which precipitated separation in 1845 and that he was one of the principal targets of important northern Baptist abolitionists.[48] If an attempt were made to name those persons in the South who provided the occasion for the separation between northern and southern Baptists, it is probable that Basil Manly should be near the top of the list.

With the death of William T. Brantly in early 1845 in the midst of the approaching storm, the Charleston church again found herself without a pastor at a critical time.

Notes

1. Funeral Sermon by E. T. Winkler, January 1, 1869, in the *Manly Papers*, Folder No. 770, on microfilm in the Library, The Southwestern Baptist Theological Seminary, Fort Worth, Texas.

2. Evidently Manly wrote the annual Circular Letter for the association at the age of twenty. See Purefoy, pp. 103-109.

3. Tupper, p. 163.

4. *Manly Papers*, Folder No. 723.

5. Tupper, p. 238.

6. John A. Broadus, *Memoir of James Pettigru Boyce D.D., L.L.D.* (New York: A. C. Armstrong and Son, 1893), pp. 16-17; see also pp. 31-32.

7. Copied in the *Alabama Baptist* (Birmingham), Vol. 138, No. 48, for December 6, 1973, p. 33.

8. See *Correspondence of Richard Furman,* on microfilm in the Library, The Southwestern Baptist Theological Seminary, Fort Worth, Texas.

9. *Manly Papers*, Folder No. 707.

10. *Minutes,* Charleston Baptist Association, 1826-37.

11. Ibid., 1835, p. 14.

12. For the Furman University story, see King, pp. 180-207, and note many entries in Manly's diary.

13. *Minutes,* South Carolina Baptist Convention, p. 10.

14. For source materials on these societies, see Baker, *Source Book,* pp. 73-74.

15. *Fourth Report of the Executive Committee of the American Baptist Home Mission Society* (New York: John Gray, 1836), p. 10.

16. *Manly Papers,* Diary for October, 1834.

17. Manly, *Discourse,* p. 53.

18. *Manly Papers,* Diary for September 30, 1832.

19. Ibid., Diary for March, 1834.

20. Through the kindness of J. Glen Clayton, Curator of the South Carolina Baptist History Society, Furman University Library, Greenville, South Carolina, I have

secured a copy of this discourse, which was printed in 1837 at the press of Knowles, Vose and Co. and titled, "Mercy and Judgment. A Discourse Containing Some Fragments of the History of the Baptist Church in Charleston, S.C.—Delivered by request of the Corporation of said Church, September 23rd and 30th, A.D. 1832." It has been referred to heretofore. Evidently Manly himself had it printed later. The *Discourse* was serialized in the *American Baptist Memorial* (New York: 1842-56), Vol. XV for July 1856 (pp. 193-198), August 1856 (pp. 228-232), September 1856 (pp. 267-272), October 1856 (pp. 292-297), and November 1856 (pp. 329-334).

21. Sprague, p. 500.

22. Cathcart, pp. 128-29.

23. Sprague, p. 504.

24. Ibid., p. 502.

25. Norman W. Cox, ed., *Encyclopedia of Southern Baptists* (Nashville: Broadman Press, 1958), I:259.

26. Sprague, p. 506.

27. Ibid., p. 501.

28. Ibid., p. 500 ff.

29. Tupper, pp. 165-66.

30. Ibid., pp. 163-64.

31. Ibid., p. 165.

32. Ibid., p. 106.

33. Ibid., p. 166.

34. Ibid., p. 168.

35. Sprague, pp. 499-505.

36. Ibid., p. 505.

37. Tupper, p. 167.

38. Cathcart, pp. 127-28.

39. Tupper, p. 171.

40. Woodrow Wilson, *Division and Reunion* (New York: Longmans, Green and Co., 1921), p. 10.

41. See Manly's letter to his wife on November 7, 1832, and his diary for November 16, 1832, *Manly Papers.*

42. Marcus Lee Hansen, *The Immigrant in American History,* ed. Arthur M. Schlesinger (Cambridge: Harvard University Press, 1940), p. 54.

43. Justin H. Smith, *The Annexation of Texas* (New York: Barnes and Noble, 1941), p. 67 f.

44. Cathcart, p. 135.

45. Through the kindness of Loulie Latimer Owens, I have secured a copy of Brisbane's address to the Female Antislavery Society of Cincinnati on February 12, 1840. It is titled, "Speech of the Rev. W. H. Brisbane, Lately a Slaveholder in South Carolina" (Cincinnati: Samuel A. Alley, 1840), 16 pages.

46. Baker, *Source Book*, p. 84.

47. Ibid., p. 90. See Baker, *Relations*, chaps. 3-4, for an extended account of the confrontation.

48. See Manly's letters to his son, Basil, Jr., in late August, 1844; September 23, 1844; October 25, 1844; and November 22, 1844.

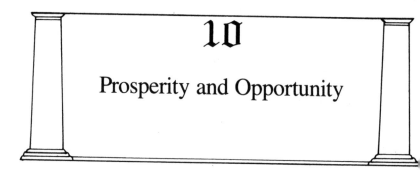

10

Prosperity and Opportunity

The First Baptist Church had experienced in Hart, Furman, Manly, and Brantly almost a century of extraordinary pastoral leadership. One could assume the church, in seeking a new pastor, would look for the strongest person available. Those charged with searching for a new pastor turned to the state of Georgia. Available records do not relate how the church was directed to Nathaniel Macon Crawford, a young man of striking promise who was pastor of First Baptist Church, Washington, Georgia. He would be called to a brief but brilliant ministry in First Baptist Church. Before his arrival in the summer of 1845, however, the church, along with many other Baptist churches in the South, would bring to pass a monumental achievement.

The year 1845 stands out as a benchmark in the life of Southern Baptists. On May 8, 1845, Baptists from across the South met in Augusta, Georgia. After five days of earnest prayer, discussion, and debate they organized the Southern Baptist Convention. William B. Johnson, pastor of the First Baptist Church, Columbia, South Carolina, was elected president, and M. T. Mendenhall, a physician and a member of First Baptist Church, Charleston, was elected treasurer. The First Baptist Church was without a pastor at the time of the Augusta meeting. William T. Brantly had resigned the pastorate in 1844 after a period of declining health, and Nathaniel M. Crawford, who was a delegate to the Augusta meeting from his Washington church, had not yet assumed his Charleston work. James Petigru Boyce, about whom more will be said, attended the meeting in Augusta but, since he had not yet joined the church, was not a delegate. J. P. Reynolds, a professor at the College of Charleston, was one of those representing the First Baptist Church. A brilliant young scholar with extraordinary gifts, Reynolds was appointed to the committee "to prepare and present rules of order for adoption by the convention." It is also noteworthy that M. T. Mendenhall was appointed to the all-important committee "to prepare and report a preamble and resolution for the action of the convention." It was this committee that would actually state the reason for bringing a convention into existence. Other First Baptist Church delegates traveling to Augusta were D. R. Lide, J. D. Debow, S.

Howe, W. Troul, A. J. Burke, W. Riley and A. Hobson, all strong and effective leaders in the church at the time.

The First Baptist Church, Charleston, had for many years played a major role in the development of Baptist work in the South and was vitally interested in the happenings of 1845. The Charleston congregation, like many other congregations, was concerned with the social and theological developments of the day and the effect these would have on the church and its mission. The organization of the Southern Baptist Convention grew out of a combination of several factors. Dr. Baker mentions these briefly in an earlier chapter of this book, and a fuller discussion can be found in his book, *The Southern Baptist Convention and Its People, 1607-1972.*[1] Any survey of the 1830s and 1840s would bring into focus those several factors, all of which would influence the formation of the Southern Baptist Convention. One of these was geographical. The nation was experiencing a great surge westward into new territories. This opened enormous opportunities for mission expansion among the Indians and the new settlers. There was a growing sentiment that the American Home Mission Society was less attentive in sending missionaries into the South and Southwest than to the midwestern states of the North and the far Northwest. This sectional rivalry would have no little effect on future developments.

Another influential factor was the antimission movement, a theological position which held in question, and even condemned, any human effort to evangelize the lost. Proponents of this position regarded it blasphemy to assume the role of God in pretending to know who should be saved. Crossing all geographical lines, the widespread movement gained strength steadily during the 1830s. Developing simultaneously with the antimission movement was the work of Alexander Campbell, a former Baptist pastor whose beliefs on a host of central doctrines including baptism and evangelism were in radical conflict with Baptist beliefs. Before it peaked in influence about 1840, the forces of the antimission movement had landed a terribly damaging blow to mission endeavors in the South. Baptists across the South felt the only way to overcome the damage of the antimission movement was to launch an aggressive advance in every available region.

Another factor of enormous influence in the founding of the Southern Baptist Convention was the issue of slavery. So critical was this issue, some contend, that even had other factors been nonexistent, there would likely have been a break with the northern brothers. Tensions had been mounting for many years. The voice of an uneasy conscience could be heard as early as the Richard Furman years when, some time between 1800 and 1810, he replied to a letter inquiring as to his thoughts on slavery: "It is undoubtedly an evil." In 1821, a brilliant young student in South Carolina College wrote a persuasive theme entitled "On the Emancipation of Slaves." His paper presented a strong and logical renunciation of the institution and based his plea for emancipation on two reasons: self-preservation for the white man and justice for the black man. His name was Basil Manly, Sr., pastor from 1826 to 1837.[2]

As so often happens, the voices of conscience are silenced or reshaped by cultural pressures and economic expediencies. The pulpits and churches acquiesced and raised virtually no moral question concerning slavery. In many instances, strange points of reasoning were employed actually to defend and support the institution. Richard Furman in 1822 wrote a paper addressed to the South Carolina governor entitled "Exposition of the Views of the Baptists Relative to the Colored Population of the U.S."[3] The South Carolina Baptist Convention regarded it as such a sound and moving document that the messengers voted to request its publication in the *Southern Intelligencer.* Furman would defend slave ownership until his death. The first Monday in February, 1825, was a cold, windy day. A group had gathered in front of the Charleston County courthouse at the corner of Broad and Meeting streets where an officer of the Probate Court would soon step forward to begin auctioning certain items from the estate of Richard Furman who only recently had died. Among the properties listed were "27 negroes some of them very prime."[4] Furman was not the only leader among Baptists who found himself reshaping personal thought patterns. As Basil Manly, Sr., stood to give the invocation at the inauguration of Jefferson Davis in 1861, he obviously had moved a long way from the convictions shared in his college theme forty years earlier.

These processes in the lives and thoughts of Furman and Manly exemplify the thought processes of the vast majority of those attending the 1845 assembly of Baptists in Augusta. Certainly those representing the First Baptist Church of Charleston at the convention would share a similar position. More will be said later regarding the relationship of the First Baptist Church to the institution of slavery. Suffice it here to say the ever-growing anxieties and stresses stemming from slavery were nowhere felt more keenly than in Charleston and specifically in the First Baptist Church.

The particular issue which brought the slavery question to the forefront was the refusal of the Home Mission Society of the General Baptist Convention to appoint any slaveholder as a missionary. In response to an inquiry on the subject made by the Alabama convention, the board stated its refusal to appoint any slave owner to serve. When word of this position reached the several state conventions in the South, a lively reaction began taking shape. Virginia requested a consultive convention of Baptists to convene as soon as possible, and the Augusta meeting resulted. It is interesting to note that those delegates who would go to Augusta from South Carolina were asked first to convene in Edgefield a few days before in order to review and plan. William

B. Johnson, pastor of the First Baptist Church, Columbia, and a loyal protégé of Richard Furman, would preside in Edgefield and would later be elected president of the Southern Baptist Convention in Augusta. Much of Johnson's thinking and conceptualizing which he shared with the brief convention of South Carolina delegates in Edgefield would become the substance of organization of the Southern Baptist Convention. Of utmost significance is the fact that despite grave political ferment, sad social upheaval, and broken denominational relationships, the delegates to the Augusta meeting would forge a preamble and charter that would pull Baptists in the South together in a commitment to evangelize and disciple men and women around the world. While the immediate crises of the day brought them together, they were able to take the long look with a profound sense of mission. The First Baptist Church was in the midst of what was transpiring. One might readily imagine with what a keen sense of anticipation the First Baptist Church delegation returned home. As Dr. M. T. Mendenhall stepped from his home at 81 Meeting Street to make his way to church the following Sunday morning, the signs of spring were everywhere. The evidence of new life filled the air and the heart of this newly-elected treasurer of the infant convention. It was his conviction, along with every other delegate, that God was at work in the midst of Baptists in the South.

When the congregation gathered for worship in May, 1845, the report from the delegates to the Augusta convention likely claimed much attention. However, another matter must have gained even higher priority. The church would soon extend a call to Nathaniel Macon Crawford of the First Baptist Church, Washington, Georgia. The details of his call and acceptance to the First Baptist Church are unknown. Could the first contact have been in Augusta? We know he represented his Washington, Georgia, church. He certainly would have spoken out in the deliberations, and it is recorded that he dismissed one of the sessions with prayer. It is not unreasonable to conjecture that those laymen from Charleston readily saw in this impressive young man a grand possibility as their next pastor. Crawford began his brilliant career quite early. Born the son of a United States Senator and treasurer of the United States, he enrolled in the University of Georgia to pursue a career in law. He graduated at eighteen as the highest honor graduate and was admitted to the bar. His family was Presbyterian, and he taught at Oglethorpe College. From his wife's winsome witness, Crawford became deeply convinced the New Testament taught believer's baptism. He became a Baptist and entered the ministry. The First Baptist Church of Charleston extended him a call during the summer of 1845, and he assumed his new post that fall.

The new pastor of the First Baptist Church embodied a striking combination of extraordinary intellect and deep spiritual fervor. So quiet was his manner that only those who knew him well recognized his capacity for appraising a situation quickly and moving to involve himself in whatever needs or opportunities were there.

One of the outstanding events to take place during his pastorate was a revival of phenomenal scope. He had asked Dr. Richard Fuller, who at the time was pastor of the Beaufort Baptist Church, to preach in a series of services in the First Baptist Church. The revival made an impact of a magnitude never before experienced not only on the church but on the entire city. Not only were more than five hundred souls brought to Christ, a large number of whom joined the First Baptist Church, but a fresh spirit of unity and cooperation developed between churches. The wholesome spirit of cooperation developed between the First Baptist Church and the Wentworth Street Baptist Church was a most noticeable example. From sketchy bits of information, it appears considerable tension had existed between the two congregations from the time the Wentworth Street work began. Although this new work began with the blessings of the mother church and her pastor, Dr. Brantly, all had not been harmonious during the ensuing years. One likely cause of the tension was the close proximity of the two churches. The location of the new church was on the north side of Wentworth Street between Meeting and King Streets. The building still stands and today houses the Centenary Methodist Church. Another possible source of tension was the close relationship of persons in the two memberships. Basil Manly, Sr., returned to Charleston as pastor of the Wentworth Street Baptist Church. Surely some who were leaders in the First Baptist Church during the Manly years were now members and leaders in the Wentworth Street Baptist Church. During the revival referred to earlier, the two churches discovered mutual bonds that would draw them together. This reunion was so meaningful that the association in its annual meeting made reference to it and offered grateful commendation to the churches for what had happened.

This season of revival also brought a surge of religious zeal that would continue for many months. For more than two years following the revival, a sizable group met every morning at sunrise for prayer. Nathaniel Crawford had a vital part in this continuing prayer meeting. H. A. Tupper, a son of First Baptist Church and for years secretary of the Foreign Mission Board of the Southern Baptist Convention, was one of many who made a personal profession of his faith in the Lord under Dr. Crawford's ministry. Tupper was asked to return to his home church in 1883 to speak during the church's bicentennial celebration. Even so many years later, he recalled vividly many happenings of the revival in "the old First Church." Recalling the sunrise prayer services which he attended regularly, he related that the services ceased only after those who led them were all called into the ministry and went away to school to study for the gospel ministry.

An illustration of what was happening in the church at this time may be seen in the experience of James Petigru Boyce, a young man reared in the First Baptist Church, whose life and work would hold such a significant place in the history of the Southern Baptist Convention. During this time of revival, Boyce was a student at Brown University. Though he had not yet made a personal profession of faith, he experienced a growing religious concern at Brown. On a voyage home aboard a steamship with his friend and classmate and another First Baptist Church youth, James K. Mendenhall, Boyce spent long hours in the solitude of his cabin. Later it was learned he had been engrossed in Bible study and prayer. Arriving in Charleston, he discovered the revival in progress. In this setting, he made public his acceptance of Jesus Christ and was baptized shortly thereafter. From that time forward, Boyce gave himself completely to the work of the Lord. Historians would agree that in the history of Southern Baptists hardly would any individual stand taller than Boyce. His life's story is a remarkable one, the full account of which can be read in his biography written by John A. Broadus.

As a youth, Boyce displayed extraordinary intellect. He was thoroughly schooled in several disciplines. While still young he served as pastor of the First Baptist Church, Columbia, and the First Baptist Church, Greenville. But his most far-reaching commitment was in the classroom, a commitment which is abundantly evident in his leadership of the founding of The Southern Baptist Theological Seminary. His father controlled extensive holdings and was regarded as the wealthiest man in the city of Charleston. The street and wharf used in his vast shipping enterprises still bear his name. He was president of the largest bank in the state and was sought out by the president of the United States for counsel in national and world financial matters. All of this becomes even more significant when it is recalled that Mr. Boyce had planned for his son a career in business and/or law. He expressed his keen disappointment in young James' decision to enter the ministry, and the senior Boyce's business and professional associates openly lamented such a "waste of talent." Although the senior Boyce never joined the First Baptist Church, he served as president of the corporation (i.e., chairman of the trustees) and gave very liberally. All other members of the Boyce family were members of the First Baptist Church. When the senior Boyce died, while there were other members of the family who might have served, James P. Boyce was designated, by his father, executor of the vast estate. His responsibilities in this role led him to give large sums of money to benevolent causes. Southern Seminary received a bequest that has stood to be one of the largest ever received in its entire history.

What happened in the life of James Petigru Boyce during the pastorate of Nathaniel Macon Crawford is but an example of what happened in the lives of many. It obviously was an exciting time to be a member of First Baptist

Church. But all these excellent happenings in the church would be overshadowed by Dr. Crawford's resignation. While these two short years affirmed Crawford's exceptional ability as a pastor, later developments in his life would affirm that his heart was in the classroom and the university setting. Dr. John L. Dagg, president of Mercer University, wanted his school to have the best department of theology possible. He knew it was necessary to secure the strongest professor to chair the department. Dagg had a keen hope that Mercer might be the location chosen for a strong Baptist seminary in the South, and a strong department in theology at Mercer would be a significant step in that direction. President Dagg succeeded in getting this brilliant young scholar to return to his native state and assume the chair of theology in Mercer University. Mercer was not chosen for the birthplace of a new seminary, but Crawford's loyal and effective service led to his election as president of the university to succeed John L. Dagg. As Dr. Crawford went about the busy tasks of getting settled in his new work in Macon, he doubtless was brought into contact with the pastor of the First Baptist Church of Macon. If this contact came about, as one might readily surmise it did, it could well have been the first in a series of events that would ultimately lead to the next pastor of the First Baptist Church. The two men would likely have had several visits, and surely the subject of the First Baptist Church, Charleston, would have come up. The pastor of the church in Macon was James Ryland Kendrick. We do not know if Crawford was the point of contact in the recommendation of James Ryland Kendrick to the First Baptist Church of Charleston, but we can safely assume the two talked about the old church. Crawford would certainly have shared his thoughts as to the great possibilities present there.

While the details and circumstances surrounding the call are hidden from us, we know it was a happy occasion when Dr. Kendrick assumed the pastorate. The *Southern Baptist*, a widely-read paper carried on its front page the announcement of the new pastor's arrival and cited the text of his first sermon preached October 17, 1847, Acts 10:29: "I ask therefore for what intent ye have sent for me?" In the same article there was printed the following hymn written by one of the members expressly for the occasion:

> Welcome, pastor, glad we meet thee.
> In this loved & hallowed spot;
> From our hearts we fondly greet thee,
> Cheered that thou wilt share our lot.
>   —On the coming,
> God's rich blessings we have sought.
>
> Welcome Shepherd! With the favor
> Of the heavenly master come;
> Lead these lambs of Christ the Savior:

Warn his sheep when e'er they roam.
—Through safe pasture
Lead thy flock to their blest home.

Welcome Watchman! On the tower
Of our Zion take thy stand;
Cry aloud when foes with power,
Gather round this little band.
—And may Jesus
Thee protect with his own hand.

Welcome Teacher! Charged from heaven,
God's whole counsel to declare:
Come, proclaim the truth as given,
Souls for life and death prepare.
—Ever grateful,
We'll uphold thy hands with prayer.

Welcome Leader! Sent to guide us
Weary pilgrim on our way,
As we journey keep beside us,
That we ne'er may faint nor stray.
—Blessed spirit
Light our path to endless day.

Welcome Brother! Bond of heaven
Of all others hold most dear;
That which God to us hath given,
Freely with thee we will share
—Holy pleasure,
To each other's burdens bear.

Welcome Pastor! Blessed ever
May to all this union prove;
And when death this tie shall sever
May we dwell with thee above.
—Welcome Pastor!
Welcome to our hearts and love.[5]

During Kendrick's pastorate, which spanned the next seven years, the First Baptist Church reached new heights in membership and related achievements. The son of a Baptist minister, James Ryland Kendrick was born in Vermont. He completed his work at Brown University and began teaching in the state of Georgia. He answered a call to the ministry and was ordained in Forsythe, Georgia. After five years as pastor of the First Baptist Church, Macon, Kendrick came to Charleston at the youthful age of twenty-six. He brought to his new charge many gifts which would greatly enhance his ministry. In preparing the annual church letter for the 1848 meeting of the Charleston Baptist Association, the clerk recorded a rather strange observation: "First Baptist Church, Charleston, reports no very unusual or interesting matters to have occurred." His observation greatly understated what in fact was happening. He adds, almost as an afterthought, "Four of the young brethren of this church . . . have been licensed to preach the gospel . . . and another, Isaac M. Springer, is pursuing a course of preparatory study, with a view to the ministry." Five young men were preparing for the ministry. The four to which reference was made included Richard Furman Whilden, who would serve, among other places, as pastor of the First Baptist Church, Kingstree; James K. Mendenhall, who would serve as pastor of the First Baptist Church, Camden; H. Allen Tupper, who for many years would serve as secretary of the Foreign Mission Board of the Southern Baptist Convention and who would later be asked to write and edit *Two Centuries of the First Baptist Church 1683-1883,* the history of the First Baptist Church written upon the occasion of the church's bicentennial; and James Petigru Boyce, who among all his other achievements, would be one of the three founders of The Southern Baptist Theological Seminary. The comment appearing in the association letter is a classic example of how prone we are to draw very limited and grossly inadequate conclusions. The licensing of these four young men came during the opening weeks of Kendrick's pastorate. Such an event was sure to set the stage for the flourishing days ahead.

During this period of her history the First Baptist Church experienced the joy of advancement in several areas. One area was the achievements in mission endeavors. October 16, 1848, stands out as one great day. On this day, the church granted letters to B. W. Whilden and his wife, who had recently been appointed missionaries to China by the new Foreign Mission Board of the Southern Baptist Convention. It was an exciting time for the entire convention since the work of the Southern Baptist Convention in foreign missions was still in its infancy. Portions of the correspondence from the Foreign Mission Board to the Whildens have been preserved. In one letter, the secretary of the Foreign Mission Board suggested that the ladies of the First Baptist Church would likely be very willing to put together a wardrobe of clothes for the Whilden's several children. It must have been an exciting experience for all those ladies who shared their sewing skills to fill a gigantic steamer trunk with lovely clothes for the Whilden's beautiful children.

The service taking place on that fall Sunday of 1848 would claim a prominent place in the memory of many. A number of pastors and other individuals gathered from across the state. Several pastors participated in the service, and W. J. Hand of Augusta preached the sermon. His text was Psalm 2:8: "Ask of me, and I shall give thee the heathen for thine inheritance, and the uttermost parts of the earth for thy possession." W. B. Johnson, president of the Southern Baptist Convention, had planned to attend but was prevented. The church minutes bear witness to the significance of the occasion:

> The meeting was one of deep and solemn interest and left impressions on the mind which the lapse of years will not efface; The sermon, the charge and the address were all excellent and the undivided attention marked the solemnity, and at times intense feelings of the vast assembly bore testimony to the strong hold which the cause of Foreign Missions, in this event, has taken upon the hearts and sympathies of our people.[6]

The Whildens sailed for Canton on the wings of the church's love and prayer, and continuing reports of their accomplishments in China were a source of much gladness back home. But the rejoicing of the church family turned to profound grief when in July, 1850, Whilden wrote that his beloved wife had died. He determined he had no other choice but to return home. Whilden buried his wife in the land where she had offered herself in love and service and, with his little children, sailed for Charleston. Family and friends gladly took the children into their families. In the providence of God, Whilden would find another lovely lady who would not only share an abiding love but express a similar commitment to foreign missions. They were married and returned to China. This partnership so abounding in grand possibilities also ended in great sadness. Whilden lost her also in death. He returned home visibly shaken by these events of extraordinary sorrow.

Whilden determined that he would not return a third time to the foreign field. The account cannot close here, however, for indeed the story did not end here. Among those at the dock preparing for departure on that first voyage was a bright-eyed, radiant-faced little girl hardly three years of age. Her name was Lula Whilden, and she was sailing with her parents to Canton. She was not yet five when the death of her mother brought her and her brothers and sisters back to Charleston, but what an indelible impression these events made! One could not possibly have looked beyond all the sorrow of B. W. Whilden to see that all his hopes and dreams of serving in China would be realized in the life and ministry of his little Lula. As the years raced by, Lula prepared herself well and quite early displayed gifts far beyond the ordinary. She taught for awhile in Greenville Female College (Women's College of Furman University), but her heart was in China. In 1872, she sailed from San Francisco, bound for the land to which her mother and father many years earlier had given their lives. At the exciting age of twenty-six, Lula was the first single woman appointed missionary to China by the Foreign Mission Board. For forty-two years, she gave her best. She worked with women and girls among the boat people. She built a home for destitute girls sold into slavery and prostitution, and on several occasions actually bought girls being sold in order to rescue them and bring them into her home. She was robbed and abused countless times, but only eternity is large enough to measure the harvest of her radiant life. Reflecting on the two generations of Whildens, one cannot help but notice that God's designs often appear to be terribly fragile, but they are never shattered beyond repair and fulfillment.

During his years as pastor of the First Baptist Church, Kendrick became an effective spokesman for the promotion of missions at home and abroad. In 1847, he was asked by the association to write a circular letter encouraging the churches to support the mission causes of the infant convention. So strong and persuasive was the letter, it was entered into the annual minutes of the association. In that same year he was asked to chair a committee to recommend a procedure to shift support from the associational committees and Board on Domestic Missions to the Board of Domestic Missions of the Southern Baptist Convention. Space is not available to describe adequately how important this shift was, and yet how delicately the matter had to be addressed. Among other concerns was the fear of a tendency toward centralization with a loss of associational control. Heretofore, most funds for domestic missions were given to and administered by an associational committee. The appeal was now made to channel this support into the new Board of Domestic Missions of the Southern Baptist Convention. The immediate concern of some was that such action would take from local churches any involvement in how and where such funds would be spent. The assignment given the committee which Kendrick chaired was to bring about an orderly shift of support from the associational Board of Domestic Missions to the more inclusive board of the Southern Baptist Convention and to convince the churches that neither their mission projects nor their autonomy were in jeopardy. The shift not only was made, but in the process enormous interest in missions, foreign and domestic, was generated. The next year, Kendrick was asked to preach the introductory sermon at the annual meeting of the association. One can readily imagine what a powerful missions message must have been heard. Probably no more moving symbol of Kendrick's influence could be found than an entry in the minutes of the 1851 session of the Charleston Baptist Association. The subject was a mission offering to educate a little Indian boy who apparently had never been named. An offering of $35.00 was taken. When it was announced, the little boy, whose home was many hundreds of miles away, was identified by a name some individual or committee in the association regarded appropriate. He was called "James Ryland Kendrick."

Another event from this period which further illustrates the vigorous role the First Baptist Church was playing in the life and work of Baptists came with the relocation of the Furman Theological Institution. Its location in Winnsboro and the scope of its academic program were matters regarded as needing immediate attention. The significant role the First Baptist Church,

Charleston, had in this matter is reflected in part by those committee members appointed by the South Carolina Baptist State Convention to study the situation and make recommendations. First Baptist Church was the only church to have two members on the committee, James Ryland Kendrick and M. T. Mendenhall. This pastor and this physician, along with B. C. Pressley, another First Baptist Church member who had served on a related assignment earlier, constituted a major force in Furman's new directions. In 1850, the State Convention adopted the committee's recommendations which included relocating the school in Greenville, changing the name to Furman University, and offering a wide academic program for all young men seeking entrance, rather than a curriculum designed exclusively for ministerial students. While the committee was comprised mainly of Baptists from lower South Carolina who could have selfishly insisted that the school be moved to the low country where Oliver Hart had begun the commitment of Baptists in the South to education and where Richard Furman had championed the cause, their magnanimity prevailed, and they all agreed Greenville was the right place. At this grand moment, Furman University entered a new era, the significance of which is still felt.

One of the more interesting things to occur during this period was the centennial celebration for the Charleston Baptist Association. In 1751, Oliver Hart, while pastor of the church, led in the founding of the Charleston Baptist Association, the first association in the South. It was only natural for the First Baptist Church to hope that the association would return to the location of its first organizational meeting. The church sent out a letter of invitation to all the churches of the association, which spread across a major part of the state. The Wentworth Street Baptist Church registered a strong protest that the invitations were sent out in the name of only one church. The members of the Wentworth Street Church so much resented the action of the First Baptist Church that they decided not to participate in the celebration. One might observe that human nature and churches change very little across passing generations. Some degree of reconciliation was brought about, and the observance took place as planned. An interesting part of the celebration came in the closing session of this associational meeting when the Lord's Supper was administered to all in attendance.[7] Since questions have been raised across the years regarding open and closed communion, it is highly significant that the First Baptist Church insisted that communion be provided for all the family of faith regardless of church membership. Across its three hundred years, the First Baptist Church has always affirmed that the Lord's Supper should be available for all professing Christians.

A noteworthy incident regarding baptism occurred during this general period. In January, 1853, as the church entered the new year, a woman who was a Methodist presented herself for membership. She had been immersed in the Methodist church and asked that this baptism be accepted. The minutes recorded, "After free expressions of opinions . . . the church voted in the affirmative."[8] In the light of controversies across the years on the subject of baptism, such a decision at this early date is interesting.

Before leaving the subject of church ordinances, it would be informative to elaborate on a few particulars of the observances. The earliest reference to baptism locates the baptistry outside the building in the northeast corner of the present Church Street property. Baptism was observed in the afternoon following the morning worship service. Many candidates, both black and white, followed their Lord in baptism, and very often it was an occasion of much exuberance and jubilation. When the present building was completed, the baptistry was located at the west end of the center aisle at the foot of the steps on the congregational level. The present steps and choir rostrum were not there originally. This placed the "font," as it was called, immediately in front of the pulpit. The pulpit at that time rose from the congregational floor level and was entered by spiraling steps. It was around this "font" that one elderly member in later years recalled gathering, as a child, with other candidates for baptism and having Dr. Furman question them on matters of the faith. This occasion gave each the opportunity to share his personal grasp of the "catechism." The service of baptism was always concluded with the observance of communion.

For many years, the Lord's Supper was taken from a common cup. In October, 1851, the church purchased a new communion service for one hundred dollars.[9] Many intriguing stories surround this lovely set. During the Civil War it was smuggled by a church member to Abbeville, South Carolina, where it was placed in the bank vault to prevent Union soldiers from taking it. In the twentieth century it was placed on loan in the Charleston Museum for safekeeping. The church has kept this service down to the present, and each communion Sunday it is placed on the table, symbolic of our heritage and the faith of our fathers. It is interesting to note that the ladies of the First Baptist Church had a communion service of virtually identical design made and sent to the First Baptist Church of Chattanooga, Tennessee. The gift was shipped on the maiden trip of the "Best Friend," America's first locomotive.

The pastorate of James Ryland Kendrick is regarded as the most prosperous period in the history of the First Baptist Church. Large numbers joined the church, raising its membership to over nineteen hundred. Some of the most influential people in the city and state were members. Tupper cites that during Kendrick's seven years as pastor liberal amounts were given to benevolent causes, not to mention large additional sums given for property improvements. The programs of the church had wide appeal. The music was "the admiration of the city," and the pastor was regarded the "most polished and popular man of the Charleston pulpit, yet not more elegant than evangelical.''[10]

Reading the history of this period, one readily perceives the vitality which characterized the work of the First Baptist Church. The apparent widespread feeling throughout the membership that things in the church were going well must have intensified the feelings of shock when on Sunday, May 28, 1854, the pastor reported to the congregation the desires and intentions of a substantial number of First Baptist Church members to withdraw for the purpose of forming a fourth Baptist church in the city. Those leaving wrote a moving letter explaining their motivation and asking for the prayers and understanding of the First Baptist Church. It stated:

> If there are any who especially need your prayers, it is those who now ask them—Pray for us that we may take our weakness to God and seek our strength in him. Pray for us that we may in this manner labor as diligently and sacrifice as cheerfully as if all depended on ourselves, and at the same time hang as absolutely on that arm on which the whole creation hangs as if our labors were in no way requisite to success.
>
> As we part from you, we crave beside your prayers, a continuance of your Christian regard—Although we leave you, our hearts will still be here; and while you stay, we entreat you go with us in your good wishes and your sympathies. Make us not offenders for ought that we have done or said—Forget if we have ever grieved you—Forgive us, if we have ever caused you pain.
>
> Yet a little while Brethren, and our work will be over—We will soon be dismissed from the church on earth to join we trust, the church in heaven—As we would depart at death in peace with all mankind—so would we part from you now. Some, many who have worshipped with us here, have gone already, and their lives of mutual love and labor here are saying to us labor in love for the reward that they now enjoy. May we meet our Sainted dead, and meet each other in the blissful presence of our Lord, as one by one, we shall be called to exchange all our houses of prayer below for God's own everlasting house of joy and praise above.
>
> As ever yours in Christ
>
> James Tupper[11]

Four Sundays later, as the church gathered for regular services, the attendance was high, with virtually every rented pew occupied and the north balcony filled with slaves. Dr. Kendrick stood to share his momentous decision to resign and go with the group beginning the new church. As the warm June sunlight filtered through those exquisitely etched Robert Mills windows, an awesome silence fell across the congregation. An occasional sigh could be heard and from the north balcony an occasional muffled mourn.

There was likely an unrecorded consensus that this development could not occur without far-reaching consequences. Across the ensuing years such concern would be substantiated. In his announcement Dr. Kendrick gave an eloquent rationalization for this decision. In his final sermon the pastor said: "Call to mind the fact that today, after having sustained the loss which you deplore, you are stronger than you ever were at any period of your history—stronger in numbers, probably in judicious counselors and pecuniary means . . . After having given off three churches, you are in fact today a more powerful body than you were before you had colonized at all."[12]

The initial response of the church seems to have been supportive and magnanimous. The church passed a resolution offering its blessing on the new venture and assuring those who would soon be leaving that the First Baptist Church wanted them to continue in attendance and worship until a new facility could be built. The church also recorded their desire for the pastor to continue as pastor until regular services had begun in the new church. Dr. Kendrick agreed to this arrangement. Soon afterward, other feelings began to surface. Full accounts of what transpired were not recorded, but the church minutes are complete enough to substantiate that very strong resentments were stated openly. So pronounced were these feelings that the pastor wrote a further letter withdrawing his offer to continue his pastoral duties until the new church was completed. His letter announced immediate cessation of pastoral functions in the First Baptist Church. This terminated his tenure with the church, and he proceeded to move his residence from 88 Broad Street to 2 Wragg Square, a lovely new residential area only a short walk from the site of the new church, later to be named the Citadel Square Baptist Church.

A brief look at the area where the new church was to be built helps one understand the excitement of those undertaking their project. During this period of time some of the loveliest residential sections ever to be developed in the city were underway. Even now, though many blocks have since been destroyed, a casual survey immediately to the east of the Citadel Square Baptist Church would help one understand the great potential. The newly constituted congregation erected a sanctuary that was acclaimed by *Harpers* to be the finest house of worship in the South. The Boyce family alone gave in excess of $40,000 toward its construction. On November 23, 1856, the Citadel Square congregation dedicated its new house of worship. First Baptist Church canceled its regular morning worship services and gathered at the new sight to join in the dedicatory services. Before its centennial celebration the Citadel Square Baptist Church would have the distinction of being the largest congregation in South Carolina. The flowering of such grand things for the Citadel Square Church, however, was also the first in a long series of events which would have a dramatic effect on the strength of "old First Church."

Notes

1. Robert A. Baker, *The Southern Baptist Convention and Its People 1607-1972* (Nashville: Broadman Press, 1974), pp. 148 ff.

2. Loulie Latimer Owens, *Banners in the Wind* (Columbia: The Women's Missionary Union of South Carolina, 1950), p. 71.

3. Ibid., p. 73.

4. Ibid., p. 74.

5. *The Southern Baptist,* October 20, 1947, p. 1.

6. *Minutes: First Baptist Church, Charleston, South Carolina,* October 16, 1848. Hereafter referred to as *Church Minutes*.

7. *Minutes: Charleston Baptist Association, South Carolina,* 1851, p. 10. Hereafter referred to as *Associational Minutes*.

8. *Church Minutes,* January 16, 1853.

9. Ibid., October 13, 1851.

10. H. A. Tupper, *Two Centuries of the First Baptist Church of South Carolina* (Baltimore: R. H. Woodward and Company, 1889), p. 178.

11. *Church Minutes*, May 27, 1854.

12. Tupper, p. 179.

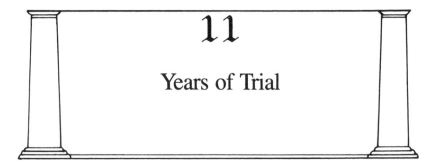

11

Years of Trial

The church once again faced the task of seeking a new pastor. Edwin Theodore Winkler had moved to Charleston in 1852 to assume the post of corresponding secretary of the Southern Baptist Publication Society, an organization with which the First Baptist Church had sustained a close relationship. M. T. Mendenhall, treasurer of the Southern Baptist Convention, had been strategic in the founding of the Society. It would be expected that Mendenhall and others were likely to encourage Winkler to unite with the First Baptist Church. The newly installed secretary and his wife Abby were received into fellowship July 29, 1852. Winkler would also assume editorship of the *Southern Baptist Journal,* a publication of wide influence also published in Charleston. Shortly after Dr. Kendrick resigned, interest rapidly developed in calling Winkler as pastor. He had supplied for Kendrick many times and likely had assisted in other pastoral work. As interest grew in Winkler, an interesting series of events ensued. In September of that year, the church in regular monthly conference appointed a committee "to confer with the committee from the corporation in selecting some suitable person to recommend as pastor."[1] The president of the corporation responded that such action was unconstitutional. Apparently, considerable effort was exerted to gain control of the procedures. Minutes related to the incident are sketchy, but on November 13, 1854, a resolution was unanimously adopted by the church to affirm the church's belief that E. T. Winkler was the proper one to be called pastor. Nothing more is recorded on the matter, and minutes of the ensuing business conferences cite E. T. Winkler as pastor/moderator. Obviously, the officers of the corporation had heard the message of the congregation's wishes and relented.

Winkler had the background to make a significant contribution in whatever post he held. A native of Savannah, Georgia, he was educated at Brown University and Newton Theological Seminary. Interested and proficient in journalism, young Winkler began his career with the *Christian Index.* Two years after leaving Charleston, he became editor of the *Alabama Baptist.* He wrote a number of books and tracts on a very wide range of topics. He was highly regarded as a scholar and literary figure, a quality which greatly enhanced his appeal and ministry in Charleston. Tupper in his bicentennial story of the church identified him as "the Chevalier Bayard of First Baptist Church: *Sans peur et sans reproche*." The Charleston pastor was an active member of the city's Literary Club, a group meeting regularly to discuss various scholarly themes. He assumed a leadership role in the group, and quite often fellow members of the club who were not members of the First Baptist Church attended the church because of impressions gained in the literary discussions. Winkler's pulpit ministry was scholarly but also powerful and persuasive. He displayed the striking combined qualities of astute intellect and physical manliness. More reference to his manliness shall be made as we see him a chaplain in the Civil War. The church continued to flourish under his leadership until the onslaught of war.

One of the several significant happenings during the Winkler period was the founding of The Southern Baptist Theological Seminary. For many years, dating back to the work of Oliver Hart, Baptists in the South had fostered a great appreciation for, and responsibility toward, ministerial education. This story has been written in other volumes and therefore will not be repeated here. Suffice it to say the pastors and members of the First Baptist Church have always given the fostering of education high priority. In the late 1850s, across the South, interest in the founding of a seminary had grown to a point that warranted action.

A series of educational conventions assembled on state levels coupled with several annual educational conventions of Baptists throughout the South gave the needed impetus to move Baptists in the direction of founding a theological school. Several Baptist schools were hoping the new seminary might be located on their campus. The date, May 7, 1857, stands out as a great day in the life of Southern Baptists. On this day in Louisville, Kentucky, the Educational Convention, after months and even years of debate and seemingly insurmountable obstacles, voted to accept a South Carolina proposal. The proposal included a commitment from South Carolina Baptists to give one hundred thousand dollars at the outset as a matching sum if the other states together would raise one hundred thousand dollars. The new school would be located in Greenville, South Carolina.

These details of the founding of The Southern Baptist Theological Seminary are included here because of First Baptist Church's fascinating involvement. Probably no other church had more individuals of its immediate past and present membership involved in this accomplishment. Basil Manly, Sr., was appointed chairman of the strategic committee that would bring the founding plans to fulfillment. As early as 1835, while pastor of the First Baptist Church, he had written an article calling for a central theological seminary for Baptists in the South. James Ryland Kendrick served on the same committee as well as Basil Manly, Jr. Edwin Theodore Winkler had a significant part in the formation, but hardly anyone gave more direction to these developments than James Petigru Boyce. It was he who convinced the South Carolina Convention in July, 1856, to approve the one hundred thousand dollar offer to the wider Educational Convention of Southern Baptists. The next year the Educational Convention, meeting in Louisville, adopted the South Carolina recommendation. Of the one hundred thousand dollars, the sum of thirty thousand dollars was already on hand at Furman University in the Department of Theology. This meant an additional seventy thousand dollars had to be raised among South Carolina Baptists. This plan was Boyce's idea from the outset, and, as would be expected, Boyce was asked to assume the responsibility for raising these funds. He traveled extensively, crisscrossing the state, seeking funds. With his close contacts and friendships in Charleston, one can readily imagine the effort he exerted there. Later Broadus would write:

> He tendered his resignation as professor in the University, but the Trustees declined to accept, and authorized him to act according to his own judgment in regard to the agency's work during the coming year. He probably had very little time for teaching in the course of the next session. We know that in his two-horse buggy, driven by a servant, he travelled far and wide over South Carolina, visiting out-of-the-way churches, and planters on remote plantations, and throwing all the energies and resources of his being into what was then and there a very large and difficult undertaking. It was no doubt often with a sense of heavy sacrifice that the young husband and father left the bright home he loved so well, with the already rich store of choice books in which he so delighted, for these laborious and not always successful journeys.[2]

Because of these and many other heroic efforts, The Southern Baptist Theological Seminary opened for its first session in the autumn of 1859, in Greenville, South Carolina with twenty-six students. Two of the faculty members had grown up together in the First Baptist Church, James P. Boyce and Basil Manly, Jr. John A. Broadus of Virginia was the third faculty member. The fourth to be elected was Edwin T. Winkler. What to do about this election posed a most difficult decision for Winkler. He had been at the center of the plans for founding the seminary. It was a singular honor to be asked to join the faculty, and yet he had a profound sense of commitment to his beloved congregation. The church minutes do not discuss the incident fully, but enough is recorded to suggest the trauma of pastor and people. The church adopted the following resolution:

> Information having been received by the membership of this Church of the election of our Pastor Revd. E. T. Winkler to a Professorship in the Furman University, we deem it a fit occasion for the expression of our

regard for him personally and our estimate of the value of his services to this Church,

Therefore

1. Resolved that we entertain for our Pastor Revd. E. T. Winkler warm and abiding affection which we could not hope to transfer to another.

2. Resolved that we would regard the dessolution of the connexion which now exists between him and this church as a serious calamity to the Church and a vital injury to our denomination in this city.

3. Resolved that a copy of the foregoing Preamble and resolution be conveyed to said Pastor. Entered upon the Minutes of this Church and published in the Southern Baptist.[3]

Winkler declined the seminary's invitation. A short time later another appeal came from the seminary prevailing on Winkler to come with them, but again his deep sense of belonging with the First Baptist Church family dictated that he stay.

The church and Winkler experienced an unusually deep affection each for the other. One of the many occasions for this esteem to be expressed came during a very difficult time for the church—indeed, for the entire city. A serious epidemic had broken out. Many were critically ill and large numbers were dying. Dr. Winkler was stricken and left Charleston temporarily, traveling to New York to recover. Both his recovery and the continued grip of the epidemic were longer than anticipated. On a number of occasions during this period of absence the pastor wrote his church family, and they replied. An example of this correspondence was entered into the minutes dated September 26, 1858.

Dear Brethren:

Since my departure from your midst, my thoughts have often reverted to you; and now while addressing him who has established the sacred bond that unites us, and making mention, as I love to think, of your absent pastor in your prayers, now it seems natural for me to speak to you and to utter as if I were among you the sentiments of pastoral affection and solicitude. It is to me, dear Brethren, a mysterious Providence which has separated us at this time. I say Providence, for I feel that a removal for a brief period from the scene of my affliction was a simple necessity; and yet it seems to me that God has prepared me as never before to weep with those that weep, and I would regard it as my highest privilege now to unite with you in the cares and occupations which the prevailing sickness has occasioned, only the protestations of others prevent me now from repairing to Charleston. Yet here I can pray in behalf of my beloved charge, and now, and hereafter, I am at your command. If you wish for me, write to me by letter or telegraph, and I will come to you without delay. Hesitate not to do so, for I would rather be with you than any where else in the world. In the mean time I pray to God, dear Brethren, that he will spare precious lives among you. If any of you become sick, remember that sickness itself is not a sign of the Divine Displeasure. He whom Jesus loved was sick. Jno. 11:3. It is enough if Jesus loves you: and then if sickness comes or even death, all is well, suffering is appointed to all. It was the lot of our dear and blessed Master: and it does not become us to shrink from what He so cheerfully bore for our sakes. But O! if suffering only brings us nearer to God we shall have reason to thank him for everything. Every tear will become as a pearl in the crown of our eternal rejoicing. And/even/now are there not supports in our divine religion adapted to support and solace the Soul under all the calamities and trials of this mortal life? Paul was afflicted with sickness. No doubt he found that mysterious "thorn in the flesh" 2 Cor. 12:7, 9 hard to bear, but what could he not bear when God said in answer to his prayer, "My grace is sufficient for thee." Wherefore if God afflict you, take to yourselves this consolation, Our prosperity, like that of Gauis 3 John vs. 2 is to be estimated by the condition of our *Souls,* not of our bodies.

O brethren, we may be required to suffer, even as David and Hezekiah and Job and Paul and Epaphroditus and so many of the most faithful servants of God have been required to bear hardness as good soldiers of the Cross for life is uncertain, and our bodies are frail and death is sure; but we have the privilige of trusting in God even though he slay us. Only be faithful, let your lamps be trimmed and burning. Abound in good works toward man and in devotion toward God, and then all things will work together for your good. I have many things to say dear brethren, but I cannot write them now, I trust to see you soon again, in the mean time I commit you to God and the word of his grace—and beg in return an interest in your prayers.

Your affectionate Pastor

E. T. Winkler[4]

The membership in conference resolved "that this church could not consent 'under any circumstance' to his return at present and would most respectfully and affectionately request him not to do so until the prevailing epidemic has entirely disappeared." On October 5, 1858, the following letter was sent from the church:

Revd. E. T. Winkler
Care Messrs. Clark Dodge & Co.,
New York.

Respected and much beloved Pastor

Your Pastoral letter of the 26th Inst to the church came duly to hand thro Bro Budd who read the same on last Sunday afternoon to a goodly number of Brethren and Sisters who had assembled in the lecture room for prayer. We can assure you the contents were earnestly and gratefully listened to, and we trust the kind affectionate lessons therein contained, will be treasured up in honest hearts and finally add to the spiritual growth of all who were present on the occasion. We kindly appreciated the disinterested and self sacrificing spirit that would prompt your return at this time, gladly would we hear from your own lips again sweet words of comfort, the earnest admonitions of truth and blessed promises of the gospel which has so often in the past supported, directed and cheered our fainting souls.

But your life and services are too valuable to us, and the cause of our Lord and Master to lead us to endanger them at present. Much as it would delight us to welcome you back, we must defer that pleasure for a season, until it is deemed safe and proper for you to return.

Before the Congregation was dismissed, the Brethren were called on to act in a church capacity, and the enclosed resolutions were unanimously adopted and a committee of the undersigned appointed to reply to your letter informing you of their action. Commending you to the care of Him "who careth for us"

We remain your Brethren in the Lord

Thos. S. Budd Chn.[5]

During the epidemic in the summer of 1858, before Winkler departed for New York, he suffered one of his greatest losses. In July of that year his wife died. Abby Turner Howe Winkler was only thirty-four at her death. The church was plunged into deep mourning. The following resolution conveys something of the feeling that prevailed. On July 12, 1858 the church wrote:

Whereas it has pleased the Almighty God of human events, to remove from the scene of her labors, her family and friends—and from her position in the Church Militant, our beloved Sister, although this event so unexpected came upon us like an electric shock in the midst of a serene sky, it found her like a faithful soldier, fully prepared with her armor on. The principles of Christianity which were so strikingly manifested in her walk and conversation through life served as "an anchor to her Soul both sure and steadfast" in the trying hour of death. Childlike and submissive she resigned her spirit into the hands of her God, and has left a bright example to the church of the efficacy of our holy religion. Like the orb of day, more mildly effulgent at its setting, it may with strict truth be said, "The day of her death was better than the day of her birth."

Therefore be it resolved,

That in the death of Sister Winkler this Church has suffered an irreparable loss.

Resolved—That we bow with submission and resignation to this dispensation of Providence and rejoice to know that our loss is her eternal gain.

Resolve—That we deeply sympathize with our beloved Pastor in this severe and trying ordeal through which he is called to pass.[6]

Mrs. Winkler was buried in the church cemetery. Her gravestone is today located in the southeast corner of the church property. The response of the church family to the death of Mrs. Winkler is a clear reminder that many a pastor of the First Baptist Church has had a faithful helpmate whose story has never been told and yet whose life likely contributed more than any other to the effectiveness of his ministry.

During the 1850s the church continued a sustained vitality. On February 13, 1860, the chairman on "the state of the church" reported in the monthly church conference:

A decided improvement in the state of our church. He was pleased to say there was no choice pews to be had and he hoped soon to be able to say that there was not one vacant in the Church, he also dwelt at some length upon the deep interest manifested in the Lectures and Sunday evening prayer meetings, firmly believing that ere long, the good God would cause his name to be magnified in the conversion of many souls.[7]

Excellent attendance notwithstanding, lesser matters requiring attention are always present. The church minutes of this period record what must have been a source of contention among the menfolk. Attention was called to "the practice of members remaining under the porch until the services had commenced as presenting a very injurious effect and of great annoyance to pastor and congregation." No action was taken in the conference, nor do any minutes of ensuing months make progress reports as to whether or not the brethren modified their pattern. For us who read of the matter many years later, there is a refreshing levity about it. It probably was much less humorous to them. The incident serves us well to show how little human nature changes. Almost a century later this writer recalls overhearing, as a youth, the complaint that "leaders" of the church often sat out on the tomb of Richard Furman, a horizontal marble slab which at that time was located over his grave approximately four feet from the southwest corner of the sanctuary. It made a perfect bench on which to sit and discuss "important" subjects. The discussions often went deep into the service time and, on occasion, were known not to have ended until the approximate time of the benediction. In more recent years, the parking lot has become the congregating point. More than once the observation has been made that the "parking lot committee" consumes more church time and energy than any other group with absolutely nothing constructive resulting.

As stated earlier, no period of her history saw the First Baptist Church experience greater attainments than those of the 1850s. But as Henry A. Tupper would in later years write, "the glory set at noonday." During the next years the church, along with the wider community, would suffer unparalleled anguish from the Civil War. No single event would more radically effect the present and future of the church than this conflict. President Lincoln's Emancipation Proclamation would profoundly effect the church both in its economic strength and its programs of ministry. The entire way of life for Charlestonians revolved around the plantation culture. Many families either operated a plantation or were engaged in related enterprises. Cotton production had made Charleston the wealthiest city from Baltimore to New Orleans, and the First Baptist Church had shared in this prosperity. Its membership included hundreds of slaves.

While some slave owners displayed a total disregard and indifference to the spiritual well-being of the slaves they owned, apparently a large percentage of slaveholders in the First Baptist Church were sincerely concerned about the spiritual condition of their slaves. Most of the minutes of the monthly church conferences record the baptizing of slaves. They were encouraged or required to attend the services. One of the most picturesque stories of the church's life during this period is of an elderly member recalling her childhood experience of hearing the Negroes who filled the north balcony peal forth in hymns of their personal faith.

The institution of slavery must be viewed as one of the darkest spots in the history of man's relationship to man. In the light of this, it is interesting to notice with what seriousness many slaveholders addressed the religious needs of their slaves. Instruction on the plantations and in the homes of Negroes started early, probably soon after the arrival of the first slaves. The endeavors of Hephzibah Townsend serves as a good example. It was not until 1847 that a structured Sunday School program, or Sabbath School as it was often called, was begun for the slaves. A similar program had been started for white children in 1816. Oliver F. Gregory states this work to be "among the first efforts made for the education of the negroes in the South."[8] The school grew to 250 "colored" students. On the first Sunday of each month the attendance was especially high. This was communion Sunday, and the "country folk" made special effort to attend. They would come for many miles either by boat or carriage. Those traveling by boat would move down the small creek touching their plantation, into the nearest river, across the harbor, and finally into the small creek which brought them within a block of the church. This creek originally followed the exact borders of present-day Water Street. Propelled by slave oarsmen, the boats moved slowly, but the time, being used for singing, fellowship, and even religious instruction, was never wasted.

Records of the church's programming indicate a variety of approaches in addressing the spiritual needs of slaves. In 1857 Dr. Winkler prepared a catechism, *Notes and Questions for Oral Instructions of Colored People.* Not only was this catechism used in the First Baptist Church but was widely accepted and utilized in many churches.[9] The work of the Sunday School for Negroes was cited earlier. In addition, the black membership was arranged in "divisions." Each division had a black leader or "overseer." These men, or women, as was sometimes the case, were devout persons deeply committed to the well-being of their people. They worked faithfully at the tasks of instruction and nurture. They gave detailed reports on the general welfare of those under their care and often prescribed discipline for those who committed moral wrongs. The church minutes reflect many instances, some in vivid details, of misconduct and the response which the church deemed appropriate. A report given by James Tupper to the monthly church conference reads:

> *London Wallace* and *Caty Siegling*—charge adultery
>
> They are both members of this Church and married persons. Eight witnesses were examined by the Committee, and the following facts proved. London as far back as seven years ago was in the constant habit of visiting Caty. They were on remarkably intimate terms. He was often seen with her in her chamber during the absence of her husband. Suspicions were excited by his frequent visits, and they were communicated to Charlotte his wife, who for a long time would not credit them. On one occasion she went to Caty's room at night; and found her seated in London's lap. This, with Caty's embarrassment upon being discovered, excited Charlotte's suspicions. Both of her parents considered Caty guilty—saying that she was in the practice of coming to their house with London, and that their conduct was entirely too intimate. The husband of Caty had frequently complained of the intimacy of London with his wife. Charlotte often complained to Caty of her conduct with London, but she refused to give up her intimacy with him, and up to this time notwithstanding the remonstrance of his wife and many members of the Church, London continues his visits as heretofore to Caty. All the Witnesses except the husband of Caty who is said to be not reliable, consider them guilty. After the above facts were adduced, Caty and London were again examined, and so contradicted themselves and each other, as to give weight to the testimony against them. The Committee after prayer, decided that London Wallace and Caty Siegling, were guilty of the sin of adultery, and were examined in recommending them to the Church for excommunication.[10]

The records of the church also reflect moments of awesome pathos. George Heyward, a slave, came seeking permission to marry again, his wife having been sold, and her new owner living some distance from Charleston. Heyward felt he would never see his wife again. The "committee on coloreds" could not agree and referred the matter to the church. The church denied Heyward's request.

In 1853 an interesting matter came before the church. The membership apparently had a concern that not enough was being done for the colored members. Dr. M. T. Mendenhall served as the first chairman of a committee to provide "a suitable place of worship for the colored people of this church, with a pastor suiting his discourses to their understanding."[11] While the exact references cannot be traced, the work of this committee likely resulted in the founding of the Morris Street Baptist Church, a grand black church which has served effectively down to the present.

One further instance concerning the relationship of the First Baptist Church to Blacks during the middle years of the nineteenth century should be cited. After the Civil War, the freed slaves were obviously at liberty to go to the church of their choice. At this time many fine churches were founded, some of which are still active. One of these was the Morris Street Church where many black people went and began a new church relationship. In this period of transition, one of the most significant things in the church's three hundred years took place. At the time it probably seemed rather minor, but the action made manifest the spirit of the church. The Morris Street Baptist Church sent a letter asking that the First Baptist Church grant to the Morris Street Baptist Church, in a blanket letter, all the colored members presently on the rolls of First Baptist Church. A committee was appointed to study the matter and recommend the proper action. The church approved the following:

> That the Clerk have authority to give such letters to those persons whose standing is unquestioned and whose names are given. A general application cannot be granted, as some of our colored members desire to retain their connection with us, and we shall be glad to have them do so. We are prepared cordially to welcome them to all the ecclesiastical privileges with us which they have heretofore been accustomed to enjoy.[12]

A number of blacks remained members of the First Baptist Church until their death. The two churches have maintained a unique relationship down to the present. In 1970 when the Morris Street Baptist Church dedicated its magnificent new edifice, the former structure having been destroyed by fire, the church invited this writer, as pastor of the First Baptist Church, to bring the dedicatory message. Christian brotherhood, shining through dark hours, had stood the test of time.

During the Civil War, the facility of the First Baptist Church was one of many buildings situated right in the line of bombardment from Union ships in the harbor. Like many other structures in the area, the church suffered extensive damage. A cannonball entered the eastern end of the building, demolishing the pulpit area and heavily damaging the fine organ. The church was without funds to repair the organ, so it was put up for sale. In exchange, the First Baptist Church acquired the Henry Erben presently being restored. The cannonball also shattered the Richard Furman tablet erected on the west wall near the pulpit. In the 1950s when renovations necessitated some excavation, a piece of the tablet was found approximately twelve feet beneath the surface, an indication of how the immediate area was pulverized. The church was so heavily damaged and the bombardments were so frequent that the building was closed. In the 1864 annual associational letter, the clerk reported the building being broken into by robbers, with looters carrying away everything of any conceivable value or use. Services were held jointly with other churches up the peninsula away from harbor bombardments. These churches included Morris Street, Wentworth Street, and Citadel Square. In 1863, the clerk of the First Baptist Church sent the following letter to the Charleston Baptist Association's Annual Meeting:

> This church has been greatly scattered, it's young men having gone into the Army, and most of it's non-combatants have removed from the beleaguered city. The pastor is serving as Senior Chaplain of Hospitals, and preaches on Sunday to the few of our denomination who remain, and to the soldiers in the Citadel Square Church, which has been cordially offered for the purpose. This edifice is less exposed to bombardment than those in the lower part of the city, and is near to several hospitals. The attendance has been quite encouraging.[13]

On the battlefields, Winkler displayed striking valor. His grandfather had fought with General Francis Marion in the same swamp lands. While he was visibly shaken by the conflict, he gave himself without calculation of risks. In his work as chaplain, Dr. Winkler would travel out to the numerous island encampments and minister to the troops. Reading issues of the *Southern Baptist* of this period, one frequently comes to those letters written by Winkler from the battlefront making passionate pleas for warm clothes and other essential items for the soldiers.

For almost exactly four years, the war went on draining the land of her men and her resources. With Lee's surrender came the enormous assignment of pulling life back together and moving toward a workable future. The church's membership and finances were radically depleted. Her building was in ruins, and the church organization was in shambles. In the fall of 1865 the clerk wrote in the Minutes, "If any meetings of the church were held after this date, August 2, 1863, the minutes are not in the possession of the undersigned, and he does not know who acted as clerk. The undersigned left the city in October 1863 and returned in August, 1865."[14] The church was closed most of that time. With the economy shattered, many who had invested heavily in Confederate bonds were now losing their homes. Plantations sold for as little as a few dollars, and foreclosures were routine. Charleston, like all of the

South, was occupied territory, and the morale of the members was extremely low. There was widespread sentiment to demolish the old edifice, selling the salvaged materials for whatever price might be had and disbanding the church. These thoughts did not prevail. Those remaining resolved to prove the church enduring, even in the face of these extremities. The immediate assignment was to have a place to worship until such time as their house of worship could be repaired. After considerable deliberation the First Baptist Church agreed to a "temporary union" with the Wentworth Street Baptist Church with Dr. Winkler serving as pastor. The deacons in the two churches would combine to form a new board. The arrangement continued for several months, during which time repairs were being made to the Church Street property. On completion of the major repairs, the two churches alternated places of worship. During this period, considerable discussion developed regarding the future of both churches. A strong sentiment surfaced favoring disposal of the property of both churches and moving north on the peninsula. A preliminary agreement was reached, and plans were underway for the move, but a considerable number of First Baptist Church members voiced reluctance. A petition made official their request that the church location not be abandoned, resulting in a mutual agreement that plans for a merger be dropped. This action posed a problem regarding pastoral leadership. The congregation of the First Baptist Church voted to ask Dr. Winkler to continue as its pastor. This left the Wentworth Street congregation without a pastor. Apparently the Wentworth Street congregation had anticipated his staying with them. The pastor's decision was to remain with the First Baptist Church, and all agreed that he would be available for special pastoral responsibilities which might arise in the Wentworth Street congregation.

Once again settled in their much beloved facility on Church Street, the congregation hoped and worked for the strength and stability it once knew, but signs of difficulty were already visible. Many members were lost in the Civil War, while others had moved away. Considerable numbers were drawn to the Citadel Square Church, and now a number of strong families were choosing to stay with the Wentworth Street congregation. All of these factors combined to deplete significantly the strength of the church. But neither she nor her pastor was without spirit. Dr. Winkler led the congregation to adopt a program of visitation, a plan which divided the city into sections, and each deacon was assigned a section. The deacon was asked to visit all the families in that section and generally to nurture them in the work of the Lord and the needs of the church. This 1867 plan might well be the first recorded attempt of a deacon family plan similar to the one which has received wide attention in our present day. This ministry, combined with other contacts within the church membership, tended to highlight the widespread poverty and distress among the members. In every monthly business meeting, the church reviewed and responded to the specific needs. It was necessary for the pastor to point out quite often that funds remained meager. The Green Fund, a fund left to the church many years earlier for the purpose of alleviating suffering within the congregation, was drawn on heavily. The pastor proposed taking a weekly offering, a custom seldom practiced, to help with some of the financial needs. He was reminded that this could not be done without affirmative action by the trustees of the corporation. Minutes of church conferences during the next several months give no indication that a practice of weekly offerings was ever instituted.

The church was laboring under great pressure during these years, but its severest jolt came June 4, 1868, when the moderator of the church read to the church conference:

Dear Brethren

The time has come when it is necessary for me to resign the Pastoral charge of your Body and to ask for myself and daughter a letter of dismission, to join the Citadel Square Baptist Church. For your kindness during long years to me and mine: God grant to you both as individuals and as a church His blessing; I cannot trust myself to speak of the past; I shall be glad to serve you if in any way I can in future—

Affectionately yours,

E. T. Winkler[15]

This was yet another in a series of events which moved the First Baptist Church from its zenith in the 1850s to the present low in which its very future was now in question. Dr. Winkler's move to Citadel Square would inevitably draw some of the leadership away from the First Baptist Church. Much to the credit of all involved, an amiable spirit prevailed between the churches. Until 1872 when Winkler accepted a call to Marion, Alabama, he was often asked to preach in the First Baptist Church. He brought the sermon the Sunday William H. Williams, his successor, was installed. Few men have made an impact equal to that of Edwin Theodore Winkler. In Alabama, he assumed the editorship of the state Baptist paper which, under his leadership, became one of the most respected Baptist papers in the South. In 1883, he was invited back to speak to the South Carolina Baptist State Convention, the highlight of which was the celebration of the 200th anniversary of the founding of the First Baptist Church, but on November 10 of that year Winkler died. On the day he was to have spoken, the evening session, convening in the Citadel Square Baptist Church, was given over completely to a memorial service. The *News and Courier,* Charleston's daily newspaper, carried a feature story describing in detail the solemnly draped pulpit and balcony. In this setting, friends and colleagues spoke eloquent words of tribute to a greatly beloved

Christian statesman. A towering tree had fallen and left a space against the sky.

Notes

1. *Minutes: First Baptist Church, Charleston, South Carolina,* November 13, 1854. Hereafter referred to as *Church Minutes.*

2. John A. Broadus, *Memoir of James Petigru Boyce, D.D., L.L.D.* (New York: A. C. Armstrong and Son, 1893), p. 149.

3. *Church Minutes,* August 11, 1856.

4. Ibid., September 13, 1858.

5. Ibid., October 5, 1858.

6. Ibid., July 12, 1858.

7. Ibid., February 13, 1860.

8. H. A. Tupper, *Two Centuries of the First Baptist Church of South Carolina* (Baltimore: R. H. Woodward and Company, 1889), p. 240.

9. "Winkler, Edwin Theodore," *Encyclopedia of Southern Baptists,* II:1505.

10. *Church Minutes,* October 13, 1851.

11. Ibid., January 10, 1853.

12. Ibid., July 1, 1866.

13. *Minutes: Charleston Baptist Association, South Carolina,* 1863, p. 22. Hereafter referred to as *Association Minutes.*

14. *Church Minutes,* August 2, 1863.

15. Ibid., June 4, 1868.

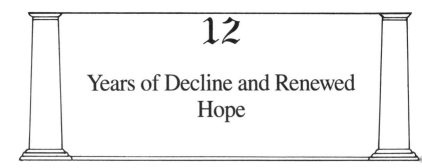

12

Years of Decline and Renewed Hope

With E. T. Winkler's decision to accept the call to the Citadel Square Church the lay leadership in the First Baptist Church now faced a compound assignment. They needed a man who would reverse the church's pattern of decline and would also bring personal and vocational qualities to the church of a strength comparable to his predecessor who was now rendering an appealing ministry just a few blocks away. William H. Williams had just completed his seminary course in May, 1868. It is reasonable to assume that anyone of the three, Boyce, Manly, or Broadus, could have recommended him to the church. They were all obviously confident regarding his ability. Dr. Basil Manly, Jr., had baptized him in the First Baptist Church, Richmond, Virginia. Dr. Broadus would later write concerning him, "He showed unusual force of character and persistency. . . . He seemed to apprehend subjects decidedly well, and to state his thoughts with clearness and vigor."[1] Williams enlisted as a chaplain in the Confederate Army, but at the close of the war he returned to the seminary to complete his work. Of those enrolled in the seminary when it was forced to close because of the war, Williams was one of only two who returned. The church extended a call to William H. Williams, and held a moving service of installation on October 11, 1868. Dr. Winkler was asked to preach the sermon that day. The members of the Citadel Square Church joined with the members of First Baptist Church for the service and in partaking of the Lord's Supper.

In December of the same year, a First Baptist Church brother was ordained deacon, and Dr. Winkler was again asked to preach the ordination sermon. The deacon ordained, Daniel H. Silcox, was the father of Mary Matilda Gillard Silcox, who very shortly would become the pastor's bride. Williams arrived in Charleston a single man. The pastor, a handsome young bachelor, had preached only a very few sermons before noticing Mary Matilda out in the Silcox family pew. He assumed the pastorate in October, and the ordination referred to came in December. It is quite likely he was already "calling by" to see Miss Mary, and it is not totally unthinkable that by December he was trying to find courage to ask Brother Silcox for his daughter's hand in marriage. If this were true, one could readily understand why the young pastor would find it terribly awkward to preach an ordination sermon focused on the man, many years his senior, whose daughter he was hoping to win in marriage. This could be the explanation for the venerable Dr. Winkler being asked to come and preach. Many years later Dr. W. J. McGlothlin, president of Furman University and the son-in-law of Dr. William H. Williams, referred to Silcox as having been the pastor's "most important deacon." Apparently there was a beautiful closeness of the two in church relationships, as well as familial relationships.

It is a credit to the young pastor that he never gave the slightest suggestion of feeling overshadowed by his predecessor. To the contrary, he frequently attested to the high esteem with which he held Dr. Winkler, and in later years would write:

> And, indeed, it was with no small degree of trepidation that I undertook to stand in the place from which Manly, Brantly, Winkler and others like them had preached the gospel. But the hearty sympathy and ready co-operation of my people were to me a source of strength and encouragement. Be it said, to the undying honor of the preceding pastors, that they had inspired the congregation with love for the Word rather than love for the man; and while these good men were regarded with highest esteem and devoted affection, yet the truth they proclaimed was more valued than the instruments through which it came. This made the work of the young pastor all the less burdensome. He was always sure of ready and appreciative hearers. Oh, that every pastor would keep in mind the duty he owes to his successors! Among the sweetest and most inspiring memories of the past are those which cluster around the 'Old First Church.'[2]

Williams enjoyed a warm and strong personal relationship with his congregation. In later years, he would share vivid recollections of his lay people's support. One example he delighted in citing was the practice of a senior deacon who set aside the time and "took the young pastor by the hand, and went with him from house to house on his first pastoral visiting tour. He thought no labor too great for the cause he loved so well." The congregation was equally as supportive in his preaching. Williams' preaching displayed a strong combination of intellectual ability and spiritual fervor. He studied faithfully and always did his utmost to be thoroughly prepared when entering the pulpit. He always wrote his sermons out in full. The First Baptist Church has in its possession two such sermons beautifully written in his personal hand.

While a strong sense of belonging was present, Dr. Williams expressed a real concern over the future of the church. He felt the poor location would ultimately destroy it. This uneasiness likely was influenced by the on-going events in the other city churches. The Citadel Square Church was flourishing and those from the Wentworth Street Church were pressing on to have an effective work in the northern part of the peninsula. Williams thought those areas were where the action was. Across ensuing years when the subject of the First Baptist Church surfaced, he always lamented its location. After having served less than ten months, he resigned and with his bride moved to Staunton, Virginia. His future work would include editing the *Central Baptist,* a strategic denominational paper in the Midwest and serving the First Baptist Churches of St. Louis, Missouri, and Charlottesville, Virginia. He was called to the First Baptist Church of Charlotte, North Carolina, but he declined the call. With William H. Williams' leaving after so short a stay, the church leadership regarded it as even more crucial that a man be found who would stay through all the woes the church was facing. The membership had continued to shrink, thus offering less and less appeal to any candidate.

After Mr. Williams' departure, only a brief time passed, and the church extended a call to Lewis H. Shuck. He assumed the pastorate in January 1870. At thirty-three years of age, Shuck came to his new work with an impressive background. The eldest son of J. Lewis and Henrietta Shuck, well known missionaries to China, he was born at Singapore on the Malay Peninsula as his parents were en route to Macao. As a missionary's child young Shuck experienced many things that would season his life. His parents had been sent out under the auspices of the Triennial Convention. In 1840 the supporting agency failed, bringing great stress upon the family, but Shuck refused to give up. He moved to Hong Kong to support himself and maintained an effective mission endeavor. In Hong Kong he operated a printing press and organized the first Baptist church in China. His work was progressing well when, in 1843, his wife died. Shuck had no choice but to return to the States with his five small children. Young Lewis was taken to the Virginia home of his maternal grandfather where he remained until college age. His father remarried and with his wife accepted appointment by the newly organized Foreign Mission Board as the first missionaries of the Southern Baptist Convention. Out of this family background, Lewis Shuck forged an excellent concept of ministry. He earned both the bachelor's and master's degrees from Wake Forest College. After having taught one year in the Oxford, North Carolina Female Institute and another year in Beulah Male Institute in the same state, Shuck moved to Barnwell, South Carolina to assume the pastorate of several small churches left vacant by the death of his father. The senior Shuck had come to Barnwell from California where he had rendered a most effective ministry with the Chinese on the west coast. The death of his third wife had resulted in Shuck's resigning his post with the Domestic Board of Missions (the Home Mission Board of the Southern Baptist Convention) and his work among the Chinese.

After a brief pastorate in his father's churches, Shuck accepted a call to the full-time pastorate of the Barnwell church, where he served until his arrival in Charleston. His close acquaintance with adversity during his formative years no doubt contributed to the spirit with which he addressed his new assignment. He found the First Baptist Church greatly reduced in numbers and in material resources. The war and its aftermath had never been felt more severely than now. From the outset, Shuck brought to his task a genuine commitment and personal affection. Family ties served to reinforce this. Like his predecessor, pastor Shuck married a young lady reared in the church. His wife's mother, Caroline Trotti, was one of the church's most faithful servants. Shuck's brother was also a resident of Charleston and a leading businessman. He, too, had married a young lady who was a member of First Baptist Church. Miss Burk's family for generations had been a loyal support in the First Baptist Church. These special relationships gave the new pastor an additional sense of belonging.

Shortly after commencing his work, the pastor succeeded in leading the church into a new religious zeal. Considerable numbers were coming for baptism, and significant happenings were occurring in the wider community. The Reverend A. B. Earle, a noted evangelist, came to Charleston offering his services. Apparently an eloquent and effective preacher, Earle joined himself to Shuck as well as to Dr. Winkler at the Citadel Square Church. The two pastors and their churches joined in mutual support and utilization of Mr. Earle's preaching with quite remarkable results. During this season of evangelistic zeal, it was not unusual on any given Sunday for twenty or more persons to move forward during the invitation and make personal professions of faith. These experiences in renewal were precisely what the church needed. While the church did not experience a great swell in membership, these events set the tone for Shuck's pastorate. For more than twelve years, he constantly worked at bringing strength and vitality to the church. The pastor's efforts in revitalization were augmented by the concern and involvement of lay people. The work of the women had noticeably increased. Prior to Shuck's arrival in Charleston, the ladies of the church organized the Ladies Industrial Society. Pastor Williams had brought to the attention of the ladies the "prostrate" condition of the church and appealed to the ladies to consider some way they might help, and their response was commendable. They resolved to meet weekly for the purpose of making articles of needlework and selling the items, the proceeds of which would go toward the purchase of anything needed in the church. Their endeavor met with much success, not only for raising funds but providing fellowship. The Society kept excellent records, a considerable portion of which have been preserved down to the present. One item entered in the record is a thank you note from Lewis Shuck for the thoughtful deed of the Society in providing his family with a ton of coal.

Another reference recorded his thanking the Society for gas lighting fixtures which so greatly improved the pastorium. Hardly did any need slip by the Society's caring eyes. In the spring of 1870 with the coming of Easter and heightened interest in those who had not yet made personal professions of faith, the Society wanted to be sure the church was ready for baptism. They presented a new baptismal robe for the pastor, two "cloaks: and curtains." [1] The following note accompanied the gift:

> My dear Pastor,
>   The Female Industrial Society request your acceptance of the accompanying baptismal robe, with the earnest prayer that you may often use it in administering the solemn ordinance to many who shall be seals to your faithful ministry.
>   With Christian regard,
>   (Miss) M. C. Budd
>   Secretary

The pastor replied:

> Miss M. C. Budd, Secretary, Ladies Industrial Society,
>   Do return thanks to the ladies of the Industrial Society for the baptismal robe received through you. I sincerely hope that I may have reason to use it frequently. Wishing the Society a career of uninterrupted prosperity, believe me sincerely and truly,
>   Your pastor,
>   L. H. Shuck[3]

The organization certainly bore the appropriate name. During a period of extreme economic pressure, the women rose to the occasion and met an untold variety of needs. In a trying time they were proved loyal and true. Such loyalty was widespread throughout the church. Although resources were seriously limited, members had a sustained interest in keeping the building attractive. In the summer of 1871, the church closed for a brief period for the purpose of painting the interior, a project of considerable expense. It could be reasonably assumed this painting was done to complete the restoration project of the mid-sixties. As is often the case, they likely exhausted the funds available during the earlier work. Such an undertaking indicates the church was definitely experiencing a period of recovery.

Another vital sign during these years was the strength of the "Sabbath School." In most of the monthly business meetings, the report was given that the Sabbath School was flourishing. During the early seventies, an average in excess of 275 "scholars" was enrolled. Each report gave encouraging remarks regarding attendance and accomplishments. One accomplishment related to the Sabbath School which received much attention was the opening of a church library. Today church libraries are commonplace, but in the 1870 such a learning resource was much less known. In addition to books, the reading materials included literature on the subjects studied in the school. One report from the library indicated subscriptions, for one year, to one hundred copies of the *Young Reaper,* a periodical with special appeal for children and youth. Mission journals were a regular accession to the collection. Such materials would inevitably heighten mission awareness among the members.

During the years of Lewis Shuck's pastorate, the First Baptist Church had a sustained interest in missions. One could readily understand the pastor's missionary heart and would not be surprised when a passionate plea came for funds to assist missionaries. Virtually every monthly financial report reflected some gift going to some distant but worthy destination. Missions concern was not limited to the romance of distant lands. Records of this period indicate the members of First Baptist gave sacrificially to victims of a severe flood locally as well as a five-dollar Christmas gift to each of a large number of poor families who were receiving continuous help from the church. The congregation also gave the Baptist Church in Beaufort, South Carolina, assistance in restoring their church from a "terribly delapidated condition," probably a carry-over from the Civil War.

Another example of the variety of mission causes espoused by the church came on the occasion of a communication received from James P. Boyce. In 1872 the trustees of Southern Seminary voted to move the seminary from Greenville, South Carolina to Louisville, Kentucky. Extensive funding was needed for the move as well as for the on-going program. The seminary was in great financial distress, and Boyce felt personal responsibility for securing funds. It was his speech before the Southern Baptist Convention that had persuaded that body to vote affirmatively on the recommendation to move. So powerful was his address that John A. Broadus, who was in the congregation, would later write, "It was a life-time concentrating itself upon one point; a great mind and a great heart surcharged with thought and feeling."[4] An offering was received and "forwarded to Dr. Boyce for the meritorious object he solicited."

Reverend Shuck was given the opportunity to broaden his ministry. He was asked to serve as assistant editor for the *The Working Christian,* the forerunner to the *Baptist Courier. The Working Christian* had moved to Charleston from Yorkville in 1870 and had opened its office at 18 Hayne Street, interestingly enough, only a stone's throw from the church's present-day activities' building. Working with the paper certainly raised Shuck's visibility and enabled him to address a much larger group. An indication of his wide appeal is seen in an invitation received in 1872 from Wake Forest College, his alma mater, to give the commencement address. On this occasion, the college conferred on him the doctor of divinity degree.

The church records for this period of the mid-seventies indicate that encouraging numbers, both members and visitors, were attending. The schedule of Sunday services had been for years morning and afternoon worship. In an effort to increase attendance, the pastor recommended the afternoon service be moved to an evening hour. An interesting provision accompanied this decision. The church resolved that seats in the evening service would be free. One surmises this action stemmed from a consensus that those inclined to attend services would do so more readily if the seats were free. Even in that day there were bargain hunters. The church records give no indication that attendance swelled because of this action. Not until the 1890s when the church was temporarily closed and then reopened did seats become free permanently.

During this period of the church's history considerable concern was focused on the decorum of individual church members. Each person was expected to walk circumspectly, and the church assumed the responsibility to discipline those who did otherwise. This practice was not unique to the First Baptist Church. The general feeling shared by most churches during this time was a responsibility to direct and control the life-style and behavior of the members. Failure to heed such direction would result in serious discipline, even excommunication, by the church. For more than one-third of the nineteenth century a recurring theme in virtually every business meeting of the church was how to bring some particular church member into compliance with what was expected or how best to deal with him or her who had defied counsel and correction. The wide range of grievances addressed in these deliberations stretched from the most trivial such as not being friendly or poor church attendance to the most serious of adultery or drunkenness. Committees were appointed to investigate allegations and recommend action. Much time was consumed in debating the right course of action, and seldom was there a division in the final vote. Excommunication meant the denial of Communion, the exclusion from voting in church conferences, and a general withdrawal of fellowship. Excommunication in a Baptist church never carried the weight of Roman Catholic excommunication because in the Baptist church nothing was said about one's salvation or Christian burial. A similar procedure was followed for those persons seeking restoration back into the church fellowship. When it had been determined that restitution had been made and a sincere desire for renewed fellowship was evidenced, the individual was restored. The service of restoration was similar to a person being received into the church at the time of baptism. The restored church member stood at the front of the congregation and received the right hand of Christian fellowship. With such concern exhibited to assure in each member a devout life-style, one might question if the effort achieved the desired ends. Based on available figures and statements, one must conclude any positive results to have been minimal. Attendance declined, attrition of new converts paralleled other periods, financial support remained static, at best, and missions awareness was unaffected. The church, faced on one side with gross laxity and on the other side with the poor results of punishment, has always struggled with the dilemma of how to discipline. In other periods of its history, the Christian community has found nurture and pastoral care as effective as more rigid procedures. The history of the First Baptist Church would attest to this fact.

Lewis Shuck's pastorate spanned some of the most trying times in the church's entire history. Not only did the Civil War and related events leave the church weak internally, but general conditions of the postwar period made recovery all but impossible. The South was occupied by Union forces, economic conditions were severely depressed, and reconstruction procedures were more destructive than constructive—all of which demoralized large numbers and plunged many into despair. Lewis Shuck must be credited not only with holding the church together during these difficult years but also with giving it a vision of what it should and could be across the years to come. In November, 1882, after having served the church for twelve fruitful years, Dr. Shuck resigned and soon moved to Paducah, Kentucky, to assume the pastorate of the First Baptist Church. In later years, he would return to South Carolina to complete his pastoral ministry, including a tenure as pastor of the First Baptist Church of Cheraw.

The church was blessed to go only a brief period without a pastor. Andrew Jackson Spears Thomas was pastor of the First Baptist Church of Batesburg, South Carolina, his first pastorate. Although he was one of eleven children, his father, a rural pastor in South Carolina, resolved that each of his children would be well prepared for whatever vocation he chose. Graduating from Furman University and The Southern Baptist Theological Seminary, Thomas displayed much self-confidence and industry. In 1877, he married Isabell Roempke, daughter of Alfred and Jess Roempke, a Charleston family of great wealth and prominence. The fact that Charleston was his wife's home made the call from the First Baptist Church very appealing. He accepted the church's call and began his work in January, 1883. He began a pastorate that would span only four and one-half years, but those years would be some of the most eventful in the church's entire history. Having assumed the pastorate, Thomas embarked immediately upon significant physical changes of the church's pulpit and baptistry. The platform was enlarged to stretch from column to column as it does at the present, and the baptistry was raised to the platform level. The pulpit, original to this building, and the sounding board which canopied the pulpit were removed, an action which was commonly regarded as quite courageous. Apparently, other pastors had thought of such action but either were thwarted or deemed it unwise to pursue. Fortunately, a number of pieces of this original pulpit were not discarded but stored in the church loft. Across the years significant pieces have been made from the aging mahogany, including a small Communion table still in the possession of the church, a gavel presented by the pastor, John A. Hamrick, to the Southern Baptist Convention in 1947, and another gavel presented by Paul J. Craven, Sr., a deacon and former president of the South Carolina Baptist Brotherhood Convention, to the Southern Baptist National Laymen's Conference in 1961. On this occasion the following statement was made:

> The solid mahogany for the pulpit from which the gavel is made was imported from the West Indies during the pastorate of Dr. Richard Furman at a cost of one thousand dollars. These materials were personally selected by Tristam Tupper, while on a business trip to St. Thomas.
>
> The pulpit was installed in the new building, which was opened for worship on January 17, 1822, and was in use for the next sixty-one years. It is interesting to note that, during this period, the deliberations of two Southern Baptist Conventions were held around this historic pulpit.
>
> The pulpit was taken down during the pastorate of the Rev. A. J. S. Thomas in July, 1883, having survived the damages effected by shells of the Civil War, which destroyed the memorial tablet to Dr. Furman, located directly beside it. This miraculous preservation of the resting place of the Word of God seemed to declare anew the truth that "Heaven and earth may pass away, but My Word shall not pass away."
>
> As the pulpit from which this gavel is made upheld the Word of God for the preaching of such giants of our faith as Furman, Manly, Brantly, Crawford, Kendrick, Winkler, Williams and Shuck, so may this same wood, in the form of a gavel, be used to direct the future deliberations of this Conference to ever uphold the Word of God.[5]

Part of the 1883 project was to purchase new pulpit furniture. This expenditure, combined with the cost of restoration, was six hundred dollars.

The work on the sanctuary was completed in time for the sixty-third session of South Carolina Baptist State Convention which met in Charleston to celebrate the bicentennial of the First Baptist Church. Since it was commonly assumed that the church, founded in Kittery, Maine, in 1682 moved to South Carolina the following year, 1883 was chosen as the date for the celebration. Not until years later was it found that the church did not move to South Carolina until the 1890s. Elaborate and appealing plans were laid for the bicentennial celebration. At the request of the pastors, several Charleston pulpits of other denominations were filled by noted Baptists who had come to participate in the commemorative services. Dr. Basil Manly preached at Second Presbyterian, and Dr. J. C. Furman preached at Bethel Methodist. A number of those Baptist leaders attending were men who had served as pastor or had spent years of their youth in the church, or for some other reason had a close relationship. These included William G. Whilden, pastor; Basil Manly, Jr., professor, Southern Baptist Theological Seminary; Charles Manly, president of Furman University; James Petigru Boyce, professor and later president of The Southern Baptist Theological Seminary; Henry A. Tupper, secretary of the Foreign Mission Board of the Southern Baptist Convention; and Oliver F. Gregory, pastor of the First Baptist Church, Charlotte, North Carolina. All of these, "sons" of the church, contributed to the significance of the event. E. T. Winkler was scheduled to speak but, as has been mentioned, died shortly before his scheduled trip. Among others attending were Dr. J. L. M. Curry, a statesman and denominational leader of extraordinary gifts, who was currently serving as professor in the University of Richmond; Dr. C. C. Bitting, a gifted preacher, pastor, and secretary of the Sunday School Board of the Southern Baptist Convention; Dr. John Lansing Burrows whose pastorates included the First Baptist Church of Richmond and the Broadway Church of Louisville, Kentucky; Dr. I. T. Tichenor, a noted pastor and college president; and Dr. G. A. Nunnally, a noted pastor and denominational leader from Georgia. Many other denominational leaders attended, but these are listed to illustrate how significant the event was regarded by Baptists in general. The addresses given in the convention covered a wide range of subjects in the church's history, including the life and work of Screven, of Hart, and of Furman; the history of the Sunday School; the history of the church's involvement with missions and education; and a review of the series of buildings occupied by the church. Five years later those addresses, augmented with additional material, were compiled into a volume by Henry A. Tupper. This volume recorded the history of the church as it celebrated its 200th birthday. The local newspapers gave extensive coverage to all the events, and the city council of Charleston in its yearbook, an official record of what transpired within a calendar year, gave significant space to the church's observance.[6]

Celebrating the bicentennial was a source of great delight, but before nine months had passed Charleston was struck in August, 1885, by a devastating cyclone. Extensive damage was done, such as the complete destruction of the steeple of the Citadel Square Baptist Church. So great was the damage stemming from this storm that the First Baptist Church could not hold services in its building for almost six months. Virtually the entire roof was blown away, leaving the building exposed to heavy rains which destroyed all the hymnals, cushions, and carpets. The congregation had hardly moved back into their restored place of worship when the terrifying earthquake of August 31, 1886 came to Charleston—one of the severest quakes ever to hit the eastern seaboard. Many structures were flattened, and many of those remaining appeared dreadfully unsafe. The first shock of the earthquake was felt at 9:50 PM. Many people, having retired for the evening, were driven from their homes and into the streets in night clothes. The streets were filled with panic-stricken citizens seeking refuge. Although property damage was extensive, miraculously few lives were lost. First Baptist Church suffered no deaths in its membership but suffered great property damage. The ceiling of the portico and the ceilings inside the building fell, as did large portions of the plastered walls. Since it was necessary to vacate the facilities, some other place for meeting had to be located. One portion of the Circular Church was unharmed, and that congregation graciously made their space available for the Sunday School to meet. Most of the churches, not having a place to gather for worship, agreed to meet on the "cistern" at the College of Charleston, a central place familiar to everyone. The Reverend John O. Wilson of the Methodist Church joined in conducting these outdoor meetings. The services were well attended and were later described by Dr. Thomas as "a most precious season of worship." Dr. Thomas assumed the pastoral care and leadership for all the Baptist churches of the city. While he tended the flocks, it was agreed that Dr. C. A. Stakely, pastor of the Citadel Square Baptist Church, would go out across the state and solicit from friends funds so critically needed in repairing their places of worship. People far and near responded to this appeal with generous contributions. More than $20,000 was raised, of which the First Baptist Church received $6,000.

During the four and one-half years of Dr. Thomas' pastorate, the congregation was forced to meet in other places for worship more than seventeen months. In July, 1887, Dr. Thomas brought to a close his work in Charleston, to accept a call to the First Baptist Church of Orangeburg, South Carolina. He remained a strong leader in the life of South Carolina Baptists. In 1891 he bought controlling interest in *The Baptist Courier,* at that time a privately-owned paper, and became its editor. Thomas served as president of the South Carolina Baptist State Convention and was one of the original members of the committee appointed to establish a Baptist orphanage in the state. A few years after his pastorate in the First Baptist Church, A. J. S. Thomas reflected on his difficult years and wrote, "The church interests during those times suffered, of course; but the Lord watched over his own . . . a more devoted, earnest, active band of disciples cannot be found."[7]

In November, 1887, when the Charleston Baptist Association convened for its annual meeting, the letter submitted by the clerk of the First Baptist Church had a distinct note of sadness about it. It referred to the unfortunate year the church had experienced as a result of the earthquake. The letter, lamenting the pastor's resignation, reported the church's "hoping and praying for a pastor to be supplied." In spite of the difficult aspects of the past year, the clerk communicated certain worthy accomplishments. The buildings had been repaired, and the church was free of debt. "A surplus of money with which the church proposes to build a mission chapel" was reported. These funds would soon be applied toward the purchase of a facility on Cannon Street which would greatly enhance the volunteer program for children and families in the northern part of the peninsula. An account of this work shall be given later in this chapter.

As the church searched for its next pastor, it turned to Darlington County and to Robert Wilkins Lide, who for approximately ten years had served the Swift Creek Baptist Church. With the exception of one brief pastorate in New Bern, North Carolina, Lide spent the entire fifty-seven years of his ministry in South Carolina. Other pastorates across the state included the First Baptist Churches of Cheraw, Barnwell, Darlington, and Georgetown.

While the exact date of his assuming the pastorate in the First Baptist Church is not certain, it was early enough in 1888 for the pastor to lead in several encouraging achievements before the autumn meeting of the association. When the Charleston Baptist Association convened for its annual meeting in November, 1888, the church clerk included in the annual church letter to the association a report of good things happening. The letter read: Our church "is actively engaged with their pastor in reaching out into new fields in the upper part of the city, where Baptist influence is much needed."[8] The letter also reported that the total given to missions in 1888 was $623.41, apparently the most to have been given in recent years.

The following year an even more encouraging letter was sent to the association. The letter, in part, related how the church "is in a growing condition with increasing attendance in religious services. The consecrated zeal of their pastor has won the hearts of his people, and the latter are not only active in all the church work, but also have an interesting mission on Cannon Street with promise of great good."[9]

The church decided to use those funds left from the 1886 earthquake fund, combined with any other available resources, to construct a "mission chapel" in the Cannon Street area. This facility would greatly strengthen the work in that area, a work that would lead to the founding of the Cannon Street Baptist Church, later to be relocated and renamed the Rutledge Avenue Baptist Church. The story of the Cannon Street work begins in 1883 when Miss Elizabeth Yoer Hyde began a volunteer program in the northern part of the city with families living in the industrial sector of Charleston. Some of the residents of the area were self-supporting factory workers, and some were underprivileged. The area had grown steadily with a number of small industries and, as such, offered an excellent mission opportunity. Miss Hyde, a member of one of the church's strongest families, had hoped for an appointment by the Foreign Mission Board. She was a contemporary with Lula Whilden whose story was told in an earlier chapter. In their youth Lula and Elizabeth were friends, and one suspects they had dreams of serving in some distant land together. Lula went to China, but Elizabeth's dreams vanished when the Foreign Mission Board deemed her health too fragile for the demands on a missionary. Such a disappointment did not take away her missionary zeal. Elizabeth gave herself completely to the work of the upper part of the peninsula, the "neck," as it was called, deriving this name from that strip of land between the Ashley and Cooper Rivers that was narrower than other sections of the peninsula. Her work consisted not only of the activities in the Cannon Street Mission but also an "industrial" school for boys located on Bogard Street. With an enrollment of sixty, the school gave instruction not only in academics but in trade skills and most of all in spiritual nurture.

Her achievements were so impressive that Miss Hyde was asked by the Citadel Square Baptist Church to add to her heavy responsibilities an additional work. The Citadel Square Baptist Church had just begun a mission work at the corner of Cooper and Blake Streets. It could be reasonably assumed that the involvement and success of the First Baptist Church in the Cannon Street area served as an encouragement for the Citadel Square Baptist Church to begin a work on the east side of town. Hardly had the church begun its project when notice came that a $5,000 bequest had been made to the Citadel Square Baptist Church by Emma Abbott (Mrs. Eugene Wetherell) whose Emma Abbott English Opera Company had appeared several times at Charleston's Academy of Music. Mrs. Wetherell, having performed in New York and London, was a noted opera singer and a colorful personality. When in Charleston, she attended the Citadel Square Baptist Church. The mission, built by the Citadel Square Baptist Church with these funds, was known as the Emma Abbott Memorial Chapel. It still stands today as the Mount Sinai Holiness Church of Deliverance.[10] The details of this story are presented here not only to point out Miss Hyde's expanded mission opportunities, but to relate the excellent growth in the work of the Citadel Square Baptist Church. As will be shown in the next chapter, the work of the Citadel Square Baptist Church soared at the same time the work of the First Baptist Church began to face decline.

Elizabeth Hyde was asked to assume the post as the first statewide secretary for Sunbeam Band work, and, as such, for twenty years she led this state mission organization in significant achievements. After her death, Sunbeam children from across the state gave their pennies in a love offering sufficient in amount to build, as a memorial to her, the original structure of the King Street Baptist Church, now the Hampton Park Baptist Church. Of all her effective work, the most far-reaching endeavor may have been the small private school she operated in the backyard of her home at 11 King Street where she taught her pastor's children. So winsome was her spirit, and so effective was her teaching, that of Pastor Lide's five sons and five daughters, Jane, Florence,

James, and Frank offered themselves to go as foreign missionaries. James' early death precluded his going, but the others were appointed and served illustrious careers. When one considers that R. W. Lide served the First Baptist Church only three years, one is constrained to feel the Lides were brought to Charleston, and Elizabeth Hyde was kept in Charleston for such a time as this. As Loulie Latimer Owens ended her treatment of this moving story, "In the providence of God one missionary was kept at home. Three were inspired to take her place!"[11]

During Lide's pastorate in Charleston, he gave significant leadership in the denomination. As chairman of the missions committee for the association, he vigorously promoted mission outreach in the state's central territory. Perhaps his most effective leadership came as chairman of the education committee. In 1890, he reported to the annual meeting of the Charleston Baptist Association not only that Furman University was flourishing but also that a number of academies were operating well. He indicated a special interest in one such academy operating in the St. Stephens area. Apparently, he had more contact with this school and had occasion personally to review its effective work. The sustained interest Robert Lide displayed in the causes of Christian education would certainly have been one reason that Furman University conferred on him the doctor of divinity degree.

Mr. Lide's effective leadership in statewide causes was found equally as strong in local mission concerns. The pastor frequently preached on Sundays at the Cannon Street Mission. By 1891, the membership in the mission numbered 150, and by 1892, it was constituted a church. As Robert W. Lide brought to a close his pastorate in Charleston toward the end of 1890, much had been done to strengthen the church, and much had been accomplished in the mission endeavors in the northern part of the city. One reading those records that are available for this period might justifiably assume a bright outlook for the last decade of the nineteenth century. But then one comes in the church letter submitted to the 1890 annual associational meeting to a brief but terribly ominous sentence: "After prayerful consideration (this church) has decided to change its location and expects soon to commence to build a new house of worship. . . . "[12] This action would lead the church into one of the saddest, most distressing periods of its entire history. An attempt would be made for the next eighteen months to close the church permanently. The church survived this, principally through the heroic efforts of a small band of women who refused to let it die. Their response is one of the most touching stories in all the church's history. The next period in the life of the First Baptist Church finds the church without a pastor and with a group of the church's leaders attempting to close the church permanently; but a group of loyal women rose to the demands of a difficult time.

Notes

1. W. J. McGlothlin, *Rev. William Harrison Williams, D.D.,* a biographical monograph. Dr. McGlothin was Rev. Williams' son-in-law.

2. H. A. Tupper, *Two Centuries of the First Baptist Church of South Carolina* (Baltimore: R. H. Woodward and Company, 1889), pp. 262-263.

3. Minutes: *The Ladies Industrial Society of the First Baptist Church, Charleston, South Carolina,* October 14, 1870.

4. John A. Broadus, *James Petigru Boyce, D.D., L.L.D.* (New York: A. C. Armstrong and Son, 1893), p. 237.

5. A monograph prepared for the service of presentation on file in the First Baptist Church.

6. *Year Book 1881 City of Charleston, South Carolina* (Charleston, South Carolina: The News and Courier Book Presses, 1881), pp. 316-324.

7. Tupper, p. 281.

8. *Associational Minutes,* 1888, p. 10.

9. Ibid. 1890, p. 5.

10. Robert P. Stockton, *The News and Courier,* March 2, 1981, p. 1-B.

11. Loulie Latimer Owens, *Banners in the Wind* (Columbia: Woman's Missionary Union of South Carolina), p. 43.

12. *Minutes* of the Charleston Baptist Association, p. 12.

13

Struggles for Survival and the Resolve to Continue

During the late spring or early summer of 1890, the First Baptist Church voted to close. Records that might give the exact date are unavailable, but the decision came early enough in the year for the action to be reported in the church letter submitted to the autumn session of the Charleston Baptist Association. As shall be discussed later in this chapter, the procedure used in making the decision was always held in serious question.

The distressing dilemma of the 1890s will be better understood against the background of several significant events which occurred in the church's life. Each of these has been discussed earlier, but, by way of review, a brief reference is repeated. First and foremost was the Civil War. Not only did the church suffer the immediate damage to its facilities and the depletion of its membership and resources, but even more difficult, the congregation faced the assignment of shaping a totally new life-style. The plantation culture was over, and the old South was vanishing. All recovery had to be accomplished in the framework of reconstruction with its demoralizing forces at work.

Another disheartening factor was the damage the church suffered from the cyclone in 1885 and the earthquake in 1886. It is enlightening to notice that after each of these three difficult experiences, there was a significant number in the congregation who thought it necessary and wise to disband or relocate the church. As late as 1920, movements surfaced to close or relocate the church. Each time the idea met stern resistance.

Still another factor which strained the church in continuing was the gradual shift of population on the peninsula. Prior to the 1840s, virtually all of the city's population was south of Calhoun Street. For example, when the Manlys and Boyces and other First Baptist Church members lived during the 1820s and 1830s on George Street, it was considered the suburbs. Then came a surge of residential development immediately north of Calhoun Street. Citadel Square Baptist Church began in the 1840s in the midst of new housing. Many of the younger families, sons and daughters of First Baptist Church families, moved north on the peninsula and built new homes. After the Civil War, many old homes in the lower peninsula were actually abandoned, only to be occupied by tenants who paid little or no rent. The setting for Dubose Heyward's opera *Porgy and Bess* was such a tenement on East Bay Street just a short distance from the church. At that time it was dilapidated housing. Today it is a part of exquisite Rainbow Row. As one strolls today through the streets in the immediate vicinity of the church, an area regarded as one of the loveliest residential areas in the country, one has difficulty imagining how badly the area deteriorated during the postwar years. Not until the 1920s was there any indication the general area might be restored to its original grandeur.

A final factor which the church faced in its struggle to remain open was the loss of membership due to death and transfer of membership. During the early 1890s there were no regular church conferences, nor was there an annual letter to the association. Consequently, there are no membership numbers available. A letter, written from one member to another in 1893 during the time of debate over closing the church, states the church had fifty-two members. During the mid-1880s a partial list of those members who died during a three-year span included not only a dramatic number but a large segment of leadership. Many names appearing in the death notices were the same names that had appeared across the years in the church minutes in roles of leadership. While the church was not depleted of leadership, it was greatly reduced at a very critical time. In addition, a considerable number of those who had been entrusted with leadership as deacons, trustees, and similar roles had taken the initiative in leading the church to disband. Some of these moved their membership to other churches in the city, and some, while not transferring their membership, ceased attending the First Baptist Church and attended other churches.

The viable programs in other churches of the city definitely and understandably influenced the thinking of many First Baptist Church members. In the 1890 minutes of the Charleston Baptist Association, the Citadel Square Church reported the finest year in its history. The church's mission gifts doubled over the preceding year, enthusiasm was high for a mission on the east side of the city, and the membership was increasing rapidly—some of the new additions coming from the First Baptist Church. The pastor of the Citadel Square Church at this time was Dr. Edwin C. Dargon, who came from a line of noted ministers and became one of the Southern Baptists' most gifted leaders. Coupled with the healthy happenings in the Citadel Square Church was the continuing development of the Cannon Street Baptist Mission. By 1891, the mission had 150 members enrolled and in 1892 was constituted a church. Like the Citadel Square Church, the Cannon Street Church inevitably drew from the membership of the First Baptist Church.

With all of the foregoing factors at work, the membership of the First Baptist Church voted around midyear 1890 to disband. If minutes were made of the meeting, they either were never left with the church or were lost. The circumstances surrounding the action have always had an element of mystery. The decision to close the church became a matter of strong contention among the members. Exactly what action the congregation took in the 1890 church conference is not clear. Apparently, the action simply called for disbanding the church with no specific action taken on disposal of the property. The church held deed not only to the Church Street property but also the Cannon Street property. While the vote passed, it was not unanimous, and those voting against disbanding continued to meet and claimed to be a bona fide congregation.

Not long after the vote to disband, the primary topic of conversation became the proper disposition regarding the properties. For many years, the First Baptist Church had followed an unusual practice regarding the church trustees. The church corporate officers were the trustees, and these individuals were not always synonymous with the deacons. The trustees were invested with extensive authority in all financial and legal matters.

One could safely assume that during the 1890s the trustees of the First Baptist Church regarded it as their responsibility to determine what disposition should be made concerning the church property. But members of the congregation also insisted on being heard. A considerable number of members voiced the desire that the Church Street property remain available for those who chose to continue the church at this location. Those advocating this policy were brought into direct conflict with the trustees who had officially ordered the church closed. Members of the church feared that if all services ceased, the property would be conveyed by the trustees to the nearest Baptist church—the Citadel Square Church. In an effort to provide a form of continuing services, a group of ladies met regularly on Thursday afternoon for prayer meeting in the lecture room or, when possible, in the sanctuary. While the number varied from week to week, the group became affectionately known as the Old Guard, and many years later the story of their faith and tenacity was still being told. Their group included Mrs. J. M. Axson, Mrs. M. C. Damon, Mrs. Mamie Bolger, Miss Juliana Watson, Miss Annie Leary, Mrs. S. A. Douglas, Miss Blanche Clacius (later to be Mrs. Harris), Mrs. Sarah Burk, and Mrs. I. F. Butler. The controversial question continued for months as to whether or not those meeting regularly for prayer did in fact compose the congregation of the church. Their meeting regularly for prayer communicated to the trustees the necessity of working out a compromise. Complications deepened when it was learned that the trustees were seriously considering conveyance of the Cannon Street property to the trustees of that work. As late as 1893, the conflict was still unresolved. A personal letter from Mrs. J. M. Axson, a member of the committee seeking a solution, to Mr. F. A. Silcox, chairman of that committee, furnishes badly needed background material. Regarding the original meeting called in the summer of 1890 to resolve the question of disbanding, Mrs. Axson pointed out that the meeting was illegally convened and the vote to disband carried less than the majority needed. The membership at this time was reported in the same letter to be fifty-two. A vote of thirty-nine was needed, and twenty-seven voted in the affirmative.

In the same letter, Mrs. Axson reviewed the essential elements of the original 1890 agreement. The Cannon Street property was to be turned over to that group for use without rent until such time as they built a new facility. At that time, the Cannon Street property would be sold with the proceeds helping fund the newly built facility. The other element of the agreement stated that those choosing to continue meeting at the 63 Church Street site would be allowed to do so. Neither aspect of the agreement was followed. Mrs. Axson's letter continued,

> . . . but you have gone beyond that agreement and have executed a deed giving the chapel to the Cannon Street Church, such was not the understanding, and you cannot find any such resolution upon the minutes of that meeting . . . but we must have the church (63 Church Street) free to do with as we think best.

The fact was later discovered that the trustees comprised of Simeon Hyde, T. T. Hyde, E. L. Wilkins, F. A. Silcox, and T. A. Nipson on April 7, 1893 registered a deed of conveyance of the Cannon Street property to the trustees of the Cannon Street Church. The entire story has great intrigue, all the elements of which were never brought into focus until 1908 some fifteen years later. Dr. B. Lacy Hoge had assumed the pastorate of the First Baptist Church in late 1907 or early 1908. In February, 1908, the First Baptist Church received a letter from the Cannon Street Church requesting the proper committees of the two churches meet to resolve the ownership problem. Probably a faulty deed appeared as the Cannon Street Church prepared to sell the property or borrow money on it. It was obviously an embarrassment to the leadership of the Cannon Street Church. One committee member from the Cannon Street Church was quoted as saying, "Gentlemen, the property is the property of the First Baptist Church, and we want you to give it to us." The final solution came with the property being placed in the ownership of the Cannon Street Church. In the work of resolving the matter, a twenty-five-page deposition was assembled for the First Baptist Church by the legal firm of Buist and Buist. The deposition is important because it gives details of the 1890s conflict that otherwise would be lost.

In 1893, the questionable deed conveying ownership of the Cannon Street property faded into the background since those meeting at the Church Street address were struggling to establish their right to be there and to gain agreement from the trustees to continue. When the trustees saw the persistence of those meeting weekly and also saw their group growing, they had little choice but to enter into an agreement to reopen the church. During the time this was being worked out, Dr. Lucius Cuthbert made known his willingness to serve the congregation as pastor without remuneration. This was precisely the provision for which the "Old Guard" had faithfully prayed. On October 6, 1892, Dr. Cuthbert preached his first sermon as pastor of the First Baptist Church. The following statement of agreement was entered into by those attending and the officers of the church:

> We, the undersigned members and officers of the First Baptist Church, being desirous of a harmonious and brotherly settlement of the differences that have existed among us, with respect to the plans and policy to be pursued in the management of the affairs of the said Church, have agreed upon the following:
>
> FIRST: That we, the members of the First Baptist Church deed to the Cannon Street Baptist Church the use of the Chapel situated on Cannon Street, to be used by them for public worship, and should they be able at any time to build another Church, to sell the Chapel and put the proceeds into the new building. But should the work fail in the Cannon Street Chapel, or after the new Church be built, the Chapel, or the amount the Chapel may bring, shall revert to the First Baptist Church, all of which will more fully appear by the deed approved by this church.
>
> SECOND: We, as officers of the Church, agree that such of the members of the Church as desire to do so may continue to worship in the Church Buildings, may hold business meetings, and may admit members under the rules and regulations of the said Church.
>
> THIRD: That none of the members, unless they desire to do so, shall be considered as under obligation to attend such services or business meetings, without prejudice to all their rights and privileges as members of the Church.
>
> FOURTH: And it is jointly agreed that those not statedly worshiping with the others, who desire to worship in said Church regularly, will assist whenever it may be deemed necessary, in holding meetings for the purpose of acting upon applications for membership in said Church.
>
> To this agreement we pledge ourselves as Brothers and Sisters of the said Church.

Mrs. J. M. Axson	Miss A. Bolger
Mrs. M. C. Damon	Miss Juliana Watson
L. F. Addison	Miss Annie E. Leary
Miss F. D. Damon	Mrs. Sarah Burk
Mrs. I. F. Butler	Simeon Hyde

Miss R. E. Finney	Thos. S. Nipson
Miss Blanche Clacius	E. L. Wilkins
Mrs. S. H. Reed	F. A. Silcox
Miss M. B. Davis	T. T. Hyde
Mrs. C. Douglas	M. Bolger

While the agreement was signed by members and officers, it did not resolve the issue. On January 9, 1893, the following article appeared in the *News and Courier:*

A DIVIDED CHURCH

A Misunderstanding Between Members of the First Baptist Church

There is serious trouble between the deacons and the president of the First Baptist Church and a number of the members. It will be remembered that some two years ago a dissension arose in the Church over moving the church located on Church Street between Tradd and Water, and the differences have never been adjusted.

About three months ago the Rev. Lucius Cuthbert of Aiken, was asked by a large number of the members, still attending prayer meeting at the church to preach to them, without compensation. This he has been doing, and the condition of the church seemed to be much more prosperous. Within the last few days, however, the deacons came to the conclusion that the services were not to the advantage of the Church, and therefore withdrew the permission previously granted to Mr. Cuthbert.

As to the exact status of affairs and what occurred at the church yesterday, the following statements were made by the gentlemen named to a Reporter for the News and Courier last night will explain. Capt. Simeon Hyde was asked for a statement of the difficulty, and replied as follows:

"I am president of the corporation of the First Baptist Church. For a long time there has been some seeming dissatisfaction with the management of the affairs of the church. No services have been had there for some time, and there is no pastor of the church because there was no congregation to support one.

"Mr. Cuthbert of Aiken, undertook to preach in the church without compensation and was granted leave to do so by the deacons of the church with the distinct understanding that the congregation to which he ministered was not to act as an organized body. When this understanding was violated, of course the permission was withdrawn. Mr. Cuthbert had been notified not to attempt to conduct services in the church because of the violation of the agreement under which he was preaching."

Mr. J. M. Axson said: "I am a warden of the First Baptist Church.

"During last October the Rev. Lucius Cuthbert of Aiken came to preach gratuitously to those standing by the church since the division some two years ago. He was granted authority to do so by the deacons of the church.

"The present members desired to have a meeting called to admit several members transferred from sister churches. To this the deacons objected and a letter was written to Mr. Cuthbert and to a lady member prominent in the Church work, saying that further worshipping in the church would be prohibited, and that Mr. Simeon Hyde, president of the congregation had the keys to the church.

"I claimed that he had no right to the keys and I opened the church for worship as usual this morning, having previously given out the regular notice for next Sunday, and while the sermon was in progress, Messrs E. L. Wilkins (a deacon of the church) and Simeon Hyde walked in. When the minister finished his sermon he read aloud their letter to him about the action of the deacons. In the letter it was stated that he would be allowed to preach there this morning, 'because the notices had been already published.'

"At this time Mr. Hyde rose in an excited manner, and said that Mr. Cuthbert had been allowed to preach there on the express condition that he would not try to increase the membership of the church, and that now he was trying to force them to call a meeting to receive members for the purpose of his getting control of the church.

"When Mr. Cuthbert started to enter the church in the afternoon for Sunday School he was met at the gate by the sexton, who handed him a note from Mr. Hyde, prohibiting him from entering the church. I invited him in, but he preferred not to come in, and so went away. The services of the afternoon were the regular Sunday services of the church."

The encounter that Sunday morning must have been a sad occasion. Witnesses would later relate that Simeon Hyde removed his coat and threatened to move Cuthbert bodily from the church. He was prevented from doing so by J. M. Axson. It appears Simeon Hyde and T. T. Hyde, his brother, felt that the life of the First Baptist Church had run its course; they thought those few who had persisted in meeting would soon die out or leave, and the trustees would then dispose of the property as they might choose. They had not anticipated individuals actually presenting themselves for membership. When this happened, their immediate reaction was to forbid any new additions. Those advocating the closing were members of strong families. For example, T. T. Hyde would later serve as mayor of the city of Charleston and president of the South Carolina State Baptist Convention. The Hyde family and other families advocating the closing had for many years been ardent supporters of the First Baptist Church. Apparently, these individuals acted out of their frustration with its decline and under the illusion that the church was actually in their trust to do with as they deemed proper.

After the incident involving Hyde and Cuthbert, Dr. Cuthbert returned to his home in Aiken, South Carolina, probably to rethink his role in the matter. While there he wrote the following letter to the editor of the *News and Courier*. It appeared in the paper January 14, 1893.

THE FIRST BAPTIST CHURCH

A card from Mr. Cuthbert concerning the
Recent Troubles

To the Editor of the News & Courier:

I beg leave to correct an assertion made by Mr. Simeon Hyde in the First Baptist Church, last Sabbath, and reported in your issue of Monday last. The assertion was, in effect, that I had violated an agreement between the committee of which he (Mr. Hyde) was chairman, on the one hand, and the members worshipping in the First Baptist Church, and myself, on the other, in simple justice to those members, as well as to myself, I now call upon Mr. Hyde to either publish, in full, the text of the agreement referred to including the conditions attached, over my signature, on their behalf,—or to make a retraction as public as was his assertion.

As nearly as I can remember (not having retained a copy of the original, which I myself handed to Mr. Hyde), permission to have public worship resumed, and conducted under my ministrations in the old Church edifice was granted upon substantially the following conditions:

1. That the committee should not be in any manner responsible for expenses incurred in consequence of such resumption of public worship.

2. That they should not, either in their official capacity or otherwise be expected to attend Divine service at the old church.

3. That those who worshipped there should not interfere with the property of the Cannon Street Mission; and

4. That no organized meeting of the members of the Church should be held unless called by the corporation, or by the deacons of the church.

These conditions having been reduced to writing, were signed by the respective parties, including all or nearly all those members of the church who desired to avail themselves of the opportunity thus afforded, and in their behalf, and with their knowledge and approval I added a memorandum to the effect that if and when it should become necessary to take official action upon business of the church, such as administering the ordinances or receiving new members by letter or otherwise they, the committee, would be duly notified and in case they failed to call such meeting or to attend the whole agreement would be deemed "null and void."

Now the question arises, in view of Mr. Hyde's assertion, wherein and how had there been any violation on the part of either the members or myself of the conditions above referred to? So far as I know and believe they have all been scrupulously observed by both minister and people and both in substance and in form. In support of this view I desire to make the following statement:

Several applications for admission as members of the First Baptist Church based upon "letters of dismissal" from sister churches in Aiken and elsewhere—were duly forwarded to the deacons in time for consideration, with a view to action thereon at the next regular meeting for church business, authorized by the rules to be held on the second Monday evening in each month, which, in the present instance, would have been the evening of Monday, the 9th. Instead of taking steps to have such meeting held and the question of receiving the applicants then and there finally disposed of, in accordance with the rules, the deacons, it would seem, took upon themselves the responsibility of exercising a function which, by Section 4 of Rule III of the By-Laws of the First Baptist Church, rests solely with the Church itself. That section provides, with regard to the admission of applicants from sister churches, that "this church being satisfied therewith, (i.e. the letter) the person so applying shall be received into membership."

Instead of allowing "this church" to have any voice in the matter the deacons caused the letter recommending three of the applicants for admission to the First Baptist Church to be returned with a communication dated the 7th. inst. signed by Deacons E. L. Wilkins, and T. T. Hyde in their official capacity, in which it is said:

"The First Baptist Church has really ceased to hold services, or meetings for business matters, and it would be an injustice to these applicants now to receive them as members therein."

I do not desire to discuss any question of fact or of law involved in the assertions contained or implied in the paragraph last quoted, but will simply remark that—in view of the fact that if the old church or what is left of it cannot be self-supporting it must go; that it is struggling for existence without outside aid, and that the situation is perfectly well known to the applicants who have been thus refused admission—it is difficult to see wherein "injustice" would be done to them by acceding to their request, is not their rejection rather an injustice to the church, which would have been, by their admission, aided in its efforts and strengthened in its work?

How strange it seems that a church which some two years ago was closed because it was then deemed impracticable to sustain it, should, after the experiment of reopening it, has been tried for a comparatively brief period, yet with a reasonable measure of success, be again closed, simply because there were seven Christian men and women who desired to join it!

In conclusion I would say, in all kindness to those displaying a spirit of hostility in this matter, why seek to thwart this remnant of the old church in their earnest, humble and sincere endeavors to revive the Lord's word in this branch of his vineyard and to again open the portals of an edifice whose venerable but sturdy walls have for generations resounded with the voice of prayer and praise, rather than allow it to become the abode of the sparrow and the spider and to crumble into final ruin and decay?

Respectfully yours,

(Signed) Lucius Cuthbert

Aiken January 11, 1893.

The incident was not sufficient to change the pastor's mind nor his commitment. He returned to the pulpit of the church with more determination than ever and involved himself in a commitment that would continue to the close of the century.

Cuthbert was gifted with unusual ability and a large capacity for commitment. He was the nephew of Richard Fuller and received much of his insight and philosophy from him. Cuthbert's brother, James H. Cuthbert, was also an ordained minister whose pastorates included the First Baptist Church of Philadelphia, Pennsylvania, and the First Baptist Church of Washington, D.C. Lucius Cuthbert had served the Citadel Square Church in 1866 and 1867 but for health reasons had moved to Aiken, South Carolina, and greatly reduced his responsibilities. In September, 1892, he was asked by the Citadel Square Baptist Church to return to Charleston as supply pastor of that church. The pastor of the Citadel Square Church, Dr. Edwin C. Dargon, had resigned to accept the professorship of homiletics in The Southern Baptist Theological Seminary. It was during this supply pastorate that Cuthbert became aware of the lamentable plight of the Old First Church. As soon as he fulfilled his commitment to the Citadel Square Church, Cuthbert came to the First Baptist Church and assumed his work in their midst.

The details of what took place in the weeks immediately following the January, 1893, confrontation of Cuthbert by the president of the corporation are hidden from us, but a general idea of what developed can be surmised. Cuthbert returned to Charleston from a brief visit to his home in Aiken more resolved than ever that those members of the First Baptist Church who desired to continue services would be assured this opportunity. He obviously found the group even more determined than he. The pastor addressed his task with keen insight.

Obviously, his strategy was not only to promote the weekly services of the church but to give it high visibility in the association. The associational minutes of this period report several committees on which Dr. Cuthbert was asked to serve.

A wide circle of Baptists throughout the association displayed concern for the well-being of the First Baptist Church. When the association convened for its regular fall meeting in November, 1894, the following resolution was adopted:

> As it has been some time since we have had any report or representation from the First Baptist Church, Charleston, South Carolina, resolved, That a committee be appointed to confer with the church that we might secure their continued cooperation and representation.

A committee of three was appointed with the understanding they would report their findings at the next session. In the 1895 session the committee relinquished its time to Lucius Cuthbert who "was then called out, and gave the association an intensely interesting account of the 'Old First Church'; of the trials, disappointments, persecutions, but final success of the faithful band of sisters who have so earnestly labored for the old mother church. It was a season of rejoicing and thanksgiving, and the association joined with Rev. David M. Ramsey in a prayer to this effect."

After this account, the clerk concluded the minutes of the occasion with a simple but highly suggestive entry. He stated the remaining reports and further deliberations were postponed until the next day, an indication that the report regarding the First Baptist Church was not only of some duration but, for the entire association, a moving experience. No further mention is made for many years on the subject of closing or disbanding the church. Those who favored its closing either moved their membership or withdrew from active involvement in the life of the church.

During the remaining years of the nineteenth century Dr. Cuthbert succeeded in stabilizing the life and work of the church. One happening that assisted him in this endeavor was the influx of new members. The increase was not dramatic, but it was steady. A. S. Willeford, an ordained minister, came into the church and volunteered his help. His daughter, Mrs. Elizabeth Burk, served as organist. Midway Dr. Cuthbert's pastorate, H. L. Baldwin joined his flock. This began a long and fruitful record of service spanning more than a half century. Reference will be made to Baldwin at a later point, but it should be mentioned here that he symbolized the determination of those committed to the survival of the church. Because of his long and faithful service, the congregation voted to have a memorial tablet to him mounted in the sanctuary as an event in the tricentennial celebration. Unlike the others whose names appear on tablets in the sanctuary, Mr. Baldwin was not a man of wide community acclaim but a man of quiet, enduring zeal for his beloved church.

As the nineteenth century drew to a close, Dr. Cuthbert had to ask for relief from his labors as pastor. No pastor could have held a church family in more genuine affection than did Lucius Cuthbert and his beloved wife, Susan. She survived him by several years and continued to serve in the church in whatever ways possible. In 1910, she, too, joined the Church Eternal. In her will, she bequeathed out of her modest estate nineteen hundred dollars to the Old First Church. Cuthbert was so highly respected and revered that one of the church's most faithful supporters, Miss Emma Ryan, bequeathed five thousand dollars to the church, a sum more than sufficient to erect a memorial tablet on the south wall of the sanctuary which reads:

In Memory
of
REVEREND LUCIUS CUTHBERT D.D.
Born Sept. 22, 1832—Died Jan. 10, 1906.
Due to financial conditions and extreme misfortune
This church closed in 1891
In answer to prayer it was reopened by
REVEREND LUCIUS CUTHBERT in 1893
His labor began asking for nothing
giving all for the glory of God.
His faithful services closed in 1900,
Crowned by the abiding love, gratitude and honor
of his congregation, who to this day do him reverence
HIS WORKS DO FOLLOW HIM
This tablet is the gift to this Church
from a bequest by
MISS EMMA RYAN
as a testimony of appreciation
for the valued services of
REVEREND LUCIUS CUTHBERT D.D.
rendered this First Baptist Church, Charleston, S. C.
Dedicated Sept. 21, 1930

As the First Baptist Church entered the twentieth century, it began a series of short pastorates which precluded any sustained growth. From 1900 to 1921, the church had nine pastors. When one considers the lapse of time between each pastorate, one readily sees the short period of time each pastor stayed. Any church would inevitably feel adverse effects from a series of such short pastorates. In 1925, Mrs. Robert Lawrence Miles was asked by the Ladies Industrial Society to write a brief summary of the history of the First Baptist Church. In this pamphlet the author began her discussion of this particular period with: "Many ministers have come and gone since Dr. Cuthbert—wise and otherwise, constructive and destructive."[1] While she and other church members were quick to praise some pastors in this period, the work of others would likely be described as less than significant. As the church entered the new century there were 139 members, a slight net increase for the years of Dr. Cuthbert's pastorate.

Early in 1900 the congregation extended a call to Arthur Ernest Crane, and the following letter was received in return:

> Plainfield, N.J.
> July 15th, 1900

The First Baptist Church
    Charleston, S. C.

Dear Brethren

Your telegram conveying the call of the church to me to become your pastor is received. In reply I beg to inform you that I have real pleasure in accepting the same, believing it to be the call of the Lord expressed through His church.

I am sure His blessing will be upon the union thus formed and that He will lead us in efforts that will be for His glory, the edification of the church and the good of the community.

I shall . . . be with you to commence pastoral duties Lord's day February 25th and pray that I may come to you in 'the fulness of the blessing of the gospel of Christ.'

Very sincerely your brother in the Lord and your servant for Christ's sake.

Arthur E. Crane

The church leadership obviously put great hopes in Crane's coming. He was born in London, England, and spent his youth in Plainfield, New Jersey. He studied in Crozier Theological Seminary and was licensed to preach by the First Baptist Church of Plainfield, New Jersey, his home church. Before accepting the call to Charleston, he served two brief pastorates in West Virginia. While we do not have his exact age at the time of his arrival in Charleston, he was ordained in 1897; therefore, he likely came to Charleston before his thirtieth birthday. No church records on Mr. Crane's tenure are known to exist. During his eighteen months of work in the First Baptist Church, he led the church in a revival which was significant enough for the annual associational letter in the fall of 1900 to make reference to it. When Mr. Crane left, the church clerk reported to the association on October 28,1901 that since October, 1899, the church had received two persons by letter and two candidates for baptism and had dismissed eleven by letter. The membership was 126 and the Sunday School enrollment was 19. Arthur Crane resigned the pastorate of the First Baptist Church on August 1, 1901.

The church was without a pastor for more than one year when, in October, 1902, the Reverend R. H. White accepted the congregation's call. Mr. White was known for his great warmth and affection, to which the following letters bear witness. These were received from the two churches in Maryland from which Mr. White resigned to assume his work in Charleston.

Eckhart Mines, Md.
Oct. 16 - 1902

The Eckhart Baptist Church to the
First Baptist Church of Charleston, S. C.
        Greeting.
Dear Brethren:
    We send this epistle as a tribute of love, confidence and of esteem in which we held our pastor Rev. R. H. White.
    It was with sincere regret and protest that we had to accept his resignation as shepherd of our flock. May his life and services among you prove as acceptable as it was among us. Adopted by the church October 15.

John Bannatyne
Church Clerk

Frostburg, Md.
Oct. 12 - 1902

To the First Baptist Ch. at
        Charleston, S. C.

Dear Brethren and Sisters,

    At a meeting of the members of Main St. Baptist Ch. at Frostburg, Md. held on above date the following letter was adopted to be sent to you.

1) The Pastor, Rev. R. H. White preached his farewell sermon to his devoted parishioners. He came to us one year ago and has endeared himself to all the members as well as made many friends every where he has gone. Bro. White presented his resignation a month ago. The ch. unanimously declined it and appointed a committee to urge him to remain. But Bro. White still thought the Lord called him to go and we regretfully accepted his resignation. He will leave us but his work will stand.

2) As a preacher of the gospel of our blessed Lord he was gladly heard by all as a pastor. He was welcomed by all alike, as a moderator in our business meetings. His counsel was always given after seeking the Lord in prayer. As a member he was all one could be. His prayer was, thine will be done O Lord. His song was What a Friend We Have in Jesus.

3) We part with him with sad hearts and while our loss is your gain, we thank God that during the past year we could always sing together and

can yet, Blest Be the Tie That Binds Our Hearts in Christian Love. May the blessing of God go with him always is our prayer.

Lawrence Coder, Clerk
John McFarland, Deacons
Edward Lewis
Samuel C. Myers
John W. Lewis
Committee

Frostburg, Md.

White displayed the same winsome spirit in his Charleston pastorate. The Rev. Bartow Harris, a product of the First Baptist Church, whose family dates back in the life of the church six generations before him shared with this writer some pleasant boyhood memories of Mr. White. The Harrises, at the time, lived at 33 Church Street, and Mr. White, who was not married when he arrived in Charleston, would quite often have meals with the Harrises. Across the years, he was remembered as a gentle man who always had time to share a good word with those children whom he met.

With the leadership of its new pastor, the congregation lifted its sights to a higher plane. This was reported in the church letter written in the fall of 1902 to the annual meeting of the Charleston Baptist Association. The letter reads, " . . . are working hard and start new year under more favorable circumstances."

Not long after arriving in Charleston, Richard White was elected to the executive board of the association where he gave excellent leadership. In 1903, a very important development was taking place on the banks of the Cooper River, a short distance north of the city. The United States Government was preparing to build a facility for the construction and repair of its ships. The talk of the community was the inevitable impact such a facility would have. Up to this time, the area along the Cooper River had been open country used in farming and timber. The 1903 report of the associational executive board to the Charleston Baptist Association attests to the vision of that group. The report, in part, stated:

> . . . territory along the Cooper River is developing very rapidly. The lands are being purchased by large lumber companies and the population is increasing. The United States Government is about to commence important work there and a railroad is soon to be built. Other denominations are fast taking possession of this territory where there are many persons anxious to be helped . . . we request help from the State Board of Missions.

This brief reference describes developments in the Charleston area that would have great significance for the entire community and to Baptists specifically. The executive board of the association was anticipating a great surge of expansion in that area, and the Baptist churches hopefully would seize the opportunity.

In 1906, R. H. White brought his work in Charleston to a close. Unfortunately, very little information about the closing years of his ministry in Charleston has survived.

Toward the end of 1907, the church was brought into touch with Beverly Lacy Hoge. At the time he was recommended, he was serving as pastor of the First Baptist Church, Onancock, Virginia. He accepted a call from the Charleston congregation and assumed his new work on January 15, 1908. A native of Virginia, Hoge came from a family of numerous ministers and lawyers. His father had been a prominent lawyer and statesman in Virginia, but the son first pursued a career in civil engineering. His first major project was building a new railroad at the young age of seventeen. But engineering lost its appeal, and young Hoge enrolled in Virginia Polytechnic Institute in Blacksburg, Virginia and proceeded to the University of Virginia to study law. This led to a productive career, but after thirteen years in the practice of law he responded to a call that would have a lifelong claim upon him.

Hoge was thirty-five when ordained and forty-four when he came to his Charleston work. On January 23, 1908, the treasurer wrote the following entry in the ledger: "Draft to Beverly Lacy Hoge freight on furniture and one horse to Charleston, as agreed, $85.00." This was a check H. L. Baldwin, the church treasurer, obviously took great satisfaction in writing. It began a warm pastor-deacon relationship of long duration. Baldwin followed Hoge's ministry with interest many years beyond Hoge's Charleston tenure. Immediately upon assuming his post, the new pastor displayed uncommon zeal and determination. Hoge was a builder and a promoter, just what the church needed. One month after his arrival the church purchased a pastor's home, 31 Church Street, for $3,554.00. Fifteen hundred and fifty-four dollars was paid down, and a note was arranged for the balance. An additional $20.00 was authorized for "fixing fence and putting up stable." The pastor's fine horse had to be taken care of properly. Apparently, the reliability of some carpentry in that day was no better than in the present day. In September of the same year, $5.40 was paid to "reroof the stable at the parsonage."

While it was difficult for the church to buy 31 Church Street, it was an excellent investment and addition. The attractive home still stands today, and on the 1982 market would be valued in excess of two hundred thousand dollars. Unfortunately, during the years intervening, the church sold it for a depressed price. The church across the years has owned several of the loveliest homes in downtown Charleston, including 11 Franklin Street and 59 Church Street, the property immediately to the south of the sanctuary. Repeatedly, however, the congregation, in some difficult period, with limited insight, would resolve to dispose of "unneeded" property, and the church suffered the loss.

B. Lacy Hoge was committed to building the church's membership. He believed in publicizing the program and getting the church before the community. In the archives of the church are pamphlets, cards, and circulars from the Hoge era, all attractively and professionally done. He believed in revivals, and each special series was well publicized. As a pulpiteer he received wide acclaim. A leading volume of biography cited him, "The silver-tongued orator of Montgomery County, Virginia."[2] During Hoge's first full year as pastor, the church's annual letter to the association reported thirty-three additions by baptism and thirty-four by letter, a phenomenal advance over recent years. The next year, the associational minutes reflected similar figures. Apparently the pastor did not suffer from a number syndrome. In the third year of his pastorate he reworked the church roll and dropped a considerable number of names.

An example of his promotional skills can be seen in a pamphlet he prepared entitled *The Baptist Improvement and Benevolent Company.*

To "ALL THEM THAT LOVE OUR LORD Jesus Christ in Sincerity" the First Baptist Church, of Charleston, S. C. sends greetings:

The Lord has richly blessed this old mother church in the past two years and made her a blessing to others. We have been permitted to lead many to Christ and have been used of the Lord to feed, cloth and in many ways administer to the needs of the poor, the sick and the afflicted. All departments of the work are growing and therefore our needs are also increasing. Let us briefly tell you of our needs and plans for the future and ask that you consider them in prayer and as the Spirit leads help us in this work which we are undertaking for the good of humanity and the glory of our Lord.

1st. We need better equipment for our Sunday School and are therefore seeking to raise the money to erect a modern Sunday School building. As our Church membership is largely composed of poor people, we are asking others to lend us a helping hand.

2nd. We realize that a home for working girls is sadly needed in our city. Many girls are working in stores and other places for salaries that are but little more than what they pay for board. In many instances they are unable to board in the most desireable places. We are undertaking to provide a home where these girls can get board at cost and at the same time brought under Christian influence. The home will be under the control of the Church, with a good Christian woman in charge, but will not be for Baptist girls only, but for all without regard to what church they belong or attend.

3rd. We expect to provide a home for old Preachers and their wives. There are many old preachers, who have spent their lives in the service of

Christ and His Church on small salaries, that find themselves in their old age without a home and the comforts they need and should have at that time of life. Many are so situated that they are deprived of the pleasure and privilege of attending church services. A home should be provided for these old servants of God, where they can be made comfortable and enjoy the happy privilege of attending the services of God's House. As the First Baptist Church is the oldest Baptist Church in the South and the church building stands up on the first tract of land ever owned by a Baptist Church in the Southern Baptist Convention, it is fitting that this Church should provide a home for the old preachers. This together with the fact that the climate in Charleston, the year round, is unsurpassed, makes this the ideal place for the old preachers home.

The reader is asked to contribute to this work. For each Five Dollars contributed a handsome engraved Certificate of Stock, containing a picture of this magnificent historic old building will be given.

Yours in the work of the Lord,
B. Lacy Hoge, Pastor

With such promotion as cited above and with such excellent additions, it is mysterious that the church's giving was virtually unchanged. In January, 1908, contributions averaged sixteen to nineteen dollars, and in the fall of 1911, Hoge's last months, the average contributions hardly varied two dollars.

In August, 1911, the finances of the church were further strained when a hurricane passed through, causing considerable damage to the church. This necessitated a special drive in which the faithful contributors were asked to give over and above their regular offerings. A church financial ledger from the period has survived, and the list of those who came forth with considerable sums for repairs were the same individuals who already were supporting the church liberally and systematically. The damage was extensive enough to gain the attention of others beyond the church membership. The church ledger carries an entry of ten dollars identified as a gift from the First Baptist Church, Union, South Carolina, sent to assist in the repairs.

The hurricane was severe enough to leave indelible impressions. Many years later, pastor Hoge's son shared with the Charleston Church a letter of recollections of his boyhood in Charleston. He was writing as a senior adult, a successful Wall Street attorney and a lay leader in the Riverside Church. His memory was that of going with his father immediately after the storm to the church for the scheduled services. He recalled that the only ones to arrive for services that day were the pastor and his young son.

The leadership of the church had hoped Mr. Hoge would continue his work in their midst for many years to come. If it were to achieve stability, the church needed his approach to ministry. In the fall of 1911, however, Emanuel

Baptist Church in Richmond, Virginia called him as pastor, a post he assumed on December 15 of that year. As he left the Charleston church, he left a church whose confidence he had won, and points of contact across the years would attest to this. In July, 1914, while pastor of Spurgeon Memorial Church in Norfolk, Virginia, he accepted an invitation to preach in the Charleston pulpit. It was a gladsome reunion. Again, in 1920 he was asked to return for a revival. This occurred during one of the church's numerous interims when morale in the congregation was low. Mr. Hoge's reply to Mr. Baldwin's inquiry read in part:

Oct. 9th, 1920

Mr. Dear Bro. Baldwin:

. . . I am sorry to hear of the trouble in the church. I am anxious to see that work go forward at the Old First Church. If I can help to pull things together again and you think it worth the expense I will gladly come down and spend 10 days or two weeks in a meeting.

Our meeting is growing in interest daily. Had 15 professions yesterday—expecting great services tomorrow (Sunday).

The Lord has richly blessed me and this work here.

The church purchase[d] since I came a beautiful Pastor House for $12,500.00 and spent $3,500.00 on the property. They can get $25,000.00 now. We have a beautiful building—new. We are all in our usual health.

With love and best wishes for you and family and all the friends at the Old First,

Yours in Christ,
B. Lacy Hoge

While we do not have Mr. Baldwin's initial letter, it is not unreasonable to conjecture that he raised the question with Mr. Hoge if there were any possibility he might consider a call to return. But in 1920, as was true in December, 1911, conditions in the church were not very appealing.

After Mr. Hoge's departure for Virginia, the congregation spent little time in locating a prospect to consider for their next pastor. On December 26, 1911, three weeks after Hoge's last sermon, there was written into the treasurer's ledger an entry for $1.00 for "one hundred postal cards—notice to members to hear brother Phillips." On December 31, Rev. T. G. Phillips preached, and on January 7, the treasurer's ledger reflects a twenty-five cents entry labeled, "telegram to Rev. T. G. Phillips confirming call to pastorate made by deacons." Obviously, he was available since, on February 11, he arrived and delivered his first sermon as pastor.

We know precious little about T. G. Phillips. Church members who recall him from their childhood days remember his having only one arm and being a person who conveyed a genuine spirit of caring. Mrs. Phillips immediately became quite involved in the Ladies Industrial Society and often had the ladies meet with her in the pastorium at 31 Church Street. While the church did not decline under his leadership, neither did it experience any significant advances. T. G. Phillips was pastor less than one year, his last Sunday being February 2, 1913.

For two Sundays after Mr. Phillips' departure the church had local ministers to supply, and on the third Sunday Dr. C. N. Donaldson of Atlanta came to preach. The point of contact with Dr. Donaldson is not clear, but when he came to supply he remained in Charleston to preach four Sundays. The church paid ten dollars for his lodging and meals during his stay. His enjoyable lodging in Miss Herriot's Inn during a delightful stay in the old city was enough to attract him to Charleston. During his stay in Charleston, he had occasion to move through the streets and shops of the city and generally to acquaint himself with the situation of the First Baptist Church. Most likely he saw some fine possibilities for the church, and the church became quite interested in him. The congregation extended him a call, and he arrived to begin his work some time in April, 1913. The treasurer's ledger has an entry on April 24, "Changing name of pastor on church sign—75¢."

During the first year Donaldson was pastor the church received nineteen members by letter, three by baptism, and two by restoration, but it lost ten by transfer, one by death, and thirty-two by erasure, for a net loss of eighteen. The membership was one hundred, with total offerings for all purposes of $1,548.

In April, 1914, Donaldson returned to Atlanta, for what reason we are not told. Before leaving Charleston, he submitted his resignation, not to be effective until July. This was disconcerting to the leadership of the First Baptist Church. The church convened a series of conferences to discuss what options were open to them. Finally, the following letter was approved:

April 26, 1914

Dr. C. N. Donaldson
Atlanta, Georgia

Dear Sir and Brother:

The church having instructed me to write to you stating that having taken action on your resignation, state that it would be better for all parties to have you quit at once and thereby save you the extra trip to this city and back home.

Very respectfully,
W. N. Tyler
Church Clerk

Dr. Donaldson replied asking that "his resignation be accepted as final and that same be published in city papers, and a copy of same to be sent to him."

The church approved paying Donaldson through April, which amounted to $105, but the treasurer was $85 short of this needed amount. In order for the congregation to meet its obligation, Mr. H. L. Baldwin made a temporary loan to the church in the amount of $85. The ledger for April was closed with a balance of 9¢.

Very soon after the departure of Dr. C. N. Donaldson, the church had the names of three men from which the next pastor would be chosen. One of these, Mr. A. J. Foster of Columbia, South Carolina, was chosen by the deacons and recommended to the church. Mr. Foster was asked to visit the church and was extended a call. While in Charleston a committee "laid the matter before Brother Foster giving him a full explanation of the conditions existing in the church and left the matter with him to decide, hoping to get an early reply." No further reference to Mr. Foster appears in the church minutes. Apparently, his reply came quickly and was negative, since two weeks later the deacons met with Mr. M. C. Cullum of Walterboro, South Carolina. He had come to supply one Sunday and returned to supply a second Sunday. After his second Sunday with the church, the deacons requested he meet to discuss his serving as supply pastor for the four remaining months of the year. The church prevailed on the Cullums to move from Walterboro into the pastor's home, an indication that the church hoped the Cullums would stay longer, even permanently. Mr. Cullum agreed to move his family to Charleston and assume the pastorate "indefinitely for the sum of $1,000.00 per year and a house to live in."

During the church year, twelve persons came into the church by baptism and three by statement, but sixteen members were lost by the transfer of their church letters. Offerings remained static, and expenses seemed always to keep the treasurer's balance near zero. During the fall of 1914, the church was faced with an additional expenditure, the charge levied by the city for paving that portion of Church Street running in front of the church property. Mr. H. L. Baldwin again advanced the church sixty-five dollars for the project. While it was an additional financial problem for the church, it was regarded as a much needed improvement.

The fall of 1914 was a busy time in the life of the First Baptist Church. The South Carolina Baptist State Convention met in Charleston in October at the Citadel Square Baptist Church. Each congregation was asked to house and entertain some of those attending from out of town. Later in the fall, the First (Scots) Presbyterian Church asked the First Baptist congregation to join with them in December for special services celebrating the bicentennial of that Presbyterian Church. Evening services were not held in the First Baptist Church on the fourth Sunday in December in order that the congregation might join with its neighboring church for this important occasion.

J. C. Cullum assumed a role of leadership in the association and was asked during his first year as pastor of the First Baptist Church to preach the sermon for the next annual associational meeting. Mrs. Cullum was also active and elected to serve as president of the Charleston Baptist Associational Woman's Missionary Union. Even though the church constantly faced the most austere financial conditions, in April, 1915, receipts from agencies and institutions indicated the following financial support from the First Baptist Church: Connie Maxwell Orphanage, $21.03; South Carolina State Mission, $20.81; Home Mission Board of the Southern Baptist Convention, $18.10; and Foreign Mission Board of the Southern Baptist Convention, $40.48. These productive signs notwithstanding, Mr. Cullum brought to a close his work in the First Baptist Church in July, 1915, one year after the first Sunday he had arrived to supply. There are no church minutes for this immediate period nor other church records that would give an account of the factors leading to his resignation.

In the summer of 1915, the First Baptist Church was again without a pastor. The deacons turned to the leaders in the offices of the South Carolina Baptist State Convention for counsel and for assistance in locating possible candidates. During this same period, the deacons had been in contact with the denominational offices exploring ideas that might bring the First Baptist Church and the Cannon Street Church into some type of merger, an idea the denominational leaders thought had merit. H. J. Langston, field worker for the Home Mission Board of the Southern Baptist Convention (a regional office of which was located in Columbia), wrote deacon H. L. Baldwin:

> . . . I think something can be done for you brethren of the First Baptist Church, and I have been anxious to find opportunity to come and talk over the situation with you. . . . I am sorry the Cannon Street Church acted so unwisely in our endeavor to unite (the two churches), but we should not be discouraged by this and conclude that nothing can be done. Something can be done.

In a letter written to deacon William Roach the same week as the letter cited above, W. T. Derieux, corresponding secretary of the State Mission Board of the South Carolina Baptist State Convention, expressed a similar thought,

> . . . I hope you and the Cannon Street people will yet get together on acceptable terms. In the mean time to help keep the Old First Church together you can secure Dr. R. W. Sanders D.D. of Greenville, S.C. to supply for you. He will come for a small remuneration. If you can raise $35.00 a month you can get him, I think.

Derieux's suggestion of Robert Wilson Sanders was extremely helpful. In response to the church's inquiry, Sanders replied in a handwritten letter:

Greenville, S. C.
Oct. 1st, 1915

Mr. H. L. Baldwin
Charleston, S. C.

Mr. Dear Brother:

I have your letter of Sept. 30th. Yes, I can "supply" for your church, the First Baptist, if the church so desires. As to the "terms" you ask me to state, I will cheerfully leave the church to decide. Only offer what you deem as right and in accordance with the ability, etc. of the church. I would remain chiefly in Charleston, and in so doing, would need a place of board; or a room simply for sleeping, reading, etc. (a quiet place preferred and a room to myself), taking meals at some "cafe" or other house tolerably convenient to my room for sleeping. Near the sea or "Battery" (for some sea-breeze) preferred; yet I would comply with your convenience in all that. . . .

In case of coming to supply, I could do so, one month or several, according to your wishes, etc. I should want, at all hazards, some whiffs of the bracing sea air, and under suitable conditions, I might sometimes go over to the Islands or Beach, for a little change.

So far as I now know, I would prefer to begin with you the 3rd Sunday or 4th Sunday of October. . . . You make out your request as a church, state your own convenient terms, and send to me; and I have no doubt that your offer will suit me. If your church is weak, I will consider all that. I can come.

Please let me hear definitely, as soon as possible, so that it will be settled and will not interfere with any other call that might be sent to me. I would not expect to come as a "candidate" for your pastorate as a permanency, and you need not feel any embarrassment as to that.

Fraternally Yours,

R. W. Sanders
241 Broadus Ave.

P.S. I have written at length, so as to make the case clear.

R.W.S.

Sanders began his work with the small but elated congregation the third Sunday in October, 1915. All the details of his coming fell into proper order. Due to the church's financial extremities, small matters normally arranged routinely posed major problems for those leaders making the arrangements. For example, what should be done about housing the supply pastor? Funds for a small salary were scarce, but funds sufficient for room and board were out of the question. Providentially, a little earlier in the same year, Mr. and Mrs.

C. R. Fogus had moved from Tye River, Virginia to assume operation of the Saint John's Hotel, the forerunner to the present Mills House. The Foguses united with the First Baptist Church and immediately saw a need in the church which they were able to meet. Dr. Sanders was provided the best in lodging and food at no cost to the church.

No one could have been more suited to the needs of the First Baptist Church than R. W. Sanders. He was retired and without heavy responsibilities. He had served in numerous posts of ministry including two terms as president of the South Carolina Baptist State Convention. He possessed patience, perseverance, and perception, all of which helped greatly in addressing the needs of this congregation. The church expressed chagrin that the compensation they provided was woefully less than that degree to which Dr. Sanders gave of himself. Though the church never sensed a trace of displeasure on the part of their supply pastor with the way the congregation dealt with its financial responsibilities, the church in April, 1916, adopted the following resolution:

> Whereas Rev. R. W. Sanders D.D. has been supply pastor of the First Baptist Church of Charleston, S. C. for about six months and the church desiring to express its appreciations of his services and the results of same have resolved:
>
> 1st. That Dr. Sanders' services have been satisfactory in every way, especially in the plain candid manner in which he has preached the pure simple gospel and for his earnest pastoral work and visitation.
>
> 2nd. That while the church feels somewhat embarrassed that it is still unable to see its way to add anything to the pastor's "salary" at present, it would be pleased to have him continue his present relation, if agreeable, and
>
> 3rd. That so soon as practicable an addition to "salary" will be cheerfully made.
>
> 4th. That Dr. Sanders be advised that the church would like him to understand that at any time he becomes dissatisfied or anything pertaining to our relations need adjustment, that he feel free to open the subject.
>
> By order of and on behalf of the First Baptist Church
>
> H.L. Baldwin Clk.

The condition of the church was stronger under the care of its supply pastor than it had been in any recent years. During the first year with Dr. Sanders as supply pastor, the church reported twelve baptisms and three additions by letter. Sanders never hedged in giving advice the church needed. On one occasion it was necessary that he be absent a few Sundays. He wrote Mr. Baldwin:

> . . . Beware of using strangers (travelers, etc.) in the pulpit always when I'm away. Of course, the "Pulpit Committee" must decide.

A stranger was wanting today to "get in." I did not know him or anything about him and gave him no encouragement whatever. It is dangerous and unwise to "tie on" to wanderers, and the churches often suffer from such fellows. So, I advise you to sleep close to the "Pulpit Committee", use Bro. Roach for good services, and "steer clear" of all entanglements with those who just happen along, yet always are ready to tell you great things about themselves when they may not be "worth a copper", and in fact may be unworthy and injurious.

Sincerely yours,
R. W. Sanders

During this time period, the church entered contracts to sell two pieces of property. Both were unusual transactions. In November, 1915, the church, after extensive debate, voted to sell for $3,000 the Meeting Street entrance to the church property. Known as 54 Meeting Street, the strip of land lay immediately north of the carriage house of the church's present 48 Meeting Street property and allowed convenient entrance to the church's cemetery as well as to the rest of the church's facility. Meeting Street residents did not like the church's owning such an entrance and continually complained about the traffic. Because of the acute shortage of church funds, the congregation found this offer, made by the owner of the property immediately to the north of the drive, a means of helping a distressful situation. Consequently, they sold the parcel and carried a mortgage on it which allowed three years for payments. Another parcel of property brought to their attention was likely unknown by the congregation even to exist. It was a 12-acre plot on Edisto Island given in 1822 by Hephzibah Townsend for the support of a clergyman of the Baptist denomination on Edisto Island. The person interested in purchasing the parcel pointed out that the trustees had been dead for many years, and there was no Baptist clergyman on the island; consequently, the will provided for the property to revert to the First Baptist Church. In November, 1916, the church completed the sale for the sum of $212.50, a vivid example of the strain under which the church was laboring.

These were trying years, not only because the First Baptist Church found itself struggling for survival, but because the whole world was in tumult. The United States was steadily becoming involved in World War I. In April, 1917, President Woodrow Wilson would lead Congress to declare war on Germany and the Central Powers. Before the War ended with victory for the Allies, the First Baptist Church, as small as its congregation was, had eleven of its members enlist for military service. One of the stars on the church service flag which hung in the sanctuary would turn to gold; one young man died in battle in France.

In later years, one church member reflecting on the ministry of Dr. Sanders during these difficult years wrote:

His gentle poetical nature, spiritual strength, depth of knowledge and

understanding created hope and courage while Christianity was held in
the balance and the world tottered physically and spiritually.

One of Dr. Sanders many gifts was the ability to compose poetry, and he
became widely read and acclaimed in those churches he served as well as
other Baptist circles. In 1921, he wrote the Centennial Hymn sung by the
South Carolina Baptist State Convention at its centennial session. Although
he left no indication when the following verse was penned, one could readily
imagine this minister of advancing years—sitting full face in the sea breezes
of the Charleston waterfront or strolling on High Battery, hardly a city block
from the old church, with its many woes heavy in his thoughts—writing his
poem, "A Song of Trust."

> God of the seas! I'm tempest-tost,
>   Grim peril's gulfs, on every side;
> Yet, in thy hands, I'll not be lost,
>   Though howling storm and waves betide.
>
> Lord of the winds! the gale is high,
>   Great ocean's roar is mad and wild;
> Yet, in thy arms, secure, I lie,
>   Serene, content, since I'm thy child.
>
> Bright hosts of saints have long sailed o'er
>   This rolling, ever-heaving deep;
> Grant me, My God, to reach 'yon shore,
>   Oh, for this boon, thy servant keep!
>
> Then, in thy presence, Lord, I'll fall
>   And worship at my Savior's feet;
> I'll shout in praise of Christ, My All,
>   And join in heavenly anthems sweet.

While the First Baptist Church had to depend on Dr. Sanders' continuing
his work in their midst for meager compensation, the church leaders never
forgot his faithfulness. Years later, in the mid-1920s, when the church was a
little more prosperous, the congregation sent him love offerings for his
personal needs. On December 21, 1925, the church received the following
note of thanks written with a feeble hand. The church had just sent him a
check.

Dec. 21, 1925
Greenville, S. C.

To the People and Pastor of the
First Baptist Church and Sunday School

Dearly Beloved:

My memories of you are precious, and my rejoicing at your prosperity and growth is great, indeed, while my love for you is immutable.

I bid you press on to the "mark of the prize of the high calling of God in Christ Jesus our Lord."

"I long to see you and to impart some spiritual gift."

I am now quite feeble and under doctors. Pray for me.

Yours in Jesus,

R. W. Sanders

It is easy to understand why the church revered him highly, but the affection was mutual. In January, 1925, some years after his pastorate in the First Baptist Church, Sanders wrote an open letter to the editor of the *News and Courier* in which he paid tribute to the "unflinching loyalty and devotions of this 'little flock'."

In 1918 Robert W. Sanders brought to a close his work with this church and bade farewell to the Low Country. While we have no way of knowing, Dr. Sanders could have used the following poem in his final message. We do know he regarded it one of his favorites.

WAITING

"Looking for the blessed hope"

Waiting to reach the "goal of life"—
The end of blighting sin and strife;
Waiting to make my task complete,
Then lay my sheaves at Jesus' feet.

Waiting to hear the glad home-call
Of him who is my "All in All";
Then know the joy He hath for me—
Joy that abides eternally.

Waiting for all my griefs to end,
Griefs that, in love, my Lord doth send;
Then in my Saviour's glory share—
Blest crown of all that 'waits me there!

In 1918, the First Baptist Church called John Bomar, and while his tenure with the church was less than two years, the brief period of ministry reflected encouraging signs of vitality. The nation generally was experiencing a rise of optimism and prosperity that would extend into the mid-twenties. In November, 1918, World War I ended, and the future looked bright. During this period, attention was given to improvements of the physical plant. Electric lights were installed to replace the gas lights. The major gas light fixtures hanging between the columns were removed. Those bracket gas light fixtures fastened to the upper columns were left and used for weddings and similar occasions until the 1950s when they too were removed.

The optimism cited earlier was evident in Baptist life in general. In 1919, the Southern Baptist Convention launched the Seventy-five Million Campaign, the most ambitious financial program ever undertaken by the Convention. It was designed to undergird a major advance in every area of Baptist causes. Dr. George W. Truett, pastor of the First Baptist Church, Dallas, Texas, was chairman for the entire Southern Baptist Convention, and Dr. W. J. McGlothlin, president of Furman University, was chairman for South Carolina. Every church was enlisted, and the pledges exceeded the goal. The First Baptist Church was one of the first to reach its goal of fourteen thousand dollars pledged. The day this was achieved the pastor sent a telegram to the national office in Nashville which read: "Mother church leads the way to victory—goal over-subscribed." It was an experience in achievement and success which the church needed.

Another area of progress under the leadership of John Bomar was his work with the youth. He and Mrs. Bomar had four children who, combined with other teenaged children, made an encouraging number of youths for a church that size. A church member, reflecting on this period many years later, regarded this focus on the nurture of youth Mr. Bomar's most lasting contribution.

Although these vital signs were evident, the question of the First Baptist Church's continuing in its present location surfaced again. In the fall of 1919, the idea was advanced that the First Baptist Church merge with the King Street Baptist Church, and the two congregations relocate to a site somewhere in the general northwest section of the city. The General Board of the South Carolina Baptist State Convention was interested in the idea materializing. The board would "aid" in the purchase of the new site and the erection of a new building. In return, the properties of both churches would be deeded to the General Board. Among others, Dr. W. J. McGlothlin, president of Furman University, appeared before the congregation to encourage an affirmative vote. On January 18, 1920, the following resolution was proposed to the congregation in conference.

> WHEREAS:
>
> The King Street Church of this city has expressed itself by a vote, willing to consolidate their church with ours, taking our name and moving to a new and rapidly growing section of our city; and
>
> WHEREAS:
>
> The judgment of some of our members is that it will be unwise to try to remain in our present location, believing that we can do nothing more than maintain our existence, with no hope for further growth and development; and
>
> WHEREAS:
>
> The residential section of our city is rapidly developing in its western portion, and thereby affording a wider and more hopeful field of labor; and

WHEREAS:

Some of our present members have already moved in or near this new section; and

WHEREAS:

This move and consolidation will not destroy our existence, but serve rather to perpetuate not only the name of the oldest white Baptist church in the State and perhaps in the south, but will also conserve the traditions and sentiments that cluster around our historic name and

WHEREAS:

It is the belief of our brethren with the State, as expressed by the Executive Committee of the Commission on Missions on a recent visit to the city, that such a move and consolidation would be wise; and

WHEREAS:

The said Commission has assured the King Street Church that it will aid in the purchase of necessary lots and the erection of the necessary building, therefore be it

RESOLVED:

That we do now assemble in God's name proceed to prayerfully and solemnly discuss the proposed move and consolidation, and express our wish and purpose by a vote now to be taken:

RESOLVED:

We propose to our King Street brethren, that the deacons of our church and the deacons of their church shall become the deacons of the consolidated church, and that the other officers of the church and Sunday School be elected after the consolidation, and

RESOLVED:

Also that we be allowed to place in the new First Baptist Church building when erected the tablets of our former pastors and leading laymen who by their character and great ability became famous in our denominational life and works: (here follow the names)

RESOLVED:

That we deed our present buildings and lot to the "General Board of the State Convention of the Baptist Denomination in South Carolina", or if by our vacation of same they become the property of any other church, that the said church shall deed the property as above, such disposition of the property is a necessary condition of our action to move and consolidate with our King Street brethren.

H. C. Moshell,   John Bomar,
  Clerk   Moderator

A spirited discussion followed. The pastor favored the proposal, as did John W. Whiteside, a worker sent by the state convention to assist with all mission needs in the Charleston area. At the time, the Whitesides resided in Charleston and were members of the First Baptist Church. When the vote was taken, seventeen voted in the affirmative, and thirty-two opposed. While the idea of closing or relocating the church would surface from time to time for general discussion, the 1920 proposal was the last formal recommendation to be addressed.

After the church's action on the proposal cited above, only a brief time elapsed, and John Bomar was called by the First Baptist Church, Winnsboro, South Carolina. The Charleston congregation passed a motion requesting that the pastor reconsider his resignation, and a committee was appointed to meet with the pastor in an effort to arrange that he stay. On the following Sunday, another church conference was called at which time a recommendation was made to raise the pastor's annual salary to twenty-five hundred dollars. The figure was higher than some thought the church should pay, while others thought it less than equitable. Mr. Bomar then insisted on the church accepting his resignation, which they did, and on March 28, 1920, the pastor brought his final message.

For a brief period between April, 1920, and July, 1921, Mr. D. O. Rivers is listed in the annual minutes of the Charleston Baptist Association as pastor. No other reference to him is found, and in 1921 and 1922 he was listed as pastor for two small churches in Bonneau, South Carolina. In a church conference in July, 1921, the congregation voted to ask Stacy P. Poag to preach two Sundays with a view toward a possible call. He was recommended by Chaplain James S. Day stationed at the United States Navy Yard in Charleston. Apparently Chaplain Day had obtained Poag's name from a Navy colleague. The following letter addressed to Chaplain Day stirred the church's interest.

Whiteville, Tenn. July 2. 1921.

Chaplain, James S. Day
Navy Yard
Charleston, S. C.

Dear Brother Day:

Your letter received some few days ago and contents noted. Have been quite busy for last few days trying to arrange for our tent meeting that starts soon.

I appreciate Brother Hammack' interest very much. He is a noble fellow. I also appreciate your inquiry concerning myself and the interest you manifest in the First Church of your city.

Yes, I am interested in a call with opportunities commensurate to a preparation for Kingdom work. I am an alumni of Union University located at Jackson, Tenn., about thirty miles from my present location. It is one of the oldest educational institutions in the Mississippi Valley. The graduates of Union University now number many of the most successful men in all walks of life throughout America, and many are prominent in other continents. I also was a student in S.W.B.T. Seminary, Ft. Worth, Texas.

. . . I came here some months ago, but did not find the opportunities for which my heart longs. This is a splendid people, with splendid house of worship, and willing to follow the preacher, all of which make it very pleasant, but the kinks are uncurled now; therefore I feel, if the Lord be pleased, that I should touch the field where I hope to settle for long pastorate.

I will soon be forty one with the growing period of my ministry before me, married, but have no children. In a pastoral way Wife is a great asset to my work and the work of the Lord.

. . . Thanking you for your consideration and trusting that our Lord shall be pleased I am

Yours for Kingdom Service

S. P. Poag

The church extended Poag a call, and he accepted.

Whiteville, Tenn. Aug. 13th. 1921.

The First Baptist Church
Charleston, S. C.
Dear Brethren:

Yesterday I sent you telegram accepting call to the pastorate of your church conditionally. I appreciate the honor and confidence imposed in me by the church, for it is a great responsibility to attempt the pastorate of any church. With you I feel that the problem is a grave undertaking, but the impression's that I received while I was there gives some assurance that God can use both preacher and church co-ordinately and co-operately to the accomplishment of a work most needed. To be sure there must be a homogeneous union of forces if the work is accomplished.

The condition is this that you pay my expense to locate on the field and the expense to all necessary Conventions. You remember that in accepting I shall receive less money and shall have to furnish my own home. The fact is I shall not move any household goods, nothing but my books, trunks and two tickets from here to your city.

Again I must have time to adjust matters here, hold some of the meetings for which I have been retained and give this church little time to secure another preacher. I might be able to come by the First of Month, but the Fifteenth of Sept. would be better.

I would like to have place there as convenient to my work as possible. Must have furnished rooms or place to board. You will do me favor to look after this matter for me as far as possible.

You will have this letter by your next prayer-meeting night; therefore let me know as soon as possible.

Yours for Kingdom Work.

S. P. Poag

Mr. Poag was probably the most unusual pastor the First Baptist Church had known. As might be detected in his letters cited above, he had a colorful style in writing as well as in preaching. Before entering the ministry he was a motorcycle policeman in Memphis, Tennessee. Some of the less appreciative members of the church expressed the belief that the pastor had brought a pronounced residue of his law enforcement days into his pulpit ministry. The teenaged boys in the church reveled in Poag's style. One such youngster, Bartow Harris, who later became a missionary to India and one of Southern Baptists' choicest ministers, reflected many years later on Stacy Poag's preaching and recalled that the young fellows in the church could never understand at the time why the pastor's preaching was regarded by many stately dear ladies to be so terribly offensive. Harris recalled a few of Poag's remarks. One long-remembered was "Some of you women have tongues so long you can sit in the parlor and lick the skillet in the kitchen." Apparently, the pastor perceived a problem with gossip. Another favorite remark of the pastor was, "You must understand I am simply a red-neck, flannel mouthed Irishman." We do not have an explanation as to the full meaning of the pastor's self-characterization, but whatever it meant, it was not palatable to the First Baptist congregation, and Mr. Poag's tenure was extremely brief. Before he left, he did lead the church in a few significant achievements. One was the licensing of Bartow Harris and Harry T. Whaley, two outstanding young men, to the gospel ministry.

The ordination service for Whaley took place in Jackson, Tennessee, where he had been called pastor. Harris' ordination did not take place until September, 1924, long after Mr. Poag's departure, but the candidate recalled a most unusual occurrence in his ordination service. The service came between his junior and senior years at Furman University. Funds were terribly short, and during the service Dr. Jesse E. Bailey, pastor of the Rutledge Avenue Baptist Church, stood to give the charge to the church. He began, "I am supposed to give the charge to the church, and frankly, I do not know how much I should charge, but I do know this young man is entering his senior year at Furman University, and I am sure he needs funds for this undertaking, so I will ask the ushers, please, to come forward with the collection plates, and we shall give a worthy offering." Harris walked home that night with his feet hardly touching the ground. Not only could he still feel the press of saintly hands having been laid on his head, but in his pocket he felt the bulge of a handsome offering provided for his enrollment in Furman University.

The idea of the offering may have been strictly that of Dr. Bailey, but this writer knew personally the young man who was pastor at this time, Oswell P. Smith, and it sounds precisely like something Oswell Smith would contrive. Under the pastorate of Oswell Smith, the church saw a new day dawning.

Notes

1. Roberta Lawrence Miles, *A Review of the History of the First Baptist Church in the South* (Charleston: J.J. Furlong & Son, 1925), p. 17.

2. B. J. W. Graham, ed., *Baptist Biography,* (Atlanta: Index Printing Company, 1917), II:146.

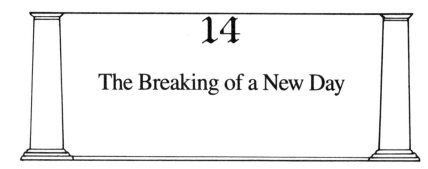

14

The Breaking of a New Day

In late 1923, the pulpit committee was glad to receive the name of a young pastor, Oswell Smith, who only recently had been discharged from the United States Navy and was serving as assistant pastor in Savannah, Georgia. After conversing with him, the pulpit committee was convinced he was the right person for the First Baptist Church. Oswell Smith assumed the pastorate of the First Baptist Church in January, 1924. Before calling Smith, the church considered several men as likely prospects. One, a "Brother Newton," replied that his physician advised against such a large assignment at that time. He suggested that the church might secure a supply pastor for six months, and at the end of that time he would consider the call. The church declined that offer. Another man to whom the church extended a call was F. O. Lomoreux, who had just completed preaching a revival in the First Baptist Church. The congregation also extended a call to John Bomar with the request that he return as its pastor, but he, too, declined. In the fall of 1923, the committee was given the name of Oswell Smith. He accepted a call with plans to begin in January.

Before Smith's arrival and during this interim, the church remained active and alert to opportunities to be the church. One example of this consciousness surfaced in an issue on public morals. This period of time was known as the Roaring Twenties, and Charleston was in the middle of all the frivolities that swept the nation. The most famous dance to survive the period and to be found, even down to the present, was named "The Charleston." The tempo and the testimony of the early 1920s bothered members of the First Baptist Church. An example of how the congregation addressed the matter can be seen in a resolution passed in a special called conference of the church, July 1, 1923.

> In view of the fact that announcement has been made relative to the Marathon Dancing Contest and whereas Miss Lattie Olney, Chief of the Woman's Bureau of the Chas. Police Dep. after Conference with the Chief of Police has declared her intention of prohibiting the contest, the members of the First Baptist Church in Conference assembled adopted

the following resolutions. That we do most heartily commend the Chief Officers of our Police Dep. on their stand in this matter. That we concur in our opinion of Miss Olney as published in Saturday's Chas. Evening Post, that these contest[s] are detrimental to the Youth and Young Womanhood of our city, and injurious physically to those participating, excepting the testimony of the leading medical specialist of the County to this effect. That we urge the parents, Churches, Civic and religious organizations of this city, to join us, in this our protest to any thing of the kind being held in our city. Resolved further, that copies of these resolutions be sent to Miss Lattie Olney Chief of the Womans Bureau of Police Dep. and to the daily press for publication.[1]

The arrival of Oswell Smith brought the church to a point of new beginning. His youthful enthusiasm, augmented with the zeal of his wife, was precisely what the Old First Church needed. Under his leadership, the congregation immediately began work in areas of church organization as well as improvements in the physical plant.

One concern in the area of organization to receive immediate attention was the need to communicate the pastor's hopes and plans to the entire membership. Smith divided the congregation into seven groups, each attended by a captain whose responsibility was to inform and motivate the members in that group. The plan met with much success, especially as the church adopted a stewardship program and an every-member canvas.

An encouraging number of young adult couples joined under Smith's ministry. This made possible a lively Baptist Young People's Union. The Paul Pridgens were one such couple. At the time, Pridgen was a railroad employee, but he became increasingly zealous in Christian service. He was ordained a deacon and soon began to supply in the area as a lay preacher. In 1925, he was licensed for the ministry, and this initiated a career that would yield outstanding results in the community. Pridgen served briefly the Mount Pleasant and Charleston Heights Baptist Churches, but for the largest portion of his ministry he was pastor of the First Baptist Church of North Charleston. His colorful and effective work in that post made an unparalleled contribution to Kingdom causes in the Charleston area.

Not only did Oswell Smith build programs and people, but he displayed strong abilities in improving facilities. Soon after his arrival, he insisted that the Sunday School rooms be wired for electricity and portable dividers be constructed for the balcony of the sanctuary to create additional Sunday School rooms. The Ladies Industrial Society was led to take under its sponsorship the refurbishing of the rooms immediately behind the pulpit area. Not long before this, the society had financed the purchase of new carpeting for the entire sanctuary at a cost of $239.70. Some church members, even today, recall the lovely olive and white carpeting which remained in service until the mid-1940s. While the church was being refurbished, the decision was made to remove one pew at the front of each of the two center sections, a modification which provided needed walking space around the rostrum.

A multitude of other improvements were made. The old benches in the Sunday School building were given to the Rosemont Baptist Church, and new chairs as well as new hymn books were purchased. The most significant achievement was the purchase of 12 Franklin Street for the pastor's home. Several other parcels had been considered, but this home was chosen and purchased at a cost of $8,400. Charles W. Parham was general chairman and worked diligently to bring about the purchase, and W. D. Murphy was chairman of the committee to furnish the new parsonage. Murphy led the church to agree that only new furniture would be put in the home. His final report cited a balance of $21 over the amount needed, and this small balance was applied to the first month's mortgage payment. As seems always too true, the project to have a home for the pastor had vocal opponents. On January 1, 1928, the Sunday bulletin carried the following paragraph:

> The report of our last Parsonage Day shows that a larger proportion of our people entered into the effort than usual. But there are still some enemies of the cause among us who never help in any way, they seem to look on and say "If you make it go you will surprise us." God will surprise all hinderers some day.[2]

Toward the end of Smith's ministry, the church received a bequest from a loyal member, Miss Emma Ryan, in the amount of five thousand dollars. Out of this bequest, the church erected the tablet in the sanctuary to Dr. Lucius Cuthbert, paid twenty-five hundred dollars on the pastorium debt, and forwarded five hundred dollars to the Baptist State Convention for missions. The church agreed that any residue from the bequest be set aside to begin an organ fund. During these years, considerable interest was expressed in regard to a new organ, and this money from Miss Ryan's bequest served as excellent seed money to start the fund.

Pastor Smith was a strong advocate of the Cooperative Program. He, like many others, felt keenly that the Cooperative Program, begun in 1925, was the answer to a great dilemma, namely, how to spread a church's mission gifts into every Kingdom endeavor. Across the years, it was not unusual to see listed in financial reports any number of separate mission accounts for which offerings had been given. Mr. Smith led the First Baptist Church to commit a minimum of 10 percent of all regular offerings to the Cooperative Program.

The new pastor believed promotion was necessary if a church was to grow. Advertisements were purchased in the tour buses and the hotel directories, and permission was sought to erect a sign at the corner of Broad and Church Streets. The pastor readily endorsed any respectable endeavor of outreach. In the mid-twenties when Evangelist Billy Sunday came to Charleston, the First Baptist Church enthusiastically supported this city-wide campaign. The evangelistic endeavor was held on the green at King and Calhoun Streets in a frame tabernacle erected for that purpose. The people of the First Baptist Church supported it well, and members were gained as a result of the endeavor. In one year, 1925, the church received fifty-three additions. In 1930, Oswell Smith's last year with the First Baptist Church, the membership had grown from 111 in 1924, the year of his arrival, to 229, and the average attendance in Sunday School had increased from 37 to 120. Financial support had also increased, though not quite as dramatically.

As the decade of the 1920s drew to a close, many significant achievements gave cause for gladness. But in October, 1929, the nation was stunned with the colossal stock market crash. This radically affected the work of the denomination and the local church as well as the life of the individual family. The First Baptist Church experienced a compound shock. In addition to the economic crash, the church experienced the resignation of her pastor. In the spring of 1930, Mr. Smith accepted the pastorate of the First Baptist Church, Fort Mill, South Carolina. As Oswell Smith departed, he left with the congregation a lingering vision of what the old church could be.

From a list of those men recommended as candidates worthy of consideration, the pulpit committee singled out one in whom it expressed immediate interest. He was Cornelius A. Westbrook, a native of Missouri. Westbrook was a graduate of William Jewell College and earned both the Th.B. and Th.M. degrees from The Southern Baptist Theological Seminary. He had served as pastor in Arkansas, Louisiana, and Texas, and his last pastorate before coming to Charleston was the Poplar Bluff Baptist Church, Poplar Bluff, Missouri. He accepted the call of the First Baptist Church and began his work in the Charleston post in June, 1930. His years in the First Baptist Church were some of the most difficult any pastor could face, for the whole nation was slipping into the worst economic depression in its history. In fact, the austere history of the First Baptist Church during recent decades probably had conditioned the congregation to endure this extreme adversity.

The new pastor and the congregation refused to allow the adverse conditions to set the tone for their new partnership. To the contrary, they embarked upon the future with an obvious enthusiasm. During the early weeks of his work the pastor led the church in a most successful revival in which he preached. He expanded the Baptist Young People's Union to include several new departments, and Mrs. Westbrook organized a junior choir. This was the first children's choir work of which any record was kept. Mrs. Westbrook brought to her husband's new work many skills acquired across the years in Missouri, where she had filled several responsible posts in statewide Baptist women's work. These skills were invaluable to the life of the church.

The congregation became increasingly concerned with the general disrepair of the church's buildings. In August, 1931, the deacons brought a carefully thought out recommendation:

> Recognizing the responsibility that rests upon the Deacon Board of our Church to be ever alert for matters that might injure not only the credit, reputation and good name of our Church, but also the physical condition of our Church property, we offer the following suggestions:
> 1st—There is a note in the South Carolina National Bank for $450.00, and outstanding bills of $528.40.
> 2nd—That current collections are of such status as to make any appreciable reduction of this indebtedness impossible.
> 3rd—The physical condition of our Church plant both interior and exterior is such as to warrant only a very rapid degree of depreciation; and in the event that such necessary repairs are not made very soon it will necessitate the spending of a much larger sum of money in the future.
> 4th—The very great need of a pipe organ is apparent to every one. The lax condition of our Church activities might be attributable to the fact that there is no definite program on foot to enlist the majority of the individuals of our congregation. We might glance into the past when we were paying for our parsonage, and gather from that experience the fact that more than one year we discounted a $1000.00 note on the parsonage and took care of a budget of nearly $6000.00 besides.
>
> In view of this information we recommend that the chair appoint a committee to make a survey of actual conditions of our Church plant, get estimates of cost of repairs, investigate the matter of installing a pipe organ, and pay off bills against the Church. The necessary money to be raised by placing a mortgage on the parsonage. The payment of such mortgage to be made on long time convenient payment plan. The matter of the amount of money to be borrowed, the terms of the mortgage, and the price to be paid for pipe organ and repairs of course must be approved by the Church in a regular or called meeting.[3]

As a result, a program of improvements was outlined and bids were sought which included extensive repair on the interior and exterior of the building. Until this date, the ceiling of the sanctuary and the ceiling of the apse over the pulpit were painted in attractive designs of blue sky and rolling clouds. Inquiry was made as to the cost of having the ceiling repainted in a similar way. It was learned that an Italian artist had done the work in the past, and the cost would be prohibitive, so the decision was reluctantly made to paint the ceilings white.

Seven contractors submitted bids, with the lowest bid being $3725. The church agreed to award the contract and begin the work as soon as financing could be arranged, but the finance committee found it extremely difficult to secure financing. Every avenue was explored. The pastor even wrote a personal letter to Mr. John D. Rockefeller, Jr., to inquire about the possibility of a loan. This being an old and historic Baptist Church and Rockefeller being an active Baptist layman, it was hoped he might be interested, but he turned down the request. Finally, arrangements were made to secure a loan for $3000 with the lender holding the first mortgage on the pastorium.

Work was completed in the early fall, and October 13, 1932, was reserved for a special program of celebration marking the reopening of the restored sanctuary. Those invited to the occasion were R. W. Sanders and Oswell Smith, former pastors, as well as all the pastors of the city. The *Baptist Courier* was invited to cover the significant event. The congregation had labored long and hard to bring this project to completion. The facilities never looked more beautiful, and everyone's thoughts were now focused on the 1933 date for the South Carolina Baptist Convention. One year from the date the restoration was completed, the state convention would meet in Charleston for the purpose of celebrating the 250th anniversary of the church's founding. The church's morale was high, and a sense of confidence was evident. The presence of optimism made more dramatic the grief and shock the congregation experienced when in February, 1933, just four months after the restoration, the church building suffered considerable damage from a fire. The blaze was caused by a faulty flue in the southeast corner of the sanctuary. The fire started in the late night hours, and had it not been for the alert attention of the church's neighbor, Mrs. F. E. Whitman, owner of 59 Church Street, the church building might have been lost. The fire burst a large number of windows and caused extensive smoke damage. In its next conference, the church wrote letters of appreciation both to Mrs. Whitman and the city fire chief. But the church was left with a heavy mortgage and a seriously damaged sanctuary. With no funds to finance repairs, this indomitable little flock called a work day and began to scrub the walls to remove the soot. Damage from the fire was almost equal to the original expenditure for restoration. In this very dismal setting, a thrilling thing happened. While volunteers were working on their all but impossible task, P. O. Mead, Sr., a member of the church, walked in and proposed that he would match one dollar with every dollar the church could raise. Although Mr. Mead dealt in large financing in his timber business, his enterprises had suffered severe blows from the Depression, and this offer was one of courageous faith. When the funds were totaled, Mr. Mead and the church had raised just under four thousand dollars. The Dawson Engineering Company was given the contract, and when the time arrived for the Baptist State Convention, the building was once again in prime condition.

At the South Carolina Baptist State Convention the history of the First Baptist Church was excellently portrayed. The Wednesday evening service of the convention met in the sanctuary of the First Baptist Church where Dr. W. W. Barnes, eminent historian, author, and professor at The Southwestern

Baptist Theological Seminary, brought an address, "The History of the First Baptist Church of Charleston," and Dr. William L. Ball of Greenville, an immediate past president of the South Carolina Baptist State Convention, brought an address, "The Significance of this History in Baptist Life Today."

Earlier the same year, Dr. W. J. McGlothlin addressed the Southern Baptist Convention meeting in Washington, D.C. and offered a moving tribute to the illustrious history of the First Baptist Church. Dr. McGlothlin, president of Furman University, was completing his third year as president of the Southern Baptist Convention. The Southern Baptist Convention meeting the previous year in St. Petersburg, Florida, had requested the committee on order of business to allot time for appropriate commemorative services to be planned for the 1933 session.

During the 1930s while funds were being sought for the church's renovation, an issue surfaced regarding the Green Fund. The fund had been established in the 1800s with a generous bequest from a member of the congregation as a continuing resource out of which the church would assist needy members of the church family, especially unmarried women. The fund had been extensively used, and during the Civil War years and similar times the corpus had been drawn upon and greatly reduced. Sometime in the early 1900s an agreement was made for the funds to be deposited with a member of the First Baptist Church for investment, with it understood the interest was to be used by the church or allowed to accumulate. While the exact figure is not known, the amount was approximately three thousand dollars. In 1932, when the church was earnestly seeking funds to finance the restoration, it decided to call in this money from the Green Fund, but the Depression had brought pressure on the holder of the funds; consequently, in spite of repeated requests, he had to deny the church's request for principal or interest. The issue was a source of contention in the church until settled in the early 1940s, at which time the loan from the church was repaid in full with accumulated interest.

During the Depression, financial resources for the church slowed to a trickle. In June, 1932, pastor Westbrook insisted his salary be reduced from $50 to $40 per week. At this time, the church owed the pastor $250 in back salary. In July, 1933, he insisted the church reduce his salary an additional five dollars to a weekly salary of $35.

In spite of such adversity, the church managed throughout the 1930s to send contributions to mission causes. Most of the time, the contribution was 10 percent of all monies received. During the Depression years, the church's membership and Sunday School enrollment dropped, as did financial support. In July, 1934, Cornelius A. Westbrook resigned to accept a call to the First Baptist Church, Ware Shoals, South Carolina. While increases during his tenure were sparce, his resolve to lead the church through one of its most difficult periods of history placed him as one of the church's most esteemed pastors.

In the summer of 1934, the question of the pulpit committee might well have been, "Where do we go from here?" The church, as well as the whole nation, was prostrate from the Depression. Banks and businesses had folded. Unemployment was at an all-time high. While Franklin D. Roosevelt had been elected on the platform of getting the nation moving again, matters were still grave. In addition, the pulpit committee could not help but think of the ghost hanging over the church, the ghost of a poor location and the ghost of so many who said, "You will never make it in that location; you really need to disband or relocate." The pulpit committee began to think in terms of the First Baptist Church becoming a strategic preaching center. *We need an effective pulpiteer, first and foremost a preacher,* they were thinking. The lay people felt they could keep the organizational part of the church going if they could find a man capable of pulling people from every section of Charleston to "preaching services."

The attention of the pulpit committee focused on a man in his mid-thirties who was pastoring two small country churches near Elizabeth City, North Carolina. The committee was perceptive enough to see in this young country preacher a rising star of uncommon promise. Vance A. Havner agreed to talk with them though not at all impressed with their pitch of heritage and honor which the church enjoyed. Besides, the country parson was receiving increasing numbers of invitations for revivals, Bible conferences, and lectureships. This format of intinerate ministry held a keen fascination for Havner, but his coolness toward the idea of coming to Charleston as their pastor only led to more persistence on the part of the committee. They appealed to him on the basis of the numbers in the greater Charleston area from which he could draw. Havner was also told that one of the church members, Louis Burk, had opened the first radio station in the Low Country, WCSC, and while he was unable to fund it during the Depression and had subsequently relinquished control of it, he might be able to assist in having a weekly religious broadcast. Religious broadcasting was in its infancy, and the idea held a fascination for Havner. Probably the deciding factor in the North Carolinian's coming to the Charleston post was the willingness of the church to provide three months leave every year for him to continue revivals and Bible conferences.

The new pastor arrived in Charleston October, 1934, and moved into the St. John's Hotel, where he stayed for the duration of his pastorate. The church paid thirty-five dollars per month for his room. Mr. Havner was not married during his tenure at First Baptist; consequently, the decision was made to sell the Franklin Street pastor's home. The church had mortgaged the home to finance restoration of the sanctuary a few years earlier and had found paying off the mortgage extremely difficult. The church first agreed to deed the 12 Franklin Street property to the mortgager with the understanding that the new owner would assume all financial encumbrances on the property. Before this agreement was consummated, however, another party agreed to buy at a slightly better figure, and the contract was signed. The transaction, made under the strain of financial expediency, was a poor arrangement for the church. Approximately ten years earlier the church had paid $8400 for the property, and now toward the end of the Great Depression the church sold it for less than half the purchase price.

Mr. Havner began his pastorate in the fellowship of a small but highly enthusiastic congregation, a group of people clearly convinced the church now had the pastor who would lead the congregation to new heights. During the first weeks of his pastorate, he presided over a sequence of events that would have a direct influence on the next forty years of the pastoral leadership of the First Baptist Church. Shortly after his arrival, Havner conducted the services in which C. T. Hamrick, Sr. was installed as a newly-elected deacon and Paul J. Craven, Sr. was ordained to the diaconate. A few weeks later in June, 1935, Havner conducted the ordination service for John A. Hamrick. Shortly before this, the new pastor had visited the Craven home, at which time he prayed a prayer of dedication for a baby boy just born, Paul J. Craven, Jr. Havner delighted to relate years later how, in that prayer of dedication, he fervently prayed that God would call this infant lad into the gospel ministry. The pastoral service of John A. Hamrick and Paul J. Craven, Jr. in the First Baptist Church would span the years 1940 through 1981.

Under Mr. Havner's leadership, the church tended to minimize organization and promotion. At one point, the church clerk entered in the minute book that no church conferences were held for a period of fifteen months. In December, 1934, the church voted "to refrain from taking an every member canvas in the future, as well as all pledges," and there was a decreased emphasis on the importance of church membership.

The midweek prayer service was rescheduled from Wednesday evening to Thursday evening, which allowed members of other churches to hear Havner preach without missing the services in their respective churches. Soon after the new pastor's arrival the First Baptist Church embarked on a weekly radio broadcast, later to be called "The Church of the Air." Mr. Havner had a radio voice with strong appeal. His homespun style of preaching was without parallel. He had a Will Rogers style of dry humor which was effectively used to drive home powerful biblical truths. His sermons were more lecture than oratory and were delivered in a drawling nasal tone. But they were absolutely fascinating to the hearer.

Attendance increased significantly. During this period the old straight back pews were tilted slightly backward, and the narrow planks serving as seats were overlaid with wider contoured seats that have remained to the present. Increased attendance brought additional young adults with young children. The church minutes record a decision to employ a nursemaid to care for young children during church services. While no reference was made to the pastor, in all likelihood it was he who insisted on organizing a nursery. He, more than most preachers, had a low tolerance for any distracting element in the service. The country preacher from North Carolina had an audacious quality about his preaching that people liked. A member of the congregation delighted in relating an incident that occurred in one of the services. A woman of senior years attending this particular service thought the temperature in the sanctuary uncomfortably high and proceeded to write a note requesting the heat be turned down. She gave the note to the usher as he passed by, but the usher, without reading it, assumed it was a prayer request to be handed to the pastor. When the pastor read the anonymous request, he shared it with the congregation and commented with much feeling, "Please, pass all such notes to the head usher. It is his job to make you comfortable; it is my job to make you uncomfortable!"

While there was a decided increase in attendance during the five years of Vance Havner's tenure, while there were a number of Bible conferences and revivals, and while individuals were converted, it was the kind of activity that provided only minimum strength and growth to the church organization. During the late 1930s, there surfaced a growing concern over the general direction in which the church was moving. First, the church became increasingly anxious that the format being followed would ultimately jeopardize the future of the church and its relationship to the denomination. It was difficult to nurture and develop any denominational loyalty. At one point during this period the church voted to distribute envelopes to the members on which would be listed all those agencies and projects which were funded by the Cooperative Program, an action which indicated a concern for lost emphasis in this area.

Another source of concern to the church was the extended absences of the pastor. As cited earlier, the church agreed that Mr. Havner would have three months leave each year for Bible conferences and similar assignments. After three such summers, a year came when commitments of work away from Charleston necessitated the pastor's absence for four months. This raised questions concerning the original agreement. The church in conference voted to ask the pastor to adhere to the original agreement, an action the congregation rescinded a few months later. The problem obviously bothered the pastor as well as the people. He felt pulled by these two aspects of his ministry, and later, when he resigned, he cited this matter as the deciding factor that moved him into full-time evangelism and Bible conference work.

In the spring of 1939, the question again arose as to the proper and equitable disposition regarding the pastor's leave. Both the church and the pastor were pleased with the solution. Mr. Havner was given four months leave, May through August, and in his absence a promising young student in his final year of seminary study was called as supply pastor. His name was John Asa Hamrick. Since he had assisted Mr. Havner on other occasions and had given his service in several needy areas of the church organization, the young seminarian felt comfortable. The summer before, while home from the seminary, he had been placed on a committee with C. W. Parham, F. J. Nepveux, Paul J. Craven, Sr., P. F. Murphy, Lyman Love, and E. L. Pannal for the purpose of raising funds with which to purchase an organ. In late summer, 1938, the church purchased a Hammond organ, and in October of that year the treasurer reported that the bill, which was $1470, was paid in full with a small balance left in the special fund. Additional appeals were made, and during the next year a total of $435 was given. These gifts were used to purchase a set of chimes.

In September, 1939, when the pastor returned from his summer circuit of Bible conferences, he found not only the organ and chimes installation completed but also an air of enthusiasm about the church's work in general. Serious discussions and plans were underway for improvements to the Sunday School facilities. This subject received even fuller attention because of damage these facilities received in a serious tornado that year. The tornado had struck Charleston in late summer and had done widespread damage.

The congregation did not know it, but Mr. Havner was struggling to make the right decision concerning his future with the Charleston congregation. After careful consideration, he announced his decision to move into evangelistic work full-time, and on November 26, 1939, he brought to a close his Charleston pastorate. Vance Havner was as unique in his departure as he had been in his life-style. On his final Sunday with the First Baptist congregation, he presented himself for membership in the church and stated that he had neglected to move his membership to the church; so as he departed, he was voted into full fellowship. He was then granted a letter to unite with any church of like faith and order.

During the final month of Mr. Havner's work, the pulpit committee began its search for the church's next pastor. Only a few days after the pastor's resignation, the congregation voted to extend a call to the Rev. Lofton Hudson, who replied that he must regretfully decline. One week later, at the next regular monthly church conference the pulpit committee presented the name of John A. Hamrick as nominee for pastor. Of the fifty-five votes cast, thirty-four were in the affirmative and twenty-one in the negative, or approximately 62 percent—which failed to give the needed two-thirds majority. A highly emotional discussion ensued. Some contended that the pulpit committee should be instructed as to the kind of pastor the church desired. The chairman of the search committee offered his resignation, but the church voted not to accept the resignation—whereupon the chairman stated emphatically his willingness to be counseled but his refusal to be dictated to by any individual. Two weeks later, in a special called conference, Robert W. Liger requested and received permission by a church vote to make a nomination from the floor. Liger nominated John A. Hamrick as pastor, and the motion carried thirty-four to eight, or an 80 percent majority.

On January 7, 1940, John A. Hamrick moderated his first business meeting as pastor of the church and at that time addressed the recent action of the church. He reported that though the church extended the call, several church leaders had written him stating their opposition to the call and prevailing on him not to accept it. Serious questions were raised about the parliamentary procedure followed in the call. The incisive young pastor had anticipated these questions and brought with him to the church conference a copy of Kerfoot's *Parliamentary Law*. Even at this early point in his ministry, Hamrick was known for his reasoning and debating skills. He had been captain of the prestigious debating team at the College of Charleston, the school from which he was a Phi Beta Kappa graduate. During his remarks before the church conference, Hamrick referred to Kerfoot several times as he presented a clear, persuasive case and concluded his remarks with the strong position that the congregation called him and that he felt deeply he should accept. He then asked for a rising vote of reaffirmation, to which the vast majority responded. But a few individuals would not allow the controversy to end. One week later a motion was made that all action in regard to Hamrick's call be rescinded. In order to bring the matter to a close, a rather ingenius motion was made to table the entire matter for five years, and the motion carried. John Hamrick began his work as pastor in January, 1940, with a salary of fifty dollars per week, hardly enough to purchase his round trip air fare to Louisville, Kentucky. He was completing his master's degree in The Southern Baptist Theological Seminary and commuted every week for five months.

From the outset, the new pastor was a builder. The church had expressed several times during the last few years the necessity for improving the educational facilities of the church. Nothing could have challenged the new pastor more. While the sanctuary was extraordinary, there was only one small "lecture room" located out from the southwest corner of the sanctuary. Mr. Hamrick led the church immediately to begin improvements. Initial plans included excavation of a half basement in the lecture room. The original ceiling was sufficiently high to allow a two-story floor plan. Just as this work was well underway, the 1940 hurricane severely damaged the roof of the building under repair. The building committee determined that an additional $2200 expended would provide a third story on this structure. This new facility could not have been completed at a more appropriate time.

On that fateful Monday, December 7, 1941, President Franklin D. Roosevelt appeared before a joint session of the Congress and announced that the United States was at war with Japan. The country had entered World War II. The Japanese attack on Pearl Harbor on Sunday, December 6, ushered in changes with staggering speed. When the church gathered for worship that Sunday morning everything was routine, but by noon the news had been flashed around the world. This writer remembers well the somber setting in the First Baptist Church that Sunday night. Those of the church membership in any branch of the military reserve returned to worship that evening in full military dress. They now were on active duty.

Charleston became a strategic location in the nation's rush to mobilize. The Charleston shipyard and similar facilities expanded geometrically, and thousands of individuals gravitated to Charleston from the Low Country and beyond. In addition, large numbers of military personnel and their families were stationed in Charleston. Many of these individuals came to the First Baptist Church. Many were single adults who found in the church a fellowship away from home, and a remarkable number of those found friends who became sweethearts and ultimately partners in marriage. By 1943, the church's membership had increased to 474, the largest number since the Civil War. Many of those uniting with the church during this period became permanent residents and assumed vital roles of leadership across the years.

The church expanded its organization not only in the conventional areas of Sunday School, Baptist Training Union, and similar groups but also into organizations of basketball teams, Boy Scouts, and a day nursery. Each new organization required additional leadership, but each also drew additional members whose personal and family needs were met. During the 1940s the pastor's work was further strengthened by his inviting individuals who had just completed their schooling, or were between graduate and undergraduate studies, to spend time with him in assistantships. This group included John A. Barry, Stanley R. Hahn, and Martha B. Barry. In 1949, the church employed its first full-time secretary, Elizabeth King, who had recently completed her work at the New Orleans Baptist Theological Seminary.

During the mid-1940s the church saw the need to repaint and refurbish the sanctuary. In addition to painting, the plans included a $1700 expenditure for new carpet and the purchase of a grand piano. With increasing numbers interested in attending the church, and with the severe scarcity of gasoline and tires, the church arranged to rent a bus to pick up those members scattered over a wide area of Charleston. The idea met with such success the church voted to purchase a bus. Since the availability of vehicles of any type was virtually nil, it was remarkable that a bus was located and the necessary gasoline coupons were acquired.

In September, 1945, the Japanese signed an unconditional surrender which brought World War II to a close, and members of the armed services returned home. Many men did not return. Across the land churches had displayed service flags. They were simple white flags on which was placed one blue star for each church member serving in the armed services. When a church member died in the service of his country that star was changed to gold. The flag of the First Baptist Church bore a large number of stars, but none.had to be changed to gold. With the end of the war came a totally new era for most of the country, and Charleston was no exception. The war had ushered in many scientific advances; it accelerated modernization in virtually every area of life. The period gave rise to new affluence and a new secularism. On the day victory was proclaimed in World War II, church bells pealed forth everywhere, but that did not mean spiritual awakening. On the contrary, the churches had a formidable task to fulfill this mission.

In 1947, John Hamrick proposed the most ambitious facility expansion to date, and less than five years later, he proposed another phase of equal magnitude. These two building programs produced virtually the entire educational plant as it stands on the Church Street property today. This, of course, did not include the Water Street and Meeting Street properties. These acquisitions came later, and their stories shall be told later in this chapter. Details of the 1947 building project are remarkable. While World War II had ended, all civilian construction remained under the scrutiny of the War Production Board. In order to obtain a permit to build, certain scarce materials had to be on hand and at the disposal of the person in charge of construction. The church was given opportunity to purchase a sizable complex of surplus barracks once used to house WAVES. Volunteers from the church membership dismantled great portions of the structures which yielded more than sufficient materials for heating, plumbing, and electrical work as well as bountiful building and finishing materials for carpentry. Only one major item was missing, the essential steel beams! No steel had been available for civilian construction since the outbreak of World War II. Steel producing companies were faced with making up those deficiencies incurred over the past seven years. Steel was ordered and purchased from handling companies long before the actual product was ever delivered. All but one such company had been contacted, and that company in Columbia, South Carolina was called. The company representative reported that the company had that very day received a shipment of steel which at the moment was uncommitted, and in the shipment were those beams needed, exact in length and weight. With the necessary steel on hand, the church received the permits to begin construction.

A glimpse into the vision shared by Hamrick and the lay leadership can be gained by relating an incident that occurred during construction in the late 1950s. For a long time, there had been attempts to acquire additional property adjoining the church. Such attempts had been futile. But when the northwest wing of the educational building was constructed across the rear line of the church property, a large beam was constructed in the wall. "One day," Hamrick said, "the church will own that property to the rear of the church, and this beam will enable us simply to make an archway there." In 1960, the church acquired the beautiful dwelling and large lot in a most remarkable sequence of events.

All of these properties were urgently needed, for in the late 1940s the church undertook one of the most challenging projects of its entire history, the founding of the First Baptist Church Day School. As earlier chapters in this book attest, across its long history the First Baptist Church has had an interesting and productive relationship with the causes of education. Several factors entered into Hamrick's rationale for a day school. First was the opportunity to have students for a major portion of each day during which time the child would be given not only Bible instruction but nurture in basic character building. The postwar years heightened the moral and spiritual dilemma of the world, and while the school was never intended to be a proselytizing instrument, it did open doors into homes for the pastor and staff that otherwise would most surely have remained closed.

Another factor in Hamrick's rationale was the opportunity to provide a program of academic excellence. The public school system had found it increasingly difficult to foster strong programs. Since Charleston traditionally had supported private schools, there was an existing market and mindset. There was never any contention between the public and private schools and, in fact, a feeling of mutual support was nurtured. The First Baptist Church Day School, from the date of its founding, never adopted any racially discriminating policies. It would be inaccurate to say this was a unanimous feeling on the part of every member. Some insisted that there be a policy clearly stating that the school was a segregated institution; and when the first black child was enrolled, some said this would be the death knell of the school. Fortunately, sound judgment always characterized the majority in policy making roles.

A third factor in the founder's rationale was the opportunity to make more secure and practical the institutional nature of the First Baptist Church. Every church must decide the image and structure it seeks to portray to the community. This usually occurs without conscious planning by the church leadership. As was related earlier in this chapter, the late 1930s saw the leadership thinking of the First Baptist Church in terms of a strong preaching station where great numbers gathered, and the life of the church was kept loosely organized with much emphasis placed on spontaneity. If such was to happen, Vance Havner was thought to be the one to bring the idea into reality. But the dream never took shape. Hamrick thought it inevitable that a downtown church must foster either a tabernacle ministry with a loosely organized, spontaneous style or an institutional ministry with a strong commitment to nurture and discipling. He envisioned the day school as an excellent vehicle with which to fulfill a commitment to an institutional ministry.

A final element in Hamrick's rationale was simply a stewardship of facilities. It bothered him that the church had such splendid facilities and used them hardly more than three or four hours per week. A day school would accumulate thousands of student hours each week, and the sanctuary would have at least one worship service six days of each week. Some church members disliked the idea of school children constantly in the facilities. Others thought the neighborhood setting did not lend itself to a school. Still other church members promoted the idea of a separate campus altogether. Had such a concept been developed, not only would it have become simply another private school with little attachment to the church, but as facility cost increased, the expenses would finally have priced the program out of existence.

A committee of the church carefully worked through all the ramifications of the matter. Finally, in the spring of 1949, a recommendation was adopted by the church. The plan was to open with a kindergarten and first grade and to add one grade per year. Mrs. Leroy Benedict was the first principal, and Mrs. W. D. Murphy, Sr. served as the first director of the kindergarten. The school opened in the fall of 1949 with an excellent enrollment and rapidly gained wide attention in the community. It graduated its first class in 1960 with every graduate enrolling in college. During the years when the high school was being structured, Mrs. O. J. Brodie served effectively as principal and gave the college preparatory program a strong foundation.

As the school gained in numbers and community acclaim, it incited the ire of its neighbors, a resentment which ultimately resulted in long and costly litigation. The problem began with a group of neighbors, none of whom were members of the First Baptist Church, but all of whom lived in the immediate proximity of the church. They saw the school growing rapidly and the increased traffic which accompanied such growth. They resolved to settle for nothing less than closing the school. The grounds for their contention were the lack of open space for playground area and the failure of the buildings to meet fire and safety codes. At one point, they further strengthened their position by having the city board of aldermen pass an ordinance which stated that before any church or school could obtain a permit to build, the applicant would first be forced to acquire the unanimous approval and consent of every resident in the block in which the church or school would be located. This, in effect, would have precluded the First Baptist Church ever acquiring another building permit.

How John Hamrick addressed the problem provides a good example of the methods he employed in many other challenges he would face. He immediately arranged for a hearing before the board of aldermen and then contacted, not only other Baptist churches, but also the Roman Catholic bishop and the three rabbis in the city. When the night for the hearing arrived, all of those mentioned, plus many other community leaders, attended, convinced the new ordinance was a grave threat to religious freedom and would be the death knell to private, parochial, and synagogue schools. The number attending necessitated moving the hearing to larger chambers. When the pastor of the First Baptist Church had completed his case, the aldermen were anxious to rescind their previous action.

With this weapon gone, the opponents continued their complaints in regard to buildings and playground. The case advanced to the South Carolina Supreme Court where the church won the case, but expensive building improvements were required—all of which made the buildings safer and more comfortable. The most significant point in the court's ruling was a numerical limitation of 270 students placed on the church school's enrollment. At this point Thomas P. Stoney, attorney for the church, exercised a stroke of genius. He succeeded in having written into the order that the limited enrollment pertained exclusively to the then existing church property, namely, 61-63 Church Street. After the court agreed to that designation, Mr. Stoney told Mr. Hamrick, "Your next step is to embark on acquisition of surrounding properties." That need would receive high priority across the next twenty-five years.

The ministry of John Hamrick would have been far less significant without his strongest ally, Margaret Kelly Hamrick, his wife. Never has there been a more dedicated and tireless worker. At the outset of his pastorate, she served as volunteer secretary and educational director. She utilized her special gifts in the most effective ways. One such talent was drama, and every Christmas she wrote and directed a pageant of major scope which, of course, generated enormous interest and drew large numbers. She was an extraordinary Bible teacher, and among other teaching assignments, she organized the My Purpose Holds (MPHs) Club which was designed to affirm and sustain young people who had given themselves to full-time church related vocations. The project was so successful that *The Baptist Program* in 1950 published a feature story on it. From 1940 to 1980, the First Baptist Church averaged approximately one person each year going into such vocations. Today many of these serve faithfully in churches, institutions, and agencies around the world. Across many years, Mrs. Hamrick worked as teacher both in the Sunday School and the Day School as well as in countless retreats and special programs, and all of this was done while rearing two fine children and caring for her aging mother who lived in the Hamrick home. One can readily understand why she was elected to the Hall of Fame of the Charleston Federation of Women's Clubs.

Part of Hamrick's achievements stemmed from his determination to give the church high visibility in the community. He was ingenious in promotional skills. He could plan a simple event like an annual Sunday School picnic and turn it into a major happening. Great crowds would meet at Chaplin's Landing to enjoy a delectable home-cooked, homecoming-type dinner. Victor Shokes, a devoted layman, and his committee would furnish barrels of lemonade, bushels of peanuts, and bags of candy. It was not unusual for the mayor, an Episcopal layman, to drive out for dinner and stay for the waterfront prayer service. Such invitations were especially important if there were some need or plan on the horizon with which the mayor might conceivably be of assistance.

As the church moved into the 1950s, the Southern Baptist Convention, in general, entered an era of unprecedented promotion and growth, and the First Baptist Church of Charleston was a part of it. In 1952, it was the simultaneous revival crusade, the first of its kind; next came the Sunday School's "A Million More in Fifty-Four" campaign; then came the drive to establish thirty thousand new churches and preaching stations. All of this strengthened and challenged the hand of the local pastor.

In the early 1950s, Mr. Lee McLeod gave the church a beachfront house on the south end of Folly Island. With a capacity for lodging sixty persons, Enter Inn became invaluable in retreats and programs for every age group in the church. The Charleston Baptist Association used it extensively, and for many years Furman University conducted a summer pastor's school there. The church found it to be an excellent facility for hosting college groups. Hamrick was the founding force in organizing Baptist student work at the College of Charleston, at the Medical University, the Nursing School, and the Citadel. He had great appeal to students and was a frequent speaker on college campuses, not only locally but regionally. Numbers of these students he met on campus visits away from Charleston came to the city later for graduate work and other assignments, and many of them looked up the First Baptist Church.

Mr. Hamrick gave high priority to denominational work and led his church in vigorous participation. He served as president of the South Carolina Pastor's Conference and president of the South Carolina Baptist State Convention. The church was continually engaged in some convention-sponsored program. An example of the degree of this participation came the year three young people from the First Baptist Church won the state Baptist Training Union junior sword drill, the intermediate sword drill, and the state Baptist Training Union better speaker's contest. At some point in his ministry, John Hamrick served on most of the institutional boards of the South Carolina Baptist State Convention, as well as the agencies of the Southern Baptist Convention. One of the most strategic posts was his membership on the board of trustees at Furman University. During his tenure on this board, the move to the new campus took place. Furman University conferred on him the doctor of divinity degree.

In the mid-1950s the church realized it must expand its facilities to house the increasing numbers in both the church and the school. With court restraints on the 61-63 Church Street facility there was no alternative but to search for new parcels, and the chance for this seemed increasingly remote. Some of those neighbors who had years earlier initiated litigation against the church and lost, now sought to have all residents in the area refuse to sell their property to the church. The church missed, by a strange set of circumstances, purchasing the house at 57 Church Street. Without forewarning, 24 Water Street was offered for sale. The four-story building would serve perfectly the facility needs of church and school. So fearful were the church leaders that their efforts to purchase the property would be thwarted, they resolved to purchase the property anonymously. A major obstacle was financing, and less than a week was available to consummate the purchase. Funds were secured when P. O. Mead, Sr., a church member for many years, and Lester L. Bates, Sr., a former member and staunch friend of the church, each agreed to put up $10,000 as temporary funding. John Hamrick negotiated a personal note for the balance needed, and the contract was completed. Soon afterward the deed of ownership was transferred to the church, and permanent financing was arranged.

In 1960, the 48 Meeting Street property was purchased in even more dramatic circumstances. The church had negotiated a purchase of the property some time earlier, but the offer was declined. Without advance notice, the property was advertised for sale, and the church entered into contract to purchase the property before noon of the first day the advertisement appeared. This parcel was the most strategic property the church could ever have negotiated to buy. It included a large three-story house, servants buildings, extensive grounds and an entrance to Water Street as well as to Meeting Street. This acquisition almost doubled the ground space and square footage of floor space of the church's educational facilities. In 1965, the church purchased the stately home at 22 Water Street which was the final acquisition during Dr. Hamrick's tenure. Not long after this final purchase, the Honorable J. Palmer Gaillard, mayor of the city of Charleston, had attended a special activity at the church. Afterward he was standing in the center of the new parking lot surrounded with the church's fine facilities and remarked, "Who would ever have dreamed that a parcel of property of this magnitude could ever have been assembled here in the heart of the city's historic district." It was more than a dream come true. It was the answer to many fervent prayers. These acquisitions, as well as many other endeavors, were not achieved without opposition. With each project, there were those in the church membership who had grave reservations as to the wisdom of such pursuits and offered considerable resistance. But in each instance progressive, positive leadership was in the majority, and each project was brought to a successful completion.

With all of Dr. Hamrick's achievements, he had not yet undertaken what would be his most dramatic challenge. For many years he had dreamed of a church-related college for the Low Country. The idea of a church-related college in coastal South Carolina was certainly a worthy and justifiable goal, but the practical problems seemed insurmountable. Colleges, generally, were feeling enormous financial pressure. Furman University, South Carolina Baptists' senior college, was in the midst of building a totally new campus. Anxiety was widespread across the state that any new institution would draw needed funds from Furman as well as other convention causes. Hamrick began talking about his dream in the 1950s. His approach was one of patient and persistent exploration. All along the way he gained the interest and support of person after person. Finally, there came the appropriate time to ask the Charleston Baptist Association to endorse the idea in concept. The association adopted the concept and appointed a committee, of which John Hamrick was chairman, to develop plans of organization and strategy. As the 1950s drew to a close, excellent progress had been made with the myriad of necessary plans, and by 1960 the charter was ready for approval. At a special meeting of the association in the sanctuary of the First Baptist Church, the same location for so many historic occurrences in the past, the charter for the Baptist College at Charleston was signed. Those in attendance that day shared a common awareness that they were experiencing another historic epoch in the ongoing story of Baptists. The document was signed in the immediate area of the two historic memorial tablets, mounted on each side of the pulpit, one to Furman and the other to Brantly. Richard Furman, for whom Furman University was later named, was the leading force among Baptists for Christian education during his Charleston pastorate, and William T. Brantly served the dual role of pastor of the First Baptist Church and president of the College of Charleston. One could readily imagine these tablets giving jubilant affirmation to the 1960 charter.

The next task for the organizational committee was to secure a site and obtain pledges for contributions. The General Board of the South Carolina Baptist State Convention agreed to bring the proposal to the Convention when a suitable site was obtained and a half-million dollars in other assets were in hand. A magnificent tract of land was secured from the city of Charleston, and a campaign was launched to raise the funds. The members of the First Baptist Church made the first pledges which initially totaled more than fifty thousand dollars. With the provisions of the General Board fulfilled, the proposal was presented to the South Carolina Baptist State Convention in 1964. The convention accepted the college and elected trustees. John Hamrick was elected chairman of the trustees and, subsequently, president of the college, a post he filled jointly with that of pastor for five years.

During the formative years of the Baptist College at Charleston the First Baptist Church filled a most supportive role. While the members of the church generally regarded the endeavor as worthy of their support, the feeling was far from unanimous. A limited number of the members resented the time the pastor was giving the project, and some even promoted the idea of calling for a decision by the pastor either to choose the work of the college or the pastorate of the church. Still others resented any of the college staff using office space in the church's facilities. Fortunately, those who harbored such feelings were always in the minority. There were others who readily acknowledged the worthiness and potential of so great an endeavor, but whose genuine affection for their pastor made their enthusiasm for the college next to nil. Amidst all these cross currents, the college began its first classes in the fall, 1965.

Dr. Hamrick soon realized he must have additional pastoral assistance in the church. He was very sensitive to the needs of the church during this period and was determined the life and program of First Baptist would not suffer. With this growing concern looming in the pastor's thoughts, he placed a very eventful telephone call on a brisk morning in the late winter of 1966. The call was to the Jackson Hill Baptist Church in Atlanta, Georgia. He was immediately put through to the pastor, Paul J. Craven, Jr. The friendship of the two spanned many years. Craven had grown up under Hamrick's ministry. After a brief exchange of greetings, the pastor of the First Baptist Church wasted little time in addressing the purpose of his call, to ascertain the Atlanta pastor's willingness to consider a return to Charleston and to the First Baptist Church as associate pastor. The idea came as a shock. Charleston was the last place Craven would have thought of as his next work. As Hamrick amplified his view of the work and how the two might address it, Craven became increasingly intrigued with the idea. As the conversation continued, Hamrick, who had already given more than twenty-five years of his ministry to the Charleston congregation, shared how he really had not intended to leave the pastorate for the presidency and even at this point had difficulty seeing himself in that dramatic change. Hamrick sought other men to assume the presidency, but while numerous individuals made known their availability, none were of sufficient strength to bring the college from an idea on paper to a concrete reality.

The conversations between Hamrick and Craven were unhurried and thorough. By mid-summer the two had agreed on the foundation for their common task. The new associate would assume considerable administrative responsibilities in the church and day school as well as supportive roles in preaching and pastoral care. Craven assumed his new Charleston post in August, 1966. The working relationship of the two men was genuinely unique. Neither ever felt uncomfortable with the role or work of the other. The preaching assignments each Sunday were divided. Dr. Hamrick usually preached in the morning worship and Mr. Craven the evening. Dr. Hamrick's work with the college necessitated his absence on some Sunday mornings, in which instances Mr. Craven preached. Many times it was imperative that Dr. Hamrick be away from the church office for a major part of the week. During such times the ministers were in constant touch by telephone. The work progressed under this arrangement with substantial growth taking place in membership and financial support.

One project taking place during this period was the complete restoration of the sanctuary and the installation of the pipe organ. During the restoration, the pulpit-choir area was slightly modified, and a new pulpit installed, designed by Mr. Albert Simons, an authority on Robert Mills' work. The original pulpit built in the 1820s had been damaged during the Civil War and finally removed in the 1880s. The pulpit of the 1960s followed a modified design of the original. Among other differences, the original pulpit had its base on the congregational level, was freestanding, and had a sounding board canopy suspended above it. During the restoration and refurbishing, the present lectern was made by Homer Peeler, a noted Charleston craftsman and a member of the First Baptist Church. On its center panel was painted the church seal which was found on a document dating from many years earlier.

Another addition during this time was a cross to hang in the baptistry, the procurement of which offers an interesting story. The pastor expressed to his associate the thought that a cross would be a meaningful addition to the baptistry area of the church. The church from time to time across the years had included crosses of various types as one of the appointments in the pulpit area. The appropriateness of the cross was shared by Fitzhugh N. Hamrick, chairman of the refurbishing committee, who proceeded to obtain a cross of proper specifications. As soon as it was known that a cross was to hang in the baptistry, sharp protestations were heard. Since Craven had been on the scene only a matter of months, it was immediately concluded that he was responsible for the strange notion and had made the decision. The chairman of the committee for refurbishing and decorating was contacted immediately. He responded with the assurance that he personally had ordered the cross. The discussion intensified, and a meeting of the deacons was called. The meeting revealed that only a limited number opposed the idea. While those opposing the idea were few in number, it was thought an open discussion would be helpful and constructive. John Hamrick masterfully led the group in an enlightening discussion and asked each deacon to write down a personal response to the following inquiry: "If the cross hanging in the sanctuary is a personal offense to you, explain why." The replies were quite interesting. No one offered a sound and persuasive response. One individual explained his opposition to the idea by saying that every time he saw the cross it made him think of the Roman Catholic Church. The pastor answered that if the cross were the only thing separating Baptists and Catholics, the two would do well to take another look at each other. Of course, the cross was left hanging. After a short time passed, one of those who had voiced serious reservations about its being there in the first place had the courage to acknowledge that its presence had become so meaningful to him that should anyone ever suggest the cross be removed, he would probably be the one to raise the severest protest.

The most significant single accomplishment during the restoration of the 1960s was the procurement of the Wicks Pipe Organ. The instrument was custom designed to have all working pipes in full view. Frederick Swann of the Riverside Church in New York was commissioned to give the dedicatory program. While in Charleston for his program, Swann acclaimed the organ for its superb tonal quality and its exquisite architectural design. It is interesting to note that in 1938 during his work as summer assistant, John Hamrick worked with a committee whose task was to raise money for a new organ. That endeavor was successful, and a new Hammond electronic organ and chimes were purchased. Thirty years later one of John Hamrick's last projects as pastor of the church was successfully to promote the purchase of the Wicks Pipe Organ which shall enhance worship for many generations to come.

In the fall of 1968, Dr. Hamrick and Mr. Craven met at the church for one of their frequent reviewing and planning sessions. Because of the complex schedules of both, the hour was typically late. During this meeting, Dr. Hamrick shared information concerning the exciting progress at the college. It was the fourth year of its operation, and the seniors were in their final year. The great news was that the Southern Association of Colleges and Secondary Schools, the accrediting agency, had notified the Baptist College that all requirements for accreditation had been met, and the seniors could graduate in the spring of 1969 from a fully accredited college, quite a phenomenal accomplishment for a senior college only four years in operation. All requirements had been met, that is, except one. The college must have a full-time president! The two discussed their options. By this time the thought of Hamrick's leaving the college presidency was out of the picture. Hamrick would have to resign the pastorate. In December, 1968, after a tenure of twenty-nine years, John A. Hamrick announced his resignation. The church planned a John A. Hamrick Day in his honor, and a testimonial dinner was held at the Gaillard Auditorium.

When one reviews the history of the First Baptist Church from 1940 to 1970, there is no way to separate it from John A. Hamrick. During these years, the church experienced growth in many areas unparalleled by any other period of its history. The following is an attempt to summarize Hamrick's philosophy and his achievements in ministry.

He had an extraordinary capacity to envision ambitious goals. So phenomenal were his ideas and dreams that on occasion he was labeled a visionary. He had the capacity to see the maximum happening in and through any person or any situation, however limited or unpromising. With his capacity to dream came Hamrick's capacity to lead and motivate. He could convince an individual to undertake the most seemingly impossible task. One staff member enjoyed relating how she entered the pastor's office to get relief from an overloaded work schedule; but before she left the study, not only had she agreed that her work load was not unreasonable, but she had also gladly agreed to assume one more small responsibility. Another story, related by W. W. Smith who, along with his talented wife, had labored faithfully in the church, illustrates Hamrick's leadership skills. Smith enjoyed saying, "If John Hamrick announced that we were to meet him at the west end of Broad Street to walk on the water across the Ashley River, I would be one of the first there. I would know the chances were remote, but nonetheless I surely would be there to try!"

Another secret of his success was Hamrick's tireless and determined effort as a worker. He never thought it beneath his dignity to do anything that needed to be done, whether it was driving a bus or even operating a construction tractor which he did when the Water Street and Meeting Street properties were being developed. On one occasion he learned that the kitchen workers in the school had threatened to quit—a threat which led him to fire the disgruntled workers and proceed to the kitchen personally, accompanied by three secretaries, and serve hot lunches to the day school children.

When John Hamrick was convinced of something, he was the most persistent and determined individual ever known. He was often characterized as headstrong or even stubborn. He was always willing to listen to opposing viewpoints, but the opponents needed always to talk fast and to be well prepared to defend the opposing position. When preparing for any controversial matter, however insignificant, one of Hamrick's routine procedures was to review the matter from every conceivable viewpoint. He frequently solicited input from others whom he would ask intentionally to oppose his position. As a result, when the time arrived for his appearance before an individual or group, he was as thoroughly prepared as any lawyer appearing in court. One of his colleagues enjoyed reflecting on those occasions when he saw John Hamrick work in situations where the stakes were high. His colleague recalled certain meetings of the Executive Committee of the General Board of the South Carolina Baptist Convention where it appeared virtually every person in attendance was in disagreement with and opposition to the proposals brought by Hamrick. When his assignment was difficult, it seemed he always wore his black, three-piece suit. On the gold chain draped from one vest pocket to the other could be seen his Phi Beta Kappa key. He was the epitome of confidence and intelligence. When he had completed his case and departed, seldom, if ever, did he leave defeated.

As a pulpiteer John Hamrick had few equals. While as a youth, he had lost totally the sight in one eye; but he remained well-read throughout his ministry and relied heavily on current events and best sellers as well as the classics for illustrative material. He did a minimum of expository preaching but rather preferred in his sermonizing to address life's situations and to base the answers on biblical truths. His appealing style of delivery was characterized by enthusiasm in which each word was delivered in a commanding, dynamic intonation. During his years at First Baptist he was continuously sought for revivals. He wrote all of his sermons out in longhand, but they were always well thought through and prepared. He readily acknowledged his complete dependence on prayer and once told a younger preacher friend, "The most important thing in sermon preparation is the preparation of the preacher's heart."

John Hamrick's pastoral skills equalled his administrative and preaching skills. His personal relationships reflected genuine caring and sensitivity. He was no respecter of persons or rank but could move comfortably in the humblest or the most prestigious circles. He developed close friendships in every sector. While not a member of the First Baptist Church, L. Mendel Rivers frequently came to hear him preach and acclaimed him as the most provocative thinker and the most effective preacher he knew.

Most of those members who joined the First Baptist Church during Hamrick's ministry were personally visited by the pastor. This partially explains why the First Baptist Church grew while at the same time many other downtown churches declined. When Hamrick assumed the pastorate in January, 1940, the church membership was approximately two hundred with an annual budget of $5000. In December, 1969, the membership was approximately fourteen hundred with a budget of $162,000. In the span of those twenty-nine years many individuals came into the church family who, across the years, gave extraordinary support and leadership. To include even a partial listing would more than fill this volume. The joy of these rests in the fact that each can claim a share in an illustrious period of the church's history.

As John Hamrick brought to a close his pastorate, he took careful measures to shift the loyalty of the lay leadership from himself to his successor. As he continued in his post as president of the Baptist College, he remained a welcomed member of the First Baptist Church. Of the entire membership no member was a more ardent supporter of Hamrick's successor than John A. Hamrick himself.

Notes

1. Church Minutes, July 1, 1923.
2. The Sunday Bulletin of the First Baptist Church, January 1, 1928, filed in the church archives.
3. *Southern Baptist Convention Annual,* 1933, p. 22.

15

God's Work Continues

For the first time in twenty-nine years, the First Baptist Church faced the assignment of searching for a new pastor. The church elected a search committee recommended by the committee on committees, and P. O. Mead, Jr., was elected chairman. As soon as John Hamrick's resignation became known, recommendations began coming to the committee. The looming question was what type of individual must be sought. The individual chosen would have to deal not only with the unique needs of an historic church in a downtown setting but also with those of a thriving day school program. The search committee formed the following profile as a guide in their work; the individual chosen

1) Must have a genuine sense of call and a commitment to that call.
2) Must be a caring pastor with the ability to counsel.
3) Must be an able preacher with a courageous, biblical message but never to embarrass the congregation, sound theologically, well-read, rejecting extremisms.
4) Must be a competent administrator with ability:
   —to select and direct a staff of forty persons,
   —to promote, fund, and follow budgets,
   —to program and evaluate effectively.
5) Must possess and utilize the following abilities:
   —inspire and motivate others,
   —willingness to carry heavy work schedules,
   —self-motivated,
   —sensitivity in matters of race and class distinctions,
   —appeal to youth.
6) Must have other personal qualities:
   —his life must back up his message.
   —dignity without aloofness.
7) His wife must be able to work with people.
8) Must have ability for good relations within the community and with the denomination.
9) Must possess a definite interest in this particular church, with its unique problems, challenges, and opportunities.

375

Early in the committee's work the question claiming primary attention was how properly to relate the fact that Paul J. Craven, Jr., was serving as the associate pastor with the church's need for a pastor. At least three lines of thought surfaced immediately. Some thought that the associate pastor should not be considered a candidate, that this was the beginning of a new era and, as such, should begin with a clean slate. Others on the committee suggested that no one be eliminated but that the committee consider all names submitted. Still others were inclined to recommend Craven to the church for immediate action. At the height of discussion, W. D. Murphy, Sr., asked to appear before the deacons. Though he had always declined election to the diaconate, his service in the church spanned more than a half century. He was highly respected for his faithfulness and his churchmanship. As he stood before the deacons, he reflected on a similar meeting thirty years earlier when the church was considering John Hamrick for pastor who at that time was associate pastor. Murphy related how it became a divisive issue with a serious aftermath. He urged the committee immediately to give serious consideration to Craven as the principal candidate.

The brisk air on that morning in late November, 1968, gave clear notice that cold weather would soon arrive, but for now, the autumn day was filled with indescribable beauty. The associate pastor had just completed plans for the annual Thanksgiving service. The phone rang in Craven's office, and the secretary indicated that P. O. Mead, Jr. was calling to make an appointment to meet with Craven. Mead had driven in from Wapola, his plantation, for the express purpose of this meeting. In a matter of minutes, Mead was seated in the associate pastor's study. After a few moments of light conversation, Mead turned their conversation to the church. "After the most careful consideration we could give," Mead began, "it is the consensus of our search committee that you should be our next pastor." While the words were not totally unexpected to Craven, they most surely were awesome and momentous. A whole world of thought surged through his mind and heart. This was the church of his boyhood! He was keenly aware of its past agonies and victories. With no little effort, he managed to give the appearance of composure. But both men were aware, though it was never verbalized, that another chapter in an ongoing story was unfolding. Craven raised the question of unanimity in the search committee. "This is my fourth church," Craven reminded Mead, "and I have always received a unanimous call." After a silence that seemed much longer than it actually was, Mead spoke: "It will not be a unanimous call because the committee is not unanimous, but I want to speak to you frankly on this matter of a unanimous call." Mead knew he could be frank. The two had spent much time together; they had hunted together; they had prayed together; they had planned church and school projects together. Their friendship ran deep; the two families had known each other for four generations. Mead continued, "I have no way of knowing what the vote will be, but I am confident you will receive a very strong majority, perhaps 85 percent or more. And while all of us would like unanimous approval from those with whom we work, what would you be saying to us who make up the majority should you reject our call?" It was the kind of straightforward question Craven needed. Other aspects of the subject were explored. The associate pastor agreed for his name to be brought to the church with the understanding that he would be told the percentages of the final vote. The congregation was notified of the date for a special business conference, at which time a secret ballot was taken. Craven had traveled to Atlanta with his family for a Thanksgiving holiday. On their way back to Charleston, they spent Saturday night in Augusta and worshiped that Sunday in the First Baptist Church in Aiken. After the service, Craven placed a call to Charleston to receive the results. The vote was 86 percent for and 14 percent against, a little more favorable than Mead had predicted. Some of those casting negative votes became faithful supporters of the new pastor and his programs. Others who opposed the call were still opposed thirteen years later when the pastor ended his work.

Craven arrived at work early that Monday morning, but Clinton Knight, the superintendent of facilities, had arrived even earlier and changed the plaque above the study door from Associate Pastor to Pastor. The transition was unique. John Hamrick preached his final sermon as pastor January 5, 1969, and the new pastor was installed the next Sunday. Preston Callison, a Columbia attorney and president of the South Carolina Baptist State Convention, brought the address. Dr. Olin T. Binkley, president of The Southeastern Baptist Theological Seminary, had accepted the invitation to bring the message, but illness prevented his coming. Craven had served as teaching fellow for Dr. Binkley during his study toward the master of theology degree.

Just as John Hamrick had been in the church as a youth and later had served as pastor to his family, so had Paul Craven spent his boyhood in the church, as the sixth generation of his mother's family. His mother, Thayer Burk, had sung in the choir from her early youth. His grandfather, Captain William Brantly Burk, had served as deacon many years. There could have been no more complete commitment to the task than Craven brought to his new post.

The single most important assignment facing the new pastor was the procurement of a staff. He needed to fill at least three key posts, minister of music, minister of education and principal of the day school. The fact was abundantly clear that a church in the setting of the First Baptist Church had to regard a vibrant music ministry as a prime concern. This ministry must not only serve the congregation but also offer wide community appeal, bringing new members and families into the church fellowship. The church had a tradition of fine music, but Craven determined that a full-time minister of music would greatly enhance the strength of the total program. William David Redd, minister of music of the First Baptist Church, Orangeburg, South Carolina, and a native Charlestonian, was called to this post. He had served as organist both in the First Baptist Church of Greenville, South Carolina, and the First Baptist Church of New Orleans, Louisiana. His ability, augmented by the talented organ work of Blanche Ellen Smith, brought the music of the church to new heights. Other individuals were attracted to the choir, and the music of the First Baptist Church was acclaimed the finest in the city. Redd also served as coordinator of all music in the church day school. The school had a long-standing reputation for its emphasis on the fine arts. In addition to classroom music, the program included several private teachers in piano, strings, organ, voice, and percussion. Spring recitals for individuals and groups further enhanced the cultural emphasis. A band was begun that won state honors, and the boys' choir, as well as other choral groups, became a popular group, performing at civic functions.

The church also needed a minister of education. Craven asked Vivian Andrews to move to this post from the office of principal of the day school. A graduate of The Southern Baptist Theological Seminary, Vivian Andrews brought the expertise needed to strengthen the educational and social ministries work of the church.

The final post to be filled was that of principal of the day school, and W. Arthur Earp was appointed to this post. A professional educator, who would soon complete his work and receive a doctorate of education from the University of Tennessee, Earp brought to this assignment an additional academic dimension which communicated the school's continued commitment to excellence.

Across the years, the church had fostered special services of worship which became increasingly important to the congregation and the community at large. One such event was the Good Friday service, which included inspiring music from the choir and observance of Communion.

The highlight of the year was the Christmas season, and of all the lovely things that comprised the Christmas season, the most celebrated was the Christmas Eve service. It began at eleven o'clock in the evening and ended promptly at twelve, with the congregation going out into Christmas morning. The church was always decorated exquisitely for the season. The processional hymn was led by the handbell choir, followed by the boys' choir and the sanctuary choir. The festive experience was electrifying. The pastor's meditation was delivered, and the final height of the candlelight service was Communion. This particular service grew in appeal so greatly that capacity crowds attended, and on one occasion *Redbook* magazine featured the service in an article on Christmas in Charleston.

In 1970, the city of Charleston celebrated its tricentennial, and in 1976 the country celebrated its bicentennial. Because of the historic character of the First Baptist Church, these two significant events provided both a reason for special celebrations and a new focus on the historic significance of the church. During the tricentennial, the pastor was asked to chair the committee that planned a service for the entire city to celebrate its religious heritage. Several events were planned, the most significant one of which was the Festival of Faith, a service which was shared by Jews, Roman Catholics, Greek Orthodox, and Protestants. The service began with a procession of more than one hundred clergy from the various groups, all attired in proper vestments. The service was an exciting celebration of the community's unparalleled religious heritage.

As Charleston made plans for observing the nation's bicentennial, the pastor of the First Baptist Church was again asked to chair a committee that would plan an appropriate community service of worship. This Thanksgiving service, held in the beautiful Citadel Chapel, brought together persons of every religious persuasion. Among other meaningful features of this service was an address brought by Dr. Benjamin Mays of Atlanta, Georgia, a native South Carolinian and a Baptist minister, one of the nation's foremost black educators, authors, and civic leaders. The event was memorable in every way and led to a similar annual service across the ensuing years. The bicentennial was celebrated in First Baptist Church with a moving service in the old historic sanctuary to which were invited all Baptists in the Charleston Association. Dr. Arthur Rutledge, Executive Secretary of the Home Mission Board of the Southern Baptist Convention, brought the address. A precise reproduction of the Liberty Bell accompanied him and was rung in the courtyard at the appropriate time.

As mentioned earlier, the celebration of these two events and the general popularizing of history during this period served to bring the history of the First Baptist Church into clear focus. Increasing numbers of individuals, both locally and nationally, turned their attention toward the Charleston church. More and more articles and references appeared from Southern Baptist writers. Locally, the prestigious Charleston Historic Foundation asked that the church be included in its spring tours. Of all the magnificent churches in the historic district, the First Baptist Church was the only church included on the tours. This resulted in thousands of persons from across the nation and around the world coming to see this Robert Mills architectural gem which Mills, in his personal writings, said, "exhibits the best specimen of correct taste in architecture in the city. It is purely Greek in its style, simply grand in its proportions, and beautiful in its detail." Other groups followed the idea of the Charleston Historic Foundation and asked that the church be included on their tours as well.

This dramatic rise in visitors to the church brought into focus a tremendous opportunity for outreach and the sharing of the faith. The church always provided church members as guides for the tours. They were prepared to tell the Baptist story, including such distinctives as the quest for religious liberty and the meaning of believer's baptism. Tourists frequently expressed surprise that the church was anything more than a lovely little museum piece, and many of those entering as tourists returned the next Sunday to share in an experience of worship.

In the early years of Craven's pastorate, he led the church in three successful property improvements, the purchase of a pastor's home on Church Street, the rebuilding of the beach house on Folly Island, and the construction of an activities building at Church and Market Streets. The development of each is a fascinating story.

The purchase of a house on Church Street for a pastor's home was not a new concept. Across the years the church had owned several homes for the pastor's residence, some of the finest of which were located on Church Street. Thirty-one Church Street and 59 Church were two such homes, both of which were sold under unfortunate circumstances. At the time he assumed his work, the pastor was provided a housing allowance with which he was purchasing a home in the suburbs some distance from the church. At the time the church began to consider the purchase of 53 Church Street, the property had been on the market for more than a year, and the price had been considerably reduced. The chairman of the deacons approached the pastor to explore the idea of purchasing the home. It was one of the finest homes on Church Street, and its back property lines joined the church's, which enhanced its importance to the church.

The plan evolved that the pastor would relinquish his housing allowance, which the church would use as part of the debt service, and in exchange the church would assume the cost of utilities. The pastor would save time and expense through reduced travel; consequently, it was an equitable arrangement for both the pastor and the church. A few months before this development, the pastor had made an interesting acquaintance with Mr. Rhett duPont, a highly successful Wall Street businessman who was residing in Charleston. A mutual friend had suggested that Craven might be of some support during a time when Mr. duPont faced some difficult health problems. Among other things stemming from this contact was an arrangement for duPont's young son to enroll in the church day school. The family obviously appreciated the assistance of the church and its staff. Before many months elapsed, Mr. duPont made an appointment to call by the pastor's office. He informed the pastor that he would like to give $25,000 for the church to use in any way it chose. The money was immediately invested in short-term saving notes. The house was listed for $65,000. The duPont money would be a sufficient down payment to assure a comfortable amortization schedule.

Everything seemed to be in order for the purchase to be made, with the exception of one obstacle. The owners had resolved that the First Baptist Church would not be allowed to purchase the property! Those church leaders sponsoring the purchase quietly arranged for a friend of the church who lived in a distant state to fly to town and purchase the house. Mr. P. O. Mead, Jr., made the necessary funds available on a temporary loan until permanent financing could be arranged, immediately upon purchase. In less than ten years, the mortgage was paid in full, and the church owned a home that on the market in the 1980s would be valued in excess of $225,000.

Unfortunately, there was strong resistance by some church members to the transaction. Some could not understand how the purchase could be made without the church incurring considerable and unnecessary expense; others resented the fact the property had to be purchased secretly; and still others simply did not like the idea of the pastor living in a neighborhood of that quality. Fortunately for the church and the pastor, these folk were in the minority. The vast majority saw it as an excellent development. As the pastor's family moved into their new home, one of the unexpected side benefits was the dramatic shift in attitude toward the church on the part of several key neighbors. As mentioned earlier, there had been across the years pronounced uneasiness and animosity toward the church. The pastor's residence in the immediate area seemed to communicate that the church was indeed concerned about the quality of life in the neighborhood, and the administration of church and school was sensitive to traffic problems and other related frustrations.

Some of the neighbors became great friends of the church and in turn served as effective bridge builders. One such individual was Mr. Ben Scott Whaley, one of Charleston's most prominent attorneys. Not only did he and Mrs. Whaley welcome the new residents on the block but constantly acted to convey to the pastor's family and to the congregation their genuine interest. One such gesture came every year. At the peak of the flower blooms, the entire congregation was invited to walk across the street to the Whaley home at 58 Church Street to view the exquisite, world-famous private garden nurtured by the Whaleys. Furthermore, it was not unusual for them to make liberal gifts to special projects undertaken by the church.

Another project of major significance for the church was building a new beach house on the front beach of Folly Island. The church had owned and utilized Enter Inn since the early 1950s, but in early September, 1971, the nostalgic old structure burned to the ground in quite a spectacular fire. The scene of many fond and cherished memories went up in smoke that day. The facility had been used extensively for retreats for groups of every age. The question now was, do we attempt to rebuild? A small but very vocal group opposed rebuilding, and a large number favored rebuilding. A committee was asked to make a preliminary study and offer a proposal to the church. The committee recommended rebuilding, and the recommendation was debated in a special church conference after the morning worship service. Those bringing the recommendation contended the new facility could be used even more effectively than the old retreat and could be used for the church membership and for an outreach ministry. Those opposing contended it had lost its usefulness and was too expensive. The church beach house was designed to provide retreat facilities for every individual both in the church membership and beyond without regard to personal financial status. The church voted overwhelming approval of the committee's recommendation.

The old structure was insured for $20,000, and the plans projected a cost of $60,000, of which $15,000 was raised immediately from special gifts. Arrangements were made to borrow the remaining $25,000. Mr. Lee McLeod had given the old facility with a stipulation in the deed that a small percentage of time each year be given to deprived children. Since this was in the original deed, it was necessary to confer with him in regard to the new facility. The chairman of the committee and the pastor arranged for a conference with him. Mr. McLeod had a fascinating way with people. He was a stern but genuinely caring individual. When the question of deprived children was raised, he answered that it was originally intended to help the financially deprived, but, with an interesting twinkle in his eye, he said, "I have noticed fewer and fewer financially deprived. Let us agree that you shall always be sensitive to any child in need financially, but let us also agree that in this day your biggest task will be to help those who are *spiritually deprived!*" So the clause "deprived children" remained in effect.

The beach house committee supervised construction of a superb facility with a capacity for sleeping sixty people. Among other amenities was the construction of a large fireplace to make possible year-round use. The facility became very popular with other churches and church related organizations. Each year, First Baptist Church reserved those weeks needed for retreats and First Baptist families, and remaining dates were made available to other churches on a cost recovery basis. The high occupancy rate resulted in the total project including debt service costing the church virtually nothing.

The final project of the three major property improvements was the construction of an activities building. The school and the church had long recognized the need for a gymnasium and activities building, but the stupendous cost had always thwarted plans. Leadership in the church continued to talk and explore. C. T. Hamrick, Jr., chairman of the board for the day school, resolved that during his one-year tenure he would exert every effort to get something started on this all-important project. At approximately the same time, E. M. Seabrook, Jr., a Presbyterian and an ardent supporter of the First Baptist Church Day School, came to the pastor and expressed a willingness to assist in every way possible. He was convinced the project was certainly feasible for the church and school and was able to offer a wealth of ideas and counsel.

These three began quietly but persistently to explore and project plans. The first essential was to acquire land. The facility could not be built on the existing campus. The idea of building the new facility over the Meeting Street parking court with one or two decks of parking underneath had been explored and brought to the city, but the board of adjustment for the city of Charleston rejected the request. Six blocks to the north of the church was the Market Street area, a terribly depressed and unattractive section of downtown Charleston. At the corner of Church and Market Streets were two small city blocks of vacant land divided by Hayne Street. The land could be purchased for $135,000. Hamrick and Craven negotiated a contract and proposed that the church borrow the funds to purchase it. Amid wails that the price was too high, that it was ridiculous to saddle the church with such a debt, and that even if the land were purchased and the building constructed, no man in his right mind would let his wife and children enter the area, the land was bought and plans were drawn for the new facility. It was determined that a gymnasium of superior quality, a number of auxiliary rooms, and a parking court for one hundred cars could be placed on the land.

Financing the project claimed top priority as a concern. Craven determined that for the first time in the history of the day school there must be an appeal to those parents whose children were enrolled in the school but whose families were not members of the First Baptist Church. The pastor asked for five men to meet with him: E. M. Seabrook, Jr.; Joseph G. Piening; J. Albert Stuhr; F. W. Ohlandt, Jr.; and H. Edward Tiencken, each of whom was asked to solicit funds. Not only did each give liberally, but within a few weeks they had raised a total in excess of $60,000 from friends of the church and school. This was the needed impetus. Simultaneously with the fund raising, plans were being completed and financing arranged.

Matters could not have developed any more rapidly or favorably. The plans and specifications were submitted to the board of adjustment to obtain one minor variance which was routinely requested and obtained for virtually all construction in the older sections of the city. The city ordinance required of all new buildings a fifteen-foot setback from street corners. This was to provide visual clearance at intersections. When the church leadership went down at the appointed hour to appear before the board of adjustment for the purpose of obtaining the variance, they were absolutely floored! The small hearing room was filled with opponents to the request. They were a residue of those in downtown Charleston who had opposed the school across the years. A quick stroke of ingenuity won the day. The board of adjustment was asked publicly by church representatives to determine if the setback at the corner of the building was the only matter for which a variance was needed. The board stated that the setback request was the only needed variance. The church, much to the surprise of everyone, proceeded immediately to withdraw its request. The pastor contacted the contractor and the engineer the same night. The building was redesigned with the required setbacks, a modification that did not impair the efficiency of the facility. The modified blueprints were ready before noon the next day, and the pastor took them to the city's permit office and requested the permit. The permit office immediately called the city attorney's office for advice. The permit office was informed that if no variance were requested, the office was legally compelled to issue the permit. With permit in hand, the pastor called the contractor, a high school classmate and friend of many years, and insisted he begin on-site grading the next day. At daybreak the next morning, much to the disbelief of the opponents, construction had begun. They sought an injunction in Circuit Court to stop the work, but their request was denied. After several other technical legal maneuvers were lost, the few opponents that remained realized the First Baptist Church Day School could not be banished from the peninsula. Six months later the church and school met in jubilation to dedicate the magnificent new facility. The church petitioned the city of Charleston to close that portion of Hayne Street which divided the two parcels. After considerable debate in the council chamber, the petition was granted. This provided the church with parking contiguous to the building. Soon after the church had purchased the Market Street property and had begun its development, the entire Market area entered a dramatic renaissance which quickly made it a prime pedestrian shopping area. Property values skyrocketed, and the church was offered more for just the parking portion of its property than the sum of its total investment. This was only one of several offers which the church declined. The new commercial developments in the area generated an urgent need for public parking. This led the city to request of the church that the church's parking court be leased to the city. A liberal contract was signed with the provision for renegotiation annually. The income from the parking lease assisted greatly with the debt service.

Not only did the Market Street project meet a long-standing need for the programs of both church and school, but ownership of such a large parcel in the city's prime real estate area provided an excellent setting for future plans and development. The pastor frequently spoke of exciting dreams of a multistoried structure with lower levels for parking and shops and upper levels for a retirement center. The income from such a project would amortize the debt and ultimately serve as much needed endowment for the day school.

A few years after the facility had been in use, the timely proposal was made that the building be officially named the John A. Hamrick Activities Building, in honor of the founder of the school. The idea received immediate support and approval from the church. Appropriate ceremonies were planned, and the Honorable J. Strom Thurmond, United States Senator, brought the principal address.

During the 1970s the church became involved with several new and significant ministries, one of which was the ports ministry, a work with the nonmilitary seamen who call at the Charleston port. While no work of an organized nature had been undertaken for many generations, the commitment of the First Baptist Church to the seamen's ministry can be traced to the early 1800s. The Mariner's Church, built with funds from communitywide sources, was a nondenominational chapel ministry where seamen attended worship and frequently visited for quietude and rest. The Mariner's Church was located on the east side of Church Street only a short distance south of the First Baptist Church, and in 1818 and in subsequent years through 1822 the congregation of the First Baptist Church used the Mariner's Church while the present sanctuary was being built.

In more recent years, members of the church frequently expressed concern that more was not being done in the area of port ministry. Charleston had rapidly become one of the busiest seaports on the eastern seaboard. By the 1970s ships from every country in the world with more than fifty thousand seamen were docking every year in Charleston, and each succeeding year experienced an increase over the preceding year. These developments provided quite literally a foreign mission field right at the church's front door. William Bishop, executive director of the Charleston Baptist Association, became keenly interested in this area of work and gained the interest of both the missions department of the South Carolina Baptist Convention and the Home Mission Board of the Southern Baptist Convention. Bishop was sharing his thoughts and dreams of a port ministry in a meeting attended by Paul Craven, Jr. The executive director's remarks immediately struck a responsive point in Craven's thinking, and Craven later called the director to express interest.

A local church was needed to work in cooperation with the denominational agencies to start the program. The pastor believed the First Baptist Church was the appropriate local church. I was within walking distance of the waterfront terminals, and the activities building was available for relaxation and recreation. The program began modestly but grew rapidly, with a Home Mission Board US-2 missionary couple assigned to the work. After four years of ministry, the Home Mission Board appointed the first career missionary couple to work, Mr. and Mrs. James Morgan. The work of the ports ministry became increasingly appealing to members of the First Baptist Church, who volunteered their help. Groups of seamen were often brought to the services of the church, and occasionally the Sunday evening sermon was interpreted into Spanish for those in attendance. When such interpretation could be planned in advance, advertisements were placed in the newspapers, and additional Spanish-speaking people attended or listened to the evening service by radio. The lay leadership of the church worked faithfully and innovatively to make the program meaningful. On one occasion, these volunteers opened the activities building on Christmas Day to those seamen whose ships were in port and provided a festive celebration for seventy-five men from around the world.

During the 1970s, another area of mission endeavor for the First Baptist Church came with the opportunity to organize and sponsor a new church east of the Cooper River. In the 1800s the church had granted letters to members, residents across the Cooper River, who desired to start a church in that area. In the 1920s the First Baptist Church had one of its members go east of the Cooper River to preach in a mission, and the converts were brought to the mother church for baptism. The request in the 1970s was at least the third such relationship. The group forming the mission was made, for the most part, of members of the First Baptist Church of Mount Pleasant, the oldest settlement east of the Cooper. The group had become displeased with some aspect of their church life in the Mount Pleasant Church and resolved to begin a new work. The small congregation first contacted the executive director of the Charleston Baptist Association, who in turn referred the lay leader to the First Baptist Church. The mission group met first in a school until a permanent location was chosen. An excellent tract of land was purchased, and within two years a most attractive and functional building was erected. On August 21, 1977, jubilant dedicatory services were held. The official publication of the mother church, *The First Baptist Builder,* printed on its front page a tribute to the East Cooper Mission which read in part,

> This Sunday will mark one of the grandest days from all the past and for all the future in the life of our East Cooper Mission. . . . The First Baptist Church salutes her youngest daughter . . . and offers thanks to God for her people and her pastor.

The mother church presented the mission a grand piano for its new sanctuary, and the work soon was constituted as a fully chartered church. In the first meeting of the East Cooper Mission and in every subsequent meeting, a percentage of all offerings was designated to the Cooperative Program and to the Charleston Baptist Association.

The story of the mission endeavors of the First Baptist Church during the 1970s would be incomplete without a reference to Boonie Doone, the Charleston Baptist Association retreat. One morning in the early 1970s Clinton Knight, the superintendent of facilities for the First Baptist Church, entered Craven's study and posed a most interesting question: "Do you think the church would be interested in receiving a donation of ninety-six acres of prime land on Wadmalaw Island?" The property was owned by Mr. Robert W.

Wolnick and the estate of his late wife. Clinton Knight had been a friend of the Wolnicks for many years and was now the executor of Mrs. Wolnick's estate which, through frugal management across the years by the Wolnicks, had grown considerably. While they were not Baptists, Mr. Wolnick wanted to leave this particular piece of property to some charitable organization in memory of his late wife. There was a stipulation that the property be developed into a camp for youth. When Knight set forth the stipulation, the pastor's countenance fell. "Clint," he said, "how could we even consider it?" Both of the men were thinking that in the immediate past the pastor had led the campaign for rebuilding the Folly Beach Retreat, and now much discussion was focused on the proposed activities building. "If we mention youth camp, both of us are likely to be run out of town." But the pastor expressed keen interest in the idea, and his strong hope that the gift not be channeled to another recipient. A thought flashed through the pastor's mind; *Why not ask the Charleston Baptist Association to accept it and develop an associational camp?* The pastor encouraged Knight to discuss the matter with Paul Craven, Sr., who was a strong associational enthusiast and who held a long-standing dream of an associational camp. The idea was next shared with the associational leadership. The immediate response of the executive director of the association was positive. The property was conveyed to the association but, with Mr. Wolnick's consent, was later sold because of zoning problems. This would prove to be providential, since the proceeds were used as seed money to purchase exquisite Boonie Doone Plantation located southwest of Charleston on the pristine Ashepoo River. The First Baptist Church, with many other churches in the association, made a substantial gift toward the purchase. The plantation mansion was named and dedicated the Arlys Johnson Wolnick Hall. During its first years of operation, the retreat experienced grave financial difficulty, but reasonable assurances came that at the death of Robert W. Wolnick a substantial bequest would secure the future of a worthy and promising ministry.

During the years of Paul J. Craven, Jr.'s, pastorate, several challenges surfaced which required the most careful pastoral leadership. One such concern was the necessity to address, perhaps for a final time, the racial issue. The specific problem that brought the issue to the forefront was the widely publicized Medical University strike in the spring of 1969. The issues that precipitated the strike were so acute and the community involvement so widespread that outside protesters gravitated to Charleston, as did numerous black civil rights leaders. One tactic employed by the strikers was to solicit moral support from churches. Some of the grievances were well-founded, and such leaders as the Roman Catholic bishop of the South Carolina diocese marched with the strikers. Those churches which did not openly support the strike faced the likelihood of a demonstration line on Sunday morning. While the First Baptist Church had not gone on record for or against the strike, there were individuals who privately promoted those reactions that could have brought unfortunate repercussions. In order to sound the congregational thought, the pastor requested a meeting with the deacons, a meeting which proved to be remarkably wholesome. There was a wide diversity of opinion. Some wanted to assume personal responsibility to meet any black person for whatever purpose he might arrive at the church and to "stop 'em at the gate." Others thought the church should debate the issue and adopt an official policy, and others strongly contended that *anyone* who came to worship should be allowed to do so.

The group was reminded that the church had never in its 287-year history adopted a policy of racial exclusion. To the contrary, the incident was cited from the church minutes in which the congregation, after the Civil War, declined a request by a sister black congregation that all black members be dismissed by letter to the black church. In the late 1860s, the First Baptist Church went on record that all blacks would be welcomed to remain members, and only those who requested such would be granted a letter for church membership elsewhere. This question was raised in that eventful deacons' meeting of 1969: Why should we wait until the twentieth century to take such a stand of exclusion? A moderate spirit prevailed, and it was agreed that no one, in labor or management, would ever be allowed to demonstrate or otherwise turn the sanctuary into a forum to espouse divisive views. At the same time, no deacon present felt comfortable to say that no black, at any time, under any circumstances, would ever be allowed entrance to the sanctuary. From that time forward, many blacks worshiped in the First Baptist Church without incident and were well received.

Another challenge to surface during Craven's pastorate was the question of ordination of women to the diaconate. Strong feelings and fixed opinions were in evidence and readily expressed. The subject was committed to prayerful study and open discussion. Again a moderate and caring spirit prevailed. The deacons recommended to the church that members of the church be elected to the diaconate without regard to gender. The church approved the recommendation unanimously and shortly afterward elected two choice church leaders who happened to be women to the office of deacon, Mrs. Mary Peeples and Mrs. Patricia Gibson. From the outset, the designation "deaconess" was thought obsolete, and each person elected was known as "deacon."

Before the decade of the 1970s ended, for the first time in its history the church ordained a woman to the Gospel ministry. It was a service of great solemnity and much jubilation when Miss Judy King knelt for the laying on of hands. More resentment toward the idea was voiced outside the membership of the First Baptist Church than inside. One local pastor sought support to expel the church from the association, an idea which suffered rejection at every juncture.

Several endeavors scattered throughout his tenure were sources of special joy to Craven. One of these was the election by the church of his predecessor, John A. Hamrick, to the post of Pastor Emeritus. Early in Craven's pastorate, A. L. Gentry, a loyal friend to both pastors, approached Craven with the idea. The pastor shared precisely the same thoughts, and the two enjoyed steering the matter through to a successful end. The election had a touch of humor about it. Someone observed that John Hamrick had achieved distinction in virtually every other area of his life, and now at fifty-four he was distinguished as the youngest "emeritus" ever to be so honored.

Another source of much joy to Craven was his denominational service in the association, the state convention, and the Southern Baptist Convention. He always expressed great satisfaction in identifying himself as a denominational man. He boasted, in jest, that he was born a Southern Baptist and would die a Southern Baptist unless he became so radical that the powers that be expelled him. He believed his service in denominational leadership not only increased his personal appreciation for Baptist endeavors but also heightened the awareness of his congregation. On the state level he spoke fondly of his service both for Furman University and the Baptist College at Charleston. He served on the board of trustees for Furman University at the time Dr. John E. Johns was elected president, and he served on the pastors' advisory board at the Baptist College during some of that school's most exciting years. The Baptist College conferred on him the degree of doctor of divinity. Craven often said that while he had earned the doctor of ministry degree from The Southeastern Baptist Theological Seminary, he felt just as honored and thankful to have had conferred on him the doctor of divinity degree from the Baptist College as any earned degree he might ever have had.

The post of convention service most fulfilling to Craven was his place on the executive committee of the Southern Baptist Convention. He expressed the wish that every pastor and every lay person might some way have the opportunity to serve in this post. He gained a totally new and dynamic insight into the work of the convention. He returned from his first session on this committee and equated the experience to a revival in its renewing and quickening power. As chairman of the strategic subcommittee on finance, he gained insight firsthand into the great opportunities Southern Baptists have at their fingertips. These experiences led him to challenge the church to double its gifts to the Cooperative Program over five years, a challenge the church accepted with enthusiasm. During Craven's two terms on the executive committee, Dr. Porter Routh retired, and the Charleston pastor regarded it as one of the high hours of his career that he should serve on the search committee that recommended Dr. Harold C. Bennett as Dr. Routh's successor.

Because of the historic significance of the Charleston church and because of the pastor's association with denominational leaders, both in the state convention and the Southern Baptist Convention, the pastor was asked to share in planning, in the late 1970s, the annual meeting of state executive secretaries, editors of state Baptist papers, and a number of other Southern Baptist leaders. The meeting convened in Charleston, and certain sessions met in the First Baptist Church. One of the highlights of the event was an evening service in the church sanctuary during which Loulie Latimer Owens brought an address on persons of historic significance in the First Baptist story. This gifted author and lecturer made the periods of Screven, Hart, and Furman come alive.

Plans for the meeting of the executive secretaries and editors had originally included a joint Communion service. The pastor thought it would be meaningful for all attending the meeting to participate in a Communion service much like earlier generations of Baptist leaders in South Carolina, who ended many associational meetings and conventions with observance of the Lord's Supper. Little did the pastor realize that of those attending some would have grave reservations about participation in the Lord's Supper away from the local church. Their concern seemingly stemmed not from personal theological or ecclesiastical position but rather the position of many constituents whom they sought to serve. The concern surfacing in the meeting of the executive secretaries and editors served to point out how diverse Southern Baptists are.

In 1977, the pastor proposed that the church elect a special committee to plan the 300th anniversary of the church in 1982. Five years were needed adequately to design the celebration. The pastor recommended the committee be chaired by Joyce Harris Murray, a choice that seemed appropriate in every way. She had been in the church her entire life; her family had been in the church for eight generations. Her father, Joseph K. Harris, Sr., was a life deacon and had given himself without reservation to service through the church. If the tercentenary celebration were to meet the high expectations, several subcommittees had to begin work immediately. A subcommittee on growth and goals was chaired by Patricia Gibson, a committee which was responsible for challenging the church to grow in numbers, in stewardship, in mission support, and in spiritual strength. A subcommittee on improvements in the sanctuary was chaired by F. N. Hamrick. A subcommittee on the Henry Erben organ, a committee to plan and fund the restoration of the 1845 instrument, was chaired by William David Redd. Though this project would be quite expensive, it was thought that the present congregation could make no more appropriate contribution to the on-going history of the church than to restore to its original grandeur this instrument which the Smithsonian Institute affirmed to be an organ of extraordinary significance.

Another committee, chaired by W. W. Smith, was budget and memorials, a committee which would secure not only funds needed for the celebration but memorial gifts out across the years to undergird the ministries of the church. A subcommittee on an archives room was chaired by Paul J. Craven, Sr., a committee to develop a proper way to exhibit items of historic significance. A subcommittee for publicity, chaired by C. R. Dominey, was responsible for telling the story of the First Baptist Church locally and far away. A subcommittee, chaired by Paul J. Craven, Jr., was commissioned to secure an authentic history of the church and to arrange for its publication. A subcommittee of special events, chaired by Martha Derrick, was responsible for meaningful services and events to be arranged for the year of celebration. A subcommittee coordinated by Arnold W. Eaves and Nancy Hart Hamrick was responsible for promotion of a pageant to be written and produced by Loulie Latimer Owens.

Each of these subcommittees began the exciting task of planning and projecting toward 1982. The subcommittee on growth led the church to adopt a five-year plan at the end of which the church would have doubled its gifts to the Cooperative Program. As 1982 approached, the subcommittee on facility improvements had already succeeded in totally redecorating the sanctuary and had planned other improvements. The subcommittee working with the Henry Erben organ had brought to completion the restoration of the cabinet which, once again, gracefully adorned the east balcony. The pipes were sent to Holland for repair, and the committee had been assured the restoration would be completed and the instrument in place for a dedicatory program during 1982. The cost for the organ restoration would be in excess of $40,000.

The subcommittee on funding and memorials succeeded in getting many commitments for immediate budget needs and laid plans to call forth a continuing support in the form of memorials across the ensuing years. The subcommittee working on an archives room was successful in collecting documents and memorabilia, much of which had never been viewed by the present generation of church members. The group was committed to giving all of the church's historic items proper display. The subcommittee on publicity worked diligently on many ideas to give the celebration wide coverage. An attempt to have printed on the cover of the 1982 city telephone directory a picture of the historic church first met with futility. But John D. Bradley, III, a brilliant young attorney in the state legislature and a faithful deacon in the First Baptist Church, presented in the legislature a resolution which acknowledged and affirmed the illustrious history of the church. After this resolution had passed both the Senate and the House of Representatives, it became increasingly evident to the Southern Bell Telephone Company that the idea of a picture of the First Baptist Church was a very sound and reasonable idea, and the church received notice that the volume would be published with the church adorning its cover.

Denominational leaders were ready to assist in every way possible with publicity. Leaders in virtually every sector of Baptist life regarded the First Baptist story as a story of importance to every Baptist. *The Baptist Program* carried an historical sketch in its January, 1982 issue with a picture of the church on the front cover. The Sunday bulletin service arranged for the

September 26, 1982 bulletin to feature the First Baptist Church. This would tell the story to multiplied thousands whose local churches used the Sunday bulletin service. As the year of celebration approached, numerous other channels for telling the story were explored and utilized. The subcommittee on the writing and publication of a history of the church resolved that no part of the tricentennial celebration was of more lasting importance than an authentic and appealing record of the church's three hundred years. While several writers had contributed significantly to specific periods in the church's history, there had never been an exhaustive work done which spanned the entire three centuries. Dr. Robert A. Baker had labored for many years in research of the First Baptist Church of Charleston, and the decision was made to commission him to write the history of the first 162 years and Paul J. Craven, Jr., pastor of the church, to address the last 138 years. A matter of utmost concern was the publication of the volume. The committee was convinced the story was important to all Southern Baptists and Baptist institutions as well as to many other persons and groups. Craven visited Broadman Press to discuss the matter and found the Broadman leadership sympathetic with the project but faced with a major obstacle. Broadman Press of necessity declines publishing the histories of all individual churches. After careful consideration, it was determined that publishing a volume on the history of this church was a unique and unparalleled project important to the entire Baptist family.

The subcommittee on special events for the year of celebration projected an impressive array of persons and programs. Those denominational leaders committed to speak included William G. Tanner, executive secretary of the Home Mission Board of the Southern Baptist Convention; Duke K. McCall, president of The Southern Baptist Theological Seminary and president of the Baptist World Alliance; and Harold C. Bennett, executive secretary of the Executive Committee of the Southern Baptist Convention. Billy Graham and Jimmy Carter were invited, and, while neither declined, both stated the necessity of waiting until the scheduled time was closer to respond. Several denominational agencies and related organizations convened in Charleston to commemorate the church's anniversary. These included the South Carolina Historical Society, the Southern Baptist Convention Historical Commission, and the Southern Baptist Convention Historical Society. The South Carolina Baptist State Convention met in Charleston in November, 1981, for the express purpose of officially launching the year of celebration. The highlight of the convention was the moving pageant written by Loulie Latimer Owens and presented to a capacity crowd in the Gaillard Auditorium. The pageant which included scores of persons in the cast and many others behind the scenes told in an indelible fashion the three-hundred-year drama.

The time was May, 1981, and although those events that would begin the tricentennial were several months away, everything about the plans for the year's celebration looked promising. Each committee was at work, and a wholesome spirit was abundantly evident. The date was May 9, and the pastor was enjoying the slow pace of Saturday morning. He soon would turn to putting the finishing touches on his Mother's Day message for the following morning. The phone rang, and the lady on the other end introduced herself as a member of the search committee of the First Baptist Church of Winston-Salem, North Carolina. She stated the purpose of her call, to inquire as to the pastor's openness to consider a call to the First Baptist Church, Winston-Salem. The pastor could not believe what he heard. He would have been speechless had the whole matter not sounded so remote. He first thought that some friend was striking up a bit of Saturday morning humor; another thought was that the caller had reached by mistake the wrong pastor. Craven had never been to Winston-Salem; he did not know anyone there; nor did he know the church was without a pastor. Here he was hearing strange inquiries about leaving Charleston for a new land. After several inquiries, all on generally the same theme, the friend on the other end asked, "Would it be useless for me to worship with you tomorrow?" The pastor found himself quoting his professor friend, Olin T. Binkley, "Don't ever say no to anything until you have taken time carefully to listen and pray." The next morning Peggy Chestnutt exchanged brief but warm greetings and left. The next week T. Winfield Blackwell, the chairman of the Winston-Salem committee, called, and the following Sunday a group visited the Charleston church. The next week still another group came, and the next week still another individual came. Though all the meetings were warm and gladsome, neither the pastor nor the committee encouraged the other. To the contrary, the committee was a little coy, and the pastor sincerely encouraged them to explore other possibilities. A minimum of communication took place during the next six weeks until on a warm Friday afternoon in July, Craven received a call from Blackwell inviting the pastor and his wife to Winston-Salem for a visit. In this conversation the chairman made it clear the committee wanted the Cravens in Winston-Salem.

To Craven the possibility of a move posed colossal problems. The tricentennial was only one of several things. All of his four daughters would be keenly affected, but one was a rising senior and had attended only one school her entire career. Another person to be considered was Joye, the pastor's wife, who had just embarked upon a new and most fulfilling career. Joye had always been willing to go where her pastor-husband felt led, but that did not lessen the trauma. Still another factor was Craven's leadership role in the conventions. One is required to resign all posts of leadership when one moves to a new state. In addition to the offices he held, Craven had been elected to preach the state convention sermon in November. Furthermore, a group had come to him earlier in the year and asked that he allow his name to go up for president of the South Carolina Baptist Convention. Craven had lost the year before in Columbia by a very slim margin to a pastor friend whose pastorate was in Columbia, and a strong feeling prevailed that he would win the election in Charleston. He had agreed to run but had stated emphatically he would not turn a finger to campaign for it. Of all these and several other foreboding factors, the most difficult was that of simply leaving the church so greatly beloved.

When it became apparent that the committee in Winston-Salem would soon seek agreement from him to place his name before the congregation, Craven realized he needed either to withdraw his name or to commence pulling in his Charleston sails. In his decision-making process, he did an unusual thing. Across the years, he had sought on many occasions the counsel of a group of friends in the church. Corporate heads and politicians would call them a brain trust. Craven preferred calling them a heart trust. He never moved on any major decision in the church without first consulting them, and this decision was no exception. There were seven in his "trust," and all made it abundantly clear they hoped he would stay, but should he go, he would go with their faithful support. The next days were agonizing. In his August journal Craven jotted down a bit of verse quoted in a sermon by the great Scottish preacher, James S. Stewart:

> Leave to His sovereign sway,
> To choose and to command;
> So shalt thou, wondering, own His way,
> How wise, how strong His hand.

On August 23, Paul J. Craven, Jr., resigned, in a most unusual way. He presented his resignation in a sermon illustration in the middle of his morning sermon. A number of people actually missed what he said. When he had assumed the pastorate there had been no letter of agreement, and when he left there was no letter of resignation, simply a statement tied in as a sermon illustration. After the service, he greeted those who came by his door, and quietly walked to the pastorium. It was his last time to preach in the historic pulpit. That afternoon many beautiful expressions of regard were received, both from the Charleston congregation and the Winston-Salem congregation—a strange mingling of joy and sorrow. The chairman of the pulpit committee from Winston-Salem called to share some beautiful words and to finalize plans for the service of installation on September 20. So came the close of Craven's pastorate. Only Screven, Hart, Furman, and Hamrick had served longer. The capable ministerial staff of David Newton, Arnold Eaves, and William David Redd were prepared to assume added responsibilities during the interim period. As the First Baptist Church prepared to celebrate its tercentenary and embark into the fourth century of its continuing story, it once again faced the task of seeking a new pastor.

Index

A

Abbeville, S. C., 284
Adams, Hugh, 83-84
Adams, William, 61, 69, 90, 93
Alabama Baptist, 288
American Home Mission Society, 273
Angel, John, 106
Andrews, Vivian, 378
Antimission movement, 273
Asbury, Francis, 181, 212-13
Ashepoo River, 387
Ashley River church, 105-07, 120-21, 148, 151, 180-81
Associational missions, 154-57
Atwell, Joseph, 27, 46, 67, 114, 116-17
Augusta, Georgia, 272
Axson, Mrs. J. M., 319
Axtell (Axill), Humphrey, 61, 63, 67, 69, 76, 90-91
Axtell, Lady Rebecca, 26, 29, 92, 104

B

Backus, Isaac, 65-66
Bailey, E. W., 250-51
Bailey, James E., 348
Bainbridge, Peter, 184
Baker, Francis, 114
Baker, Sarah, 106
Baker, Susanna, 106
Baker, William, 104
Baker family, 28
Baldwin, H. L., 327, 332, 337
Ball, William L., 356
Baptism, 283
Baptist College of Charleston, 369, 389
Baptist Religious Society, 143, 160-62, 217
Baptist World Alliance, 392
Baptistry, 284
Baptists, British, 13-17, 22, 33-40
Baptists, General, 15-16, 28, 81-82, 94-95, 107-19, 133, 181
Baptists, Particular, 15-16, 95, 108-19, 133
Baptists, Separate, 124, 127, 134, 156
Barker, Charles, 106
Barker family, 28
Barnes, W. W., 13, 355
Barry, John A., 362
Barry, Martha, 362
Bates, Lester Sr., 368
Beaufort Baptist Church, 276
Bedgegood, Nicholas, 133, 139, 158
Bedon, Elizabeth, 106
Bedon, John R., 114
Bedon, Richard, Jr., 105
Bedon, Richard, Sr., 105
Bedon, Ruth, 129
Benedict, Mrs. Leroy, 365
Bennett, Harold C., 389, 392
Best Friend, 284

Bethel Methodist, 310
Binkley, Olin T., 393
Bishop, William, 385
Bitting, C. C., 311
Black members at Charleston, 212-13
Blackwell, T. Winfield, 393
Blake, Benjamin, 24-25, 69
Blake, Lady Elizabeth Axtell, 26, 29, 85, 92, 104, 111
Blake, Joseph, 25-26, 69
Blake, Rebecca, 26
Board on Domestic Missions, 282
Bolger, Mamie, 319
Bomar, John, 343, 350
Bonneau, Ann, 109
Boonie Doone, 386
Booth, Robert, 105
Boston Baptist church, 47-61, 68, 86, 88-90
Botsford, Edmund, 130-32, 135, 139, 144-45, 158-59, 179, 181-83, 210
Boyce, James P., 48, 272, 277, 280, 290, 307, 311
Boyce, Ker, 248
Bradley, John D., III, 391
Bradwell, Jacob, 106
Bradwell, Susan, 106
Brantly, William T., 369
Brisbane, William, 114, 117, 119
Brisbane, James, 119
Brisbane, William H., 219, 268-69
Broadman Press, 392
Broadus, John A., 277, 290, 302
Brodie, Mrs. O. J., 365
Brown, Christine, 106
Brown, Jeremiah, 180
Brown, John, 105
Brown University, 279, 288
Budd, Thomas S., 293
Bullein, Elizabeth, 106
Bullein, Nathaniel, 119
Bulline, John, 91, 105
Bulline, Thomas, 77, 81, 90-117
Bulline family, 28, 75
Burk, Elizabeth, 327
Burk, Sarah, 319
Burk, Thayer, 377
Burk, William Brantly, 377
Burke, A. J., 273
Burns, Dorothea Maria, 209
Burrows, John Lansing, 311
Butler, Elisha, 116-17
Butler, Mrs. I. F., 319
Butler, Richard, 90, 91, 105, 109
Butler, William, 116-18
Butler family, 29

C

Callender, Ellis, 88
Callison, Preston, 377

395